ACTS OF THE TAPESTRY SYMPOSIUM

NOVEMBER 1976

THE FINE ARTS MUSEUMS OF SAN FRANCISCO

This publication is supported by
generous grants from The San
Francisco Foundation and
The Museum Society.

CONTENTS

FOREWORD

On November 20–21, 1976, a distinguished group of tapestry specialists met at the California Palace of the Legion of Honor to exchange information. The focus of their attention was the hitherto unpublished and almost unknown group of tapestries belonging to The Fine Arts Museums of San Francisco. The symposium marked the opening of an exhibition and the publication of a catalogue of this collection, *Five Centuries of Tapestry*.

Those invited to participate in the symposium had contributed in various ways to this double event. The lectures they delivered further extended this supporting role by expanding understanding and appreciation of the collection. The Fine Arts Museums are happy to be able to publish their supporting research papers and to provide a permanent record of the lectures for future study.

The idea of a tapestry symposium was not new. The San Francisco symposium, however, broke with tradition by including papers of a technical as well as art historical nature. Thus the first four papers in this volume are concerned with the physical aspects of tapestries and scientific measures of preservation. Wendy Hefford and Geneviève Souchal have contributed additional papers to this publication which enrich the symposium corpus. It is a matter of regret, however, that Mark Adams' delightful lecture on tapestry design is not included in this record.

The papers are arranged in three sections. The first, dealing with the medium and materials of tapestry weaving, is composed of three articles. Christa Thurman creates a unifying frame with an overview of the history of tapestry weaving. Harold Lundgren informs us about tapestry's basic material, wool, giving its structure, properties, and responses to changing conditions. Liliane Masschelein-Kleiner identifies dyes in a group of late medieval tapestries and describes those regulations which contributed to the remarkable survival of medieval colors.

Conservation, present and past, is the subject of the second section. Nobuko Kajitani's comprehensive review amounts to an explicit manual of tapestry conservation. Wendy Hefford reconstructs from historical evidence some of the conservation procedures of the seventeenth and eighteenth centuries. Her article leads naturally to the last section devoted to art historical discussions.

Two great Flemish tapestry series of the fifteenth and sixteenth centuries are studied in the first half of Part III. Larry Salmon traces the inter-relationship of several panels illustrating the Passion of Christ with reference to the culture that produced them. Geneviève Souchal and Guy Delmarcel present different aspects of the Renaissance series, *The Triumph of the Seven Virtues*. Souchal gives exhaustive coverage to its iconographical program; Delmarcel reveals the overall plan and purpose by referring to prototypes.

The three papers of the final chapter deal with tapestries woven in France. Madeleine Jarry surveys the activity of Parisian ateliers just before the establishment of the Gobelins Manufactory. Bertrand Jestaz reports on newly discovered documents which expand our concept of the production of Beauvais at the end of the seventeenth century. The symposium papers conclude with Edith Standen's discussion of tapestries related to the designs of Berain. Her easy informality of style recalls her delightful lecture and belies the formidable supporting research.

The Fine Arts Museums express deep appreciation to the busy authors who took time from regular duties to prepare these papers for publication. Acknowledgment is made of the assistance of Anne Durand and Scott Bryson who began the translation of manuscripts submitted in French. Special thanks are due Antoinette Knapton for her painstaking review and completion of the translation project. Editing the manuscripts, Brian Williams faced the problem of bringing the required degree of conformity to this complex publication of multiple authorship, and his work was immensely helpful. Sally Blair and Karen Lum spent hours of much appreciated volunteer time following up at the stage of proofs and corrections. The ultimate responsibility for this volume rested with our Publications Manager, Ann Karlstrom, who inherited the task from Ned Engle. Her patience and skill were critical in bringing the *Acts* to press.

The San Francisco Foundation made two grants toward the publication. This generous support and that of The Museum Society have given the Tapestry Symposium a permanent form and insured its availability as a study resource.

ANNA G. BENNETT

PART I
MEDIUM AND MATERIALS

PART I
MEDIUM AND MATERIALS

Tapestry: The Purposes, Form, and Function of the Medium from Its Inception until Today

Christa C. M. Thurman

When we hear the word "tapestry," we think of the large wall coverings that have adorned castles and churches for centuries. Indeed, in this sense, the origin of the tapestry-woven wall covering is essentially European. When the weave was used in the Near East, it was not only for making furnishing items for tents, but also for making "travel weavings"—bedspreads in which personal possessions could be bundled up.[1] In addition, the European tapestry-woven wall hanging has always featured pictorial subject matter, whereas the Near Eastern counterpart has generally presented non-pictorial patterns.

Technically, the weave in a tapestry is a weft-faced plain weave, achieved through the use of a discontinuous weft.[2] The warp threads are never visible and appear only in the form of widely spaced, undyed ribs; their function is to support the much finer, colored weft threads. Since the wefts are discontinuous, they appear only where required for coloration; they do not run through the entire fabric as it is being constructed on the loom. Yet, because the hanging usually had to be large, an item of immense weight, it therefore had to be well constructed. The critical place was where adjacent color areas met. It was solved in one of three ways—by dovetailing the wefts of the first and second color around one and the same warp thread, by linking the wefts in an interlocking technique, or by returning the weft on itself (without either dovetailing or interlocking, which would have left slits). If the third approach was taken, it required subsequent sewing up of the slits. Regardless of which joining or nonjoining technique was used, the weave produced a fabric that was totally reversible.

In addition, in large tapestry-woven hangings the concealed warp threads run counter to one's expectation; in other words, in the finished product they run from right to left in the horizontal direction rather than from top to bottom. The same is true if one looks for the so-called selvages; they, too, go counter to one's expectation, appearing at the top and bottom of the finished piece instead of at both sides. The reason for this puzzle is that most tapestries are woven on their sides. If the ribs were to run vertically, they would produce tremendous distortion, whereas horizontal ridges catch the light and in doing so unify the design. Thus, the horizontal lines, the concealed warps, create relief, while the vertical lines, the color-carrying wefts, provide the color.[3] Shadows in the tapestry could be provided by slits. Middle light, as well as a feeling of three-dimensionality, was provided by hatching, which could be achieved by inserting wedges or lighter colored weft threads into darker color areas, so as to produce a color blend (a faster and cheaper method was to weave two adjacent color patches, but this could not really be compared in quality to the hatching techniques).

The weaving process was carried out on two types of looms: the high-warp loom (*haute-lisse*) and the low-warp loom (*basse-lisse*).[4] (For an illustration of an earlier loom, from around 1500, one should see the border of the Passion Tapestry in Bamberg.[5]) The high-warp loom was the older of the two and was apparently not changed much during the Middle Ages. It was a vertical loom constructed out of two upright beams between which rested the warp and cloth beams. The tension and weight lay between these beams. As the weaver wove, the finished part of the tapestry was rolled onto the cloth beam. The heddles—parallel cords used to guide the warp threads—hung in front of the warp threads and were manipulated by the weaver with one hand while he inserted the weft threads with the other. Wooden guards protected the finished part of the tapestry from dirt.

The low-warp loom was essentially a table or horizontal loom, and the weaver was able to use both hands since the manipulation of the heddles was controlled by foot pedals. Weaving on this loom was consequently much faster.

With either loom the weaver worked from full-size designs called cartoons (the word derives from the Italian *cartone*, a large piece of paper). The cartoon idea started with *petits patrons* (sketches) supplied by a designer, which were in turn worked up by a painter into full-scaled *patrons* or cartoons, usually drawn on linen sheets or on wide strips of paper subsequently attached to one another.

In the case of the high-warp loom the cartoon was placed behind the weaver, easily accessible for reference at all times. In addition, he worked with a tracing of the main outlines of the design on his warp threads, at least until the seventeenth century when tracing paper was invented. For the weaver on the low-warp loom, on the other hand,

the cartoon was cut into strips about a yard wide and placed under the warp threads. In neither case could the weaver see the finished side of the tapestry unless he walked around the loom, crawled under it, or used a mirror. None of the cartoons from the low-warp loom have survived, since the cut-up strips were rolled into the finished portion of the tapestry as the work progressed and were exposed to a great deal of wear. One can imagine the dedication required of the poor weavers. Not only were they always having to look at the back of their glorious creations and weave them on their sides, they also had to work the design itself in reverse, based on a cartoon that was either hanging behind them or cut up into strips.

The materials employed in tapestry weaving over the centuries have been wool, linen, and silk, as well as gold and silver threads. Wool was used for the warp and weft, linen occasionally for the warp, silk for highlights, and the glittering yarns were added for further emphasis. Cotton did not appear

until sometime during the nineteenth century, when it was used as a cheaper warp; later even the weft became cotton when mechanized-loom woven panels began to be mass produced.

During earlier centuries, the colors needed to dye the wool weft threads were limited in scope and were made entirely from natural substances. It was not until the eighteenth century that the weaver could choose from many shades of colors, and after the introduction of chemical dyes in the 1850s the palette knew no limitations. Yet, the limitations were very definitely there, to be discussed later.

One of the tools used today for thoroughly investigating and examining tapestries is infrared photography, which can reveal aspects of restoration through varying densities too difficult to be recognized by the unaided eye. Such photos were taken of two tapestries (one of which is illustrated here) at The Art Institute of Chicago, with startling results. As Figs. 1, 2, and 3 show, the dark areas indicate the original sections; the light

Fig. 2. Infrared photograph of Fig. 1. Courtesy of The Art Institute of Chicago.

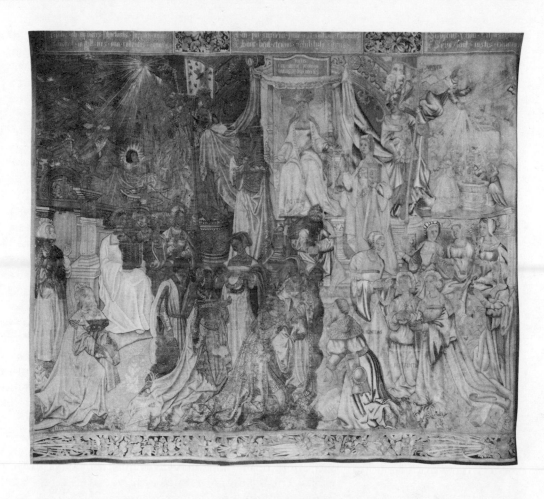

Fig. 3. One-quarter detail of infrared photograph of Fig. 1. Courtesy of The Art Institute of Chicago.

areas show where restoration had taken place. Through the work of Guy Delmarcel of the Royal Museums of Art and History in Brussels, the restoration can be pinpointed as having taken place in part during 1897. Additional restoration was carried out during the beginning of the twentieth century. As other versions of the tapestries were woven and are still in existence, it was fairly simple for the restorers to reconstruct these vast portions. The tapestry itself is a later version of *Los Honores,* kept at La Granja de San Ildefonso, in Segovia, Spain. The later set was woven around 1530 in Brussels and consisted of seven panels, although two were lost sometime during the seventeenth century and only five now survive.

Another tool for examining tapestries is thin-layer chromotography, the examination of threads, yarns, and their dyes. But as conservation and dye analysis are covered in detail by Nobuko Kajitani, Harold P. Lundgren, and Liliane Masschelein-Kleiner in this volume, I shall not take further time on these aspects.

In search of the tapestry-woven panel's origin, we find that no conclusive evidence exists. The technique as such is universal and appears in Egypt or the East in general and even in South America. However, the concept of the large decorative hanging is, perhaps, another matter. Why did this kind of hanging suddenly appear during the fourteenth century? Although there are isolated earlier examples—such as the Baldishol panel portraying the months of April and May, which was made in 1175 as part of a pew decoration of a church in that Norwegian town, and another piece made in Halberstadt, dating between the twelfth and thirteenth centuries, which illustrates Abraham and Saint Michael—from these we jump to the *Angers Apocalypse,* probably woven in the 1370s (since it is mentioned in the account books of Louis I, Duke of Anjou, as first having been ordered between 1377 and 1379, with references of payment as late as 1381).[6] In all three early instances the subjects lent themselves to being executed in cycles or stories. After all, if April and May have survived in the Baldishol panel, it stands to reason that other months would have existed as well; and if Abraham and Saint Michael were portrayed in a panel, perhaps other saints were, too. The Angers set, which is far more complete, gives us the storied interpretation of scenes from the New Testament, the book of Revelation. Often, as in the Angers instance, tapestries were inspired and in parts copied from illuminated manuscript pages. (In the Angers case, in fact, it is known that Charles V lent a manuscript to his brother, Louis of Anjou,[7] although the comparison to other extant manuscript pages—whether they are from the libraries in Cambrai, from Metz, or even from the Bibliothèque Nationale—indicates that the Master Hennequin of Bruges must have used them as references.)

Fig. 4. *Painted Wall Hanging from Deir-El-Bahari.* Tempera on linen. Egypt., XVII-XIX Dynasty. The Heckscher Museum, Huntington, New York; August Heckscher Collection, 1959.294.

Fig. 5. *Sion Tapestry*. Printed
linen. Italy, fourteenth century.
Historisches Museum, Basel,
1897.48.

In origin the storied wall decoration was
nothing new. An early example exists from
Deir-El-Bahari (Fig. 4). Another is the so-
called Sion hanging of Italian origin (Fig. 5),
which dates from the fourteenth century and
is almost contemporary with the Angers
tapestries. Would it not have been easier to
have *painted* the Angers compositions in a
similar fashion?

To use the tapestry weave in the form of
woven insertions and in the making of large
hangings can also be found within the history of textiles of the sixth century (Fig. 6).
The Coptic curtains that have survived are
numerous;[8] in isolated instances the entire
hanging was woven in the tapestry technique (Fig. 7). Another example is the *Cloth
of Saint Gereon,* once part of a hanging used

Fig. 6. *Coptic Curtain*. Linen,
plain weave with tapestry-woven
decorations in wool. Egypt, sixth
century. The Royal Ontario
Museum, Toronto, 910.125.32.

Fig. 7. *Icon of the Virgin*. Wool,
tapestry weave. Egypt, sixth century. The Cleveland Museum of
Art, Purchase, Leonard C. Hanna
Jr. Bequest, 1967.144.

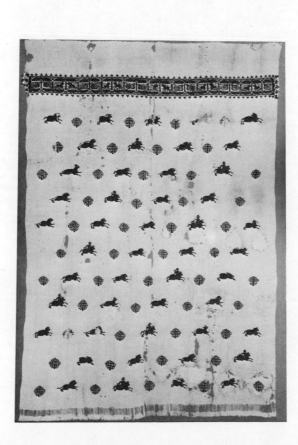

in the choir of that church in Cologne. Thus, the tapestry-woven panel, curtain, or hanging was truly nothing new.

As an item of decoration and of tremendous expense, the tapestry would have had to have been first used within places of worship. After the Christian church had moved out of its underground period, its members had the natural human desire to make the church interior as luxurious as possible. As early as A.D. 200 there arose the need for precise spatial divisions, and it was required that the assembly room be large, easily accessible, and divided between clergy and laymen. As a result, curtains and hangings were used to divide interiors for maximum flexibility and at the same time provide structural elements of separation between clergy and congregation, congregation and Emperor, Emperor and court, and, finally, God and man, as expressed in the altar, which was symbolically separated from the nave and the rest of the church. Curtains were drawn while the Eucharist was being celebrated within the ciborium.[9] Today manuscript pages, painted frescoes, and the mosaics from Ravenna show these curtains and hangings, which by the time of the Renaissance were replaced by large and splendid woven tapestries. Soon coming into use in the church, tapestries also began

to be used in the royal quarters, possibly, as one authority believes, because of the change in castle interiors, when the simple donjon or keep was replaced by large rooms with equally large walls.[10] Thus, the occupants were looking for a means of decoration that at the same time would provide warmth in the drafty, poorly heated castles. In southern climates frescoes could be used for these decorative purposes, but in northern countries ''woven murals'' were required. Since only heavy hangings would do, it was only natural that the royal interiors would be furnished with secular counterparts of a medium that was used in the churches. After this, the tapestry-woven hanging made inroads everywhere, even into the bed chambers in the form of curtains around the royal canopied bed. Indeed, it almost became an extension of the wealthy man's being, and when he traveled he brought his tapestries along with his other furnishings. Tapestries were also found at outdoor tournaments, as depicted in an engraving of 1509 (Fig. 8) by Lucas Cranach the Elder (1472–1553).

Whether used within the religious or the secular interior, the medium required rich patronage. Ownership of a tapestry signified power, wealth, and grandeur, and so the royal collections grew. One wonders

Fig. 8. *The Tournament with Samson and the Lion*, woodcut by Lucas Cranach the Elder. Germany, 1509. Courtesy of The Art Institute of Chicago, Gift of Mr. and Mrs. Potter Palmer, 1956.929.

if most tapestries were hanging most of the time or if there were many members of royalty who kept them locked up, as did Philip the Good, who had a vaulted storage to which he assigned six guards, twelve servants, and countless menders.[11] How many tapestries would one person own? Philip the Bold owned seventy-five,[12] Francis I owned 200 at the time of his death, and Henry VIII had 2,000 at one time.[13] Tapestries often constituted royal or papal gifts and more than once were exchanged for political or diplomatic reasons. Quite obviously, then, the centers of tapestry production throughout the centuries were to be found in countries where wealthy kings and monarchs of the church held forth and where the wool trade flourished.

A map gives us a quick overview. The beginnings of tapestry weaving were to be found in what is today Belgium and the Franco-Belgian border area, formerly known as the Spanish Netherlands provinces. The provinces, which once belonged to the powerful Dukes of Burgundy, were annexed to France in 1668 and from then on were known as French Flanders. In time sequence, the tapestry weaving centers were found in Brussels, Antwerp, Arras, Tournai, Lille, Douai, Valenciennes, Cambrai, Ghent, Oudenaarde, Mechelen, Enghien, Leuven, Tienen, St. Truiden, Bruges, and Mons. From here the influence of tapestry weaving spread to France, Holland, England, Italy, Spain, and Denmark. In France the following centers were of importance: Paris, Touraine (or Tours), Angers, Aubusson, Felletin, Charleville, Nancy, and Beauvais. The influence was further felt in southeast and northern Germany, Bohemia, Spanish Netherlands, Sweden, and Russia.

Germany as a whole was not a creative tapestry-weaving country. In Italy the entire production was under Flemish leadership, while in Holland tapestry weaving was influenced by the Spanish Netherlands. England was essentially directed by the Flemish until the studios at Surrey and Mortlake appeared. The Spaniards were also exposed to Netherlandish influence, until the eighteenth century, when Pastrana and Madrid became important. Denmark was under Netherlandish leadership, while Sweden and Russia succumbed to the French style.

Because the woolen coverings had to clothe vast expanses of wall, it was essential for the designers to find subjects complex enough so that more than one panel could be created. Thus, they searched for motifs by going through miniatures, adventure romances, historic and classical accounts, mystery and miracle plays, *chansons de geste*, and, of course, the Bible. Yet before these stories could be woven they had to be cast by a so-called author into a script, frequently with inscriptions that appear in most instances in either Latin or French or both at the top and bottom of tapestries. Thereafter, the author depended upon the painter, who had to interpret the script and, under the author's guidance, translate it onto paper. During the later centuries the painter frequently became the author. With this development a decline in the actual subject matter occurred.

Subjects were, of course, selected by those who commissioned the sets. One cannot help but think that often an association determined the selection, even if it was just symbolic and perhaps subconscious, and the patron would favor Alexander the Great at battle or King Arthur and the Knights of the Round Table, or express particular preferences for certain characters out of mystery or miracle plays. Religious subjects continued to be interpreted, but to the educated members of royalty, who were in fact reading the romances and attending the mystery or miracle plays, these new themes gained in personal importance.

By the end of the fourteenth century, tapestry-weaving establishments were found throughout Europe, and each center became known for certain characteristics or specific styles. Best known were the studios of Paris and Arras; smaller ones were found in Tournai. Arras operated during the reign of Louis XI until 1477, and its wall hangings became so famous that the town's name translated in Italian to Arazzo became synonymous with "tapestry."

One great difficulty is the task of dating tapestries and accurately attributing them to specific weaving centers, especially if no marks exist and one is making a purely visual analysis. Occasionally, coats of arms are of help, although they are to be explored with caution, since often when a tapestry changed hands the coats of arms were cut out and rewoven with the new owner's coat of arms, as seen in *The Annunciation*, woven during the Renaissance in Italy (Fig. 9). On the basis of the two coats of arms shown at the top of the tapestry, the panel can be dated. They are those of the Gonzaga family

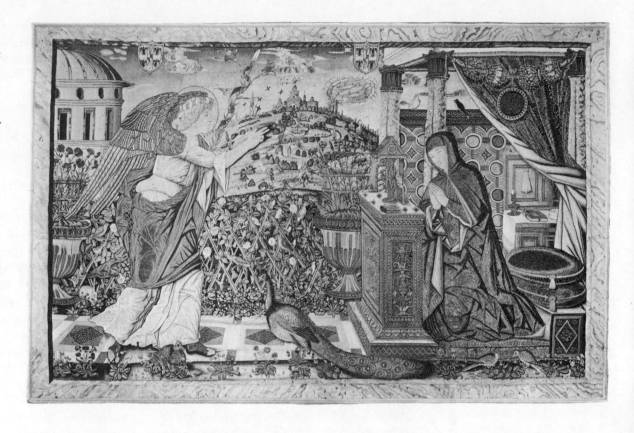

and bear the device of a gonfalonier of the church. The coats of arms point to Francesco Gonzaga, fourth marquess of Mantua, who was the recipient of the appointment bestowed upon him by Pope Julius II before 1510. This appointment gave him supreme command over the papal armies. Andrea Mantegna (1431–1506), who worked as a painter for the Gonzagas from 1459 to 1506, is believed to have been the designer for this tapestry. The weaver, as usual, is unknown. As Mantegna died in 1506, the design must have been executed before then. Since Francesco Gonzaga died in 1519, the tapestry can be dated somewhere between the years 1506 and 1519.[14]

Sometimes textile patterns are used for identification, as are the costumes and uniforms portrayed in the tapestry. Architectural elements such as buildings can aid occasionally; but if the subject matter belongs to the past, so would the architecture, the costumes and uniforms, and the textile patterns. Trying to use a particular episode portrayed within a given cycle as a means of identification can be unreliable because provincial interpretations occasionally made their ways into the sketches and cartoons. During the early centuries the author was the local priest, since he was often one of the few people in a small community who could read. Sometimes also, historic events or scenes taken from several sources were fused into these panels, and it almost requires a detective's mind to decipher the plots, guided occasionally by the so-called "labels."

Royal inventories prove most helpful in the study of tapestries, and for that matter they often become the foremost source of information. The account books of the Duke of Anjou, for instance, reveal not only the men who worked for him but also the specific sums paid to them. Indeed, sometimes tapestries now known to be lost can be documented only in that way. Inventories can tell us that, for example in the case of Philip the Good (1419–1467), who in 1449 ordered *The Story of Gideon,* the tapestry was to be executed in a set of eight panels by Robert Dary and Jean del'Ortie, tapestry manufacturers from Tournai, and that these eight panels were to cost 8,960 gold crowns for a total area of 630 square yards made of wool, silk, gold and silver, to be delivered within four years.[15] It is generally assumed that the average size of the tapestry was around 16×40 feet. The payment was probably made with a coin known as *ecu d'or*, royal coinage. (Today's value in gold content is $2.25 per *ecu*

d'or, which for 8,960 would total $20,160.
What the actual purchasing power of this
amount would have been cannot be determined.) A set such as the *Gideon* was of immense importance and would have been
used at times of marriages—in this instance,
the marriage of Charles the Bold in 1468 at
Bruges to Margaret of York—or at times of
baptisms, as for the baptism of Eleanor,
daughter of Philip the Handsome, in 1498.
Thereafter, in 1555 at the occasion of Charles
V's abdication it was used again. Unfortunately, toward the end of the eighteenth
century the set disappeared, a fact often bemoaned, for the *Gideon* tapestries could
perhaps have clarified the Tournai style.[16]

In the Lowlands all aspects of tapestry manufacture were governed by guild regulations.
Because so many problems had arisen, the
tapestry weavers and the wool workers had,
by the middle of the fifteenth century, formed
their own separate corporations.[17] Guild
rules became very specific. They required, for
example, that the master weaver had to be a
citizen of Brussels, that he could employ only
one apprentice aside from those drawn from
his legitimate children, that his working
hours had to start with the morning bell and
end with the evening bell, and that he could
not weave on Sundays or holidays. The regulations included warnings against the use of
goat and cow hair, since it was considered inferior.[18] No weaving workshop was allowed
to sell chambers or sets of tapestries unless

they had passed inspection by the so-called
jurors, who met on the average three times a
year in every workshop.[19]

Toward the end of the fifteenth century the
center for tapestry weaving shifted to Brussels. Today anyone referring to Flemish
tapestries woven at that time usually means
tapestries woven at Brussels. Commissions
kept the looms busy and the orders came
from all over Europe.

The re-using of original cartoons resulted in
additional sets. The cartoons, based on the
petits patrons, were the work of painters, but
after they were completed and delivered to
the weaving studio they became the property of the studio. On occasion the owner
would purchase the cartoon along with the
tapestry to ensure against any further dupli-
cation. At other times, especially if the cartoon had been drawn on linen sheets, the
patron would purchase it for the mere reason of saving this very expensive original.
Pinchart mentions an account of the town of
Lille, where in 1480 *les rich patrons haute-lice*
were hung in the great hall at the time when
the Chatelain of Lille took oath.[20]

An example of repeated and modified cartoon use is to be found in *The Redemption of
Man* series. The series contains ten designs
of which *The Resurrection* in The Fine Arts
Museums of San Francisco is number eight
(Fig. 10). Of this subject three related tapestries exist—one in the Vatican, another at

the Cathedral in Burgos, Spain (Fig. 11), and yet another in Chicago (Fig. 12). The Chicago version is six feet narrower, and one notes deletion of cartoons such as the Gates of Hell and a group of soldiers. Christ shown with his staff no longer has any meaning. What is even stranger are two angel wingtips which appear unattached, as the angel to whom they once belonged has disappeared. So has the fountain in front of which he knelt. The center axis of Christ has been moved to the left, and a totally unknown female figure replaces *Pulchritudo*. The Burgos panel must be looked upon as

Fig. 11. *The Resurrection*, from *The Redemption of Man* series. Wool and silk, tapestry weave. Flanders, Brussels, ca. 1500. Burgos Cathedral, Spain. (Photograph: The Photo Club, Burgos, Spain)

Fig. 12. *The Resurrection*, from *The Redemption of Man* series. A reduced version of the eighth in a series of ten. Wool and silk, tapestry weave. Flanders, Brussels, ca. 1500–1510. Courtesy of The Art Institute of Chicago, Gift of Mrs. Chauncey McCormick, Mrs. Richard Ely Danielson and William Deering Howe, 1947.47.

Fig. 13. (a) Two B's, separated by the red escutcheon, one for Brabant and the other for Brussels—mark used by Brussels weavers. (b) Instance of two B's used in Beauvais during seventeenth and eighteenth centuries.

a

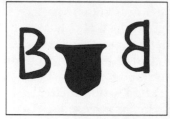

b

the most complete version of the cartoon. The most striking difference between the San Francisco and Chicago tapestries and the Burgos panel are inscriptions contained within scrolls in the outer floral border of the latter. Also, another figure appears in front of the architectural unit to the right.

Perhaps one of the most famous sets woven in Brussels was *The Acts of the Apostles*, designed by Raphael (1483–1520) for Pope Leo X. Pieter van Aelst received the order in 1515, and the set of ten panels was completed within three to four years. The cartoons, drawn in distemper this time, are still to be seen today at the Victoria and Albert Museum. For nearly one hundred years they had remained in Brussels, and during that period the set was copied an additional four to five times. As many as fifty-five full or partial sets can today be traced to the cartoons. The original set was destined to hang in the Sistine Chapel on the lower level, where the panel with the Miraculous Draught of Fishes hung to the right of the altar. The upper level was decorated with frescoes. In 1630 Charles I purchased the cartoons and had them transferred to Mortlake, a factory established in 1619 in London. The painter Anthony van Dyck (1599–1641) was ordered at that time to design more elaborate borders for them.[21]

What is of interest is the fact that the original order and the cartoons for these tapestries came from Italy. The influence of Raphael's cartoons on the Brussels artisans was extensive.[22] They introduced perspective at last to the North, which, up to this point, had treated group scenes by assembling people in tiers or by crowding them together. From then on we find expansive vistas. A liaison between Italian painters and northern weavers was established. In turn, Flemish painters went to Italy and returned fully trained and capable of providing cartoons incorporating the phenomenon of perspective.[23] One only has to think of men such as Bernard van Orley (1471–1541), who subsequently was made superintendent at the Brussels workshop and under whose supervision the famous *Acts of the Apostles* were woven, as well as the splendid *Jacob* series now belonging to the Royal Museums of Art and History in Brussels; Jan Vermeyen (1500–1559); and Pieter Coecke van Aelst (active 1495–1532).

During the sixteenth century, religious wars occurred throughout Europe, and Protestants were moving to escape persecution. Although religious subjects were still in demand and being woven, a change in attitude and subject matter found its way into the cartoons and tapestries. Other changes also occurred: borders, which gained in importance and in width, providing space for smaller scenes, can be compared to the predella paintings of Italian origin of centuries before. From 1528 on, there appear within these borders or just above them the famous two B's separated by a red escutcheon, one for Brabant and the other for Brussels (Fig. 13a). For nearly three hundred years this mark was used by the Brussels weavers under orders from the municipality of Brussels, which required that all tapestries woven in the Netherlands carry these marks along with the weaver's monogram. One must be careful, however, not to confuse this mark with other markings close to it, such as the two B's used at Beauvais during the seventeenth and eighteenth centuries (Fig. 13b). Occasionally, the marks turn into three sets of initials, as in the San Francisco tapestry showing the *Execution of Joan of Arc* of 1905–1907 (Fig. 14).

Toward the end of the sixteenth century and during the early seventeenth century, difficulties of identification often puzzle us again as the designers once more became unknown entities. With the need for borders it became common practice to combine center panels with border designs not necessarily done by one and the same hand. As engravings became available, it was often left to the weaver's discretion which border he wished to use with which panel.

With the introduction of distemper- and oil-painted cartoons by Raphael and, later, by Peter Paul Rubens (1577–1640), the weavers were faced with problems in duplicating translucent colors and light effects in general, and variation of tones of color were needed. In addition, the compositions changed once again, this time to accommodate enormous figures, which were placed into settings reminiscent of stage sets. It was the Baroque style which now had conquered the tapestries, as so clearly seen in the *History of Zenobia*, designed by Justus van Egmont (1601–1674) and woven by G. Peemans (active 1660–1705), in Brussels. Borders and their function found new meaning, this time as guarding enframements beyond which nothing must fall, as it were, from the main scene. Frequently they became columns and were very much part of the compositions.

14

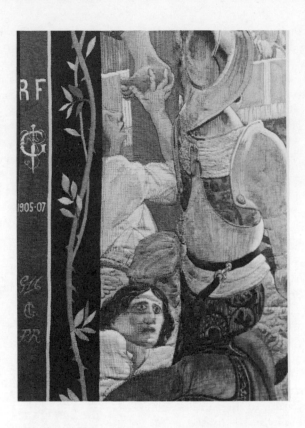

Fig. 14. Full set of marks from *Execution of Joan of Arc*. France, Gobelins, 1905–1907. The Fine Arts Museums of San Francisco, Gift of the French Government, 1924.32.3.

Fig. 15. Fleur-de-lis mark of identification from Paris workshops, on a tapestry showing *Le Festin* from *L'Histoire d'Artemise*. France, early seventeenth century. Courtesy of The Art Institute of Chicago.

In France at this point Arras and Tournai had been phased out, and the tapestry workshop established at Fontainebleau by Francis I during the sixteenth century began slowly to pass into oblivion. Now the leading workshops were to be found in Paris. As marks of identification the fleur-de-lis was used (Fig. 15). In 1601 two Flemish tapestry makers, Comans (active 1601–1627) and van der Planken (active 1601–1627), opened a workshop where, among other panels, *entrefenêtres* were created after drawings by Antoine Caron (1521?–1599?), today kept at the Cabinet des Dessins, Musée du Louvre in Paris (Fig. 16). The subject matter can be traced to the allegory of Queen Artemise with King Ligdamis, based on the text by Nicolas Houel (1520–1584), who, however, actually portrayed Catherine de Médicis in the role of Artemise.

The weavers employed in Paris were religious refugees. After Henry IV proclaimed the Edict of Nantes in 1598, many a Huguenot was allowed to return to his homeland without being prosecuted. Comans and van der Planken enlarged their workshop through the partial purchase of a property established since the fifteenth century by the Gobelins, a dyer family in Faubourg-Saint-Marcel. In 1662, by the order of Louis XIV, this property was purchased through his minister of finance, Jean-

Baptiste Colbert (1619–1683), so that all the Parisian workshops could be moved to the area. In 1667 the site was named La Manufacture Royale des Meubles de la Couronne, known also by its much shorter name, to this day, as the Gobelins. It worked exclusively for royal commissions. A weaver was trained for fourteen years and wove two and one-half square yards per year. Because of this slow rate, the need for additional French workshops became quite an issue, and so Beauvais was established in 1664 and Aubusson in 1665.

The first director of the Gobelins was Charles Le Brun (1619–1690), who managed 250 weavers. Trained as a painter, he followed Raphael's monumental and life-size style. Guided by Le Brun's knowledge as a decorator and designer, the Gobelins produced tapestries that balanced intellectualism with an understanding of the human figure; they came to stand for the best the seventeenth century had to offer. After Le Brun died, the Gobelins was closed for five years, from 1694 to 1699.

Beauvais, meanwhile, was directed from 1684 by Philippe Béhagle (active 1684–1704), the merchant and tapestry weaver under whose leadership the *Grotesques* series was made. Berainesque in style but designed by Jean

Fig. 16. *Le Festin* from *L'Histoire d'Artemise*. Wool and silk, tapestry weave. France, early seventeenth century. Courtesy of The Art Institute of Chicago, Gift of Charles J. Singer to The Antiquarian Society, 1890.10.

tified in insisting that his coloring and the effects of light and shade be duplicated exactly or whether such matters should be left for the weavers to decide, as they were perhaps better judges since they knew the practical limitations of their craft. [24] According to Weigert, the controversy resulted in a broadened color palette that would provide for proper shadings. However, some of these faint tones faded in a very short time, and today many a tapestry of that epoch has changed in character so totally that color harmony has been entirely thrown off balance.

Oudry's influence was tremendous, and both the Gobelins and the Beauvais factories changed their styles of cartoon interpretations to that of rendering paintings exactly, thereby producing tapestries unimagined in former centuries. Although painting had always influenced tapestry design and the industry could not have existed without it, painting had previously led, while the tapestry medium had followed. Once they became one and the same, however, decline was inevitable.

The seventeenth century came to be called the Age of Reason, for philosophy, mathematics, and astronomy came to be the subjects that concerned the questioning and reasoning mind. Such a mind, which questioned the Creation and saw in God the First Cause, so to speak, was no longer interested, when looking at tapestries, in seeing extensive episodes taken from the Bible. Indeed, if for instance the story of Moses was portrayed, it was used mainly for introducing vast country scenes.

The first half of the seventeenth century belongs to the Baroque. During that time the scenes became highly theatrical and illustrated exuberance, albeit at all times controlled by rationale. During the second half of the century, generally known as the Age of Louis XIV, these new-founded philosophies, thoughts, and ideas were solidified. Tapestries were concerned with subjects from ancient history and mythology as well as with allegories. The hunting tapestries with enormous and far-reaching vistas were popular, but so also were the portrayals of dancing, smoking peasants, reminders of everyday life.

During the eighteenth century, called the Age of Enlightenment, the interest in classical subjects and allegories declined, and there arose a demand for light, relatively happy

Baptiste Monnoyer (1636–1699), these tapestries foreshadow the eighteenth century in lightness and gaiety. (The *Grotesques* series and the Beauvais factory are described in detail in this book by Edith Standen and Bertrand Jestaz.) As the factory ran low-warp looms, the tapestries it produced were somewhat less expensive than those woven at the Gobelins.

After the Gobelins reopened, its focus was changed and the artistic and administrative sides were separated. Under the artistic direction of men such as Jean Baptiste Oudry (1696–1765), the Gobelins factory produced tapestries that were as exact an interpretation of a painting as was technically and humanly possible. This accomplishment became quite an issue, and more than once the question was raised as to whether a painter was jus-

episodes that earlier tapestry patrons would have thought frivolous and superficial. The attitudes of the century are best represented in the thinking of men such as Frederick the Great (1712–1786), who regarded himself as a servant of the state, as compared to Louis XIV (1638–1715), who thought he was the state.

The tapestry-weaving establishments of that century were nourished by the cartoons and paintings of men such as Antoine Watteau (1684–1721), François Boucher (1703–1770), and Jean Pillement (1727–1808). The subjects portrayed were light, far removed from historical and religious happenings, since the demand was merely for decorative panels. Thus, we see portrayed *The Loves of the Gods*, *The Bird Snatcher*, and *The Village Festival* by Boucher, as well as scenes from opera and the *Commedia dell'Arte*. Many a panel was also influenced by Far Eastern motifs, as are found in those woven at Aubusson after Pillement.

The demand for tapestries was extensive. Indeed, on special occasions the streets would be lined with them. A painting by Giovanni Pannini (1691–1765) shows the Piazza Farnese as it was decorated for the marriage of the Dauphin. The painting dates from 1745 and is today part of the Chrysler Museum's collection in Norfolk, Virginia.

By the end of the eighteenth century most tapestry studios found themselves in trouble. Although some artisans still survived and supplied cartoons, such as Francisco Goya (1746–1828), who had created his forty-three cartoons portraying country life, in general the economic situation in Europe, with its repeated wars and revolutions, was very unsettled—not at all conducive to the expensive production of these large masterpieces.

By the last quarter of the eighteenth century another matter had begun to influence tapestries. The size of living quarters changed, creating a demand for smaller tapestries. Often the large tapestries of preceding centuries would be cut down, with a rather awkward result for panels showing foremost historic events contained, as it were, in large, impressive, woven frames. Out of this and the general *Zeitgeist* there eventually grew an attitude in which tapestries were treated much as one would treat wallpaper—by using them to line walls and surround doors and windows.

The most splendid example of this concept within tapestry manufacture is the famous Croome Court Room, today part of the Metropolitan Museum's collection in New York but originally designed by Robert Adam (1728–1792) in the 1760s for Croome Court in Worcestershire, the country establishment of the Earls of Coventry.[25] Woven to measure and actual room specifications at the Manufacture Royale, the panels incorporated designs by François Boucher, known as First Painter to the King in 1765, against a background imitating panels in the damask weave.

The weaver was Jacques Neilson (active 1749–1788), in charge of the low-warp looms at the Gobelins. It was he who, along with Jacques Soufflot (1713–1780), introduced in 1757—after the engineer Jacques de Vaucanson (1709–1782) had made it possible—the translation of the low-warp loom procedure into a vertical loom operated by foot pedals. This loom was able to produce tapestries one-third less in price than those produced on the high-warp loom. Furthermore, weaving on it was much faster; thus the royal factory found itself in competition with the Beauvais establishment in that it could produce Gobelins-quality tapestries but at Beauvais prices.

Along with these interiors went matching firescreen and furniture coverings. Going to ovals or roundels—paintings, in fact, which could be woven separately and then inserted into an allover background—was a way of achieving faster production at lesser expense, for the master weavers could create the figures while lower-paid men or even apprentices could produce the rest of the panels. The weaving of covers for furniture became an industry in itself, for they required much less time than did tapestry making and so became a means by which the factories were kept going. Beauvais produced quantities of firescreen panels and chair and sofa covers; similar efforts went on at Aubusson, including the weaving of carpets. Another art that emerged was the woven portrait, utilizing painted portraits and easel paintings in general. François Gérard's (1770–1837) painting of Napoleon I was woven at the Gobelins in 1811, first in full size, thereafter just as a portrait.

The arrival of the Industrial Revolution brought with it a concern for mass production

Fig. 17. *Pomona*, designed by Sir Edward Burne-Jones (1833–1898) and William Morris (1834–1896). Woven at Morris Workshop. England, Surrey, late nineteenth century. Courtesy of The Art Institute of Chicago, Purchase, Ida E. Noyes Fund, 1919.792.

and speed of execution, leaving less time for worry about quality and something called taste. The situation became devastating until voices began to be raised—in France by Eugene Violet-le-Duc (1814–1879), in England by Augustus Welby Northmore Pugin (1812–1852), John Ruskin (1819–1900), and Edward Burne-Jones (1833–1898). William Morris (1834–1896) and other members of the arts and crafts movement broke away from the practice of senseless verbatim copying of paintings and engravings on mechanized looms, and Morris and Burne-Jones began to draw their own designs at Merton Abbey in Surrey and wove them on hand-operated looms. In Burne-Jones' *Pomona* (Fig. 17), we see the subject matter was inspired by the Roman goddess of the fruit of trees. Placing her against a floral background undoubtedly was intentional, as it was reminiscent of the *mille-fleurs*, the thousand-flower tapestries of the fifteenth century.

In the United States, men such as Albert Herter (1871–1950) began to be concerned with American interior decoration and to design textiles and tapestries for such purposes. The subjects became strictly American, as, for instance, in a portrait of George Washington, included in a panel of a series of twenty-six intended for the mezzanine of the Hotel McAlpin in New York. As in Surrey, this was woven on hand-operated looms. Candace Wheeler (1827–1923), dismayed that there had been more accomplishments of the loom than of handwork,[26] referred to tapestries as simply "needle weavings"[27] and preferred to think of her own needle weaving as real tapestry. American tapestries, she felt, should be made "by embroidery alone, carrying personal thought into method."[28] Out of her deep involvement grew her desire to copy in needle weaving the *Miraculous Draught of Fishes*, based on the Raphael cartoon she had seen in London. In her own estimation the accomplishment was to be looked upon as "by far the most important work accomplished by needle weaving which has ever been made in America." Raphael and Pieter van Aelst must have turned in their respective graves!

In Europe the Art Nouveau, Art Deco, and the Wiener and Deutsche Werkstaette movements, as well as the Bauhaus, changed and influenced the basically good intentions of the nineteenth century. The 1919 Bauhaus proclamation by Walter Gropius (1883–1969) urged a return to crafts, and the unification

between the arts and crafts was preached constantly. The Scandinavian countries also made important contributions, particularly Sweden, whose crafts survived without having to cope with the Industrial Revolution, probably because of their strong tie to folk art. Within the tapestry field Márta Mäas-Fjetterström (1873–1941) and Anne Marie Forsberg will never be forgotten, nor will the Saarinens in Finland. In the 1930's their thinking, philosophies, approach to composition, design, color, and technique influenced artists in the United States as did those of the Bauhaus.

Artists in New York, Chicago, and Los Angeles, as well as those at Black Mountain College in North Carolina, began to affect the design of American tapestries or "wall hangings," as they now began to be called. For instance, Anni Albers (b. 1899) influenced many when she said, "I think of my wall hangings as an attempt to arrive at art, that is, giving the material used for their realization a sense beyond itself. . . . Breathing does not express anything; one's work should be like breathing, essential to just being."[29]

It is of interest to note that in France not one of the Impressionist or Post-Impressionist painters drew a cartoon for a tapestry during the nineteenth century. The mechanized looms were fed with seventeenth- and eighteenth-century subjects of the kind still available today by mail order. But rebirth of the medium found its way into the old Aubusson workshops, at first through the tutelage of Jean Lurçat (1892–1966), and later through the support of the Association des Peintres-Cartonniers de Tapisserie, established in 1947. Lurçat returned to the *Apocalypse of Angers* and the principles that governed its creation. Coarse textures and a color scale reduced to about a score of shades restored to tapestry an appearance of boldness and vigor.[30] Once again it became important to think of the purpose of a tapestry—to remember, as Roger-Armand Weigert states, ". . . that the purpose of tapestry-hangings is to adorn large areas of wall and that they should therefore give the impression of an unbroken, decorative, coloured surface. Deep perspectives, distant backgrounds, and even patches of pale colour must be avoided, for they create 'holes' in the wall, which ruin the harmony and balance of the effect."[31]

Once again, painting became the source of tapestry subjects, although its concept compared to that in the eighteenth century was entirely different. The tapestry became a woven mural rather than something copied from painting and contained within a frame. The woven frame disappeared entirely. In addition, the color range was limited to about twenty-five tones, as opposed to the 14,000 shades with which dyers and weavers had to cope at the end of the eighteenth century.

Artists such as Pablo Picasso (1881–1973) and many others designed the cartoons themselves, keeping technique and technology of the woven medium in mind. Others, such as the Scandinavian Jan Groth (b. 1938), created the entire tapestry themselves; Groth, for instance, not only creates his own *petits patrons* and the full cartoon, but he and his wife weave their own tapestries rather than make arrangements to have them woven at Aubusson or elsewhere. Groth is particularly fortunate in that he can weave on a turn-of-the-century Danish loom, originally used to weave copies of the Karel van Man-

der tapestries in the Frederiksborg Castle, and since his wife was trained on the *basse-lisse* loom, with the cartoon under the warp threads, the Groths are able to adapt their cartoons and hang them behind the high-warp loom. A further modification is the fact that the heddles are operated by a foot pedal and are hanging behind the warp threads. MM. Soufflot, Neilson, and Vaucanson of 1757 would be delighted could they see the Groths weave today.

In the 1960's wall hangings were essentially conceived as having nonutilitarian purposes, and their appearance as wall linings was considered new and inventive. Of course this was not true, as we have seen. However, what *was* new was the idea of free-standing walls made of tapestry-woven panels, to be viewed from more than one side. In America in the 1960's there occurred a vast and influential change brought about quite independently by two of tapestry's most prominent artisans, Lenore Tawney (b. 1925) and Claire Zeisler (b. 1903). One began to speak of "woven forms," and the once flat wall decorations acquired a third dimension which removed them from the wall entirely and brought them out into the interior. The Biennale in Lausanne was quick in acknowledging the change and continued to include the creations in its biannual tapestry exhibitions. A search for better and clearer terminology for referring to such pieces began—and is not entirely resolved even today. "Woven forms," "art fabric," and "fiber sculpture" are all attempts in that direction. Some utilize the tapestry weave totally while others employ it only in parts, but when used it is interpreted with a freedom undreamed of in earlier times.

The latest attempt in terminology is *la nouvelle tapisserie,* as André Kuenzi refers to the medium in a recent publication: "La nouvelle tapisserie nous a paru le terme convenant le mieux à des ouvres murales ou spatiales—ne ressortissant plus aux conceptions de la tapisserie traditionnelle de haute et de basse lisse."[32] To the Biennale the medium remains *la tapisserie*.

When we look at the creations of recent years it is evident that we have moved far from the tapestries of the fourteenth through the eighteenth centuries. Still, there is one aspect the old and the new have in common: a concern for an aesthetic result.

NOTES

1. Arthur Urbane Dilley, *Oriental Rugs and Carpets* (New York: Charles Scribner's Sons, 1931), p. 250.

2. Irene Emery, *The Primary Structures of Fabrics* (Washington, D. C.: The Textile Museum, 1966), p. 78.

3. George Leland Hunter, *The Practical Book of Tapestries* (Philadelphia: J. B. Lippincott Company, 1925), p. 231.

4. Denis Diderot, *A Diderot Pictorial Encyclopedia of Trades and Industry*, vol. 2, Charles C. Gillispie, ed. (New York: Dover Publications, 1959) pls. 331, 336.

5. Mercedes Viale, *Tapestries* (London: Paul Hamlyn, 1966), p. 17.

6. Geneviève Souchal, *Masterpieces of Tapestry from the Fourteenth to the Sixteenth Century* (New York: The Metropolitan Museum of Art, 1973), pp. 31–32.

7. Ibid., p. 31.

8. Veronika Gervers, "An Early Christian Curtain in the Royal Ontario Museum," in V. Gervers, ed., *Studies in Textile History, In Memory of Harold B. Burnham* (Toronto: Royal Ontario Museum, 1977).

9. Richard Krautheimer, *Early Christian and Byzantine Architecture* (Harmondsworth, England: Penguin Books, 1965), pp. 158–60.

10. W. S. Sevensma, *Tapestries* (New York: Universe Books, 1965), pp. 40–41.

11. Souchal, p. 17.

12. Ibid., p. 16.

13. Ibid., p. 17.

14. Christa Charlotte Mayer, *Masterpieces of Western Textiles* (Chicago: The Art Institute of Chicago, 1969), p. 29.

15. Hunter, p. 264.

16. Ibid.

17. Alphonse Wauters, *Les Tapisseries Bruxelloises* (Brussels, 1878), pp. 32–33.

18. Ibid., pp. 34–35.

19. Ibid., pp. 35, 41–45.

20. Alexandre Pinchart, *Histoire Générale de la Tapisserie,* Pt. III (Paris, 1878–85), p. 46.

21. Hunter, p. 222.

22. Viale, p. 65.

23. Ibid., p. 67.

24. Roger-Armand Weigert, *French Tapestry.* Translated by Donald and Monique King. (Newton, Mass.: Charles T. Branford Company, 1962), p. 120.

25. Edith Standen, "Croome Court, The Tapestries," *Bulletin, The Metropolitan Museum of Art* 18, no. 3 (November 1959): 97.

26. Candace Wheeler, *The Development of Embroidery in America* (New York: Harper & Brothers, 1921), p. 126.

27. Ibid., p. 133.

28. Ibid., p. 126.

29. Mildred Constantine and Jack Lenor Larsen, *Beyond Craft: The Art Fabric* (New York: Van Nostrand Reinhold Co., 1972), p. 24.

30. Weigert, p. 160.

31. Ibid., p. 162.

32. André Kuenzi, *La Nouvelle Tapisserie* (Geneva: Les Editions de Bonvent, 1973), p. 17.

Tapestry Wools, Ancient to Modern

Harold P. Lundgren

Tapestry weaving goes back to ancient times and was discovered and carried out independently by different cultural groups in the New World as well as the Old. Although the oldest tapestries have all but disappeared, mainly by deteriorating and falling apart, there are still a few preserved which are not quite so old and not so damaged. Among these are the woven products made in Egypt by the Copts, members of a Christian sect who in the early centuries after Christ wove large quantities of tapestries, usually with Christian symbols. Many of the woven materials were used as burial shrouds. They are in relatively fair condition today because they were preserved under dry, dark, less damaging conditions than fabrics stored elsewhere. Another example of tapestry in good condi-tion is shown in Fig. 1. This 1200-year-old Peruvian fabric was found buried in a copper mine.

Many fibers have been used in making tapestries, including cotton, linen, silk, and threads of gold and silver. Animal hairs have also been used, notably mohair from the Angora goat of Asia Minor and the hair of the llama and alpaca of South America. Yet over time, the predominant material has been wool.

Why is wool so desirable? What are its limitations in tapestry art? What differences are there between ancient and modern wools? What has been and is being done to preserve and improve its qualities? Here I will try to answer some of these questions.

Fig. 1. A 1200-year-old wool cloth found in a copper mine in Peru. Fibers from fabrics such as these have been compared with corresponding fibers of today.

Wool has an intuitive appeal to people, especially today. In trying to get away from much of the sameness of modern life, people are seeking out things made creatively by skilled hands, things that carry the implications of time, tradition, and individuality.

As traditionally defined, tapestries are hand-woven textiles used for hangings, curtains, and upholstery. As artistic creations, they are the medium of expression of the artist who designed them. They are produced by the interweaving of weft threads into a prepared warp (threads that run the long way in the loom), with the weaver using a bobbin held in the hand. The weaver may or may not be the same person as the artist; indeed, frequently the two are not the same.

The whole surface of the tapestry is patterned with the weft threads, which the weaver inserts, as appropriate, alternatively over and under the warp threads. The weft threads are not inserted across the whole of the surface as in shuttle weaving, but only to the extent dictated by the artist's design (or cartoon, as it is called by the tapestry weavers). In the finished tapestry, the warp becomes covered by the inserted weft. Thus, it is the weft that determines the design, color, and texture of the product.

It is as the weft threads that wool is predominantly used in tapestries. The reason wool is not generally used as warp threads is due to its elasticity. This elasticity can result in a product uneven in shape unless the weaving process is done with extreme care. More often warp threads are made of linen and cotton, which are less elastic than wool. On the other hand, it is the elastic character of wool that contributes to its ease of manipulation and to the springiness of the yarn and subsequently to the aesthetics of the finished product.

SHEEP AND WOOL

Wool is, of course, the animal hair that provides the protective outer covering of sheep. Sheep were among the first animals to be domesticated by humans for food and fiber. Although little is known about the remote ancestors of present-day sheep, undoubtedly they are related to the wild sheep now found in different parts of the world, such as the Rocky Mountain Big Horn sheep in the United States. Wild sheep have an overcoating of long, coarse hair and an undercoat of soft, shorter wool fibers. Over the centuries, through selective breeding

humans have improved sheep and wool, developing breeds to thrive in specific climates, eliminating the wild hair, and producing wools of varying grades ranging from fine and short to coarse and long. Each level of fineness and length can produce a specific type of yarn, and it is from the finer wools that the finer yarns can be spun.

In addition, the qualities of crimp (fiber waviness) and luster are important to the feel and appearance of wool products. Wools differ in luster, depending on the smoothness of the fiber surface and the straightness of the fibers. Luster can be silvery (or silky) and glassy. The mild silvery luster is found in the fine, highly crimped merino wool. The silvery luster comes from the long wool of the Lincoln and Leicester sheep. The mohair from the Angora goat produces what is described as glassy luster.

WOOL PROCESSING

The first step toward making yarn involves shearing the fiber from the animal. Special skill is required; otherwise there will be flaws in the end product. A poor shearer may take a second or more cuts, resulting in very short fibers that, when blended with the longer, more desirable fibers, can reduce yarn quality.

After shearing, the wool is sorted into separate qualities and grades. Despite all the work by breeders in improving fleeces, there are inevitable differences in lengths and finenesses of fibers, even on the same animal. Furthermore, there may be faults present such as stains from urine or feces or from microorganisms growing in the fleece. There can also be damage to the tips of fibers from the action of sunlight. Those skilled in hand-sorting shorn wool can quickly judge differences in qualities by the appearance and feel of the fiber locks; in fact, most of the wool in the world is bought and sold on the basis of such subjective judgments. However, we cannot be certain that the wools used in tapestries in the past were sorted for highest quality.

After sorting, each lot is washed ("scoured") to remove lanolin and other grease constituents, vegetable matter, sand, and dirt. Improper washing can lead to fiber matting (felting), and this results in breakage of fibers in subsequent carding. Earlier, soap and soda washing agents were used, but because washing solutions that are too alkaline can

Fig. 2. Schematic illustration of the hair follicle, the structure in which the wool fiber is made.

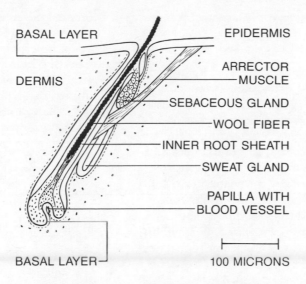

BASAL LAYER
EPIDERMIS
DERMIS
ARRECTOR MUSCLE
SEBACEOUS GLAND
WOOL FIBER
INNER ROOT SHEATH
SWEAT GLAND
PAPILLA WITH BLOOD VESSEL
BASAL LAYER
100 MICRONS

cult problems was to match the unique and flexible control that the skilled hand-spinner exerts when he or she maintains the needed variable or constant tension as the fibers pass between first finger and thumb.

UNDERSTANDING WOOL FIBER

In order to understand the behavior of wool fibers in their long and potentially damaging route from the sheep's back through processing and into use, it is necessary to consider the evidence obtained by scientists working on wool and other mammalian hairs. These researchers use highly sophisticated techniques, such as electron microscopy, x-ray diffraction, ultraviolet- and infrared-light absorption, electron-spin resonance, chromatographic methods, ultracentrifuging, and even analysis of sound produced when fibers are rubbed together.

It is well established that all hairs, including human hair, are similar in chemical composition, physical structure, and properties. The hairs are the product of a remarkable process that begins at the base of a tubelike sac, the follicle, located in the outer layers of the skin (Fig. 2). The process starts with the generation of living spherically shaped cells. As these cells are pushed outward by newly formed cells, they undergo a remarkable transformation. The cell nucleus disintegrates and the liquid protoplasm within the cells turns solid and then into fibrillar units and matrix substances. The finished wool fiber comes out of the follicle as a cemented-together, elongated cellular structure composed of a cuticle and cortex (Figs. 3 and 4).

seriously damage wool qualities, today neutral, nonionic synthetic detergents are used.

After washing and drying, the wool is carded in order to separate, open out, and initiate alignment of the fibers in preparation for spinning. Carding involves passing the wool between the wires of a brush on a flat or cylindrical surface. Woolen yarns are made directly from the carded wool (the "card sliver"). Worsted yarns are made from the "top"—that is, carded wool from which shorter fibers have been combed out, leaving the remaining longer fibers highly aligned.

Spinning woolen and worsted yarns requires special skills. Developers of modern spinning machinery found that one of the most diffi-

Fig. 3. Enlarged electron micrograph of wool fiber showing the overlapping surface-scale (cuticle) structure.

Fig. 4. Schematic illustration of the composite structure of the wool fiber showing the hierarchy of units from the keratin molecule unit (the alpha helix) and its relation to the levels of organization that form the fiber cortex. The cortex is shown surrounded by the three-layered cells.

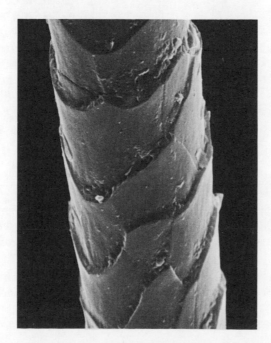

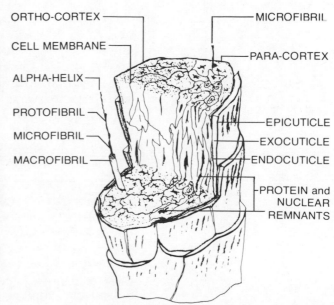

ORTHO-CORTEX
CELL MEMBRANE
ALPHA-HELIX
PROTOFIBRIL
MICROFIBRIL
MACROFIBRIL
MICROFIBRIL
PARA-CORTEX
EPICUTICLE
EXOCUTICLE
ENDOCUTICLE
PROTEIN and NUCLEAR REMNANTS

The same process occurs in a generation of human hair.

THE CUTICLE

The surface covering of the wool fiber, the cuticle, consists of relatively hard units, the so-called "scales" (Fig. 3). These structures overlap each other like tiles on a roof. Depending on the breed of the animal, the scales vary in size, shape, and thickness. In general, they are made up of three suprimposed layers, all of the protein material called keratin (Fig. 4). The layers are the *epicuticle,* the *exocuticle,* and the *endocuticle*. The epicuticle is the outer layer and, despite the fact that it is protein, it has water repellency. Unless the epicuticle is damaged, it enables wool to shed drops of liquid water, even though wool has high moisture-vapor absorbing power. Moreover, the frictional characteristics of the surface of wool contribute to its excellent spinning quality, its tendency to felt, and the appearance and "hand" (feel) of products made from it.

THE CORTEX

Underneath the cuticle and comprising about 90 percent of the wool fiber substance is the cortex. It is made of an amazing hierarchy of structures, all of *keratin protein molecules.* Some of the molecules are coiled and assembled in groups of two or three into units called *protofibrils* (Fig. 3). These, in turn, are united in groups of nine or ten into *microfibrils.* The microfibrils are embedded in a less organized matrix of keratin and make up the *macrofibrils* (frequently called fibrils). The macrofibrils are packed together into the long, needle-shaped *cortical cells.* Finally, the cortical cells are cemented together, forming the *cortex.*

In general, the cortex of wool fibers divides into two areas, the *ortho* cortex and *para* cortex (Fig. 4). The amount and placement of these determine the fiber crimp. The presence of crimp relates directly to differences in the elasticity and, in turn, to differences in the amino acid composition of the keratin molecules that comprise the ortho and para cortical cells (Fig. 5 and 6).

COMPARISONS OF FIBERS

As mentioned, all of wool substance is keratin protein. The silk fiber is also of protein, but its amino acid composition and structure are entirely different from wool. Since silk and wool are both protein substances, they have similarities in stability and chemical reactivity. On the other hand, linen and cotton are built of cellulose molecules which are entirely different chemically from protein. Nevertheless, both the protein and cellulosic fibers are biodegradable. In other words, with time, and especially under adverse conditions, these fibers can stiffen, crack, yellow, and fall apart. Among the conditions that promote degradation are warm and moist atmospheres, sunlight, and chemically alkaline, acidic, oxidizing, and reducing environments. The natural fibers can also be destroyed by insects and microorganisms.

CHEMICALLY SENSITIVE CENTERS IN WOOL

Three kinds of areas in the protein molecules of wool are susceptible to chemical breakdown: (1) *the peptide linkage,* (2) *the chemically reactive centers along the keratin chain molecule,* and (3) *the disulfide crosslinks.*

The peptide links[1] serve to tie together the amino acid building units into the protein chain molecules. These linkages are susceptible to breaking down if kept in acidic or alkaline conditions or exposed to the presence of enzymes (for example, those of moth larvae). The ultimate breakdown of the protein produces the original amino acid building units.

The chemically reactive centers, which are situated like ribs along the backbone chain, are also susceptible to modification (Fig. 7). Some of these centers are acidic in nature (for example, the carboxyl groups, $-COOH$), others are basic (for example, the amino groups, $-NH_2$), and still others are chemically neutral but also chemically reactive (for example, $-OH$). These several kinds of reactive sites are susceptible not only to chemical damage but also to modification for improvement. For example, dyes and/or other desired agents can be chemically attached at these sites.

The third and most characteristic sites of keratin proteins are the disulfide crosslinks,[2] the linkages that tie together the keratin molecules into networks and thus provide the properties of strength, toughness, and insolubility in water. Although these linkages are relatively strong, they nevertheless can be severed by insects, microorganisms, oxidizing and reducing chemicals, and sunlight and heat.

Wool was not intended to be used by humans. If we wish to make use of it, it is up to us to improve it to meet our requirements. This is being done. Significant progress has

Fig. 5. Enlarged photograph of cortical cells isolated from wool and suspended in water. The cells exhibit special optical properties (birefringence) in polarized light because the keratin molecules that compose the cells lie in one direction. The two kinds of cells, the ortho and para, are not directly distinguished.

Fig. 6. Separation of the ortho and para cells of wool. The ortho and para cells mixture has been put into a density gradient column in which the liquid varies from highly dense at the bottom to less dense at the top. The less dense ortho cells float above the more dense para cells. It thus becomes an easy matter to separate them for comparative study.

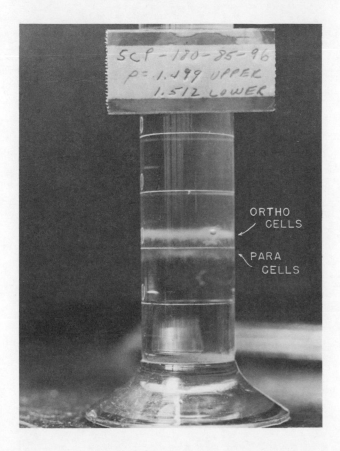

Fig. 7. Enlarged schematic illustration showing the "heart" of the wool fiber. The coiled, thread-like keratin molecules are crosslinked by disulfide bonds. The molecules are built from amino acids that have been tied together by peptide bonds (not shown). The X, Y, and Z symbols represent chemically reactive centers contributed by different kinds of amino acids.

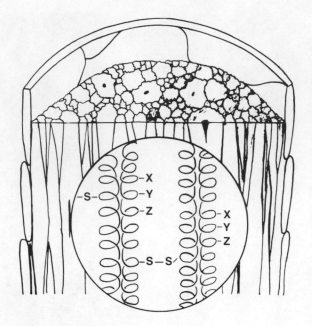

been made toward improving the resistance of wool to soiling, flame, and insects and microorganisms, as well as to damage in washing.

But it is not possible to repair wool fibers that are severely embrittled and weakened over time. One of the author's students, Susan Spritz, finds that, in general, all the ancient wool fibers (up to two and three thousand years old) she examined are weak and brittle even though the fibers have been in the dark and also in dry conditions. Evidence indicates that oxidation of the keratin protein is mainly responsible for the damage.

As researchers become more able to pinpoint chemical damage, they will be in a better position to develop treatments that will help offset further damage with time.

ACKNOWLEDGMENTS

The author wishes to thank Dr. Wilfred H. Ward of the Western Regional Research Center, Albany, California, for permission to use his photographs of the wool fiber (Fig. 3) and Dr. Jan Sikorski of the University of Leeds, England, for permission to use his schematic illustration of the wool fiber (Fig. 4).

NOTES

1. Chemically, $-\begin{bmatrix} H-O \\ | \| \\ N C \end{bmatrix}-$

2. Chemically, $-[S-S]-$

REFERENCES

The following are recommended for further details on the structure, chemistry, and processing of wool and modifications for improvement.

H. Mark, N. S. Wooding and S. M. Atlas, *Chemical Aftertreatment of Textiles*. New York: Wiley-Interscience, 1971.

Proceedings, International Wool Textile Research Conferences. I (Melbourne: Commonwealth Scientific and Industrial Research Organization, 1956), II (Manchester, England: *Journal of the Textile Institute*, Transactions vol. 51, no. 12, 1960), III (Paris: CIRTEL, L'Institut Textile de France, 1965), IV (New York: *Journal of Applied Polymer Science —* Applied Polymer Symposia Number 18, Wiley-Interscience, 1971), V (Aachen, e.V., West Germany: Schriftenreihe, I-V, Klaus Zeigler, ed. Deutsches Wollforschungsinstitut an der Technischen Hochschule, 1976).

M. L. Ryder and S. K. Stephenson, *Wool Growth*. London: Academic Press, 1968.

W. Von Bergen, *Wool Handbook,* 3rd ed. New York: Wiley-Interscience, vol 1, 1963; vol. 2, pt. 1, 1969; pt. 2, 1969.

Wool Science Review. London: International Wool Secretariat, 1949–present.

Dyeing Techniques of Tapestries in the Southern Netherlands during the Fifteenth and Sixteenth Centuries

Liliane Masschelein-Kleiner

THE DYERS' CRAFT

The southern Netherlands of the fifteenth century had roughly the same borders as has Belgium today, but in the Middle Ages it was joined to other Burgundian territories such as Artois and Picardy. A flourishing craft of dyers existed in Western Europe as far back as the eighth century, when Charlemagne had ordered the cultivation of madder throughout the empire.[1] Most townsmen belonged to a guild, as did the dyers,[2] who were separated into two distinct classes: dyers of blue (Blauwevaerwers) and dyers of red (Rootvaerwers). In Flanders their emblem was a bicephalous eagle—blue on a silver background for the dyers of blue, golden on a red background for the dyers of red.[3]

The guilds not only helped their members when they were in difficulty; through rigorous regulations they also held them to a high

standard of production. Dyers were told exactly what dyes and what mordants they should use. The use of materials of inferior quality was prohibited. Working on Sunday was forbidden, as was working before dawn and after sunset because, it was thought, "high-quality work could not be done by candlelight." Bad workmanship was punished with fines for small infractions and expulsion for major ones. The number of workers or apprentices a master could employ was severely limited, often to no more than three or four, and their wages were regulated. Competition between dyers was forbidden, and the guilds made sure that nobody became either too rich or too poor. As a result of all this, the same customs were imposed on craftsmen for generations, and there was no change in technique until the end of the sixteenth century.

Fig. 1. The dyers' workshop. From Denis Diderot and Jean Le Rond d'Alemberts, eds., *Encyclopédie. Recueil des Planches*, vol. 10 (Paris: Briasson, 1772), and vol. 31 (Stuttgart: Frommann-Holzboog, 1967).

Teinturier de Riviere, Attelier et différentes Opérations pour la Teinture des Soies.

THE DYERS'
WORKSHOPS

Dyers generally built their workshops near a river or a well in order to obtain the large quantities of water necessary. The mordant or dye liquors were heated on stone stoves, often in stone vats on top of the stove, and the fibers, in the form of skeins, were stirred in the liquid with a wooden stick (Fig. 1). After the dyeing, the wool or silk was rinsed in the river or was laid in a basket and pressed with feet. Sometimes the water was squeezed out by wringing the skeins on a pole (*espart*) (Fig. 2). Finally, the skeins were spread over racks for drying.

MATERIALS AND
TECHNIQUES
OF DYEING

The techniques of dyeing were different for blue dyers and red dyers. The blue dyers were called vat dyers, from the large wooden vats in which, through a sophisticated fermentation process, the dye bath was prepared. The red dyers dyed in all colors except blue. Because most of the dyestuffs the red dyers used were mordant dyes fixed on the fiber in boiling water, they were called "teinturiers de bouillon."

Most natural mordant dyes have a polygenetic character; that is, an individual dye can have a range of different shades with different mordants. The best mordants are metalic salts which form soluble oxides or hydroxides, such as aluminum, iron, tin, copper or chromium, which are only very slightly soluble in water. In the Middle Ages, the only mordants used by dyers were alum and ferrous sulfate. Tartar was often added to alum to effect an even deposition of the aluminum hydroxide on the wool.[4] When wool is boiled in a solution of alum, the solution converts into aluminum hydroxide, a sticky jelly. This sticky hydroxide is maintained, through Van der Waals attractions and ionic bonds, on the surface and in the pores of the wool, and the wool is thus able to form very

stable complexes with most phenolic dyes. These complexes are called "chelates" because the metal ion can be pictured as being held by the dye molecule as though by the pincer (*chela* in Greek) of a crab. After dyeing with alum, copperas, a green ferrous sulfate, was often used in order to obtain duller shades, a process called "saddening."

Although there are great numbers of dyes available in nature, chiefly for yellow shades, nevertheless the dyers of the fifteenth and sixteenth centuries had to work with a quite limited range of dyestuffs. Let us consider some of these.

THE RED DYESTUFFS

MADDER Madder plants (*Rubia tinctorum*, Fig. 3) were cultivated from early times in Western Europe. In the fifteenth century, Dutch growers became the first producers of madder in Western Europe.

Madder is a perennial with reddish roots, which contain the dyestuffs, and leaves that grow in groups of four or six and also in circles at regular intervals on the stem. In June small yellowish flowers appear. The fruits are black shiny berries. It takes three years for the madder roots to reach their peak yield in dyestuffs. Records show that in Lille in northern France, roots were harvested between September 8th and April 15th and had to be oven-dried before May 15th.[5]

The first quality of madder, the "cropmadder" was found in the inner part of the root; the outer part of the root had to be scraped off because of its high tannin content which would impart a brown color to it. Madder contains several chemical compounds, of which the most important for dyeing purposes are alizarin and purpurin.

Fig. 2. Rinsing and wringing the skeins after dyeing. (From Diderot and d'Alembert, vol. 31).

Fig. 3. Madder *(Rubia tinctorum)*. (From Louis Figuier, *Les Merveilles de l'Industrie*, vol. 2 [Paris: Furne, Jouvet et Cie, 1876], p. 640).

Fig. 4. Kermes *(Coccus ilicis)*.

Dyeing with madder was usually done on alum-mordanted wool or silk. The roots were powdered and soaked overnight, then boiled and strained through a gauze into water. The bath was heated to a lukewarm temperature, wet yarns were then added, and the temperature was slowly raised to 80°C. After a half-hour of simmering, the yarns were left in the bath to cool. In the final rinse, slaked lime was added, which produced a more purple color. Indeed, madder is the only dyestuff that is best used in hard water.

KERMES The red dyestuff kermes is extracted from the dried bodies of the female insect *Coccus ilicis* or *Coccus vermilio*, which feeds on the stalks of the oak *Quercus ilex* or *Quercus coccifera*. The dried body looks like a bluish berry. (Fig. 4).

Kermes must be gathered just before the insects lay their eggs. The insects are killed in boiling vinegar and dried, and the resulting "grains" look reddish brown and are often covered with a whitish powder. The principal colored compound of kermes is kermesic acid (5kg of insects would produce 50g of this acid). It seems to have been a very expensive dye.[6]

With alum mordant, kermes produce pretty scarlet lakes. In the past, they were called "Venetian scarlet" or "grain red." These insects once lived throughout the Mediterranean region—in southern France, Spain, northern Africa, and so on—but they are now in process of disappearing.

BRAZILWOOD Brazilwood is a collective name that was used for many red woods. Various leguminous trees, including the lima, sapan and peachwoods, are classed as brazilwoods or so-called "soluble red woods" to distinguish them from the barwood family of trees, which yield coloring matters that dissolve only in boiling water. It is very difficult to determine the real origin of the dyes used in the old methods.

Until the fifteenth century, the southern Netherlands obtained its brazilwood from India, Sumatra, and Ceylon by way of Venice. The country of Brazil not yet having been discovered, the name Brazil comes from an Arabic word *braza*, meaning fire or red; the country of Brazil takes its name from the tree because it grew there abundantly.

Brazilin is the main component of the *Caesalpinia* species. It is colorless but is oxidized to the colored brazilein by exposure to air (Fig. 5). The red dye santalin is one of the known components of the *Pterocarpus* or sandalwood trees.

Fig. 5. Brazilwood *(Caesalpinia braziliensis)*. (From Figuier, p. 654.)

Fig. 6. Weld *(Reseda luteola)*. (From Figuier, p. 658.)

Fig. 7. Dyer's-broom *(Genista tinctoria)*.

Fig. 8. Woad *(Isatis tinctoria)*. (From Figuier, p. 664.)

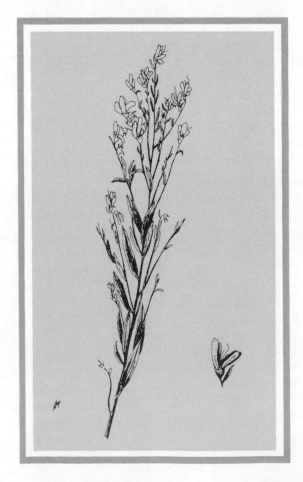

Pretty hues varying from blood-red to dark brown were obtained from brazilwood using alum and iron mordants. However, because of its poor fastness to light, brazilwood was used only for shading another, more stable dyestuff. Indeed, the dye faded so quickly on exposure to air that the chips of wood had to be cut just before use.

THE YELLOW DYESTUFFS

WELD Weld—dyer's mignonette or dyer's weed (*Reseda luteola*)—is an herb, an annual native to Western Europe that grows wild in many places. It reaches about 1m in height and has upright stalks; long, narrow leaves; and small, yellowish flowers that grow in long, slender spikes at the top of the stalk (Fig. 6). The plant (except the roots) contains the yellow dyestuff luteolin.

The plant was harvested in June when in full flower and could be used at once or dried for future dyeing. It was often sold in sheaves like straw. Bright yellow shades were achieved with alum mordant; olive shades were obtained with iron.

In the southern Netherlands weld was the only dyestuff named by the guilds' regulations.[7]

DYER'S-BROOM. Dyer's-broom, also known as dyer's-greenweed or woodwaxen, is a shrub, *Genista tinctoria*, found in sandy soils on the shores of the Mediterranean. The flowering tops were used to make a green by dyeing over indigo (Fig. 7).

The plant contains two dyestuffs: luteolin (also found in weld) and genistein. Although genistein has never been found in any tapestry of the southern Netherlands from the fifteenth or sixteenth centuries, it may have disappeared because of aging.

THE BLUE DYESTUFFS

WOAD Woad, *Isatis tinctoria*, belongs to the *Cruciferae* family. It is a biennial or perennial herb with an erect stem bearing yellow flowers (Fig. 8).

In the Middle Ages it was widely cultivated in Europe, but sometimes very strictly regulated. In certain countries peasants were permitted to grow only a certain amount of woad, and no dyer was permitted to buy it up ahead of his colleagues. Prior to being sold it had to be tested, and often it was sold only to citizens of the same town.[8]

In France large quantities of woad were produced. In the Languedoc it was called "Guesde" or "Guède," in Normandy it was called "Vouède" or "Pastel," and in Picardy it was called "Waide."

Woad was sown in February and harvested from the end of June until October. Four or five gatherings of the leaves were often possible although the first crop; "virgin woad," was thought to be the best. The mature leaves were then brought to a horse- (or water- or wind-) driven mill,[9] reduced to a pulp, drained, and thrown into a heap. After fifteen days, the paste was thoroughly mixed and pressed into a wooden mould to form the famous balls called "Cocagnes" or "Tourteaux." Languedoc, which was the main producer of woad, was often called "Pays de Cocagne," a term that had come to mean a country of unusual wealth. (Figure 9 shows sellers of woad balls, from a sculpture on an exterior wall of Saint Amiens Cathedral.[10])

The final and most difficult stage of manufacture was the fermentation. The balls were reduced to powder, the pulverized mass piled into a layer about 1m deep called "Tourtes," and left to ferment for nine weeks. One of the difficulties of this process was exact regulation of temperature, which was not supposed to exceed 50°C. The paste was therefore frequently sprinkled with water and turned over. During this process the glucosides of indoxyl (indican or isatan) were hydrolyzed by a ferment present in the plants (isatase or indemulsin), and oxidation then transformed the indoxyl into indigo (Fig. 10a). Five hundred grams of woad leaves yield about 1.5g of indigo. Because the efficiency of indigo was said to improve with age, barrels of dried, fermented indigo were marked according to quantity and year of production and stored. They were usually used after four years. Indigo was applied on textiles by a rather sophisticated procedure known as the vat process (Fig. 10b). Since indigo is insoluble in water, reducing agents were used to convert the dye into an alkali-soluble compound, leucoindigo, by the addition of hydrogen (Fig. 10c). Leucoindigo has a good affinity for wool and can be absorbed by the fibers, and in the presence of air is quickly oxidized to insoluble indigo. In the past, reducing agents consisted of bran, starch, honey, molasses, or any other goods containing glucose. Some plants giving reducing enzymes, such as weld or madder, were often added. Glucose is transformed by fermentation into lactic acid, which in turn gives butyric acid, carbon dioxide, and hydrogen.

Fig. 9. Sellers of woad balls. Saint Amiens Cathedral, exterior wall, southern face of the nave.

Alkalis were provided by wood ashes, the best ones imported from the Baltic towns of Koenigsberg and Riga.[11] Managing the vat required great experience and continual attention. The temperature had to be carefully maintained at 45°C, and so the vat was covered with a lid and with blankets. Reducing agents and alkalis also had to be maintained at the right concentration during the dyeing.

The wool was immersed in the bath for about ten to thirty minutes, and on being removed the fibers were greenish yellow and turned to blue with exposure to the air. This operation was repeated at least three times in order to obtain an even dyeing, and the fibers were then rinsed in acidic water and finally in pure water.

In the past, the woad vat could be used only for three days; today the vat can be kept in good condition at least fifteen days. In Ypres a dyer might work with three vats a week, whereas in Leyde and in Bruges only two vats were allowed.[12]

Fig. 10. Chemical process of making and applying woad dye.

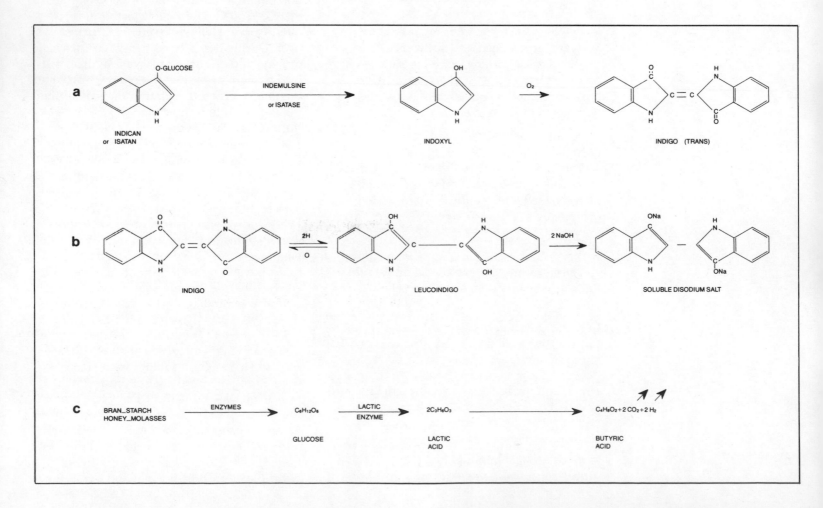

Fig. 11. Eastern indigo *(Indigo-fera)*. (From Figuier, p. 620.)

Fig. 12. Archil *(Roccella tinctoria)*. (From Figuier, p. 641.)

EASTERN INDIGO Eastern indigo is extracted from several shrubs that are varieties of the leguminous *Indigofera*, indigenous to Eastern Asia, Central America, Brazil and Java. They have oval leaves and tiny, reddish-yellow flowers (Fig. 11). The plant was sown in spring or autumn and harvested three or four times a year, although the quality of the crop declined throughout the year.

The dye, indigo, is just the same as that extracted from woad. Another dye, indirubin, is present in Bengal indigo (2.4 per cent) and in Java indigo (15 per cent). The yield in indigo is ten times superior in eastern indigo than in woad: 500g of leaves produce 15g of dye. The fermentation process is also much quicker: the branches and leaves are immersed for about thirteen hours in water, the surface of the liquid is beaten with wooden sticks to promote oxidation, and the paste that settles on the vat bottom is pressed into cakes, which are ready to be used by the dyer.

Although in Venice eastern indigo was imported since the first centuries A.D. and freely used,[13] woad growers in other parts of Europe succeeded for a long time in prohibiting the use of this dangerous competitor, enacting numerous laws until the eighteenth century. In 1609 Henry IV condemned to death the users of this "devil's dye," which was reported to be injurious to cloth fabrics,[14] and even in 1671 Colbert still ordered French dyers to use one hundred times more woad than Eastern indigo.[15] Records of the quantities of woad and of Eastern indigo sold in Antwerp show that general use of the latter

began only at the end of the sixteenth century in the southern Netherlands.[16]

THE PURPLE DYESTUFFS

ARCHIL is derived from a lichen, *Roccella tinctoria* that grows on rocks along the shores of the Canaries, the Azores, and Mediterranean islands (Fig. 12). Other kinds of lichens such as *Variolaria* or *Lecanora* were used to make dyes called litmus, turnsole, or cudbear.

All these lichens contain some common constituents, among them azolitmin, erythrolitmin, lecanoric acid, and orcin. When fermented in urine, orcin is transformed into the purple dyestuff orcein, which can be fixed directly on wool without mordant; it needs only a short boiling. However, the red, pink and purple shades so obtained show a poor fastness to light. This dye, called "fuel" in the Middle Ages, was forbidden by the guilds' regulations.[17]

THE BROWN DYESTUFFS

TANNINS Tannins have been used since early times for tanning, mordanting, and dyeing. They are found in a wide variety of plant species. Gallnuts are one good source of tannins. These are abnormal growths on the leaves and branches of certain trees where the tannin content has been increased by the feeding activities of an insect larva. Tannins have also been obtained from walnut shells, walnut bark, alder bark, and oak bark. Tannins consist of two classes of polyphenols, the so-called "hydrolyzable tannins" and "condensed tannins."[18]

Light brown shades are obtained by simmering wool for thirty minutes in a water solution of the dye. Darker colors may be achieved by adding ferrous sulfate to the bath. In the Middle Ages dyeing with tannins was tolerated only for darkening other fast dyes or for dyeing cheap textiles, since a high concentration of iron catalyzes the oxidation of wool and shortens drastically the life of the fibers.

ANALYTICAL METHODS

Samples taken from the back of tapestries must be analyzed in a different way from those taken from modern textiles analyzed for industrial purposes. Mordants and dyestuffs must be analyzed on threads that are often no longer than half a centimeter. Moreover, the analysis must be done accurately but quickly enough to enable the study of many samples from each tapestry. This is necessary so as to get a general idea of the dyeings of one piece.

We found that thin-layer chromatography was the most suitable method for this kind of analysis, although ultraviolet, visible, and infrared spectroscopy may sometimes be used also.[19] The process we proposed in 1967[20] has been applied successfully to most natural red, yellow, and blue dyestuffs. Indigo and orcein have to be confirmed by an additional testing. Tannins are, so far, still difficult to identify.

Thin-layer chromatography works as follows. Little bits of wool or silk are cut off from the back of the tapestry. Whenever possible, each shade is gathered from different areas. These areas are localized on a photograph. The yarns are washed and examined by X-ray fluorescence[21] in order to determine the metallic mordant. The same samples are then put into a small test tube. Two drops of hydrochloric acid (1/1) are added and brought to a boil. The residue is diluted with 0.5ml of water and the latter is evaporated. The result of this process is the hydrolysis of the colored lake from the fibers. The dyestuff can now be dissolved in ethanol and dropped on the thin-layer chromatography plate.

When the presence of archil is suspected or when an infrared spectrum must be taken, it may be necessary to purify the dyestuff a little more. Instead of evaporating the aqueous phase, one adds 1ml of amyl alcohol to the solution and shakes it. The dyestuffs are dissolved in this organic phase, but the sugars that accompany most dyestuffs in the solution remain in the aqueous phase and can be eliminated. This process does not extract indigo. When the fibers are still blue at this stage, they are placed into a new test tube and boiled in the presence of pyridine, which dissolves indigo.

The solutions of dyestuffs are now ready to be analyzed by thin-layer chromatography. After many attempts we found that the conditions proposed by Wollenweber[22] for the analysis of synthetic anthraquinones were the most suitable for natural anthraquinones such as those present in madder, kermes, and cochineal, for natural flavonoids such as those present in weld, dyer's-broom, old and young fustic, and even for indigo.[23] Layers of acetylated cellulose are laid down on glass plates (2.5 by 7cm). The dyestuff solution is applied by means of a micropipet as a little spot about 0.5cm from the edge of the plate. The latter is then placed in a chromatography tank filled to a depth of about 0.2cm with a developing solvent: ethylacetate, tetrahydrofurane, and water in the proportions of 1 to 5 to 7. The solvent rises up and the individual substances from the applied solution are transported upward at different rates because there is a competition between attracting forces of the acetylated cellulose and the eluting forces of the solvent.

When the solvent front has advanced a sufficient distance, 6cm from the starting line, the plate is removed and dried. The separated spots are made visible by spraying with beta-aminoethyldiphenylboric ester (1 per cent in methanol). This reagent forms colored compounds with anthraquinones and flavonoids that are particularly visible in ultraviolet light.

It is always advisable to run a known comparison compound on the same plate because various factors influence the rate of elution and cannot be closely controlled. Ultraviolet and visible spectroscopy are sometimes useful to complete the identification of a dye. Cochineal can be differentiated from kermes. Weld and dyer's-broom are easily recognizable. This analysis does not need a new sample; the same solution that has been prepared for the thin-layer chromatography only needs to be diluted.

Infrared spectroscopy can seldom be used because it needs a perfect elimination of the sugars from the glucosides of the dyestuffs. Longer threads, about 10cm long, are therefore necessary. Nevertheless, most pure dyestuffs show a specific infrared spectrum.

RESULTS AND
DISCUSSION

Gas-liquid chromatography has limited applications for the same reasons as infrared spectroscopy.

The present study deals with about seventy tapestries made in the southern Netherlands. Most of them were tapestries attributed to Tournai workshops from the fifteenth and sixteenth centuries, which were exhibited at Tournai's Cathedral in 1967, 1970, and 1971.[24] M. Jean-Paul Asselberghs from the Royal Art and History Museums of Brussels, whose sudden death shocked all who knew and worked with him, was the promoter of this work. Margaret B. Freeman from The Metropolitan Museum of Art in New York entrusted us with the analysis of the dyestuffs of the beautiful series *The Story of the Hunt of the Unicorn*. We also had the opportunity to complete this study with five Tournai tapestries from The Fine Arts Museums of San Francisco, thanks to the kindness of Anna G. Bennett. Another important series of tapestries was Antwerp's tapestries from the sixteenth and seventeenth centuries; the study of their dyestuffs allowed us to compare the techniques of the two centuries within a fairly limited area of production.[25] We are now studying the Brussels tapestries exhibited at the Royal Art and History Museums in 1976 with the collaboration of Guy Delmarcel.

Let us take the tapestries from The Fine Arts Museums of San Francisco as an example of the results usually found for tapestries from the southern Netherlands and also as an example of the difficulties sometimes encountered (Fig. 13).

THE RED SHADES

Madder is by far the most usual red dyestuff we found in all the tapestries from the southern Netherlands. Madder is used alone or mixed with weld, brazilwood, and (very rarely) kermes. It is fixed on alum mordant for the light shades and on iron for the darkest shades.

We found kermes in only one thread gathered on *Hector and Andromache* from The Metropolitan Museum of Art of New York. However, it was mixed with madder. This dyestuff was no doubt very expensive in the southern Netherlands. We found it in very precious clothes and embroideries such as the famous *Antependium of Rupertsberg* (thirteenth century),[26] and also in the dress of the bishop Erard de la Marck buried at Saint Paul's Cathedral of Liège in 1538. It has been claimed that the red backgrounds of the tapestries of the series *Apocalypse of Angers* contain kermes.[27] We were unable to find this dyestuff in the threads given to us for examination by the conservator, Pierre-Marie Auzas.

Fig. 13. Analysis of dyestuffs in tapestries of The Fine Arts Museums of San Francisco.

TAPESTRIES	DATE	RED	ORANGE	YELLOW	BROWN	BEIGE	BLUE	GREEN	PURPLE
SIMON THE MAGICIAN ARRAS? TOURNAI?	ca 1475	b1_d8_e5_e2_ e1 MADDER AL	c4_f3 MADDER AL	c1_e7_d5 QUERCETIN AL	b2_e8 MADDER Fe	c5 LUTEOLIN AL	e4_b7_d6 INDIGO	c4_g3_c8 QUERCETIN +INDIGO Zn	f1_e6_f5 ARCHIL ?
					b3_(f6)_d4_f1_ e8 MODERN Cu	c1_c8_c3 ?			
ABRAHAM AND MELCHIZEDEK TOURNAI	ca 1475	c3 MADDER AL	g2_e2 LUTEOLIN AL	d7_c5_f5 LUTEOLIN AL	c4_b1 MADDER + LUTEOLIN Fe		g7_d3_c4 INDIGO	c6_c5_g1 LUTEOLIN + INDIGO	
		f4_b2_h6 MADDER Sn_(Cu)			a6_e4 TANNIN Fe				
CHRIST BEFORE PILATE ARRAS? TOURNAI?	ca 1500 1525	d4_b8_h1_g6 MADDER Fe Zn	e7 LUTEOLIN Zn Fe	d1_h4_e7_b1 LUTEOLIN AL (Zn)	b6 MADDER	e6 TANNIN Fe Zn	d3_g8_g4 INDIGO	d1_b8_h1_f4 LUTEOLIN+ INDIGO Fe_ Zn	b7 ARCHIL ?
		e8 MADDER + LUTEOLIN AL	c8_e2_c5 ?		d1_e3 TANNIN Fe Zn	b1_d4 ?	b8 INDIGO + LUTEOLIN Fe Zn		
SPANISH BISHOP SAINTS TOURNAI	ca 1490 1500	f3_e1_d2_d6_e4 MADDER AL			b1 MADDER e1 M.+LUTEOLIN b5_d1_b3_d3_c2_d2 ?		a4_c2 INDIGO	a6_f1 INDIGO + LUTEOLIN	
THE ARMING OF HECTOR AND OTHER SCENES TOURNAI	ca 1500 1525							c1_b4 LUTEOLIN INDIGO Fe Zn	

Brazilwood was rarely found in the Tournai and in Brussels tapestries but more often in the Antwerp ones. The guilds' regulations seem to have been less rigorous there. As a matter of fact, brazilwood was tolerated only for shading a fast dye because of its poor fastness to light.

The detection of tin in three red samples gathered from *Abraham and Melchizedek* from The Fine Arts Museums of San Francisco and in a red sample from the tenth piece of Saint Remi's life from the Museum of Reims was quite surprising. Until now we have not found any mention of this metal in dyers' regulations during the fifteenth and sixteenth centuries. Although tin was well known in the Middle Ages, it was quoted as a mordant only in the seventeenth century. Consequently, in this case, two hypotheses are possible: tin was seldom used in the Middle Ages, or these threads originate from areas that have been repaired.

Zinc is another metal sometimes found in tapestries. As far as we know, it was not used as a mordant before the eighteenth century.[28] Zinc exists in some places in Belgium as calamine, a natural zinc silicate. Some of its salts are very hygroscopic and are used to increase the weight of fibers.[29] This modern falsification was perhaps known in the past. On the other hand, zinc may also originate from the clay used by the fullers for scouring wool; fraipontite, a clay containing zinc, is indeed found in the eastern part of Belgium.

The Yellow Shades

The only yellow mentioned by the guilds' regulations in the northern region is weld. On the other hand, in Italy some other dyestuffs seem to have been commonly used. The *Plictho*, one of the first books on dyeing, reports the use of curcuma, dyer's-broom, fustet, saffron, and fenugreek.[30]

We found weld in all the original threads gathered from the tapestries. The metallic mordants were aluminum and iron. Only one sample contained tin: it came from a piece of *The Passion* series, *Jesus' Condemnation*, from the Tapestries Museum of Angers.

Quercitron was found in some threads of *Simon the Magician* from The Fine Arts Museums of San Francisco. This dyestuff was imported in Europe by Edward Bancroft in 1785.[31] These samples come from old restorations.

The Orange Shades

The orange shades are obtained by dyeing with madder alone or mixed with weld. Weld alone was found in some yellowish oranges.

The Brown and Beige Shades

Real black did not exist in old tapestries. The darkest shades were dark brown or dark blue. Dark brown was usually a mixture of three basic dyes: madder, weld, and indigo. Very often, of course, tannins and iron were used, too, although these matters were regarded as dangerous by the guilds' regulations.

The brown threads of the tapestries have proved particularly sensitive to aging. Often they have been replaced several times and are still the most damaged area of the piece. The high concentrations of dyes and of iron may be the cause of this quicker decay of the wool. Some recent studies prove that bound metal ions are at least partly responsible for photodamaging.[32]

Most beige threads do not contain dyestuffs anymore. They have the color of aged wool or silk.

The Blue Shades

We found indigo in every blue thread we had the opportunity to analyze. Sometimes madder or weld were used at the same time. It is difficult to state if this indigo comes from woad or from *Indigoferae* species. Indirubin, which is present in some eastern indigo, was never found. According to Schweppe,[33] kaempferitrin should accompany indigo in *Isatis tinctoria*. In our opinion that remains doubtful; we did not find this yellow dye in the leaves of *Isatis tinctoria* in our possession nor in any threads of blue wool or silk gathered from tapestries. Besides, kaemferitrin exists in many species of plants and among others in some tannins often used to obtain dark shades. This fact makes analysis difficult.

The Green Shades

Greens are always a mixture of weld and indigo. Some olive shades are dyed with weld with iron mordant.

The Purple Shades

This color is obtained by mixing madder and indigo. Nevertheless, some threads contained archil, although this dye was forbidden by the guilds. Many dyers seem to have transgressed this law.

CONCLUSIONS

The colors of the tapestries from the fifteenth and sixteenth centuries remain surprisingly bright and beautiful. They are often better maintained than those in some tapestries from the eighteenth century, although they are at least two hundred years older. This longevity is no doubt largely due to the choice of the trio of weld, madder, and indigo as basic dyestuffs.

After several centuries of aging, this choice still appears very wise. These three dyes age very well together. Weld shows a rather poor fastness to light, madder is fairly stable, and indigo is very fast to light.[34] The pale areas of the tapestries—that is, those with the pale yellow, beige, pink, and orange hues—are made up with low concentrations of weld and madder. They become paler and paler on aging. On the other hand, the dark areas more often contain a good deal of indigo; thus, they keep their darkness. The contrasts will improve on aging and the pattern will remain distinct.

In the Middle Ages the cartoons took into account not only the weaving techniques but also the materials—wool and silk and their dyestuffs. Although the weaver had great liberty in interpreting the sketches, he had to conform to a fairly narrow range of shades—about thirty for most workshops. The shadow working was not the result of a sophisticated mixture of dyes: a system of hatching was woven, generally with three shades of the same hue. These factors gave the tapestries a striking originality. From the seventeenth century on, and above all in the eighteenth century, the painters forced the dyers more and more to copy the colors of oil paintings, and the number of shades increased in an unreasonable way: more than 30,000 hues were used in the Gobelins in 1773.[35] Mixtures of four and still more different dyestuffs were sometimes necessary in order to obtain an exact match to the color of the painted cartoon.

As a result, a lot of new dyes were introduced in the dyers' workshops without care being taken of their light-fastness. The use of indigo carmine, for instance, was a real catastrophe for the tapestry. The aniline dyestuffs of the nineteenth century had even poorer fastness to light.

Fortunately, modern chemistry offers dyers a wide range of fast dyestuffs. Let us hope that the dyers of today will be as wise as their ancestors of the fifteenth and sixteenth centuries in selecting their materials.

ACKNOWLEDGMENTS

The author wishes to express her gratitude to The Fine Arts Museums of San Francisco and to Anna G. Bennett, Curator of Textiles, for giving her precious samples and for allowing her the opportunity to present this study. She is also grateful to Luc Maes, *ingénieur technicien,* for his extensive analysis of metallic mordants, and to Roger Versteegen for taking the photographs.

NOTES:

1. Franco Brunello, *The Art of Dyeing*, trans. Bernard Hickey, (Vicenza, Italy: Neri Pozza, 1973).

2. Neil Grant, *Guilds* (New York: Franklin Watts, 1972), pp. 1-4.

3. G. De Poerck, *La draperie médiévale en Flandre et en Artois* (Bruges, Belgium: De Tempel, 1951), p. 168; and Marcelle Derwa, *L'Héraldique* (Liège, Belgium: Bibliothèque de l'Université de Liège, 1964), p. 19.

4. De Poerck, p. 171.

5. Ibid., p. 177.

6. Felicien Favresse, *Etude sur les métiers bruxellois au moyen âge* (Brussels: Institut de Sociologie, Université Libre de Bruxelles, 1961), p. 109.

7. De Poerck, p. 187.

8. Jamieson B. Hurry, *The Woad Plant and Its Dye* (London: Oxford University Press, Humphrey Milford, 1930).

9. Paule Roy, "Moulins à vent de Picardie," *Bulletin de la Société des Antiquaires de Picardie*, 1967-68, pp. 99-118.

10. Jacques Le Goff, *La Civilisation de l'Occident Médiéval* (Paris: Arthaud, 1964), p. 282.

11. De Poerck, p. 163.

12. Ibid., p. 165.

13. Gioventura Rosetti, *The Plictho*, trans. Sidney M. Edelstein and Hector C. Borgetty, translation of first edition of 1548 (Cambridge, Mass., and London: M.I.T. Press, 1969), p. 111.

14. Louis Figuier, *Les Merveilles de l'Industrie*, vol. 2 (Paris: Furne, Jouvet et Cie, 1876), p. 621.

15. Lucien Reverd, "La Manufacture des Gobelins et les colorants naturels, I. Historique de la teinture à la Manufacture des Gobelins," *Hyphe. Teppiche, Wandteppiche, Stoffe. Internationale Zeitschrift* 1 (1946): 91-104.

16. Emile Coornaert, *Les Francais et le commerce international à Anvers fin des XV, XVI siècles*, vol. 2 (Paris: M. Rivière et Cie, 1961), p. 114.

17. De Poerck, p. 182.

18. E. Haslam, *Chemistry of Vegetable Tannins* (London and New York: Academic Press, 1966), p. 10.

19. Liliane Masschelein-Kleiner and Josef B. Heylen, "Analyse des laques rouges anciennes," *Studies in Conservation* 13 (1968): 87-97; and David H. Abrahams and Sidney M. Edelstein, "New Method for the Analysis of Ancient Dyed Textiles," *American Dyestuff Reporter* 55 (1964): 19-25.

20. Liliane Masschelein-Kleiner, "Microanalysis of Hydroxyquinones in Red Lakes," *Mikrochimica Acta* 6 (1967): 1080-85.

21. The analyses of mordants by X-ray fluorescence were made by Mr. Luc R. Maes, *ingénieur technicien*.

22. Paul Wollenweber, "Dünnschicht-chromatographische Trennungen von Farbstoffen an Cellulose-Schichten," *Journal of Chromatography* 7 (1962): 557-60.

23. Liliane Masschelein-Kleiner, Nicole Znamensky-Festraet, and Luc Maes, "Les colorants des tapisseries tournaisiennes au XV siècle," *Bulletin de l'Institut Royal du Patrimoine Artistique* 10 (1967-68): 126-40.

24. Ibid; Liliane Masschelein-Kleiner, Nicole Znamensky-Festraets, and Luc Maes, "Etude technique de la tapisserie tournaisienne au XV siècle. Les colorants," *Bulletin de l'Institut Royal du Patrimoine Artistique* 11 (1969): 34-41; Liliane Masschelein-Kleiner and Luc Maes, "Etude technique de la tapisserie tournaisienne aux XV et XVI siècles. Les colorants," *Bulletin de l'Institut Royal du Patrimoine Artistique* 12 (1970): 269-79; and Liliane Masschelein-Kleiner and Luc Maes, "Etude technique de la tapisserie des Pays-Bas Méridionaux aux XV et XVI siècles. Les colorants," *Bulletin de l'Institut Royal du Patrimoine Artistique* 14 (1973-74): 193-99.

25. Liliane Masschelein-Kleiner and Luc Maes, "Etude technique de la tapisserie des Pays-Bas Méridionaux. Les tapisseries anversoises des XVI et XVII siècles. Les teintures," *Bulletin de l'Institut Royal du Patrimoine Artistique* 16 (1976-77): 143-47.

26. Marguerite Calberg, *Broderies historiées du Moyen Age et de la Renaissance* (Liège, Belgium: Georges Thone), p. 7.

27. René Planchenault, *L'Apocalypse d'Angers* (Paris: Caisse Nationale des Monuments Historiques et des Sites, 1966), p. 19.

28. Reverd, p. 98.

29. Henri Spétebroot, *Traité de la teinture moderne* (Paris: Dunod, 1927), p. 33.

30. Rosetti, p. 198.

31. Brunello, p. 253.

32. G. J. Smith, "The Effect of Metal Ions on the Photoyellowing of Wool," *Textile Research Journal* 45 (1975): 483-85.

33. Helmut Schweppe, "Untersuchung alter Textilfärbungen," *Die BASF* 26 (1976): 29-36.

34. Tim Padfield and Sheila Landi, "The Light-Fastness of the Natural Dyes," *Studies in Conservation* 11 (1966): 181-93.

35. Lucien Rever, "La manufacture des Gobelins et les colorants naturels, II. Evolution de la technique," *Hyphe. Teppiche, Wandteppiche, Stoffe. Internationale Zeitschrift* 1 (1946): 141-47.

PART II
CONSERVATION AND
RESTORATION

The Preservation of Medieval Tapestries

Nobuko Kajitani

For centuries, tapestries[1] were made to cover architectural interiors and functioned mainly as barriers against the cold. Then, as they gradually became more colorful and pictorial, they were used as decorative wall hangings, and their possession became a popular status symbol in the West. Today, their aesthetic and historical value has been recognized, and museological philosophy regards them no longer as mere draperies but as pure works of art. Here I will present an approach to the preservation of medieval tapestries which, though extremely generalized and condensed, emphasizes objective information based on practical scientific and technical work. The relevant principles may be found in the publications listed in the Selected Bibliography.

At first glance, a typical medieval tapestry appears to be a fabric with an unrepeated pictorial design in many colors. Its creation, however, was a long process that started with growing or gathering raw materials for yarn and dyes, preparing the fiber, making the yarn, coloring, designing, weaving, and finishing. Specialists in widely distributed areas assumed the execution of these processes, which were affected by nature, socio-economic conditions, cultural trends, trade, and the progress of science and technology.

Tapestries are normally rectangular, woven fabrics ranging in size up to 40m² and 50kg in weight and are made primarily of organic fibers and dyes of plant or animal origin. Although these materials are characterized by pliability and absorbency, which distinguish fabrics from other works of art, they are also physically and chemically sensitive to their environment. Today, after several hundred years, many medieval tapestries have lost their original strength and are incapable of supporting their weight.

Essentially, preservation and conservation require, first, a study of the chemical, physical, and photochemical compatibility of any object with all aspects of its environment and, second, an approach to controlling the interaction between them in order to maintain the intrinsic quality of the object. If a tapestry is provided with chemical stability, laid flat and undisturbed on a supportive platform made of chemically inert material in clean air with proper climatic control, without light, and under a good maintenance program, then the present state will be preserved as well as possible. But, of course, tapestries are constantly exposed to the threat of deterioration—on the wall, in storage, and while being transported, studied, and treated—from physical strain, chemical interference, and photochemical degradation in an atmosphere created for human comfort rather than for tapestries. Mechanical movement, unsuitable contacting material, climate, air contaminants, and light impose physical, chemical, thermochemical, and photochemical deterioration that can easily be accelerated by negligence caused by a lack of scientific and technical knowledge. To provide proper environmental conditions that will prevent or at least retard such deterioration, we must determine the nature of the tapestry. Fiber, yarn, colorants, and fabric structure must be studied, and the tapestry must be given chemical stability and physical support with well-selected conservation materials and the use of sensible techniques. Then a steady maintenance program must be instituted in order to assure the tapestry's long-range preservation.

TAPESTRY AS MATERIAL

FIBERS IN MEDIEVAL TAPESTRIES

The natural fibers used to form the primary elements from which fabrics are constructed can be classified either according to their physical form (continuous length, limited length, and processed) or according to their chemical composition (protein, cellulose, or mineral, which indicate the fiber's animal, plant, or mineral origin). Continuous-length fibers are obtained from cocoons made by the larvae of certain types of insects and from bast, leaf, and bark fibers of plants. Limited-length fibers are obtained from external hairs of mammals, plant seed hairs, and fibrous minerals. Materials that are processed into fiberlike forms include parchment, membrane, and leather from mammals, paper from plants, and metal from minerals. Each group has characteristic physical and chemical properties that determine its appropriate care. Among these, silk, wool, flax, and metallic material are found in medieval tapestries.

Silk filament is obtained from the cocoon of lepidopterous insects, generally a cultivated species. The morphological features of silk include a pair of filaments—brins—in the center that are surrounded by a gummy substance. Chemically, the brins are fibroin and the gum, sericin. Silk is essentially protein, consisting of bundles of various amino-acid molecules; it is also porous, a characteristic of all fibers. Being protein, it is easily affected by water, strong alkalis, and various inorganic acids. Silk and most of its dyes are easily damaged by any type of light. It is especially vulnerable to weathering, deterioration caused by a combination of sunlight, soil, and drastic fluctuations of temperature and humidity.

The outstanding morphological characteristic of wool fiber is its exterior scales, which overlap in one direction toward the tip of the fiber. The scales can be chemically and mechanically damaged and can deteriorate through time, falling off as the wool degrades. Wool is essentially protein, primarily keratin, which is characterized by the presence of sulfur. Unfortunately, certain insects are attracted by sulfur and consequently thrive on wool. Being protein, wool fiber is also easily affected by alkalis and strong acids. In a humid atmosphere, wool readily absorbs moisture up to 20 percent of its own weight, and when wet it loses its physical strength. In the presence of water, with mechanical agitation, high temperature, and increased acidity or alkalinity, wool fabric felts, creases, and shapes into various forms. Thus, when subjected to wet cleaning, tapestries are exposed to potential shrinkage, felting, and fiber loss. Because of its physico-chemical nature, wool fiber accepts dyes and mordants better than any other fiber—hence its predominant use in pictorial tapestries.

Among the many bast fibers used in fabrics, flax, which is called linen after it has been spun, is occasionally found in medieval tapestries. Its morphological characteristics include ridges along its length and cross marks at many points; a canal runs through the center. Linen is sensitive to humidity; moisture penetrates and moves quickly in the fiber, increasing its dimensions, weight, and tensile strength. Being cellulose, linen withstands moderate alkaline conditions but is affected by acids. It has practically no affinity for metallic oxides and thus for most dyes. Harvested flax must undergo numerous fiber-extraction processes, and chemical methods recently introduced by a profit-oriented industry tend to reduce fiber longevity. Thus, if linen fabric is to be used as a long-term conservation material, its longevity must be ascertained before its use.

Metallic yarn, itself a subject of study, comes in a number of varieties that reflect the level of technology and trade of the time. Most metallic yarn in medieval tapestries was made by cutting prepared metallic material into strips, which were then wound around a core thread of silk or linen. The metallic materials were either gold or silver leaf adhered to membrane or soft metal. Membrane is adversely affected by water and alkaline conditions. The soft metals contain silver, the corrosion of which can completely cover its surface.

YARNS

There are two major yarn types. One is formed from relatively long- to continuous-length fibers by combining and then splicing them. The other is made from limited-length fibers by spinning. Silk filaments and relatively long fibrous materials such as flax are generally made into yarn by combining several fibers while twisting them under moist conditions. A mass of loosened, relatively short fibers, such as cotton, hair, and cut continuous-length fibers, is made into yarn by spinning; that is, a portion of the mass is drawn out at a certain speed and force as it is simultaneously twisted. Though both methods of making yarn are essentially the same, techniques and tools vary according to the type of raw material and the quality and makeup of the yarn desired. The amount of fibers fed in, the way the fibers are laid down, the balance of drawing-out speed, and the number of twists all affect the quality of the yarn. These two yarn-making processes create a *single yarn,* which can be used alone or combined with two or more others either without adding twist (combined yarn) or twisted (*plied yarn*) to better meet the requirements of a fabric.

Either of two twisting directions may be used to form yarn, Z or S, as may be seen by examining the trend of twist by holding the yarn in a vertical position. When two or more *single yarns* of the same twist are twisted together again, usually in the opposite direction, the resultant *plied yarn* has greater tensile strength but less flexibility than its component *singles*. The type and quality of fiber used, how it is made into yarn and then into fabric, determine the type and quality of fabric produced. In most medieval tapestries *plied yarn* of hairy, undyed wool was used for the warp, and plied and dyed wooly yarn was used for the weft. Most dyeing was done after fibers had been made into yarn.

COLORANT

There are two types of colorants for fibers: pigments and dyes. Pigments are, for the most part, inorganic compounds that come in colors, are insoluble in water, and have no affinity for fibers. After being ground into small particles and mixed with a binding medium, they are used to color the flat surface of fabrics; when applied they affect the surface only, immediately displaying the intended colors. Any affinity they have for the fabric is dependent on the binding medium, which is often water-soluble. Dyes are, for the most part, water-soluble organic compounds, the colors of which differ in solution from the final color desired. When immersed in a dye bath, fibers, yarns, or fabrics absorb the dissolved dyes. Various physical and chemical treatments are carried out to extract the dye from the plant, to transfer it to the fiber, and to bring out the desired color. When the dyed yarn has been transformed into fabric, it has a rich, penetrating tone, in sharp contrast to the flat tone of surface-covering pigment colors.

The dyes found in medieval tapestries are or-

ganic compounds from nature that occurred during a particular stage of growth in a plant or insect, some only from a specific locality. Harvesting the plant at the optimum stage of the dye is only the beginning of an extremely complex process. This includes extracting the dye compound, as well as ascertaining the relationship between the dye, fiber, metallic oxides, color-inducing agents, specific gravity, temperature, and the hydrogen-ion concentration level. The order of dyeing procedures will depend on these relationships as well as on the yarn to be dyed, the quality of dye in the plants, climatic conditions during the course of dyeing, the quality of water for the dye bath, and so forth.

Dyes are either monogenetic or polygenetic. The former produce one hue on fibers; the latter provide different hues according to the additives used. Among the dyes found in medieval tapestries, indigotin is monogenetic and all the rest are polygenetic.

One of the prime considerations in dealing with both natural and synthetic dyes is their fastness. The chemical composition of each dye, additive, and fiber causes a different fastness to light, water, and abrasion. In addition, the dyer's skill in manipulating the complex process of dyeing affects not only the color's initial appearance but also its subsequent fading. When dealing with medieval tapestries and selecting modern, synthetically dyed yarns and fabrics for conservation laboratory work, therefore, one must examine the fastness of all dyed colors.

Some general characteristics of major dyes found on the wool in medieval tapestries are presented below,[2] organized according to a rough category of colors still identifiable on the backs of tapestries. These dyes when applied on silk should be considered more fugitive.

BLUE Chemically this is indigotin, an indole derivative from woad (*Isatis tinctoria L.*). Dark blue is light fast, but the lighter the color the lesser the degree of fastness. Being an oxidizing dye, indigotin blue is refreshed when it is washed. Since it occurs in pigmentlike form, it may not have initially been abrasion fast but is now stable.

RED Principally this is alizarin, an anthraquinone derivative, from madder (*Rubia tinctorum L.*), used with the metallic oxides (mordant), alum, and occasionally iron. It has been said to be quite fast but has been

48

found faded on medieval tapestries, particularly the light hue. It is fast to water.

YELLOW-BROWN RED   This is brasilin, a dihydropyran derivative, from brazilwood (*Caesalpinia braziliensis L.*), with alum. (With iron, brasilin appears grey or grey black, and with alum and iron, dark brown.) It is highly fugitive to light.

RED-PURPLE   This is orcin, dihydroxytoluene, from archil, or orseille, *(Roccella tinctoria D.C.)*, with alum or iron. It is very fugitive to light and fades to light beige.

YELLOW   This is luteolin, flavonoid group, mainly from weld (*Reseda luteola L.*), with alum. It has a low fastness to light and medium one to water.

BROWN   This is tannin from bark and nutshells of a variety of trees, or a combination of weld yellow and madder red with alum or iron. Browns are generally fast to light, water, and abrasion. Iron-mordanted yarns, however, deteriorate quickly by accelerated oxidation and are now found turning to powder in medieval tapestries.

GREEN   This is a combination of woad blue and weld yellow. Since yellow fades faster than blue, greens become much more blue than originally intended.

FABRIC

A tapestry is a pictorial wall hanging made of woven fabric. Its fabric structure is based on *plain weave*, which is not only the most fundamental and simplest of all fabric structures but also creates fabrics of many different qualities, varying in thickness, strength, pliability, handle, and texture. The fabrication technique that refines *plain weave* into so-called *tapestry weave* is *weft-faced plain weave in discontinuous wefts*.[3]

When weaving a fabric of any given structure, one can achieve different surface effects —*warp-faced*, *balanced*, and *weft-faced*—by the selection of type and quality of yarn and compactness and tension of warps and wefts on the loom. For instance, to make a weave *weft-faced*, thick, strong warps are set tautly and spaced apart and are compactly interlaced with finer, resilient wefts which are laid in a somewhat looser tension. The color of the fabric is determined by the color of the set of elements, warps or wefts, that appear on the surface. In medieval tapestries the pictorial designs were best executed with *weft-faced plain weave* because it allowed the

use of *discontinuous wefts* in desired colors and textures from area to area in the sturdiest, simplest fabric structure. This is why *tapestry weave* has developed into the most suitable fabrication structure and technique for tapestries.

When *discontinuous wefts* are used in a base structure of a fabric, junctures occur between horizontally juxtaposed areas as the fabric is being woven. Several types of structure can be employed at each juncture of the two areas that gives variety to the pictorial design elements and affects, more or less, the integrity and strength of the tapestry. In medieval tapestries, *slit*, *dovetailing*, and *double-interlock* juncture structures are found which have been selectively used according to the design. (Open slits were sewn after the tapestry was removed from the loom.) Structurally, each area of color in a tapestry is independently constructed with discontinuous wefts; because of the structure, *tapestry weave* is stronger in its warp direction than in its weft direction.

From earliest times, many types of looms have been invented, and their development has depended on the type of weaving elements available, the demand for specific types of fabric suited for particular uses, and the level of mechanical technology in a culture at a given time. To weave a *tapestry weave* fabric, whether on a simple frame or on an electromechanically operated treadle loom, the same three conditions are necessary: (1) the warps must be beamed tautly, (2) wefts must interlace discontinuously in considerably looser tension from area to area, and (3) any type of juncture structure may be interlaced between independently woven areas as desired. (This interlacement can only be accomplished by manual means.) Because the pictorial designs for medieval tapestries were drawn with vertical lines emphasized more than horizontal lines, it was a natural technological development for medieval tapestries to be woven with the pictorial design sideways on the loom, so that uninterrupted rectilinear and curvilinear weft lines were exploited to execute the vertical lines. Whether the looms on which medieval tapestries were woven were beamed horizontally or vertically, the weaving was done in a manner that allowed tapestries to be any length, although the maximum width (height as it hangs) was restricted by the width of the loom.

We have observed that physical and chemical characteristics of fibers, yarn makeup, colorant, fabric structure, and fabrication technique influence the quality of tapestry as fabric. A fabric is by nature pliable and absorbent and is strongly affected by atmosphere, light, mechanical handling and conservation laboratory work. To bring tapestries up to their optimum state, therefore, we must create for them a suitable environment.

PRESERVATION OF TAPESTRIES

ADMINISTRATION

Preservation of tapestries should begin immediately upon their acquisition by a museum. Figure 1 shows an idealized relationship between the collection, its guardians, and the public. People in these positions, as well as members of the board of trustees and administrators, should carry out the functions of acquisition, study, conservation, and presentation with due consideration for the impact of these functions on the preservation of the tapestries. Indeed, only with their combined effort can preservation be guaranteed.

Preservation of tapestries must be considered at all times wherever they are located—while hanging on the wall, resting in storage, being moved on a cart, being studied, and being handled. Figure 2 shows possible locations of tapestries in a museum building. The architectural layout of the entire building should be designed for safety and maintenance of tapestries. Fire, dust, water leaks, fungus and insect attack, polluted air, drafts, and light damage tapestries instantaneously as well as over the long term. Floors of hallways and galleries should be smooth, and the truck or dolly used for transport should be supportive and equipped with shock-absorbing, swiveling casters.

ATMOSPHERE

The ideal climate range for tapestries in the eastern United States is said to be a relative humidity of 50 percent, plus or minus 5 percent, and temperature of 20°C plus or minus 2 degrees. The temperature may be adjusted to maintain a constant relative humidity. Sudden changes as well as extremes of either one are damaging to tapestries. Other factors can also be involved; for instance, if the temperature rises above 20°C, there is a chance of insect infestation, and if the relative humidity goes over 70 percent fungus growth may occur.

It is essential for everyone to be concerned with providing a good environment for tapestries—that is, of stable relative humidity level and temperature, clean air, and moderate air circulation. Intake and exhaust ducts for air-conditioning must be properly positioned to avoid a direct draft on stored or exhibited tapestries. For example, in the gallery, ducts along the wall in either the ceiling or the floor are not acceptable, since a draft directly reaches the tapestries and dust in the gallery gathers around the intake duct. Air is contaminated by sulfur dioxide, hydrogen sulfide, and other gases, which hasten chemical deterioration of tapestries by combining with moisture and dirt. Windows must function properly, filter out ultraviolet rays, and otherwise prevent the entry of unnecessary heat and light.

ILLUMINATION

Without light, tapestries cannot be seen, enjoyed, and studied. Light is, however, one of the most destructive elements of the environment for organic fibers and colorants, causing photochemical degradation. Light produced by the sun as well as by artificial means reaches tapestries in a variety of wave lengths (or colors). The type of light and quantity must be controlled for both viewing and preservation. The photochemical damage caused by the ordinary use of light in the course of a year or so is not discernible to our eyes, but over five, ten, or fifty years it is quite deleterious. The basic step in minimizing photochemical damage is to conscientiously eliminate light whenever the tapestries are not being viewed. Although illumination science and technique is a complex matter, we can summarize some practical steps that should be taken.

All three types of light—visible, ultraviolet, and infrared—cause photochemical degradation of fibers and dyes. Among these three, only visible light is necessary for viewing tapestries; the invisible ultraviolet and infrared rays do nothing but harm them. Visible light is present in sunlight, fluorescent, and incandescent light; ultraviolet rays are present in sunlight, fluorescent light, and a small quantity is found in incandescent light; infrared rays are found in both sunlight and incandescent light. Although the richness of color in tapestries is best illuminated by sunlight, we must totally eliminate it and substitute properly selected and conscientiously controlled artificial light. Period rooms in a large museum building, for instance, should have false windows with artificial light. Daylight through skylights should never be the source of light; while ultraviolet rays may be nearly eliminated with filters, the level of daylight on bright sunny days is far beyond the bearable level, and the fluctuation affects visibility, which is relative to illumination in neighboring areas. Furthermore, exposure to light from sunrise to gallery opening, from gallery closing to sunset, and on days when the museum is closed, in effect trebles exposure.[4]

There are various types of ultraviolet-ray filters available for fluorescent bulbs and for windows, and their effectiveness, percentage of elimination, and filtering life vary. Since ultraviolet rays pass through regular fabrics, one should use special UV-shielding drapery for windows. The elimination of ultraviolet rays by filtering does not give tapestries complete protection against photochemical deterioration; it only helps to retard it. Heat caused by the infrared rays emitted from incandescent light bulbs must be kept at a sufficient distance to avoid thermochemical damage.

Photochemical degradation occurs the moment a tapestry is exposed to any type of light. Some exposure to light is unavoidable, but the reduction of exposure levels and time is feasible and essential, since degradation is determined by the level of illumination multiplied by the duration of exposure. Thus, if a tapestry is exposed to 300 lux (10.67 lux equals 1 footcandle), it will suffer as much photochemical damage in 100 days as another tapestry would when exposed to 100 lux for as long as 300 days. The level in the exhibition area should be restricted to a maximum of 100 lux.

In the galleries three types of lighting systems are necessary: ambient, for installation and maintenance; spot, for exhibition; and night light for the safety of night watch personnel (close to the floor and only where necessary). Since the perception of colors and the degree of shadow (tapestries are structurally three-dimensional) is affected by the type of light bulb used, it is important to select the appropriate bulb for a particular fixture in a particular position. The produced light should be used to its full advantage: the viewer's eye level and focal point on a displayed tapestry must be calculated to determine the optimum position and angle of light bulbs.

For successful illumination, an important factor to take into account is relative light strengths. The human eye needs time to adjust when light levels change. For instance,

on walking from the bright outdoors into a building illuminated in 100 lux, one would be almost blinded for a short time. If one were led gradually through progressively dimmer lobbies and galleries displaying inorganic objects, light levels for tapestries would become acceptable to one's eyes. Similarly, the areas immediately surrounding a tapestry must be lit at the same level or, preferably, more dimly.

Lighting for photography causes considerable damage. If a tapestry is to be photographed, one should take all details with a variety of film. This should be done only once; not only is repeated exposure to photographic light harmful, but it necessitates mechanical handling.

PHYSICAL ORGANIZATION, EXAMINATION AND PRESERVATION

Good physical organization can make it possible to monitor a tapestry collection effectively and efficiently, enabling long-range plans for research, exhibition, and particularly preservation to be carried out satisfactorily. First, the physical characteristics of the entire collection must be understood and classification categories established such as the following:

1. Classification as wall hanging or as fragment
2. Classification according to historical, art historical, technical, and material characteristics
3. Classification according to condition— very fragile, fragile, fair, or good, in consideration of age
4. Classification according to first, second, and third quality

After each tapestry has been categorized according to all of the above, decisions can be made as to how it will be preserved, handled, exhibited, and conservation work performed. Undertaking such classification and organization exposes the guardians to the collections; this is the first step in working toward a long-range preservation, conservation, and study plan.

In the course of organization, basic technical information should be compiled and a long-range preservation plan for each tapestry proposed, as follows:

EXAMINATION
1. Fiber: type and condition
2. Yarn: makeup, angle of twist, and diameter

3. Colorant: color identification viewed from front and back, dye, mordant, and fastness against water and light

4. Fabric: warp and weft count, structure, dimensions (width and length of field, border, subborder, and so on), and condition

5. Former treatment: evidence of washing; pH level; restoration; replacement; reweaving; conservation material added, its method, and an evaluation of its effectiveness

PRESERVATION PLAN

1. Air: cleanliness and degree of circulation
2. Climate: temperature and relative humidity levels
3. Illumination: length of exposure time and strength of light
4. Treatment: cleaning and restoring
5. Support: type of support, strapping, lining, webbing, and hanging slat
6. Handling: systematic handling and hanging procedures
7. Storage preparation: proper material for support and to give physical and chemical stability; technique to prepare for storage
8. Storage: safety, accessibility, and study space
9. Exhibition: good location in relation to climate, air, light, and protection from visitors

Well-trained visual perception and aesthetic senses are essential for an appraisal of material quality, color, and condition. For example, a tapestry may contain a different type of yarn or an unusual dye, which should first be identified visually, and then could be brought under further scrutiny by microscopic and chemical analysis. In the analysis record the method of fiber identification—visual, microscopic (magnification), and/or chemical (process and reaction)—should be indicated.

The present color should be identified from the front and back of the tapestry under designated light by using a reference color chart. Dye and mordant analysis requires complex organic chemistry and a great deal of laboratory experience involving botanical chemistry and ethnobotanical history. To obtain an accurate analysis, a sample of minimum 1.5g or 2cm of yarn, which will be consumed, should be supplied to the researcher who organizes both dye and mordant analysis. The record should indicate the method of analysis, the name of the chemical compound detected and/or the name of the plant or animal deduced, when possible, and the name of the researcher.

The unit for warp and weft count is per 1 or 2.5cm. The count and description of condition of weft should be made for each identifiable type of yarn.

An assessment of former treatment, identifying materials and methods and deducing the chronology of restoration, often indicates original designs, colors, and dimensions of the tapestry. The type and material used for restoration and support should be examined whether such previous work was an aid to preservation or, rather, damaging to the tapestry.

Handling of tapestries must be systematic. Without a plan for a handling procedure a tapestry package should not be opened. The plan includes provision for ample space; a manner of opening the package; protective and supportive materials; methods for turning the tapestry around and over, for reaching to the center area, for moving it safely between storeroom and gallery, then from floor to wall; and so forth.

As the examination is developed, the when, how, what, and then of a long-range comprehensive preservation plan can be made, such as the following:

1. Schedule of periodic condition checks in storage and on exhibition
2. Plans for periodic renewal of storing material
3. Conservation laboratory work
4. Rules and conditions for exhibitions and loans (including "not for loan")

GENERAL APPROACH TO CONSERVATION LABORATORY WORK

Conservation laboratory work is intended to put tapestries into their best possible condition, recapturing their original beauty with the least possible alteration. All tapestries in a collection should be comparatively studied by a curator, conservator, restorer, and caretaker, and the final form for their physical presentation should be determined and a preservation method planned. Laboratory treatment is often thought of as "improvement," but it exposes the tapestry to the greatest dangers of major chemical and physical changes. The basis for decisions for conservation laboratory work is a logical approach to the science and technology of tapestries, present state, conservation materials and methods, visual impact, safekeeping procedures, and the environment wherever they are to be kept. A medieval tapestry requires a great deal of conservation laboratory work to enable it to support its weight, correct its chemical state, revive its pictorial integrity, and prepare it for storage and exhibition.

To practice conservation laboratory work, it is essential to start on an experimental basis, such as with a mock tapestry fragment from a modern fabric, then a medieval fragment, finally "graduating" to a complete tapestry. Under no circumstances should one start with a complete medieval tapestry, particularly one of first quality.

Conservation laboratory work should be performed step by step according to the condition of tapestry. Although there are exceptions, one concrete rule that applies in doing conservation laboratory work is "all or nothing, under a long-range plan." A tapestry must not be subjected to haphazard washing and mending. Work should be done at different times, according to the stage of deterioration, but by only one method envisioned under a long-range plan. The work must be done with a thorough understanding of the chemical, physical, and technical nature of all components—materials in the tapestry, unwanted foreign matter, conservation materials—and the compatibility of all three with each other. For instance, in deciding whether to wash a tapestry, the chemical and physical compatibility of fiber, soil, and cleaning medium must be weighed for fiber protection versus removal of soil.

Longevity, local insect habits, and aesthetics also play roles in the selection of conservation materials and techniques for cleaning, reweaving, backing, lining, webbing, and storing, which in turn determine climate, handling requirements and methods, and storage facilities. It should be understood that selection and preparation of materials for conservation and preservation work, and procedures in handling and storing tapestries are time-consuming and tedious. It should also be understood that the effects of conservation treatment and preservation work can be seen only after twenty to fifty years. This is why it is important to evaluate periodically past as well as recent conservation work.

Laboratory work should be performed only to counteract natural deterioration. A tapestry should not be subjected to repeated washing and mending because of accumulated dust and soiling owing to mishandling and negligence in the gallery or in storage. Strict adherence to a sensible handling procedure alone considerably reduces damage to tapestries.

During the course of conservation laboratory work, precise records must be kept for future reference. For example, three states of work on the tapestry itself—with previous repair, after removal of unacceptable previous repair, and the final state—should be recorded photographically. To aid curatorial study, a line-drawing or a photostat, indicating restoration and missing areas in colored pencil, should also be prepared. Every step of vacuum cleaning, spot cleaning, wet cleaning, and dry work needs documentation with samples of conservation material used.

Handling

Because of their organic, fibrous components and their fabrication structure, tapestries are flexible and absorbent. The degradation of the components owing to age makes a medieval tapestry vulnerable to various types of damage to the point that its strength can no longer support its own weight. Medieval tapestries, therefore, often have supportive strappings and linings. Although these are intended mainly to support the hanging tapestries, under conditions of stress, they can be damaging. Each time the tapestry on which modern supporting material is attached is moved to be hung or rolled, the medieval and modern materials are forced to compete with each other, resulting in the yielding of medieval materials to the modern addition. No matter how well strapping and lining materials are selected and how skillfully added, they can, in effect, harm the tapestry when it is handled. The act of handling the tapestry, therefore, must be well planned and systematically and carefully executed.

Handling a tapestry includes such actions as grasping, pulling, stretching, and folding, all of which may occur during unwrapping, unrolling, rolling, moving, and all the other routines necessary for study, periodic checking, preparation for storage, or hanging. In principle, when a tapestry is being handled, it should be held at both ends of the same warp or weft at the same time. When one end needs to be moved, its opposite end, whether or not that end has to be moved, should also be handled and the handling movement maintained straight across along the warp or weft. One should remember, however, that a tapestry has more strength in its warp direction and less in the weft direction; thus, if tension is necessary the warps should receive the greater amount. When a tapestry is rolled on a tube or folded during handling, therefore, it is the warp that should be bent, folded, and pulled, while the weft should be kept straight along the length of the tube or along the fold. If it is necessary to pull in the weft direction, it should be done where the strappings are attached.

All surfaces with which medieval tapestries will be in contact—hands, worktable, floor, and wall—must be clean, inert, smooth-sliding, and securely supportive. Tubes, boards, and worktables used for transportation and treating tapestries, must be able to accommodate the full weft width of the tapestry. The floor used for examination (but never for treatment) must be larger than the full dimensions of the tapestry. The stationary work area, floor or worktables, must be completely covered with a movable surface such as paper or polyethylene film, and the tapestry should be opened out directly onto this paper or film. The opened tapestry can then be moved, even for as little as 10cm, by moving or sliding the paper, thus avoiding strain on the tapestry.

When a tapestry is brought out rolled, it has usually been rolled right side out (Fig. 3a). If this is unrolled in the usual manner, it will lie with the wrong side up (Fig. 3b). Depending on the condition and dimension of the tapestry, one should select a method from the three suggested below in order to have the right side up. To understand the procedures and how the tapestry's position changes, one should practice following the steps using a piece of paper or fabric. Never practice with a medieval tapestry.

The first method is to unroll the tapestry right side up directly from the tube. Have the right side of the tapestry up and the tube under the portion to be unrolled (Fig. 4a). Proceed to unroll the tube until the entire tapestry is unrolled (Fig. 4b).

The second method (Fig. 5) requires a space at least one-third larger than the tapestry in the warp direction. First unroll the tapestry in the usual manner (Fig. 5a); the wrong side of the tapestry will be up (Fig. 5b). To turn it over, one person is required at each corner (* in Fig. 5b) of the warp end farthest from the extra space allowed. Walking outside each edge of the tapestry, two people can move this end over the portion on the floor toward the extra space, until two-thirds or more of the tapestry is turned over (Fig. 5c), with one-third still left lying wrong side up under the portion that has been turned over. Next the two persons should go back to the fold just created (** in Fig. 5c) and move it over the portion turned until the other warp end underneath (*** in Fig. 5c) is on the top (Fig. 5d); thus, two layers will have been moved, and the tapestry is now right side up but folded into three layers. The final step is to move the top two layers completely out by holding the two top corners (*** in Fig. 5d) and walking them in the opposite direction (Fig. 5e). Smaller tapestries (3m or shorter in the warp direction) can be turned over almost completely by the method shown in Fig. 5c; only about 50cm will be left lying wrong side up and will then be turned over by the succeeding steps. This requires twice as much space as the area of the tapestry.

The third method (Fig. 6) may be used in a limited space such as on a worktable. While being unrolled (Fig. 6a), the tapestry is folded back and forth like accordion pleats in 50cm widths. When the pleating is completed it is then ready to open right side up (Fig. 6b). There is a specific position and direction to pleat; one direction opens the tapestry right side up and the other, wrong side up. If it has to be repositioned, either the tapestry has to be moved to the opposite end of the work area or the whole pleated tapestry should be turned upside down by turning each pleat, one by one, like pages in a book (Fig. 6c), and then opened flat (Fig. 6d).

Soil

Soil has been defined as "matter out of place." For instance, soup in a bowl is soup but if spilled on a rug it is soil. Analysis of the soil leads to an identification of the nature of its adhesion. This identification along with an assessment of the nature of fiber and the condition of the tapestry determines if and how the soil should be removed.

Six categories of soil are encountered in conservation laboratory work:
1. Air removable soils adhere to the tapestry

only weakly or not at all, and may be removed by vacuum cleaning.

2. Mechanically removable soils are crystallized deposits such as earthy substances adhering to the tapestry surface, which may be partially removed by painstaking work under microscope with a pipette-tipped vacuum cleaner.[5]

3. Dry-solvent removable soils are candle wax, grease, and other oil-based substances.

4. Wet-solvent removable soils are generally airborne and decomposed fibers from the tapestry itself.

5. Special-agent removable soils are all types that require additional carriers with solvents, such as polyphosphate, detergent, acids, and alkalis.

6. Unremovable soils.

All these types of soil may be scattered in combination on a tapestry, and removal requires a knowledge of basic chemistry and skill in handling flexible, fragile tapestries particularly in aqueous solution.

VACUUM CLEANING

Most tapestries covered with air-removable soils, including their own deteriorated fiber particles, are vacuum cleaned. The strength of vacuum suction and method of cleaning should be selected according to the condition of tapestry and soil.

Three types of vacuum cleaners supply the suction strength necessary: a two-horsepower machine equipped with a special dust bucket that holds water; a medium-strength, one-half-horsepower household machine; and a specially constructed suction pipette attached to a faucet.[6]

To withstand the pressure of the vacuum-cleaning work, the area to be cleaned should be kept flat against the floor or the worktable, and either space should accommodate the full weft width of the tapestry. The area being cleaned must be close enough for the worker to be able to check constantly the effectiveness of the vacuum-cleaning action and the condition of the tapestry.

A screening, woven of nylon or saran monofilament (about four warps and wefts per centimeter) is laid on the area to be cleaned. Before attempting vacuum cleaning, one should check the strength of the suction and manner in which the brush on the nozzle touches the tapestry through the screening by placing a hand underneath the screen. Because the surface of the monofilament screening is harsher than that of the tapestry, the screening must be placed in an up-and-down manner on each area to be cleaned. Once placed, it should be held securely without sliding (rubbing) on the surface of the tapestry. The nozzle also should be moved up and down during the cleaning.

WET CLEANING

When submerged in water, all fiber-made products change their physical and chemical state, handle, and appearance. Water is a remarkable solvent in the way it changes the character and condition of fabrics, improving some while degrading others. Thus, it is a serious decision to wet-clean a tapestry. A standard should be established after observation of the long-term effects of soiling, vacuum cleaning, wet cleaning, routine handling, exhibition, and storage. If a tapestry is to be wet-cleaned, which should properly stabilize its chemical state, the conservator must accurately remember its prewash physical character and condition so as to be able to assess the inevitable visual and tactile changes. Since the majority of medieval tapestries appear to have been washed in the past, they must have changed dimensions, handle, and appearance since they were presented to the first patron without undergoing wet finishing like woolen fabrics for garment. If a tapestry had never been subjected to water, a change in character from washing is virtually certain to occur, even with maximum scientific precautions and control.

Washing must be done only under complete submergence with temperature-controlled, demineralized water in fast and plentiful supply and with the aid of an electronic pH meter with a surface electrode in an optimum-sized, fast-draining bath. Without these, washing may damage tapestries even with the proper chemicals and procedures.

Dye fastness and soil reactions to water and washing agents should be tested first. Lay a blotting paper underneath a selected color or a stain in an inconspicuous area. Start with a drop (1 to 3ml) of water in which the tapestry is to be washed on each different yarn, including repairs. After a few minutes, when the water has penetrated, check the pH level and press over the area with another blotting paper. (For testing color fastness, if water does not penetrate the soiled tapestry, add a tiny drop of detergent solution—a surface-active agent—to decrease the surface tension of water.) The tapestry should not be rubbed with the blotting paper, as particles of fiber will transfer onto it and interfere with the assessment of dye fastness. When the tapestry is subjected to water, decomposed organic substances dissolve, coloring the water brown. Brown color spotted on the blotting paper is often this substance or soil from the long-unwashed tapestry rather than dye. If the dye does not run, then try, one by one, all the cleaning agents that will be used. The alkalinity, acidity, detergency, and other chemicals in each cleaning agent may bleed an otherwise water-fast dye. The testing agent solutions should be concentrations slightly stronger than the solution to be used in actual cleaning. It should not, however, be a saturated solution, since that renders the agent less active than it would be in optimum ratio. Medieval tapestry dyes are normally fast to water and water-based cleaning agents which are in the range of use suggested for museum fabrics.

Before washing, one should remove all alien materials and undesirable repairs, do spot cleaning if necessary, and vacuum clean. Spotting is a method of removing localized heavy soil and stains prior to overall vacuum cleaning and wet cleaning. If a tapestry were to be immersed in wash water without preliminary spotting, dissolved soil deposits could disperse in the wash water and resettle on other parts of the tapestry.

A pipette-tipped vacuum system is used to remove particles of soil deposit adhering to the surface of the tapestry. One can mechanically break up a soil deposit in a crystalline formation by pricking (not scraping) it with a needle held in one hand while vacuuming up the broken particles with the pipette-tipped vacuum suction in the other hand. The use of a wide-field, stereo-zoom microscope with a magnification of 10 to 30× ensures a safe and efficient operation.

Wax and other oil-based soils that respond to dry solvent must be individually treated before those that respond to water-based agents. The dry-solvent-penetrated area should not be in contact with water or vice versa until complete drying has taken place. Water and water-based agents, including acids, alkalis, detergents, and digesters, should not be used for spotting unless thorough wet cleaning follows immediately; otherwise, accumulated soil and decomposed protein would be dissolved by the spotting

solution and carried to the edge of the wet area by capillary action, possibly settling as a new stain. Use of steam, digesters, and rust removers may be appropriate for certain cleaning needs, but they require extremely sensitive scientific control, technical skill, and knowledge of the nature of medieval fabric materials and aged soils.

To protect edges, holes, and weakened areas against the flow of water during washing, cotton net should be sewn over the areas in a sandwichlike manner. (Cotton net adheres to the tapestry when wet, protecting yarn from fraying, whereas nylon net does not.) Another layer of nylon or saran woven screening covers the entire tapestry. The preparation for washing is time-consuming but contributes to its success.

During wet cleaning, the tapestry must be kept flat, open, and completely submerged in water. There is no alternative method for wet cleaning or for rinsing out soils and cleaning agents safely and thoroughly. (Tapestries and any other museum fabrics should never be "surface cleaned" with wet-cleaning detergents.) Keep in mind that when a wet fiber is exposed to the air, it is known to oxidize more rapidly than when it is dry or in the water. Thus, during wet cleaning, each draining and refilling of the bath as well as drying should be done as quickly as possible.

The washing facility should be prepared as follows:

1. A bath should be made to the dimensions of each tapestry to minimize the time needed to drain and fill the bath water. Such a versatile bath can be constructed with industrial, clear polyethylene film placed within barricading channels.
2. The color of the washing floor should be white to allow constant monitoring of the color of the water.
3. The washing floor should slant toward one end. There a trough at least 2m long should be built to drain the bath water, which is done by pulling the polyethylene film down into the trough. To help speed the draining, a tank should be built under the trough to accommodate a large quantity of water until it is gradually taken into the low-capacity sewer. The trough itself could be the drain to the tank.
4. A large water-demineralizing unit(s) with two or more faucets is necessary so that the water can be fed into the bath quickly.

5. To avoid having soils and moisture trapped underneath, washing screens to support the tapestry during washing and drying are necessary. They should be constructed in 18/8 stainless-steel or nylon mesh on frames on 1:2 ratio modular units, with connecting hooks. (No corrosive metal should be used.)

6. A bridge of sturdy construction on casters should extend over the entire width of the bath. It must be able to support at least two people and allow them to work closely to the center of the tapestry in the bath.

Water has two characteristic actions: chemical and physical. Although both can effectively clean and stabilize the chemical condition of tapestries, they can also do harm if improperly manipulated. For instance, the flow of water separates fibers and frays yarns more easily than it removes soils. During washing, one must continually observe the strength of the tapestry (wool and silk become weaker when wet); the dyes; color of the water (decomposed fibers, soils, and dyes will discolor it); the pH of the water, the cleaning agent(s), and the tapestry; temperature (optimum range for fibers, water, and cleaning agent); and water flow.

The generalized washing procedure outlined below is for a medieval tapestry in good condition. It should be modified to suit the condition of each tapestry; each tapestry is limited in its ability to withstand various operations.

First, water-soluble soils should be removed. The tapestry should be laid flat on the washing screens, with the wrong side up, completely submerged, the water level just above the surface of the tapestry. (If the tapestry is too large or too weak to be turned over while wet, it should have the right side up throughout.) Water temperature should be approximately 26°C. The pH level of fresh demineralized water should be checked (the pH should be between 6 and 8). After a while, check that of the tapestry (a surface electrode must be used) and bath water also. Depending on the type and quantity of soil and condition of fiber, immersion for about ten to thirty minutes should be sufficient to remove water-soluble soils. If the water becomes considerably brown in color within a short time, the water should be completely changed and the process repeated. Agitating the water by sponging up and down or by rolling a paint roller on the surface of the tapestry helps increase the effectiveness of soil removal, but it must be done carefully.

Occasionally, one may encounter residue from a previous washing such as "surface cleaning"; that is, after about half an hour or more of submergence in initial rinsing water, a slimy, slippery chemical condition with bubbles may occur. In this case, the pH of the tapestry should be checked; there may be surprisingly high alkalinity which did not register earlier. If this is so, one should rinse by continuously supplying fresh water, until the pH level comes down to the level of the fresh water. (Use of acid as a counterleveling neutralizer is not recommended.)

In the next fresh-water bath, sodium hexametaphosphate may be added to remove more soils before the detergent treatment. Since polyphosphate increases the pH level and cleaning action, fragile tapestries should not be treated in this solution.

The detergent for wool and silk should be either a non-ionic or anionic synthetic, with a pH range between 7 and 8, and a solubility temperature of about 26°C. (The optimum amount of detergent in solution differs depending on the detergent.) The detergent solution should be prepared in a container and then applied to the tapestry with the sponge or paint roller (the tapestry should never be rubbed). The tapestry does not have to be submerged during the detergent application. The detergent is then flushed out with fresh water poured slowly from a small container as sponging progresses from area to area in an orderly manner. (A running faucet has too high a pressure for the tapestry.)

The wet tapestry should then be turned over with the aid of a water-resistant tube or a rolled nylon or saran screening that accommodates the full weft width. The free end of the rolled screening should be laid underneath, along the weft edge of the wet tapestry, the tapestry rolled onto the tube and then unrolled in reverse, with the tube now underneath, turning the tapestry right side up. Sponging with the detergent solution should be resumed.

During the three to five rinses that follow, the tapestry must be submerged and sponged. When the wet cleaning has been completed, a tapestry with protein fibers alone should be in the range of pH 6.5 to 7, and one with protein and cellulose fibers, pH 7.

For a medium-sized medieval tapestry, the washing operation takes six to seven hours with four people.

DRYING

When exposed to the air, fibers oxidize faster when they are wet than when they are dry, and so a wet tapestry must be dried as quickly as possible. Thus, the room should be equipped with an exhaust unit, auxiliary fans, and a heater to create a temperature of about 30° C, with air blowing at a velocity of up to 1km per hour.

After the water has been drained from the bath, excess water from the tapestry should be removed by toweling it with gentle hand pressure or by using a paint roller. Both the tapestry and toweling must be kept absolutely flat, with no wrinkles. If a wrinkle of toweling is pressed against the tapestry, the thick area of the wrinkle will damage the tapestry, and a wrinkle in the tapestry can develop into a break. Toweling should be changed as often as possible until the tapestry feels almost dry. If the tapestry is left to dry without sufficient toweling, the water may continue to dissolve chemically decomposed organic substances, that have been carried out by the capillary action of water, which will leave brown staining on the edges and surface of the tapestry.

Next, the tapestry must be air-dried. If the room does not have a climate control, electric fans may be turned on for air circulation, if they are not aimed directly at the tapestry, and interior door should be opened for ventilation. With such ventilation, a tapestry left on the washing screen will dry in about eight to ten hours.

While drying, fabrics shape themselves as they are placed. Thus, warp and weft positions should be lined up, and when the tapestry is medium dry, blocking may be done. To prevent stiffening, a natural matting effect of water, repeated, gentle hand pressure may be applied.

After it has been dried, the tapestry should be left flat in a controlled climate for about three weeks before needlework and storage preparation are begun.

NEEDLEWORK

Since tapestries are pictorial art objects rendered in a fiber medium, "face-lifting" restoration work, reweaving, has been an accepted practice. Considerable experience is necessary to determine the extent to which pictorial elements should be recreated and degraded yarns substituted and the choices of color rendition. Preparation for hanging—attaching strappings, lining, webbing, and slat—requires knowledge of the compatibility of conservation materials and the tapestry, and needlework skill.

Medieval fiber materials are weaker than modern ones, and—as can be seen under high magnification—are easily damaged by the abrasion and vibration of a needle and thread. Nevertheless, most tapestries must be needleworked to be rewoven and supported. Areas being worked must at all times be supported flat, kept from being moved or bent by the sewing action, force, and strength of the needle and thread. The thickness, length, and shape of the needles and quality and strength of the threads must be properly selected for sewing and reweaving, and the needlework should then be done smoothly, without jiggling and yanking that will disturb the tapestry. Stitches on the tapestry surface should blend as inconspicuously as possible into the picture, catching the stronger elements, the warps.

The following must be considered in the selection of conservation materials:
1. Quality of color and fastness of dyes against light and washing
2. Longevity
3. Compatible strength and thickness
4. Texture

To reweave a *weft-faced* weave, the warps of the tapestry must be kept taut, and both the front and the back of any area to be worked must be accessible. A roller frame with two parallel rollers supported at worktable height is generally used for reweaving. It should be devised to enable the warps of each working area to be tensioned tautly and independently.

Large areas that are completely missing from a tapestry may be filled with either a non-textured or a tapestry-weave textured, monotone, dyed fabric to make the missing area less conspicuous and its functional strength compatible with the rest of the tapestry. The color should blend well with the surrounding area and be selected from high-quality cotton fabric. If the selected fabric is too thin to be compatible with the tapestry, it should be used with a second layer of a sturdy fabric underneath, exploiting the surface effect of the first fabric and functional strength of the second. Warps and wefts of the tapestry should be stitched down in their original positions on the fill-in fabric, while the tapestry and the fill-in fabric are

58

kept under tension on a temporary stretcher frame.

The tapestry must then be strengthened by supportive strapping. Straps, nonstretching and of a compatible strength, should be attached in a complementary tension to the tapestry along the weft direction at regular intervals as well as at points where the tapestry is structurally and physically weak. Sewing should be a combination of zigzag and backstitches and should be kept under 3cm on the back so they will not be caught.

A loose lining of a lightweight fabric with a slippery finish will protect the tapestry against dust coming from behind. It should be sewn around the two sides and the top but left open at the bottom and strung to the tapestry with 5cm-long chained thread at about 50cm intervals.

For hanging, a heavy webbing tape about 8cm wide, such as that of a racing-car seat belt, must be sewn at the top edge of the tapestry. The tape in turn should be nailed onto a wooden slat that will hang from the moulding by S-hooks and wires. The sturdiness of the webbing tape should be directly related to the weight of the tapestry so that when it is hanging, the tapestry's weight will be held evenly across the top by the tape.

To attach the webbing tape, open the tapestry out wrong side up on a flat surface, and determine the position of a straight line across the top edge. The webbing tape must be laid along this straight line, not along the wavy edge often found on tapestries. The webbing tape should be sewn with linen thread in two rows, with the upper line 1.5cm from the top edge of the tape and the lower line 1.5cm from the lower edge. Each stitch in the front should catch two to three warps of the tapestry, and on the back should be about 3cm long. Every stitch (or every other stitch, at least) should be knotted by hitching it onto the previous stitch.

Slats should be of poplar or another low-resin wood, sanded, and finished with a double coating of polyurethane resin. The length of the slat should equal the length of the webbing; the width should be 8cm and the thickness 2cm. Hanging plates (Fig. 7) should be attached to the slat, two for tapestries up to 4m and three or four for longer ones. The tapestry should then be laid on a flat surface

right side up and the webbing tape attached to the slat by opening the edge of the tape above the top row of stitches and pushing a noncorrosive upholstery tack through the tape (the head of the tack rests between the tapestry and the webbing tape), each about 3cm apart.

On lightweight tapestries, Velcro tape (check the manufacturer's specifications for weight endurance) can be used instead of upholstery tacks. The tape's compact weave does not allow a threaded needle to pass through it; forcing a needle to sew the tape and tapestry together will damage the tapestry. Thus the Velcro tape should first be machine-sewn onto a webbing tape, which can then be handsewn onto the tapestry. The hook is nailed directly onto the slat without being sewn to the webbing tape. To heighten security against theft, metal rings may be sewn on the webbing tape and secured by fasteners to the slat.

EXHIBITION
The tapestry should hang in areas that receive no daylight, drafts, or dust. It should not hang near passage openings where viewers can come closer than 1m. Barricading bars (if ropes are used, they should be stretched tightly, without slack) and kickboards must be placed at least 1m away from tapestries.

Tapestries should hang from S-hooks attached to built-in picture hangers or to moldings by the wires attached to the hanging plates on the slat. The process of hanging a large tapestry requires pulleys and ropes and two rigs with at least five people—two on each rig, two on each rope, and one directing the operation and watching out for the safety of the tapestry.

The tapestry is ready when the webbing is nailed onto the slat. In preparing it for the hanging operation, it should be folded back and forth in 30cm widths from the bottom up, ending with the slat on the top, placed on a sturdy board, and moved to the floor against the wall where the tapestry is to be hung, with the back of the tapestry facing the wall. Wires approximating the distance between the molding and the slat when hung should be cut and attached to the hanging plates on the slat and allowed to hang on the front side of the tapestry.

Hanging the tapestry should be done as follows: With the rigs placed close to the wall, the tapestry laid between the wall and the rigs, hook the roped pulleys to the molding and tie each end of the rope to each hanging plate on the slat. Hoist the tapestry until it reaches the correct hanging position. Be sure the slat is raised slowly and evenly horizontal with utmost caution. Attach S-hooks on each end of the hanging wire, the length of which is now determined, and hook them to the moulding. Loosen the tension of the ropes. The tapestry should now be flat, slightly away from the wall with the center vertical line straight up and the focal point at a good viewing position. If the height needs to be changed, put tension on the rope again, adjust for the correct position, and reset the position of the S-hooks on the wires. Remove the ropes from the slat, the pulleys from the molding, and the rigs.

For taking tapestries down, the procedures are reversed.

Both hanging and taking down require utmost caution. The tapestries are being exposed to an extremely dangerous situation. Ample time, an adequate number of workers, and a comfortable working atmosphere will ensure a safe operation.

STORAGE

Tapestries must be stored independently of other art objects, such as paintings, metal, porcelains, glass, and wood, and the storeroom must not be combined with a curator's office, caretaker's workroom, or conservation laboratory. This is to avoid the dust from tapestries falling onto other objects, unnecessary exposure to light, changes in atmospheric conditions resulting from people's coming and going, and security and safety risks. Considering the bulky dimensions and weight of tapestries, however, their study room and storeroom may be combined.

Good storage preparation, housekeeping, and periodic checking in the storeroom are keys to good preservation. Storage preparation should be done only by responsible, trained caretakers, who should use this opportunity to check the condition of the tapestries, the storage preparation materials, and the storage units.

Tapestries should be stored in a resting position. If they have been hung, they should first be vacuum cleaned and left opened flat in the storeroom for at least two weeks before they are rolled for storage. Tapestries should be in direct contact only with chemically inert and physically suitable storing materials: washed, desized unbleached muslin (cotton) and acid-free paper. The person in charge of the storage should assess the environmental conditions and decide whether to use paper or fabric for storage preparation, carefully weighing the characteristics of each in relation to the tapestries. For example, paper has a slippery surface, while fabric does not, and paper is less pliable than fabric.

Tapestries must be rolled on tubes with diameters of 15 to 20cm. The material, length, and thickness of the wall of the tube are determined according to the storage system and the weight and weft width of the tapestry. Rolling tapestries is, of course, not simply a matter of winding something around a tube; it is an operation that requires skill and care. Tapestries must be rolled in the direction of the warp, with the weft parallel to the tube. (The slat, therefore, must be removed.) If the tapestry has been strapped and lined, it must be rolled right side out.

The procedure for rolling is as follows: Lay the tapestry open wrong side up on a clean surface with the warps and wefts properly aligned. The tube is completely covered with buffered, acid-free paper. Then it is wrapped with several rounds of desized, unbleached muslin, the same length as the weft width of the tapestry as a starter. Place the edge of the tapestry on top of the end of the starter, overlapping about 30cm, and begin rolling; this ensures that the edge of the tapestry will not be creased at the start of rolling. As rolling proceeds, the lining, which is facing up, will begin to ripple. Do not attempt to smooth the ripple away; instead, lift up the tube to allow it to be rolled in with the tapestry. Because of the uneveness of the tapestry, occasionally one end of the tube must be lifted up to allow one side to be rolled slightly looser in order to keep the warps perpendicular to the tube at all times. As the rolling proceeds, a ridge may be gradually created in the section of the tapestry yet to be rolled. Pull the rolled tube back as much as necessary to remove the ridge without loosening the rolled tapestry on the tube or pulling the unrolled portion too tightly. At all times make sure the tension of the rolled tapestry is neither too tight nor too loose, and check that the face of the tapestry is rolled without wrinkles and creases. If a webbing tape is attached, padding made of cotton or polyester nonwoven fabric should be rolled in to compensate for the thickness of the webbing tape.

60

CONCLUSION

Preservation practices are both numerous and perpetual. To preserve a tapestry collection effectively, a long-range preservation plan must be formulated in which a day-to-day monitoring schedule, incorporating attention to each tapestry, must be implemented. It is no easy matter, regardless of the quantity and quality of the collection or its financing, facilities, and personnel. Neither dramatic nor fanciful, it demands a specific philosophy, commitment, and concerted action by everyone who loves and enjoys tapestries.

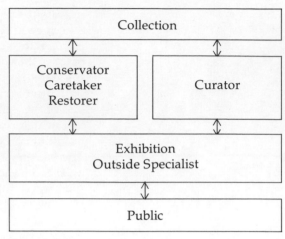

Fig. 1

Fig. 1. Idealized relationship between the collection, its guardians, and the public.

Fig. 2. Possible locations of the collection in a museum building.

Fig. 2

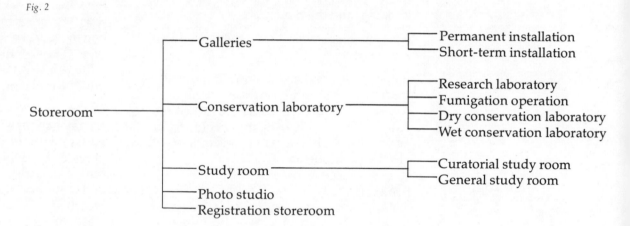

Fig. 3. Unrolling a tapestry wrong side up. (Drawing by Emiko Matsumoto)

a

b

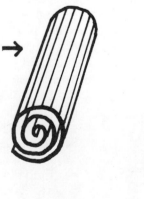
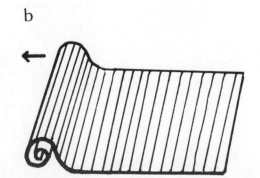

Fig. 4. Unrolling a tapestry right side up. (E.M.)

a

b

Fig. 5. Unrolling a tapestry and
turning over by folding. (E.M.)

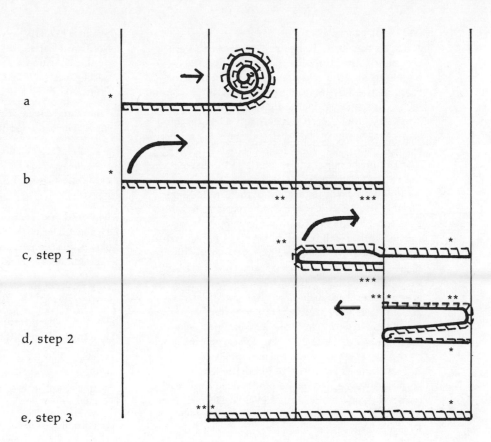

a

b

c, step 1

d, step 2

e, step 3

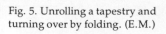

Fig. 6. Unrolling a tapestry and
turning over by pleating. (E.M.)

Fig. 7. Hanging plate on a slat.
(E.M.)

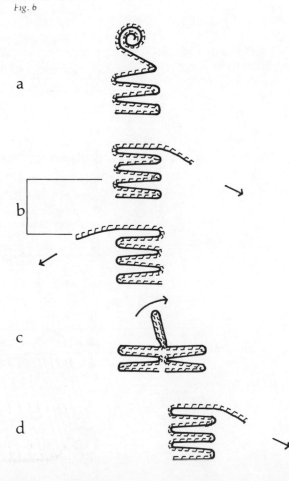

a

b

c

d

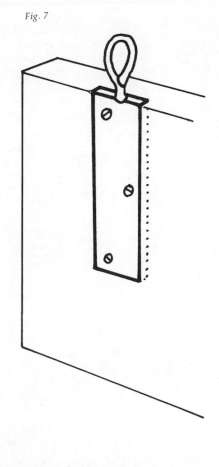

Fig. 7

NOTES

1. Today the word "tapestry" has two different meanings: one connotes the fabric's function as a wall hanging, the other as a specific fabric structure. As used by laymen unable to distinguish one technique of fabric technology from another, "tapestry" most often refers to any fiber-medium work that hangs on the wall—that is, any fabric, embroidery, patchwork, pigment-patterned, dye-patterned, or combination of different techniques and constructions in two- or three-dimensional form regardless of the intended use. On the other hand, when the term refers to fabric structure, a tapestry need not have been transformed into a wall hanging but may be in any form (such as a band or bag) as long as the fabric has been executed in a particular structure. In describing fabric structure, therefore, *tapestry weave* is the accepted term for *weft-faced plain weave in discontinuous wefts*; it is preferable to limit the use of the word tapestry only to those wall hangings executed in *tapestry weave* having certain quality, such as medieval Western European tapestries.

2. The name of plants included in the list are commonly accepted as the plants used in the organized dyers' work in medieval Western Europe. The same dye compounds, however, may be found in other plants.

3. *Discontinuous wefts* can be woven in other basic fabric structures, *twill weave*, *satin weave*, and *gauze weave*. Unless otherwise noted (for example, *twill tapestry weave*), *tapestry weave*, because of its predominant use, refers to the use of *discontinuous wefts* in *weft-faced plain weave*.

4. Ambient light from a skylight in a gallery should be converted by installing fluorescent lighting above the lower skylight ceiling and covering the entire skylight roof with a light-proof roofing material.

5. Joseph V. Columbus, "A Specialized Vacuum Device for Fragile Textiles," *Textile Museum Journal* (1962): 56.

6. Ibid.

SELECTED BIBLIOGRAPHY

Medieval Tapestries

Bennett, Anna G. *Five Centuries of Tapestry*. San Francisco: The Fine Arts Museums of San Francisco and Charles E. Tuttle, 1976.

Freeman, Margaret B. *The Unicorn Tapestries*. New York: The Metropolitan Museum of Art, 1976.

Souchal, Geneviève. *Masterpieces of Tapestry from the Fourteenth to Sixteenth Century* (exhibition catalogue). New York: The Metropolitan Museum of Art, 1974.

Material and Technology

Diderot, Denis. *A Diderot Pictorial Encyclopedia of Trades and Industry*, Vol. 2. Edited by Charles C. Gillispie. New York: Dover Publications, 1959.

Emery, Irene. *Primary Structures of Fabrics*. Washington, D.C.: The Textile Museum, 1966.

Fannin, Allen. *Handspinning*. New York: Van Nostrand Reinhold Co. 1970.

Hofenk-de-Graaff, Judith H. *Natural Dyestuffs— Origin, Chemical Constitution, and Identification*. Amsterdam: International Council of Museums, 1969.

Inventaire Général des Monuments et des Richesses Artistiques de la France, Ministère des Affaires Culturelles. *Principes d'Analyse Scientifique Tapisserie*. Imprimerie Nationale, Paris: 1971.

Masschelein-Kleiner, Liliane; Znamensky-Festraets, Nicole; and Maes, Luc. "Les Colorants des Tapisseries Tournaisiennes au XVe Siècle." *Bulletin de l'Institut royal du Patrimoine artistique* (Brussels) X, 1967/68.

Mauersberger, H.R. *Matthew's Textile Fibers*, 6th ed. New York: John Wiley & Sons, 1954.

Tidball, Harriet. *Contemporary Tapestry*, Shuttle Craft Monograph 12. Lansing, Mich.: Shuttle Craft Guild, 1964.

Administration

Conservation of Cultural Property in the United States. Washington, D.C.: The National Conservation Advisory Council, 1976.

Professional Practices in Art Museums. New York: The Association of Art Museum Directors, 1971.

Environment

Feller, Robert. "The Deteriorating Effect of Light on Museum Objects." *Museum News Technical Supplement*, no. 3. Washington, D.C.: American Association of Museums, 1964.

Hueck, H.J. "Textile Pests and Their Control." In *Textile Conservation*, edited by Jentina E. Leene. Washington, D.C.: Smithsonian Institution, 1972.

Thomson, Garry. "Textiles in the Museum Environment." In *Textile Conservation*, edited by Jentina E. Leene. Washington, D.C.: Smithsonian Institution, 1972.

Examination, Conservation, and Preservation

AATCC Technical Manual. Research Triangle Park, N.C.: American Association of Textile Chemists and Colorists, 1976.

Bennett, Ralph D. "Tapestry Conservation Equipment in The Fine Arts Museums of San Francisco." Unpublished manuscript, The Fine Arts Museums of San Francisco, 1975.

Fulton, George. *Applied Science for Drycleaners*. Silver Spring, Md.: National Institute of Cleaning and Dyeing, 1951.

Identification of Textile Materials, 7th ed. Manchester, England: The Textile Institute, 1975.

Kajitani, Nobuko. "Care of Fabrics in the Museum." In *Preservation of Paper and Textiles of Historic and Artistic Value*, Advances in Chemistry Series No. 164. Washington, D.C.: American Chemical Society, 1977.

Rice, James W. "Principles of Textile Conservation Science." *Textile Museum Journal*, 1962, 1963, 1964, 1967, 1968, 1969, 1970, and 1973. Washington, D.C.

"BREAD, BRUSHES, AND BROOMS": ASPECTS OF TAPESTRY RESTORATION IN ENGLAND, 1660-1760

Wendy Hefford

In the summer of 1710, Zacharias Conrad von Uffenbach of Frankfurt, an inveterate tourist, was visiting London. One of his two guide books to the city had been emphatic in its praise of the tapestries in the House of Lords, which von Uffenbach naturally went to see. Alas for his expectations! He wrote in his journal:

Finally we saw the House of Lords or Upper House, which is described in some detail in the Vieu of London. . . .[1] The room is much smaller even than that of the Commons, and one finds that the great expectations formed of all these things are monstrously disappointed. The 'Tapistry accounted the finest in Europe' may once have been very handsome, but it now looks so wretched and tarnished with smoke that neither gold nor silver, colours nor figures, can be recognised. All the same it is curious on account of the intrinsic value of the gold and silver with which it is lavishly worked, and of the story of the invincible Spanish Armada.[2]

Looking at a tapestry, our first, natural response is appreciation of the art and workmanship of the time when the tapestry was made. In some unfortunate cases this may be combined with sadness or revulsion, similar to von Uffenbach's reaction, caused by the condition of the tapestry. This is particularly so when a tapestry is disfigured by obtrusive repairs. Such repair, immediately evident to an observer, is of comparatively recent date, resulting from the commercial revival of tapestry in the late nineteenth century and increasing with the inflating prices of the twentieth. So that tapestries could be sold and hung, their missing portions and areas where the weft was weak were rewoven, at best using dyes which then faded at a different rate to the older work, at worst with complete lack of feeling for the style of the tapestry or understanding of the lost design.

Reweaving is one way of restoring a tapestry. A different approach, often favored by museums and by discriminating collectors, is of conservation rather than restoration, carefully preserving all that is left of the old material, removing unsightly repairs, and adding to the remains of the original only so much as is necessary to prevent the structure from disintegrating or the missing parts from hindering enjoyment of the whole. Nobuko Kajitani's paper delivered to the San Francisco Symposium[3] demonstrated the great care and sensitivity with which the repair of tapestry is now approached.

But what of the hundreds of years that may have elapsed between the making of a tapestry and its most recent repair? When we look at a tapestry we tend to forget that it must have been cleaned and repaired many times in the course of its existence. Repairs of the sixteenth to the eighteenth century may not be easily detected from the general appearance of a tapestry: the natural dyes used for the wools and silks may have faded to much the same degree as those used in the original work; and the men who made these repairs usually did so before the original weaving had completely perished, so that it could be accurately copied. A recent article by Bertrand Jestaz, revealing the extensive restoration made in the late seventeenth century to the famous tapestries of the *Galerie de Fontainebleau*, shows that more attention should be given to the many documents recording repairs so that we may understand just how frequent and how drastic the earlier restoration of some tapestries may have been.[4]

Tapestries were used by their owners for show and display. Great store was set by the famous tapestries of the past, as can be seen from the inventory of Charles I's possessions in which the fine sixteenth-century sets at Hampton Court were given values equal to or higher than the new, expensive tapestries made at Mortlake. But they had to be usable and so, if they deteriorated, they had to be rewoven and restored to look like new.

The English Crown, like most monarchies, had its own staff for the restoration of "arras" tapestries. They were under the control of the Master of the Great Wardrobe and were directed by the Yeoman Arrasworker. The latter was often chosen from among the leading owners of tapestry workshops. His own workshop might provide new tapestries for the Crown which figured in the Wardrobe accounts, but his chief function on the Wardrobe staff was to supervise the cleaning and repair of tapestries by six or more men employed at daily rates solely for this purpose.

The Public Record Office in London holds numerous Wardrobe accounts detailing quarterly payments to the tapestry workers and for the rent of offices at the yeoman arrasworker's premises, also amounts spent on materials for the work done. Some yeoman arrasworkers when making their claims specified which tapestries they had repaired. The accounts of the late seventeenth and early eighteenth centuries are particularly detailed, enabling us to see how much work was entailed and how frequently any particular set was cleaned and repaired. For example, tapestry hangings of *Romulus and Remus* were cleaned and repaired in 1676–77,[5] with more work on some of the pieces in 1680 and again in 1696.[6] Nine tapestries of *The Sciences* were also cleaned and mended in that year,[7] with further treatment in 1710–11[8] and in the early 1730s.[9] The Mortlake sets of *Hero and Leander* and *Vulcan and Venus* were named in lists of tapestries repaired in 1677–78, 1707–8, 1732–33 and 1760–61.[10]

These records indicate that tapestries in constant use in the royal collection tended to be cleaned and repaired every twenty or thirty years. To be certain of this, considering that the tapestries cited could have belonged to different sets of the same name, it is necessary to return to the tapestries of the *History of the Spanish Armada*, for which von Uffenbach provided such a rare eyewitness account of condition. This series of designs was woven only once, and any record of that name, or of the alternative title, *The Story of Eighty-eight*, must apply to the one set.

The tapestries were commissioned by England's victorious Lord High Admiral, Lord Howard of Effingham, from the Delft workshop of Frans Spierings. Queen Elizabeth could afford no such extravagances, and her disappointment must have been greater than the surprise of her court when, visiting Howard at Arundel House in December 1602, "The Lord Admiralls feasting the Quene had nothing extraordinarie, neither were his presents so precious as was expected; being only a whole suit of apparell, whereas it was thought he wold have bestowed his rich hangings of all the fights with the Spanish Armada in eighty-eight."[11] It was left to James I to buy these hangings for the royal collection for the sum of £1,628.8s. in 1611/12. The tapestries were used in the House of Lords as early as 1644, for Wenceslaus Hollar showed them in his engraving of the trial of Archbishop Laud; but in 1649 the inventory of Charles I recorded them as part of the furnishings of the Tower.[12] When much of the royal collection was sold under the Commonwealth, the Armada tapestries were reserved for the use of the State, and

in 1651 they were hung in "the late Lords' House" which served for meetings of the Committee of Parliament.[13]

In 1710, therefore, these rich tapestries of wool, silk and metal thread were over a hundred years old and had seen public service in a place of assembly. From the description of their filthy condition, either they had not been cleaned for a long time, or the smoke from open fires, flaming torches and candles quickly dimmed the lustre of such precious hangings, necessitating very frequent cleaning. The records of the Great Wardrobe show that some pieces were cleaned more frequently than the average discussed above. In 1668 Charles II acquired a new set of tapestries "being the first after the design" called the *Bacchanals*.[14] These tapestries were cleaned in 1678,[15] ten years after their manufacture, and again only three years later, in 1681.[16] But the *Armada* tapestries, "wretched and tarnished," may possibly have been neglected since before the 1670s, for they are not named in the Wardrobe accounts until 1693. In that year the tapestries were mended; but the account did not charge for cleaning or for cleaning materials. John Vanderbank, yeoman arrasworker, simply claimed: "For Crewle and Silke to mend the tapistry hangings of Eighty-eight—£7.0.0."[17] With silk costing eighteen pence an ounce and wool at about five shillings per pound weight, the total sum was about average for mending a fairly large set of tapestries needing only minor repairs. Perhaps Vanderbank did little more on that occasion than sew up the slits which appeared along joins between colors where the original sewing threads had perished.

The first recorded cleaning of the set took place two years after von Uffenbach expressed his disapproval. Vanderbank's account for 1712 includes the significant words "bread" and "brushes." The Wardrobe accounts leave no doubt that in the seventeenth and eighteenth centuries the usual method of cleaning a tapestry was by brushing crumbled bread across its surface. The moist bread would have taken dirt from the tapestry rather in the way that a gum rubber takes pencil marks from the surface of paper. In 1691 Vanderbank cleaned four of his own newly made tapestries, recording; "for bread to clean the hangings—£1.2s.0d."[18] In 1693 another ingredient was added to the cleansing feast for the ten *Abraham* tapestries at

Hampton Court, with "Bread and Branne and other Materialls to cleane the said pieces."[19] The same cleaning methods were still being used in the 1770s. The leading tapestry maker, Paul Saunders, charged in 1771 for cleaning tapestry in eight rooms at St. James's Palace for "Bread, Brushes and Brooms used for the purpose—£1.4s.0d.,"[20] an exceptionally economical use of bread in an operation said to have taken seven men five days.

If one imagines the effect of brooms brushing over tapestries in which the silk especially was no doubt already weakened by acids in the dirt and by exposure to light, it is not surprising that the repairs needed by the *Armada* tapestries in 1712 cost more than the £7 of 1693. The sum quoted, however, is staggering. "For the House of Peers—for ffine Silke Worsted Warps Crewle Bread Brushes Tacks and other materialls to mend cleane and line Eight large pieces of Tapestry hangings of the Spanish Invasion—£205."[21] This sum is even more amazing in that only eight of the ten pieces were repaired and that no gold or silver, the most expensive items in tapestry repair, were included in the list of materials used. The specification of worsted warp implies some extensive repair where rewarping, and therefore reweaving of the weft, were necessary.

Vanderbank rarely charged more than £5 an ell[22] for the tapestries made in his workshop; a charge which included all the costs of the materials, wages of his weavers, overheads and, presumably, profit. Of the £205 spent on the restoration of the *Armada* tapestries, some £15 may have been for the relining of the eight pieces with canvas or linen,[23] some £5 for materials for cleaning. The rest must have been accounted for by sewing and reweaving which, at one of Vanderbank's higher rates, could have equalled over 35 ells of newly worked tapestry. This amount in a set which contained 704 ells was the equivalent of half a tapestry. The valuation of the *Armada* tapestries at £3 an ell some sixty years before could mean that Vanderbank charged only £3 an ell for his replacements, and therefore rewove proportionately more. The only alternative supposition to a considerable amount of reweaving is that the yeoman arrasworker was embezzling Wardrobe funds.

In spite of this great amount of work done on them, within twenty years these tapes-

tries had to undergo another cycle of cleaning and repair, presumably because they had become dirty again. In the 1730s the accounts submitted by John Ellys, successor to the Vanderbanks, were for less than that of 1712 but again included warp material and had a certain amount of reweaving specifically noted:

In the House of Peers. John Ellys craves Allowance . . . For fine Silk, Thread Woosted Warp Crewell, Bread, Brushes Tacks and Canvas with other Materials, to mend, clean and new Line in Several places Eight large pieces of Tapistry Hangings called the History of the Spanish Invasion and for Adding and Interweaving Pieces where worn out—£80.0.0.[24]

A year or so later, Ellys dealt with two pieces of the *Armada* tapestries. One would expect these to be the other two pieces from the set of ten, omitted from the repairs of 1712 and 1730. When John Pine published the series in 1739[25] he wrote, "Some of these are now in the Royal Wardrobe, others in the House of Lords"; and in the 1760s the set was still divided into eight and two pieces—but Ellys' second bill was also headed "In the House of Peers." Either the two pieces were normally kept in store but were occasionally used in some smaller chamber of the House of Lords, or John Pine mistook their usual location, or Ellys repaired separately two of the eight pieces that he had cleaned in 1730. His bill was for silk, warp, wool, thread and other unspecified materials "to repair 2 large pieces of Tapestry Hangings called the Spanish Invasion Several pieces of New Tapestry added—£34.2s.6d."[26] At £17 per tapestry compared with the £10 that was the average for the eight restored in 1730, it does seem likely that these two tapestries were the ones not previously restored.

When Lempriere drew and John Pine engraved the ten tapestries of the *Spanish Armada* in 1739, how much of what they recorded was the work of Vanderbank and Ellys? Possibly, from the rough computations which are all that we can make, some 48 ells of tapestry. Pine apparently found the tapestries in fair condition after their cleaning and repair, for his introduction to the engravings made no mention of dirt or dilapidation. His whole concern (with reason, as events transpired) was with the future condition of the tapestries:

. . . because Time or Accidents or Moths may deface these valuable Shadows, we have endeavour'd to preserve their Likeness in the Prints

68

annexed, which being multiplied and dispersed in various Hands, may meet with that Security . . . which the Originals must . . . scarcely . . . hope for, even from the Sanctity of the Places they are kept in.

The prints are very detailed, which could reflect the precision of the woven detail at that time (see Figs. 1 and 2). From Pine's willingness, "for more Variety," to have the tapestries embellished with a newly invented and decidedly rococo border (Fig. 1), one must, however, be prepared to suppose that what could not be seen was quite simply supplied from the imagination.

The third eighteenth-century restoration of the *Armada* tapestries came around 1760–61. This was possibly a rushed job for the coronation of George III, since the bill mentions a special rate of pay for the workers "on Account of working Day and Night." The account, submitted by Paul Saunders, stated, "For the House of Lords; Paid for Cleaning and Repairing also Restoring the Colours and new lining 8 pieces of Tapestry Called the Spanish Armada used fine silks worsteds Threads Stains etc. the whole containing 580 Ells at 4/2 on Account of working Day and Night—£120.16s."[27]

Here, for the first time in this sorry tale, is the ominous word "stain." Painting or otherwise coloring rather than weaving the details in tapestry had been so common in the early sixteenth century that regulations had to be made to deal with the abuse. Dr. Schneebalg-Perelman has shown how widespread was the practice of painting or chalking certain details, either of faces and flesh or of background scenery, in tapestries supplied even by some of the leading Brussels manufacturers of the time. A regulation of 1525 forbade painting only in Brussels tapestries that cost more than 20 sous the ell. A more sweeping edict of 1544 still allowed the use of ink and chalk for outlining or enhancing areas already woven into the fabric and for retouching mistakes in weaving. The complaints which led to these regulations condemned not the use of paint in itself, but painting "more than usual" on newly woven tapestry. For restoring old tapestries the use of coloring materials was generally accepted, and Dr. Schneebalg-Perelman found numerous mentions of the practice in the accounts of the period.[28]

Probably a certain amount of painting went on in every century. In the late seventeenth

century one of the leading tapestry dealers in Antwerp wrote to his son in Vienna, "it is dirty work, and what has been painted . . . and is exposed to dampness must surely deteriorate."[29] John Vanderbank does not seem to have used this means of restoration; at least, no charge for it appears in his detailed accounts. But in the second half of the eighteenth century, when tapestry weaving in England was declining, Paul Saunders, the last of the great yeoman arrasworkers, had recourse to paint or stain for "restoring the colours" in almost every set of tapestries which he repaired for the Crown. As he charged by the ell, it sounds as though his use of stain was fairly comprehensive.

Scoured, rewarped, rewoven, painted, the *Armada* tapestries perished in the fire that destroyed the Houses of Parliament in 1834. An eyewitness recorded what he imaginatively conceived to be the moment of their consumption:

At about half past nine an immense column of flame burst forth through the roof and windows of the House of Lords; . . . bright blue corruscations, as of electric fire, played in the volume of the flames [Note: This singular appearance proceeded perhaps from the coloring matter in the materials of the tapestry of the House of Lords, which represented the destruction of the Armada], and so struck were the bye-standers with the grandeur of the sight at this moment, that they involuntarily (and from no bad feeling) clapped their hands as though they had been present at the closing scene of some dramatic spectacle.[30]

Before the *Armada* tapestries met the fate feared for them by John Pine, they were illustrated by Rowlandson and Pugin in a view of the interior of the House of Lords in Ackermann's *Microcosm of London*.[31] Unfortunately, there is not sufficient detail in the illustration to show how well or ill the tapestries looked as the result of their restoration. Perhaps the accounts of the eighteenth-century work seem more drastic than they would have appeared to the eye. The weaving in gold and silver must have been hard enough to withstand the friction of the bristles, for no replacement of metal thread was recorded in this set; wool and silk may have been rewoven with craftsmanship, and were in colors made from natural dyes which blended with the original work; and the stain may have been removable. Nevertheless, the case of the *Armada* tapestries shows that hangings in constant use did need cleaning and quite considerable repair every twenty to thirty years.

Fig. 1. Engraving by John Pine, 1739, of the tapestry in the House of Lords showing the approach of the Spanish Armada. The border is an eighteenth-century invention; the original border design can be seen below, in Fig. 2. (Photograph courtesy of the Victoria and Albert Museum, London)

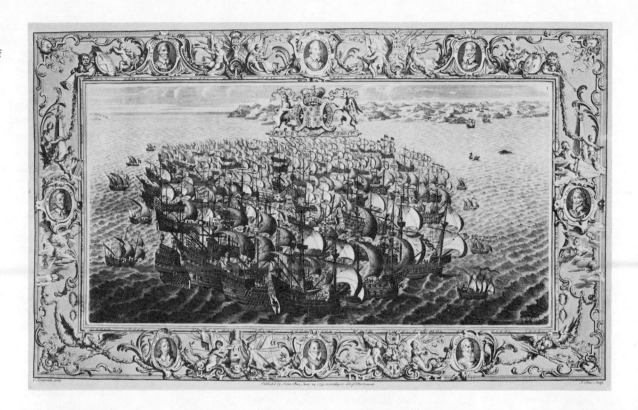

Fig. 2. Engraving by John Pine, 1739, of the tapestry in the House of Lords showing the English fleet pursuing the Armada. (Photograph courtesy of the Victoria and Albert Museum, London)

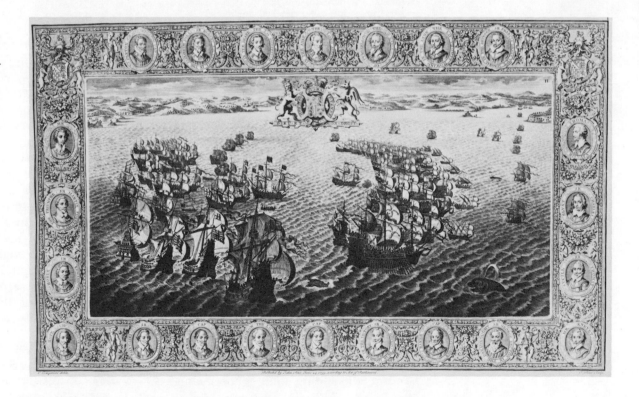

To a contemporary of John Vanderbank it would have seemed entirely natural not only to have rewoven such parts of a tapestry as were in need of repair but to have added to the length or breadth of the pieces in a set and even to have made whole new tapestries of matching subject in order to make an existing set fit a different room.

Many cases of such alterations combined with repairs occur in the Wardrobe accounts. Following the union of England and Scotland under Queen Anne in 1706, Vanderbank submitted this account:[32]

For Kensington.	£	s.	d.
ffor bread, Brushes, Tacks, and all materials to clean and make bright the gold and silver in 4 pieces of Tapestry hangings (called) the Children of Israell	10	0	0
Gold, Silver etc & workmanship for the middle of the said 4 pces of hangings	13	0	0
ffor altering and dismantling, Joyning and fitting the said 4 peices to the Room both in Depth and breadth	12	0	0
ffor working, in Gold and Silver, her Majesty's Armes and Badges according to the Union in Several places in the Borders of the said hangings which together makes 27 Ells flemish of New Arras Tapestry at £6 p. ell . . .	162	0	0
For Gold and Silver to work in the borders of the said 4 peices of hangings to fill up the Vacancies between the Arms and the Badges	70	0	0
For workmanship to work the said Gold and Silver in all the Borders	35	0	0

To this altered set of tapestries Vanderbank also added three completely new pieces: "At Kensington. ffor Three new peices of Tapestry hangings Arras (called the Story of Moses) being Addicons for and Suitable to the hangings in the Princes Bed Chamber (called the Children of Israell) cont. 58 Ells ¾ at £6 p. ell flemish—£352.10.00."[33]

In 1720 the workshop of John Vanderbank, run by his family after his death, cleaned and repaired these seven pieces of tapestry and increased the height of the three made by Vanderbank, adding another 10¼ Flemish ells.[34]

The *Children of Israel* was described as "new" in 1671, and so was some thirty years old at the time of its transformation by Vanderbank; but he was also called upon to make radical alterations to his own newly woven tapestries. In August 1690 he supplied "4 Peeces of

fine Tapestry Hangings designed and workt after the Indian Manner" for the withdrawing room at Kensington Palace. At that time the set measured 99 square Flemish ells.[35] In the next year or so Vanderbank added two more pieces to the set and lengthened some of the "old" pieces, making in all 54¼ new ells of tapestry. In 1696 "Another piece of the same Indian work is made entirely, two ells flemish and half in breadth and 4 ells ½ Flemish in depth makes 11½ ells at £5 p. ell". At the same time two other pieces from the set were widened by small amounts.[36] The set which had started at 99 square ells increased in the first six years of its existence to 177 square ells.

When Vanderbank enlarged a tapestry, part of the border had to be removed and pieced together with new sections of border. Any addition to the width of the scene was not simply sewn to the edge of the old tapestry but was joined by knotting each warp thread of the old tapestry to the corresponding warp thread in the new piece, making a join almost invisible from the front of the tapestry. Vanderbank made this clear in his account of 1707–08 for enlarging the "winter" and "harvest" tapestries of *Dutch Boors* for Kensington Palace: "knotting ye warp threads together of all the said pces with the materials to make it like old work."[37] On this occasion too he made a small new tapestry to add to the set. As he made no charge for the drawings from which to work the 44½ additional ells, it may perhaps be assumed that Vanderbank here, as with the Indian pieces, was augmenting his own earlier work rather than altering a set of Flemish tapestries. This assumption is strengthened by a comment in a guide book of 1761 not usually given to the attribution of tapestries, which described a room in Kensington Palace "adorned with very beautiful tapestry, representing a Dutch winter piece, and the various diversions peculiar to the natives of Holland, done by Mr. Vanderbank."[38]

If Vanderbank had no access to the original cartoons of a series, the pieces which he made "suitable" may have differed quite noticeably in style from the tapestries in the set he was enlarging. Vanderbank worked for private patrons as well as for the Crown, and among his best customers was Ralph, Earl and later Duke of Montagu, who was Master of the Great Wardrobe and so Vanderbank's official paymaster. In Boughton House, Northamptonshire, inherited from the

Fig. 3. Tapestry from a set of *Bacchanals,* second half of the seventeenth century; with alterations dating from 1700 by John Vanderbank. (Photograph courtesy of the Victoria and Albert Museum, London, and His Grace the Duke of Buccleuch and Queensberry)

Montagus by the Dukes of Buccleuch, a large part of Ralph Montagu's impressive collection of tapestries still remains. Among them is a set depicting Bacchanalian children reveling in formal gardens, surrounded by a deep border with snakes each biting the tail of the snake in front. Six of these tapestries have applied borders with mitred corners, and at the bottom of each scene a strip of grass and plants has clearly been added (Fig. 3). The other two pieces, both narrow upright panels, have integral borders and show no signs of additions in their length (Fig. 4). In these two pieces the figures are closer in style to the boys in the Mortlake series of the *Story of the Boys* (Fig. 5) than to the Bacchanalian boys of the other six tapestries, and the backgrounds show distant mountains in place of the decorative formal gardens.

The alterations to the six pieces and the differences in the two narrow tapestries are explained by bills from Vanderbank at

Boughton detailing his work. In 1700 he asked £29 "ffor lengthening 6 pieces bachannells att top and bottom 14 ells and ½ at 40s.," and in 1704 "ffor making 2 new pieces of Bachannells to suit wth the 6 pieces I lengthened top and bottom wch 2 pieces contained 24 ells at 40s. p. ell—£48.0.0."[39] Clearly in this case he had not owned the cartoons of the *Bacchanals* but adapted designs of a similar subject.

Between 1695 and 1705 Vanderbank's work for Montagu amounted to the weaving of six entire tapestries, altering three existing sets and cleaning and repairing seven sets of tapestries. The cost of repairs and minor alterations equalled one-third of the amount earned for new work, and most of that new work was for pieces to enlarge existing sets. In the same period, the proportionate cost of Vanderbank's repair and alteration work compared with the prices of new tapestries made for the Crown is less easy to estimate,

72

Fig. 4. Tapestry woven to add to a set of *Bacchanals* by John Vanderbank, 1704. (Photograph courtesy of the Victoria and Albert Museum, London, and His Grace the Duke of Buccleuch and Queensberry)

Fig. 5. Tapestry of the *Story of the Boys*, woven at Mortlake in the second half of the seventeenth century. (Photograph courtesy of the Victoria and Albert Museum, London, and His Grace the Duke of Buccleuch and Queensberry)

as the record may be incomplete. Roughly, however, Vanderbank claimed less than £100 for new tapestries made between 1695 and 1705, while materials for repairs and alterations in that period cost over £500.

From the Wardrobe accounts and from private bills such as those at Boughton, it is obvious that the income of a tapestry workshop depended quite substantially on repairs and alterations. The importance of this sort of work should therefore always be considered when assessing the production of a particular workshop. The enormous amount of recorded restoration should also be remembered when looking at any tapestry made before the eighteenth century. Many treasured tapestries in the great collections of today may owe their comparatively fair state of preservation to the tapestry restorers of the seventeenth and eighteenth centuries. Conversely, many of those tapestries in constant use over the centuries, calling for cleaning and some substantial repair every thirty years or so, may have been restored to such an extent that it is now difficult to tell what is original work. More recent tapestries, too, may have been so altered that they would be unrecognizable from their bill of sale. Whatever the case, a study of the records concerning these repairs can add appreciably to our knowledge both of the tapestries and of the workshops concerned.

NOTES

1. He refers to the guidebook *A New View of London*, 2 vols. (London, 1708), 2: 629.
2. W. H. Quarrell and M. Mare, eds. and trans., *London in 1710 from the travels of Zacharias Conrad von Uffenbach* (London: Faber & Faber, 1934), p. 74.
3. See pp. 45-63, this volume.
4. Bertrand Jestaz, "La tenture de la Galerie de Fontainebleau et sa restauration à Vienne à la fin du XVIIe siècle," *Revue de l'Art* 22 (1973): 50-56.
5. The Lord Chamberlain's Books. Great Wardrobe (bill books, tradesmen, etc.). L.C. 9/275, account no. 30. London: Public Record Office.
6. Ibid., L.C. 9/280, account no. 66.
7. Ibid., L.C. 9/280, account no. 66.
8. Ibid., L.C. 9/283, account no. 79.
9. Ibid., L.C. 9/288, account no. 118.
10. Ibid., L.C. 9/275, account nos. 113, 163; L.C. 9/282, account no. 55; L.C. 9/288, account no. 29; L.C. 9/292, account no. 89.
11. Letter from John Chamberlain to Dudley Carleton, 23 December 1602, Sarah Williams, ed., *Letters of John Chamberlain during the reign of Queen Elizabeth* (London: The Camden Society, 1861), pp. 169-70.
12. The tapestries were then valued at £2113.10s., more than James I had paid. See Oliver Millar, ed. and introd., *The Inventories and Valuations of the King's Goods, The Walpole Society,* Annual Volume 43 (1970-72): 5-6.
13. Calendar of State Papers Domestic. Commonwealth. Vol 15 (January-June 1651), p. 1. (London, 1877).
14. The Lord Chamberlain's Books, L.C. 9/271, account no. 284.
15. Ibid., L.C. 9/275, account no. 163.
16. Ibid., L.C. 9/276, account no. 102.
17. Ibid., L.C. 9/280, account no. 22.
18. Ibid., L.C. 9/280, account no. 79.
19. Ibid., L.C. 9/280, account no. 22. The cleaning agents for the ten large tapestries cost £6, new brushes, £1.10s.
20. Ibid., L.C. 9/318, account no. 94.
21. Ibid., L.C. 9/284, account no. 66.
22. The charge was by the square ell. The linear Flemish ell by which tapestries were measured was 27 inches.
23. In 1760-61, eight of the *Armada* tapestries were lined with Osnaburgh linen by Paul Saunders at a cost of £15.4s.0d. (L.C. 9/292, account no. 89.)
24. The Lord Chamberlain's Books, L.C. 9/288, account no. 41.
25. John Pine, *The Tapestry Hangings of the House of Lords: Representing the several Engagements between the English and Spanish Fleets, in the ever memorable Year MDLXXXVIII . . . (London, 1739).*
26. The Lord Chamberlain's Books, L.C. 9/289, account no. 42.
27. Ibid., L.C. 9/292, account no. 89.
28. Sophie Schneebalg-Perelman, "'Le retouchage' dans la tapisserie bruxelloise ou les origines de l'édit impérial de 1544," *Annales de la Société royale d'Archéologie de Bruxelles* 50 (1956-61): 191-210.
29. J. Denucé, *Antwerp Art-Tapestry and Trade, Historical Sources for the Study of Flemish Art,* vol. 4 (Antwerp, 1936), p. xl.
30. Letter of 17 October, 1834 by A.J.K. to *The Gentleman's Magazine* 156, New Series II (1834): 477-80.
31. Rudolph Ackermann, *The Microcosm of London* (London, 1808-11), vol. 2, Pl. 52 opposite p. 183. The acquatint was published 1 January, 1809.
32. The Lord Chamberlain's Books, L.C. 9/282, account no. 57.
33. Ibid., L.C. 9/282, account no. 56.
34. Ibid., L.C. 9/286, account no. 68.
35. Ibid., L.C. 9/279, account no. 94.
36. Ibid., L.C. 9/280, account nos. 44, 66.
37. Ibid., L.C. 9/282, account no. 55.
38. *London and its environs described,* vol. 3 (London, 1761), p. 269. On the other hand, an account in the name of John Vanderbank submitted by his widow in 1720 charged for cleaning seven pieces of the *Dutch Boors* at Kensington and for adding 50 ells of "new ffine Tapistry" to the set with a charge "ffor Expenses in drawing the patterns and painting the designs of the said hangings—£27.0.0" (L.C. 9/286, account no. 68). But perhaps the family had run out of subjects at the previous enlargement of the set.
39. Manuscript bills at Boughton House, quoted by kind permission of His Grace the Duke of Buccleuch and Queensberry.

PART III
SUBJECTS AND HISTORY

PART III
SUBJECTS AND HISTORY

The Passion of Christ in Medieval Tapestries

Larry Salmon

INTRODUCTION

The exhibition and publication of the European tapestry collections of The Fine Arts Museums of San Francisco in the fall of 1976 were events of major significance for textile scholars throughout the world because they brought to public attention for the first time so many beautiful and important weavings. Among the previously unpublished examples was a tapestry of the late medieval period showing two scenes from The Passion of Christ, *Christ and Barabbas and Pilate Washing His Hands* (Fig. 7).[1] The ultimate design source for this San Francisco hanging is the same as that drawn on for several other tapestries with scenes from Christ's Passion, which are in various European and American collections. These other weavings have been the subject of frequent study, and the placing of the San Francisco piece with this group presents the perfect opportunity to review the main facts and hypotheses advanced over the years regarding them. Not only can past research be reevaluated and consolidated here, but all these tapestries and a related set of embroideries can be reproduced together for the first time in this book.

First, we will present the cultural context in which these tapestries were produced and then describe their narrative scenes as they relate to each other and to this background. We can then better tackle the problems of the relationships these hangings bear to each other, the time period in which they were produced, and the attribution of them to one or more weaving centers.

THE PASSION OF CHRIST IN MEDIEVAL EUROPE.

Christ's Passion was one of the most popular religious themes in European literature and drama in the fifteenth and sixteenth centuries, and it was equally favored in contemporary art.[2] The story of The Passion was drawn from the Scriptures of Matthew, Mark, Luke, and John, but it was added to substantially from many other sources throughout the Middle Ages. Apocryphal sources such as the thirteenth-century *Golden Legend* of Jacobus de Voragine and the *Meditations on the Life of Christ* steadily grew in fame and popularity, and they influenced the relating of Christian thought to the people as it appeared in literature and the arts.

It is no surprise that these apocryphal sources served as the bases for many of the mystery plays that developed in the Middle Ages. The *Meditations* typified a gradual turning away from an intellectual contemplation of The Passion to an exploitation of its emotional possibilities, and this approach was ideally suited to dramatic presentations. The Passion of Christ was a favored subject for the mystery plays, and a great many versions of it are known. It was apparently a standard in the dramatic repertoire by 1400, and in 1402 a special patent was granted a group to stage it in Paris. At one time or another, performances were held in major cities throughout Europe, over eighty being recorded in France between 1400 and 1550, with almost half of them taking place between 1480 and 1510.[3]

Performances of these medieval mysteries were occasions for local holidays, calling upon the energies of whole cities. Most work came to a halt as people gathered in large outdoor public areas for the performances. People of many classes made up the cast, and the audience often came from great distances to watch and to join in the celebration. The textual material was continually expanded to allow for greater definition of the characters and for more conversations, so that by the mid-fifteenth century four days were commonly required for one complete performance of The Passion. In later years the addition of new material reached extremes, and an expanded version of The Passion of Christ staged in Valenciennes in 1547 required twenty-five days to perform. These plays made good theater, however, and they were enthusiastically received. A manuscript note discovered by William Hone in a *Passion* published in Paris in 1490, describes some of the events of one such performance and conveys the high regard in which it was held by a spectator:

. . . in the year 1437, on the 3rd of July was represented the game or play, *de la Passion, N.S.* in the plain of Veximiel, when the park was arranged in a very noble manner, for there were nine ranges of seats in height rising by degrees; all around and behind were great and long seats for the lords and ladies. To represent God was the Lord Nicolle, Lord of Neufchatel, in Lorraine, who was curate of St. Victor of Metz; he was nigh dead upon the cross if he had not been assisted, and it was determined that another priest should be placed on the cross to counterfeit the personage of the crucifixion for that day; but on the following day the said curate of St. Victor counterfeited the resurrection, and performed his part very highly during the play. Another priest, who was called Messire Jean de Nicey, and was chaplain of Metrange, played Judas, and was nearly dead while hanging, for his heart failed him, wherefore he was very quickly unhung and carried off: and there *the Mouth of Hell* was very well done; for it opened and shut when the devils required to enter and come out, and had two large eyes of steel.[4]

Two fifteenth-century Passion plays are especially well known and appear to have been the bases for most versions that followed. Completed just before 1450 by Arnoul Greban, the first is written in good verse and includes music composed for it by the author.[5] Jean Michel is the author of the second version, apparently written for a 1486 performance of The Passion in Angers.[6] Michel often stretches scenes out to great lengths, but he does achieve a heightened dramatic sense and a fuller development of the characters. The advent of printing was to ensure his fame and serve as a measure of his version's popularity, with at least fifteen editions known to have been printed between 1490 and 1542.[7]

The designer of the group of Passion tapestries to which the San Francisco hanging belongs would hardly have slavishly followed the text of one or another of the many dramatic versions of The Passion in composing his scenes. However, these mystery plays were so well known in their own time that collectively they would have been part of the designer's experience, and he would have drawn on them consciously or subconsciously for narrative ideas. Often details began to appear in contemporary art which, although present in earlier narrative literature, had been passed over until incorporated into the dramas. The art of tapestry weaving shared an additional strong bond with medieval drama, moreover. Tapestry design of the late Middle Ages more than any other art form paralleled design of the stage settings for these mystery plays. Action took place on a long stage, moving from left to right, with summary architectural elements and a piece of furniture or two indicating settings but with little or no internal division between scenes. One should be aware of this kinship of drama and tapestry design in studying the San Francisco tapestry and the others of its group, in the event that the dramas can shed any light on the composition, narrative detail, and relationship of the weavings to one another.

TEXTILES RELATED TO THE SAN FRANCISCO TAPESTRY

The San Francisco Passion tapestry shares a common design source with four hangings owned by the Tapestry Museum of the Château of Angers and displayed at present in the chapel of the château, with a weaving in the Museum of Fine Arts, Boston, and with two large fragments, one owned by the Rijksmuseum in Amsterdam and the second in the collection of the Musée des Arts Décoratifs in Paris. In addition to these tapestries, a set of nine monumental embroideries is preserved in the collegiate church of Saint Barnard in Romans, Drôme, which is apparently based on the same cartoons. The scenes represented in these textiles are *The Agony in the Garden and the Kiss of Judas* (Fig. 1), *Christ before Annas and Caiaphas* (Fig. 2), *Christ before Pilate and Herod* (Figs. 3–6), *Christ and Barabbas and Pilate Washing His Hands* (Figs. 7–9), *Road to Calvary* (Figs. 10, 11), *Crucifixion and Harrowing of Hell* (Figs. 12–15)[8], and *Entombment of Christ, Resurrection, and Christ Appearing to the Virgin, the Magdalene, and Saint Peter* (Figs. 16, 17).

The complete set of original cartoons would surely have included additional scenes, not preserved in either the tapestries or the embroideries, but any reconstruction of the whole sequence would be speculative. We can more profitably study the existing textiles in an effort to determine their provenances and relationships to each other.

The Passion tapestries in Angers and Boston have detailed provenances credited to them, which bear reviewing. The four Angers hangings (Figs. 6, 10, 13, 16) have been identified since 1889 as four of the six tapestries of The Passion of Christ known to have been in the Church of Saint Saturnin in Tours around 1792–93. These six tapestries measured a total of thirty-eight *aunes* or about 45.6m in length. They were said to have been sold to the Church of Saint Etienne in Chinon and then later to Angers.[9] L. de Farcy wrote in 1897 that these same six tapestries were recorded in an inventory of Saint Saturnin dated 1727 and that they had been left to the church in 1505 by Pierre Morin, treasurer general of the bureau of finances.[10] In 1923 Ch. Urseau wrote that the date of purchase of these tapestries from Saint Etienne was 1824,[11] and he agreed that these were four of the tapestries given Saint Saturnin in Tours in 1505 and evaluated in 1792–93.

Recently, however, this provenance has been questioned by the present curator of the Angers tapestry collection, Antoine Ruais.[12]

Ruais writes that these hangings were purchased in 1854 (not 1824) from the Church of Saint Maurice in Chinon rather than the Church of Saint Etienne,[13] and he further notes that there is no proof that the four Angers tapestries are part of the set of six Passion tapestries of Saint Saturnin of Tours.[14] Finally, Ruais has discovered the date "1621" woven on the cope of Christ in the scene of his descent to Hell, on the right side of the hanging featuring his Crucifixion, which Ruais suggests could be the date of a restoration. The accounts of Saint Saturnin of Tours deserve close examination not only because of any information they might reveal that would help to prove or disprove these two sets to be identical, but also because they might show if any record exists there of payments for the restorations suggested by the woven date "1621," which would place the Angers set in Tours.

The provenance of the Boston hanging (Fig. 5) is as follows. According to family tradition at the time the tapestry was sold to Robert Treat Paine, 2nd, the hanging was brought to Knole, in Kent, by either Archbishop Warham, between 1503 and 1532, or by his successor, Archbishop Cranmer, who built the chapel where it had hung continuously until the time of its purchase. No contemporary records exist to substantiate this tradition, however, and several circumstances make it seem unlikely. The chapel is not large enough to hold more than one tapestry of this size, and a single scene from the middle of the Passion story, either new or secondhand, would seem a peculiar choice for Archbishop Cranmer to have made to furnish his new chapel. Moreover, the estate and goods of Knole were confiscated by the king in 1645 for nonpayment of advance taxes, then were appraised and sold. On 30 September 1645 "ffive peeces of Orris hangeinge" from the chapel chamber were appraised,[15] and these may well have been the only hangings for which there was space in the chapel. At least seventy-five tapestries in all were appraised at Knole and dispersed as a result of this confiscation. It is unlikely that such a large hanging as that now in Boston could have been overlooked in such a disposition, no matter where in the house it was displayed or stored.

Whether or not this tapestry was brought to Knole in the early sixteenth century or at some time after the English Civil Wars, it did not hang there continuously until its removal to Boston. At the 17 May 1882 meeting of the British Archaeological Association, Rev. G. B. Lewis discussed this tapestry and showed photographs of it, saying that "it was found rolled up, and laid aside, among other old things, in Knole, about sixteen years ago. The late Lady Delawarr and Baroness Buckhurst had it cleaned and repaired, and placed it in its present position, along the north-east wall of Knole Chapel."[16] It should also be noted that this tapestry did not fit perfectly into its space in the chapel, and a depth of about 23cm along the bottom edge had been turned under to permit its installation there.[17]

From this review it is obvious that the traditional provenances for the Angers and Boston tapestries cannot be accepted at present and, therefore, afford no insights regarding their possible date of manufacture. Hence, we must turn to a study of the hangings themselves in search of internal evidence for dating.

DESCRIPTION OF THE TEXTILES
In *The Agony in the Garden and the Kiss of Judas* are the first extant scenes of Christ's Passion in this series, represented by one of the Romans embroideries (Fig. 1). To the upper left Christ kneels in prayer in the Garden of Gethsemane with the cup of sorrow resting on a nearby hillock and the archangel Michael coming toward him, holding a cross. From left to right below Christ, James, Peter, and John are sleeping, and below them the remaining eight disciples sleep. Through a gate in the upper left corner, Judas leads a band of soldiers into the garden. At the lower right Judas kisses Christ while Peter cuts off the ear of the soldier Malchus. In the upper right the bound Christ is being led back to Jerusalem.

The second embroidery (Fig. 2) appears once to have extended to the left, as fragmentary soldiers are engaged in some activity there. In the upper left appear two arches with interior scenes beneath them. In the left one, Peter and John are confronted by a woman, while James stands outside to the left. A cock appears just below this scene, identifying it as the denial of Peter. In the right arch Christ stands bound before Annas. In the hanging's main scene in the lower center Christ is brought before Caiaphas for questioning. In the upper right corner a crowd of men mock the blindfolded Christ in the high priest's house.

82

The next scenes place Christ before Pilate and Herod (Figs. 3, 5, 6). To the lower left a group of men stand watching Christ being led before Pilate. In the Angers and Boston tapestries four small figures, whose significance is unclear, stand in the background above the heads of Christ and the soldiers accompanying him. In the next scene to the right Christ stands before Herod. The moment portrayed here was a favorite with the writers of the mystery plays. A man slips a white robe, the dress of a fool or idiot, over Christ's head after he has refused to answer Herod's questions or to perform miracles. In Greban's play this robe is place over a nude body, but Michel has the white robe placed over the clothes Christ is wearing, and it is this version that the designer has followed.[18] While no conclusion based on this observation should be hazarded, it is of interest that the cartoons might date after 1486, the date of the first performance of Michel's play, a possibility strengthened by internal evidence in the hangings.

As these are the first scenes shared by more than one extant hanging, observations of variations and similarities among the three examples are in order at this time. The costumes in the Angers tapestry (Fig. 6) suggest a date between 1490 and 1500. The length of the jacket or jerkin worn by many of the men is quite short and rarely drops to mid-thigh length. No one in this tapestry is wearing shoes or boots with pointed toes, a style which had some currency until almost 1490. Of course, it is difficult to make any close assignment of date on the basis of these costumes, as the figures represented would have been both historical and Oriental from the point of view of a medieval European, and exotic or fanciful details might be introduced to suggest these differences.[19]

A comparison of costumes and of design and technical details of the Angers and Boston tapestries suggests an earlier date for the former of these two. The jackets of all men in the Boston piece who are not wearing full robes are longer, but they are still well above mid-calf, a length they reached about 1510. A parallel modification of costume can be noted in the Boston hanging for the architectural figure standing on the bracket between Christ and Pilate in the upper left corner. Many figures of the Boston weaving have longer hair, especially those standing behind Pilate, another indication of a slightly later date. A third point that favors the hypothesis of an

earlier date for the Angers example is the greater amount of detail in it. The number of patterned textiles used as costumes is greater, the patterns are more complex, and the jeweled ornaments are fussier and less mechanical. Moreover, the individual faces are generally more expressive in the Angers hanging. All of these points are evident in a comparison of the group of men standing in the left foreground of each hanging. While these points are not proof of a sequence, one would expect the first uses of a cartoon to be the most important and, therefore, the most carefully executed.

Although neither tapestry gives a strong sense of a third dimension, the Angers example does have more of a suggestion of a depth of field. For example, the design of the Angers hanging places the four tiny figures in the upper left corner more successfully in a receding background. More important in creating this illusion of depth are the proportions of the architecture to the figures in the Angers weaving. The Angers arch under which Pilate stands is much higher than that in the Boston weaving, a peculiarity that could be the result of using slightly different cartoons for the two tapestries. The flatter arch of the Boston hanging is not paralleled by a lessening of the total height of this weaving, however. In fact, it is almost 40cm taller than the Angers hanging, making its figures larger in scale and therefore slightly more imposing. If the Angers tapestry can be dated about 1490 to 1500 on the combined evidence of these various points, the Boston hanging must date from about 1495–1505, based on the comparison of its costumes and design details with those of the Angers weaving.

The Romans embroidery of this same scene (Fig. 3) shows no significant compositional difference from the tapestries; however, certain details suggest that it might not have been copied from either the Angers or Boston hangings but rather from still another version. The height of the arch above Pilate's head and its ornamentation are more similar to those in the Boston hanging, as are some of the costume details, such as the hem decoration of the dark robe in the lower left corner. However, the length of the jackets or jerkins is that of the Angers hanging. More importantly, however, the patterns of the figured textiles and costumes of the Romans embroidery are those of a date later in the sixteenth century, as are the types of floral plants appearing along its base. These later designs are to be expected, as the Romans hanging depicting the Resurrection of Christ has the date "1555" embroidered on the roof of one of the buildings in the left background, which may well be the date the set was completed.[20]

No circumstances of the Romans embroideries' history are known until 1677 when a citizen of Romans, Hélène Tardy, the widow of Pierre de Loulle, left the hangings in her will to the convent of Ursuline nuns there.[21] Their ownership reverted to her nephew, Laurent Gitton, however, who sold them in 1684 to Charles de Lyonne de Lesseins, sacristan of the chapter house of Saint Barnard. Upon his death the embroideries of The Passion were left to the church, while seven others in the series were sold in Paris.[22] Together these embroideries were said to form a "Life of Christ" series, but no listing of the subjects of the seven missing hangings is known.

The tapestry owned by the Museum of Fine Arts, Boston, portraying *Christ before Pilate and Herod* has several more scenes than that in Angers, and these scenes appear in another of the Romans embroideries as well (Fig. 4). In the upper center of the Boston hanging, Judas returns the thirty pieces of silver, at which point in the mystery plays he attempts unsuccessfully to bargain for Christ's life. Below this scene, Christ is returned to Pilate. The next scene to the right is that of the flagellation of Christ, which the mysteries treat in great detail, acting out the removal of Christ's clothing, his being tied to a column, and his brutal punishment at the hands of four men. In the lower right corner the crowning of Christ with thorns and the offering of a reed as a scepter take place in the presence of Pilate, who is seated to the right with a *mille-fleurs* tapestry nailed to the wall behind him. In the upper right corner appears the *ecce homo* scene, with Christ being presented to the crowd. An attendant pulls back his cloak to show his wounds, while the crowd gestures for his crucifixion, three of the men holding out their arms, hands crossed at the wrists.[23] One significant decorative detail occurs in the Boston tapestry which is not present in any of the other tapestries under examination except that in San Francisco. Spaced along the bottom foreground at intervals are two large lily and two large carnation plants, all with broken stalks, which might symbolize the sorrow of the events of the Passion taking place above. No

major changes are present in the Romans embroidery of these last scenes of Christ before Pilate; but again the jacket lengths in the embroidery are those of the Angers, and not the Boston, tapestry, and the flowers and textile patterns are those current later in the sixteenth century.

The next two scenes represented in this group of hangings appear in the tapestry in the collection of The Fine Arts Museums of San Francisco, left to the California Palace of the Legion of Honor as the bequest of Hélène Irwin Fagan (Fig. 7). The left half is devoted to *Christ and Barabbas before Pilate,* with Pilate standing under an arch, Barabbas to his right and Christ in the foreground to his left. A group of men stands in the left foreground apparently pointing toward Christ as if to indicate their desire to have him crucified. The right half is devoted to the scene of *Pilate Washing His Hands,* with Pilate enthroned to the right and with Christ standing on his right side. A woman, possibly Pilate's wife, enters through a doorway in the background, and a figure to Pilate's right leans toward him to speak, while a man in the foreground holds a basin of water up to Pilate, who washes his hands in it. The canopy above Pilate's head carries an inscription: "PILATUS • ES • CV ___ ___ • B[or G?]ATUS." Again a crowd of men is gathered to the left foreground of this scene. These men hold both hands to their chests in an apparent gesture of acceptance of the blame for Christ's crucifixion. Among the flowers positioned along the bottom edge of the hanging are one large iris plant and a carnation plant with a broken stalk.

These scenes do present a sequence problem with regard to the other tapestries from this set of designs. The scene of Barabbas and Christ is reported in all four Gospels,[24] where it always precedes the flagellation and crowning with thorns. In only one instance in the Scriptures is it mentioned that Pilate washes his hands to absolve himself of any responsibility for Christ's death,[25] where it too precedes the flagellation and mocking of Christ. Yet it is clear in the San Francisco tapestry that these events have already taken place, for here Christ wears his crown of thorns. One possible reason for this shifted sequence may be found in the mystery plays of Greban and Michel. In both versions the scene of Christ and Barabbas takes place before the flagellation and the mocking, as it does in the Scriptures,[26] but the washing of Pilate's hands takes place after the *ecce homo* scene,[27] as it does here. It may be that, in yet another version of the Passion play which might have been popular at the time this hanging was woven, both of these events were shifted to a position following the *ecco homo*.

Another possibility is suggested in the fact that these two scenes are very similar in their composition to those of the first two scenes of *Christ before Pilate and Herod,* represented by hangings in Angers, Boston, and Romans. The architectural background is similar; Pilate stands in the same place in the left half, and he assumes Herod's seated position to the right. The bound Barabbas replaces the bound Christ to the left, and the large figure groups occupy roughly the same space in both designs. This might also explain Christ's subordinate position in both scenes. It would seem possible that the San Francisco subjects were not part of the original cartoons but rather were added, based on the existing design for the previous subjects, possibly to enlarge the number of weavings available. Whatever the reason, it is worth noting that all the scenes in question are represented in the Romans embroideries (Figs. 3, 4, 8, 9), and they most likely, therefore, coexisted in at least one tapestry-woven version of the designs as well. The San Francisco tapestry appears not to have extended further to the left, as that scene comes to a natural end. However, figures do run off the right side, indicating that the weaving once continued in this direction. It may only have had another figure or two, as does the comparable Romans embroidery (Fig 4), or it might have had one or more additional scenes.

Lacking any provenance for the San Francisco weaving prior to its bequest, we can attempt to place it chronologically only through a comparison of its design and workmanship to those of the other related hangings. The length of the figures' costumes and hair appears to be closer to that of the Angers hangings than to that of Boston, and indeed the rendering of intricately patterned textiles and jeweled ornaments is also closer to that of the Angers weavings. However, the San Francisco tapestry most probably is not part of the Angers set, as the modeling of faces and costumes is flatter and less skillful in the San Francisco weaving, the faces show less individuality, and the rendering of fur and hair is less that of individual strands than of an accumulated whole. However, it is unwise to be dogmatic about these observations, in view of

the great amount of reweaving and repair the San Francisco tapestry has endured, especially in the areas of hats and other costume parts, a circumstance certain to change the look of the whole.

Before we attempt to draw other conclusions about these tapestries, it is appropriate to study the three remaining tapestries in the Angers set, as well as the other tapestry fragments and embroideries sharing their scenes. The *Road to Calvary* is depicted on an Angers tapestry and an embroidery (Figs. 10 and 11). As the figures run off the left side of both hangings, this design must be considered incomplete. In the left background Pilate and his entourage, mounted on horseback, leave the city through a gate carrying the inscription "HERUSALEM" overhead, with Christ and Simon of Cyrene carrying the cross in the foreground. In the center background Judas hangs dead from a tree, and in the right background the Virgin faints in grief. Farther to the right two men carry the other two crosses toward the site of the Crucifixion. Below them the two robbers are led off. The embroidery remains basically true to this design, with the expected modification of flowers and fabric patterns and with the intriguing addition of a windmill on the right horizon.

The third Angers tapestry shows scenes from the *Crucifixion and Harrowing of Hell* (Fig. 13). At the left Jesus is led in and stripped of his clothes, with Pilate standing in the background. In the left foreground Jesus is nailed to the cross while men quarrel over possession of his garments. The central scene is that of the Crucifixion itself, with an angel and a devil above the two robbers' crosses, taking away the souls of these men, and with the Virgin Mary, supported by John the Evangelist, fainting at the foot of the cross as Mary Magdalene kneels in prayer to the right. While Pilate looks on, the blind Longinus pierces Christ's side with a lance, while another man known as Stephaton offers Christ a vinegar-soaked sponge on a stake. Behind the crosses rest the bones of Adam on the hillside, from which Calvary takes its name, while to the right of the hill Joseph of Arimathia and Nicodemus plead with Pilate for permission to have Christ's body in order to bury him before sundown. Farther to the right they head off, near a man carrying a ladder for use in the deposition. Meanwhile, in the lower right corner of the tapestry, Christ descends to hell in order to free the souls trapped there, led by Adam and Eve. The door itself is rendered in the shape of a huge monster's mouth, one eye of which may be seen to the extreme right of the hanging, while a demon lies crushed under the lowered door.

Other fragments of this design exist in tapestry technique, a large one in the Rijksmuseum in Amsterdam (Fig. 14)[28] and a smaller one in the Musée des Arts Décoratifs in Paris (Fig. 15),[29] as well as in an embroidery in Romans (Fig. 12). None of these other textiles shows Christ's harrowing of hell, and only the Paris fragment shows Joseph and Nicodemus talking with Pilate. The Amsterdam panel is well executed, but there are many signs that indicate that it might not represent an early use of the cartoons. The sponge offered Christ on a stake has now assumed the shape and character of a tree similar to those dotting the weaving's landscape. An angel and demon appear over the robbers, but no souls are present for them to gather up. With regard to costume details, this hanging is closer to the Boston rather than the Angers design, but there is relatively little on which to base such a judgment. The fragment from Paris is even more difficult to compare to the other weavings because it is so abbreviated. One can be certain, however, that it was never part of the Amsterdam fragment, as there are overlapping pattern areas. The Paris piece shows evidence that it once included the left arm and foot of the rightmost robber, parts of which are also present in the Amsterdam hanging. This fragment once continued to the right as well, for halfway up the right edge is a single curve of the banderole attached to Christ's staff, which he carries in the rightmost scene of the related Angers tapestry.

The final Angers tapestry and a Romans embroidery (Figs. 16 and 17) show the entombment of Christ by Joseph and Nicodemus, while the Virgin Mary, Mary Magdalene, and others look on. In the center the risen Christ surprises the guards around the tomb, behind which advance the three Marys guided by an angel. At the right Christ appears as a gardener to Mary Magdalene, and he appears to the Virgin Mary at the upper right. In the extreme upper right corner he appears to Saint Peter, a scene providing proof of his word for the foundation of the Church and an especially popular scene in the mystery plays. The related embroidery is similar to the tapestry in all important details of the story,

although here Christ's crown of thorns has fallen off as he is laid in his tomb and rests on the ground in the lower left corner.

ORIGIN OF THE TAPESTRIES
The number of scenes which might have made up the complete set of Passion tapestries based on these designs cannot be reconstructed from the evidence now at hand. We can be certain, however, that more scenes existed originally than have come down to us in these tapestries or the Romans embroideries, for a few narrative events that are missing here but that were extremely popular in contemporary art would surely have been included. One such scene is the Deposition of Christ, which is suggested by the man carrying a ladder in the upper right corner of the *Crucifixion* tapestry. In the tapestries from this series which do survive and which have just been reviewed, we can see that they come from four or five distinct sets, indicating the great popularity these cartoons must have enjoyed at the time they were prepared.

A more difficult hypotheses to develop is that regarding a place of manufacture for this group of Passion tapestries. Similar depictions of the Passion appear with great frequency in Flemish art of this same time, which points both to the great popularity of this subject and to a sympathetic artistic climate in which the tapestries could have been produced. A sculptural fragment of a retable in the Church of Saint Denis, Liège, which shows the crowning of Christ with thorns and Christ carrying the cross, is but one stylistically similar example.[30] A page in a book of hours in the Bodleian Library, Oxford, attributed to the Master of the David Scenes in the Grimani Breviary, places several scenes of Christ's Passion around a central one of Moses and the serpent.[31] Painted in the early sixteenth century, the small scenes share many features of composition and detail with the tapestries. Another illuminated manuscript with scenes from the Passion, preserved in the University Library, Ghent, is less similar to the hangings stylistically but does have certain narrative details in common with them.[32] In the scene of Pilate washing his hands, Christ is already wearing the crown of thorns, and after his resurrection Christ appears to Mary Magdalene with a spade in His Hands.[33] However, no paintings or other art objects have been discovered which would help pinpoint the origin of these tapestries' designs more closely than to Flanders in general.

Let us turn next to an examination of past attributions that have been made for these Passion weavings. A. Thiéry believed the Angers hangings contained the names of the painter Jan von Roome and the weaver Pierre van Aelst, and he therefore stated they have been woven in Brussels.[34] Although his attribution enjoyed a certain amount of acceptance in the early decades of this century, virtually no recent opinion has agreed with his conclusions.[35] Many contemporary scholars, on the other hand, have tended to attribute this group of hangings to Tournai, one of the major tapestry weaving centers of the late Middle Ages, based on stylistic and technical comparisons with other weavings attributed to this town.

No one can question the vast quantities of tapestries that were produced in this Flemish city in the fifteenth and sixteenth centuries, as great numbers are recorded in documents.[36] Tournai must have been a major center indeed for Philip the Good to have purchased from Pasquier Grenier in 1461–62 a number of Tournai tapestries in one set, L'Histoire du Chevalier au Chine, and six hangings in another set, L'Histoire du roy Assuere et de la royne Hester, to give to the Cardinal of Arras, which was itself another very important tapestry-weaving city.[37] However, we cannot be certain that all tapestries sold in Tournai were manufactured there. Pasquier Grenier himself, who figures in so many of the documentary references for this town, was in all probability a merchant, with resources capable of carrying on trade over a wide geographic area. Moreover, Philippe Scellier, a tapestry merchant of Tournai, is known to have provided cartoons to both Brussels and Audenarde toward the end of the fifteenth century.[38] If such activity were at all common, a definition of one center's style over another based on designs alone can never be achieved. Perhaps the interpretation of the cartoons or weaving characteristics differed from one place to another, but such distinctions would be difficult if not impossible to identify unless all the hangings in questions were to be brought together for close study.

Only a very few documents catalogued by Soil can be positively linked to any late medieval hangings that exist today. One exception is that of a major series of eleven tapestries of The Trojan War, from which series parts of various sets exist in Europe and America.[39] But as the cartoons for this set were most likely prepared before 1467,[40] the resulting tapestries cannot be expected to resemble in style the Passion hangings. More to the point are three tapestries from a set depicting The Life of Saint Ursin, now in the collection of the Musées de Bourges. In an obituary of Guillaume du Breuil mention is made of this set, which he gave to the collegiate church of Saint Ursin in Bourges around 1500, and the obituary states that the hangings were made in Tournai.[41] These tapestries date from approximately the same period as do those of The Passion, but unfortunately the designs and format are nothing alike.

The late Jean-Paul Asselberghs performed a great service in bringing together so many tapestries attributed to Tournai for the exhibition "La tapisserie tournaisienne au XVe siècle" held in that city in 1967, and in his catalogue he was able to advance many plausible arguments for possible Tournai attributions for tapestries belonging to certain sets other than those of The Trojan War and The Life of Saint Ursin.[42] However, other tapestries in the exhibition, among them six of the Passion tapestries discussed here, are included in a group possibly woven in Tournai because they are similar to The Trojan War hangings.[43] Until research has been able to establish the existence of a style or styles typical of this weaving center distinct from those of any other centers in that part of Flanders, we should beware the temptation to advance a Tournai attribution for weavings similar in style or technique to those that can possibly be attributed to that town on other grounds.

Additional information may eventually come to light, allowing us to be more definite in an attribution of the Passion tapestries under consideration here. However, at present it is more prudent to acknowledge the intense activity of tapestry weavers throughout the section of Flanders between Brussels and Paris, which supplied so much of Europe's demand for fine and not-so-fine weavings during the last years of the Middle Ages, without attempting to assign these Passion hangings to one center or another within this area. This reservation takes nothing away from their grandeur or from the interest they hold as monuments to religious thought and dramatic expression as interpreted in late medieval art.

Fig. 1. *The Agony in the Garden* and *the Kiss of Judas*. Wool and silk yarns embroidered on linen with painted details. H: 2.80m W: 2.28m. Church of Saint Barnard, Romans (Dróme), Bequest of Charles de Lyonne de Lesseins, 1701. (Photograph: Caisse Nationale des Monuments Historiques)

ACKNOWLEDGMENTS

The author gratefully acknowledges the generous help that Anna G. Bennett of The Fine Arts Museums of San Francisco, Guy Delmarcel of the Musées Royaux d'Art et d'Histoire in Brussels, and Wendy Hefford of the Victoria and Albert Museum in London gave him during the research leading up to this paper. His work was made much easier by the thorough studies his predecessors, Gertrude Townsend and Adolph S. Cavallo, had made of the related tapestry in Boston.

Fig. 2. *Christ before Annas and Caiaphas*. Wool and silk yarns embroidered on linen with painted details. Dimensions unknown.* Church of Saint Barnard, Romans (Drôme), Bequest of Charles de Lyonne de Lesseins, 1701. (Photograph: Caisse National des Monuments Historiques)

Fig. 3. *Christ before Pilate and Herod* (part 1). Wool and silk yarns embroidered on linen with painted details. H: 2.80m W: 2.28m. Church of Saint Barnard, Romans (Drôme), Bequest of Charles de Lyonne de Lesseins, 1701. (Photograph: Caisse Nationale des Monuments Historiques).

Fig. 4. *Christ before Pilate and Herod* (part 2). Wool and silk yarns embroidered on linen with painted details. Dimensions unknown.* Church of Saint Barnard, Romans (Drôme), Bequest of Charles de Lyonne de Lesseins, 1701. (Photograph: Caisse Nationale des Monuments Historiques)

Fig. 5. *Christ before Pilate and Herod*. Tapestry. Wool warp, wool and silk weft. H: 4.17m W: 9.01m. Courtesy Museum of Fine Arts, Boston, Gift of Robert Treat Paine, 2nd, in memory of his son, Walter Cabot Paine, 29.1046. (Photograph: Museum of Fine Arts, Boston).

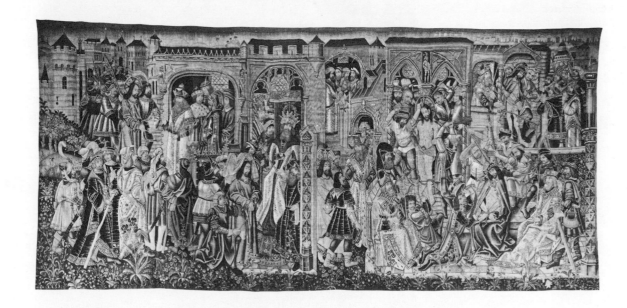

Fig. 6. *Christ before Pilate and Herod*. Tapestry. Wool warp, wook and silk weft. H: 3.80m W:4.13m. Musée des Tapisseries, Château d'Angers, Purchase, 1854. (Photograph: Caisse Nationale des Monuments Historiques)

Fig. 7. *Christ and Barabbas and Pilate Washing His Hands*. Tapestry. Wool warp, wool and silk weft. H: 4.01m W: 4.34m. The Fine Arts Museums of San Francisco, Bequest of Hélène Irwin Fagan to the California Palace of the Legion of Honor, 1975.5.25.

Fig. 8. *Christ and Barabbas*. Wool and silk yarns embroidered on linen with painted details. Dimensions unknown.* Church of Saint Barnard, Romans (Drôme), Bequest of Charles de Lyonne de Lesseins, 1701. (Photograph: Caisse Nationale des Monuments Historiques)

Fig. 9. *Pilate Washing His Hands*. Wool and silk yarns embroidered on linen with painted details. Dimensions unknown.* Church of Saint Barnard, Romans (Drôme), Bequest of Charles de Lyonne de Lesseins, 1701. (Photograph: Caisse Nationale des Monuments Historiques)

Fig. 10. *Road to Calvary*. Tapestry. Wool warp, wool and silk weft. H: 3.80m W: 4.16m. Musée des Tapisseries, Château d'Angers, Purchase, 1854. (Photograph: Caisse Nationale des Monuments Historiques)

Fig. 11. *Road to Calvary*. Wool and
silk yarns embroidered on linen
with painted details. H: 2.80m W:
3.60m. Church of Saint Barnard,
Romans (Drôme), Bequest of
Charles de Lyonne de Lesseins,
1701. (Photograph: Caisse
Nationale des Monuments
Historiques)

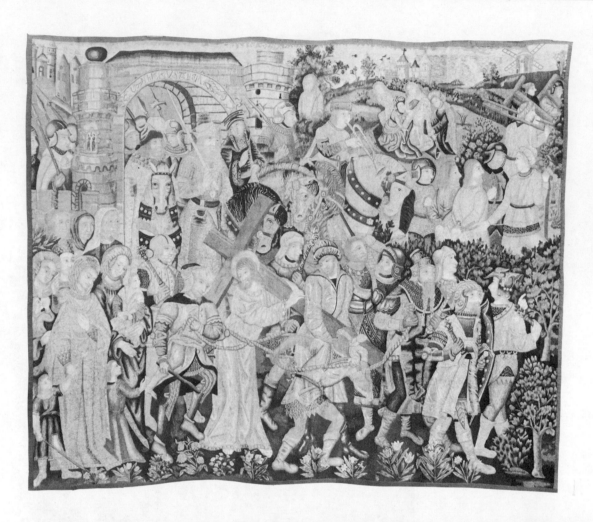

Fig. 12. *Crucifixion*. Wool and silk
yarns embroidered on linen with
painted details. H: 2.80m W:
3.60m. Church of Saint Barnard,
Romans (Drôme), Bequest of
Charles de Lyonne de Lesseins,
1701. (Photograph: Caisse
Nationale des Monuments
Historiques)

Fig. 13. *Crucifixion and Harrowing of Hell*. Tapestry. Wool warp, wool and silk weft. H: 3.91m W: 7.16m. Musée des Tapisseries, Château d'Angers, Purchase, 1854. (Photograph: Caisse Nationale des Monuments Historiques)

Fig. 14. *Crucifixion* (fragmentary).
Tapestry. Wool warp, wool and
silk weft. H: 3.00m W: 4.60m.
Rijksmuseum, Amsterdam, Purchase, R.B.K. 1958–16. (Photograph: Rijksmuseum, Amsterdam)

Fig. 15. *Crucifixion* (fragmentary).
Tapestry. Wool warp, wool and
silk weft. H:3.60m W: 1.64m.
Musée des Arts Décoratifs, Paris,
Gift of M. Jules Maciet, inv. no.
8350. (Photograph: Musée des
Arts Décoratifs, Paris)

98

Fig. 16. *Entombment of Christ, Resurrection, and Christ Appearing to the Virgin, the Magdalene, and Saint Peter*. Tapestry. Wool warp, wool and silk weft. H: 3.76m W:4.65m. Musée des Tapisseries, Château d'Angers, Purchase, 1854. (Photograph: Caisse Nationale des Monuments Historiques)

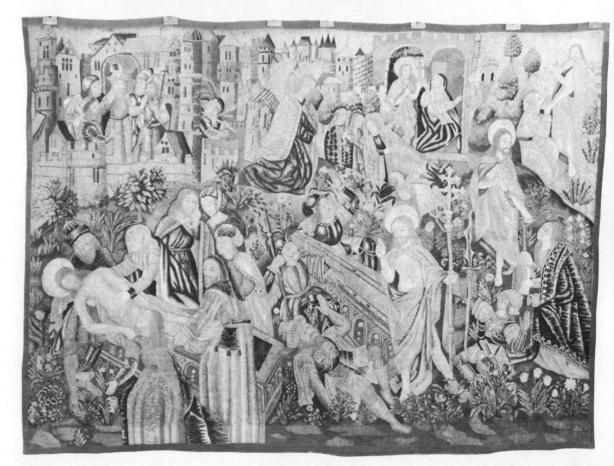

Fig. 17. *Entombment of Christ, Resurrection, and Christ Appearing to the Virgin, the Magdalene, and Saint Peter*. Wool and silk yarns embroidered on linen with painted details. Dimensions unknown.* Church of Saint Barnard, Romans (Drôme), Bequest of Charles de Lyonne de Lesseins, 1701. (Photograph: Caisse Nationale des Monuments Historiques)

*Dimensions for all of these embroideries are given in the catalogue for an exhibition *Exposition de la Passion de Christ dan l'Art Français* (Paris: Musée de Sculpture Comparée, 1934), p. 123; but they are obviously inaccurate, as they do not reflect the proper proportions of height to width when compared to the figures.

NOTES

1. Anna G. Bennett, *Five Centuries of Tapestry* (San Francisco: The Fine Arts Museums of San Francisco and Charles E. Tuttle Co., 1976), cat. no. 6; pp. 42, 44; ill. p. 43.
2. An example of the popularity of the Passion may be seen in the inventory taken of Henry VIII of England's possessions at the time of his death in 1547 (British Museum, Bibl. Harl. no. 1419). W.G. Thomson, *A History of Tapestry from the Earliest Times until the Present Day* (London: Hodder and Stoughton, Ltd., 1930), pp. 245-60, lists tapestries in this inventory to which titles were assigned, and sixty-nine tapestries with scenes of The Passion are included, grouped as if from seventeen different sets.
3. L. Petit de Julleville, *Les Mystères* (Paris, 1880), vol. 2, pp. 183–84. This source and Emile Roy, *Le Mystère de la Passion en France du XIVe au XVIe siècle* (Dijon: Damidot frères [1903–04]), are useful for an introduction to these Passion plays. Grace Frank, *The Medieval French Drama* (Oxford: Clarendon Press, 1954), also discusses the various Passion plays briefly.
4. William Hone, *Ancient Mysteries Described* (London: 1823), pp. 172–73.
5. Gaston Paris and Gaston Raynaud, eds., *Le Mystère de la Passion d'Arnoul Greban* (Paris, 1878).
6. Jean Michel, *Le Mystère de la Passion*, ed. Omer Jodogne (Gembloux: Duculot, 1959).
7. Frank, p. 175.
8. Two other *Crucifixion* tapestries based on the same cartoons are known. One with several significant variations was sold at auction at Christie, Manson & Woods, London, 17 November 1938, lot 83, ill. opp. p. 35. This tapestry was formerly at Rufford Abbey, and its present location is unknown. A second, which shows approximately the left two-thirds of the Angers design, was sold at auction at Sotheby Parke Bernet & Co., London, 7 July 1978, lot 159, ill. p. 105, from a German private collection, purchased anonymously to be given on permanent loan to Leeds Castle, nr. Maidstone, England. The author would like to thank George Hughes-Hartman of Sotheby Parke Bernet & Co. for bringing this second weaving to his attention.
9. Ch. de Grandmaison, "Estimation des anciennes tapisseries de Saint-Saturnin de Tours aujourd'hui à la cathédrale d'Angers . . . ," *Nouvelles archives de l'art français*, 3e serie, 5 (1889): 330–31.
10. L. de Farcy, *Histoire et Description des Tapisseries de la Cathédrale d'Angers* (Lille and Angers: Desclée, de Brouwer et Cie., n.d.), p. 52.
11. Ch. Urseau, "Historique de la Collection," *Beaux-Arts* no. 15 (1923): 228.
12. The author is extremely grateful to M. Ruais for his assistance and for providing this information.
13. M. Barbier-Montault, *Les Tapisseries de Sacre d'Angers* (Paris, 1863), p. 58, also stated these tapestries were once the property of the Church of Saint Maurice of Chinon.
14. Although it has no bearing on the provenance of these tapestries, the fact that the Angers tapestries arrived there in many fragments and had to be rejoined to make four hangings is of interest. This information was also furnished by M. Ruais in correspondence with the author.
15. Charles J. Phillips, *History of the Sackville Family* (London: Cassell and Company, Ltd., [1930]), vol. 1, p. 355.
16. Rev. G.B. Lewis, "The Tapestry Scenes from the Passion of Christ in Knole Chapel," *The Journal of the British Archaeological Association* 38 (1882): 216.
17. Phillips, vol. 2, ill. opp. p. 354 shows the Boston tapestry *in situ* in Knole Chapel.
18. See G[ertrude] T[ownsend], "The Passion Tapestry from Knole," *Bulletin of the Museum of Fine Arts, Boston* 29 (1931): 99–100, for a more detailed description of the scenes in the Boston tapestry.
19. The bizarre turban-hat of Pilate and the turban and crown combination worn by Herod are examples of this practice.
20. These embroideries were worked in wool and silk yarns on linen cloth, with painted faces and hands, in pieces that were joined together upon completion. They are most likely the work of many different hands, possibly talented amateurs, and the quality of workmanship varies greatly.
21. Paris, Musée des Arts Décoratifs, *Les Trésors des Eglises de France* (Paris: Musée des Arts Décoratifs, 1965), p. 373, states that the coat of arms that appears in the embroidery of the Crucifixion is that of Pierre de Loulle.
22. *La Chapelle du Saint-Sacrement et ses tentures* (Romans, n.d.), pp. [3–4]. The spelling of the principals' names in this history are rendered as follows in *Les Trésors*: Hélène Tardif, Pierre Deloulle, Charles de Lionne-Lesseing. Laurent Gitton is not mentioned.
23. This gesture of crossed hands appears frequently in contemporary depictions of the *ecce homo* scene. In the following paintings, for example, one or more spectators hold their hands in this position: *Christ Shown to the People* by Jerome Bosch (?), Museum of Fine Arts, Boston [Max J. Friedländer, *Early Netherlandish Painting*, trans. Heinz Norden (Leyden: Sijthoff, 1969), vol. 5, add. 149, pl. 123]; *Christ Shown to the People* by a Dutch master, loan to the Museum Boymans-van Bueningen, Rotterdam, from the J.W. Frederiks Collection [Friedländer, vol. 5, supp. 119, pl. 109]; *Scenes of the Passion* by Hans Memling, Galleria Sabauda, Turin [Friedländer, vol. 6, pt. 1 (1971), no. 34, pl. 86]; *Christ Shown to the People* by the Master of the Morrison Triptych, Kunsthaus, Zürich [Friedländer, vol. 7 (1971), add. 198, pl. 131]; *Ecce Homo* by Colijn de Coter, National Museum, Warsaw [Jan Bialostocki, *Les Musées de Pologne, Les Primitifs Flamands. I. Corpus. ... No. 9* (Brussels: Centre National de Recherches, 1966), no. 119, pl. LXXII]. A facial expression of astonishment rather than brutality or vengeance

often accompanies this gesture, and it may therefore have more significance than merely the symbolic demand for crucifixion.

24. Matthew 27: 15–26; Mark 15: 6–15; Luke 23: 18–25; John 18: 39–40.

25. Matthew 27:24.

26. Paris and Raynaud, pp. 294ff.; Michel, pp. 355ff.

27. Paris and Raynaud, p. 309; Michel, p. 378.

28. Acquired in 1958 by purchase. Ex. coll. James Watts, Jr., Abney Hall near Manchester. Sold at auction at Christie, Manson & Woods, Ltd., London, on 18 July 1957.

29. Git to the Musée des Arts Décoratifs in 1896 from M. Jules Maciet.

30. Comte J. de Borchgrave d'Altena, *La Passion du Christ dans la Sculpture en Belgique du XI au XVIe S.* (Paris, [1946]), p. 114, figs. 28, 29.

31. Otto Pächt and J.J.G. Alexander, *Illuminated Manuscripts in the Bodleian Library, Oxford* (Oxford: Clarendon Press, 1966), vol. 1, p. 30, cat. no. 396, Douce 112, fol. 3. No published illustration known.

32. Monotessoron Venerabilis doctoris Johannis de Gerson. St. Bavon, 1480–1505. Ghent, Université Bibliothèque, 11. No published illustrations known.

33. These are fol. c and fol. e of the manuscript. See Brussels, Musées Royaux d'Art et d'Histoire, *Tapisseries bruxelloises de la pré-Renaissance* (Brussels: Musées Royaux d'Art et d'Histoire 1976), cat. no. 16, ill. p. 69, for another example of Christ wearing a crown of thorns while Pilate washes his hands, here in a Brussels tapestry dating from about 1520 or a little later.

34. A. Thiéry, *Les inscriptions et signatures des tapisseries du peintre bruxellois Jean de Bruxelles appelé aussi Jean de Rome ...* (Louvain: Nova et Vetera 1907), pp. 10ff.

35. Adolph S. Cavallo, *Tapestries of Europe and of Colonial Peru in the Museum of Fine Arts, Boston* (Boston: Museum of Fine Arts, Boston, 1967), vol. 1, p. 81 summarizes prior attributions. For more recent opinions of Thiéry's hypothesis see J.-P. Asselberghs, *La tapisserie tournaisienne au XVe siècle* (Tournai: 1967), p. 11; S. Schneebalg-Perelman, "Un grand tapissier bruxellois: Pierre d'Enghien, dit Pierre van Aelst," *L'Age d'or de la tapisserie flamande* (Brussels: 1969), pp. 286–87; Jan-Karal Steppe, "Inscriptions décoratives contenant des signatures et des mentions du lieu d'origine sur des tapisseries bruxelloises ...," *Tapisseries bruxelloises*, p. 202; and Bennett, p. 44.

36. The main source for these published documents is Eugène Soil, *Les tapisseries de Tournai* (Tournai, 1891).

37. Ibid., pp. 240–42.

38. Francis Salet, "Introduction," *Masterpieces of Tapestry from the Fourteenth to the Sixteenth Century*, trans. Richard A.H. Oxby (New York: The Metropolitan Museum of Art, 1973), p. 13. Salet's essay gives an excellent introduction to the difficulties of attributing late medieval tapestries to specific weaving centers.

39. See J.-P. Asselberghs, *Les tapisseries tournaisiennes de la guerre de Troie, Artes Belgicae* (Brussels: Musées Royaux d'Art et d'Histoire, 1972), for proof allowing the attribution of these weavings to Tournai.

40. Geneviève Souchal in *Masterpieces of Tapestry from the Fourteenth to the Sixteenth Century*, p. 56.

41. Asselberghs, *La tapisserie tournaisienne*, p. 39, fig. 34.

42. Ibid.

43. Ibid., p. 12. The Passion tapestries included are the four from Angers (cat. nos. 23–26), that of Amsterdam (cat. no. 27), and the fragment from Paris (cat. no. 28).

101

SELECTED BIBLIOGRAPHY

Asselberghs, J.-P. *La tapisserie tournaisienne au XVe siècle*. Tournai, 1967.

Bennett, Anna G. *Five Centuries of Tapestry*. San Francisco: The Fine Arts Museums of San Francisco and Charles E. Tuttle Co., 1976.

Cavallo, Adolph S. *Tapestries of Europe and of Colonial Peru in the Museum of Fine Arts*. Boston: Museum of Fine Arts, Boston, 1967.

de Farcy, L. *Histoire et Description des Tapisseries de la Cathédrale d'Angers*. Lille and Angers: Desclée, de Brouwer et Cie., n.d.

T[ownsend], G[ertrude]. "The Passion Tapestry from Knole." *Bulletin of the Museum of Fine Arts, Boston* 29, 1931.

Urseau, Ch. "La tapisserie de la *Passion* d'Angers et la tenture brodée de Saint-Barnard de Romans." *Bulletin Archéologique du Comité des Travaux Historiques et Scientifiques*, no. 1, 1917.

The Triumph of the Seven Virtues: Reconstruction of a Brussels Series (ca. 1520-1535)

Geneviève Souchal

Scattered throughout Europe and America are seventeen tapestries (one incomplete) which allow us to reconstruct almost in its entirety an important early Renaissance series—the seven panels devoted to *The Triumph of the Three Theological Virtues and the Four Cardinal Virtues*. Today *Temperance* is missing,[1] but most of the other virtues are known because several versions exist, notably the virtue *Fortitude*, for which there are five versions (see Table 1), demonstrating the success of the series.

The Triumph of the Seven Virtues is one of the great Brussels sets of the sixteenth century, yet it is nearly unknown, as its stray panels have never been regrouped.[2] Since I have been able to examine most of them, I would like to "revive" the *Triumph* in this study.

Let me say first that we know we are dealing with tapestries woven in Brussels, since eight of the seventeen—the *Hope* of Pittsburgh, the *Charities* of Chenonceaux and Toledo, the *Prudences* of Asheville and San Francisco, the *Justice* of San Francisco, and the *Fortitudes* of San Francisco and Toledo—still display on the lower edge a coat of arms placed between the two B's of Brabant-Brussels, mark of the duchy's capital. This mark was decreed obligatory on 16 May 1528, which proves that these tapestries were woven after that date.[3] The nine others were also certainly woven in Brussels, despite the absence of the city's mark, for they offer exactly the same characteristics. They do not have the mark, however, because their lower portion is missing (in *Hope* of Cluny and *Fortitude* of Langeais), or the edge has been rewoven (*Faith* and *Charity* of Asheville, *Fortitude* of Chenonceaux), or else (as with the *Hope* of Moscow, the *Prudences* of Edinburgh and Vienna, the *Fortitude* of Liverpool, and the incomplete *Hope* of Cluny) their border is compartmented, different from that on pieces bearing the arms of Brussels (which show a continuous band of green plants), a design used in a slightly earlier period and probably predating 1528.[4]

As a matter of fact, in this first type of border we find long repeated patterns on a midnight-blue field, broken on the sides by a sort of fleuron or by a vase on a light-blue field, at the bottom by ornamental motifs enclosing a head (Fig. 1), and at the top by a red banderole inscribed with clear Gothic letters flanked by stylized vegetal ornaments. Within this repeating design are enclosed large fruit and flowers: pomegranates, grapes, cherries, strawberries, irises, red roses, and so on. These patterns alternate with repeated tiny circles in which a brown bird perches on a branch against the blond silk (Fig. 2). In the corners are inset medallions containing a woman's profile or that of a bearded warrior. A triple green-beige-green galloon separates this border from the central scene as well as from the guard. In the second type of border, vegetation of the same order (grapes, pomegranates, pears, apples, almonds, cherries, roses, pansies, irises, thistles . . .) abounds between two blond-beige-reddish galloons, suggesting a wooden frame set against a very deep blue field in which a red central axis can be discerned; this is interrupted only by the scroll at the top.

This second border belongs to the style that was popular in Brussels tapestry during the second quarter of the sixteenth century or, more precisely, during the 1530s. It appears, for example, in the *Salve Regina* hanging, a gift to the Palencia Cathedral in 1535,[5] and in the *Mythological Episode* of the former Somzée collection.[6] The repeating border design, which is much less common,[7] acted as the transition between the above-mentioned border and one consisting of alternating rectangles and squares, which is of earlier date and was the successor of the thin, continuous garland of the beginning of the century. Examples of this alternating geometric motif are found in the *Miraculous Communion of Herkenbald* (1513, Brussels),[8] the *Saint Jerome at Prayer*, or the *Burial of Turnus* of the Patrimonio Nacional of Madrid.[9]

Therefore, if the last versions were woven after 1528,[10] we may surmise that the first predate them by several years. As we shall see, this hypothesis is confirmed by study of the style and iconography of the scenes. Their iconography is based, for more than one good reason, on still another iconography, that of the famous *Honors* hanging of Madrid, executed around 1520.[11] Many proofs to this effect were furnished by Guy

---

AUTHOR'S NOTE: As this article went to press, I learned of one more tapestry in this series belonging to the Kunsthistorisches Museum, Vienna: a *Prudence* of the type with the repeated design border. It has been taken into account in my mention of the number of tapestries involved, but the information arrived too late to allow for full discussion of this particular example.

Delmarcel, successor to the late J.-P. Asselberghs at the Royal Museums of Art and History. Another proof that the last sets cannot be dated much later than 1528 is given by the presence of Gothic letters in the upper inscription, since even before 1540 this type of lettering had been replaced by Roman capitals,[12] already used here for the central figures (Fig. 3).

Therefore, lacking information about the person for whom the set was conceived, its precise date, or other circumstances of its commission, we may say that *The Triumph of the Seven Virtues* was planned around 1520–1525 and actually woven up until 1530–1535 because of its popularity.

All the panels are large and of about equal size, around 4.5 m in height by 5.5 m in width, except for those pieces with a border of repeating design, which is narrower.[13]

Woven in wool and silk, their composition is for the most part the same: below the Latin distich of the upper border, which defines its character, is a life-sized virtue seated in a chariot (except for *Hope*, who is borne by a ship) and who, possessing those attributes generally given her by sixteenth-century French and Flemish artists,[14] arrives from the right or left of the upper half of the tapestry. The virtue is flanked by a crowd of

skillfully superimposed men and women, identified by their inscriptions woven in beige, pink or brown (Fig. 3), often along the edges of their clothes. The size of these men and women decreases toward the top of the tapestry, which, along with a landscape in which a cloudy sky tops an elevated horizon, tends to restore some perspective and introduce a certain clarity into the mob. *Faith*, however, is on a smaller scale than are the other virtues. It occupies the center and faces forward. Because *Charity*, *Justice*, and *Fortitude* arrive from the right and *Hope* and *Prudence* arrive from the left, we may infer that the missing *Temperance* also arrived from the left, and that the six virtues converged on the central *Faith*. This means the hanging must have been designed for a vast room, with the first theological virtue probably occupying one of the smaller sides (perhaps facing the entrance) and flanked by the other virtues, three on each long wall.

The figures accompanying these virtues are taken mainly from the Old Testament, but also from mythology, antiquity, and, to a much lesser extent, Christian history. Their distribution varies, however, from one piece to another. There are no pagans in *Faith*, as was to be expected. There are no Christians in *Hope*, probably because the coming of the Messiah was fulfilling the essential expecta-

Fig. 1. Detail of a repeated pattern border, lower section of the border of *Hope* in Moscow. (Photograph: Pushkin Museum of Fine Arts, Moscow.)

Fig. 2. Detail of a repeated pattern border, right section of the border of *Hope* in Moscow. (Photograph: Pushkin Museum of Fine Arts, Moscow.)

Fig. 3. Sample of inscription, detail of *Hope* in Moscow, Judith's sword. (Photograph: Pushkin Museum of Fine Arts, Moscow.)

The border of this hanging consists of great bouquets of leaves, flowers, and fruit, interrupted in the upper part of the piece with the inscription:
Verbo sancta fides divino credit et omni
officiosa Deum religione colit
("The holy Faith trusts in the divine Word and honors God with all the respect due Him.")
However, the tapestry has lost it original edge and therefore bears no marks.

In the center, a misspelled inscription (EIDES for FIDES) identifies the virtue Faith, who is facing the viewer and wears a wimple, a red dress, and a cloak of a color ranging from yellow to blue (in accordance with the procedure for expressing green typical of Brussels). Backed by an elliptic halo, Faith holds a church in her right hand and in her left a chalice with the host and a large cross topped by the inscription INRI. Above her, in the sky, appear the three members of the Trinity, dressed in red, wearing crowns and holding the orb and cross. At her feet is the lamb of God, flanked by cherubs holding torches. Because she is depicted in the upper part of the tapestry, as though she were arriving from the back, she is therefore on a smaller scale than are the figures in the foreground. She is seated in a red chariot with beige motifs, flanked by anonymous figures and pulled along by the symbols of the Evangelists: the lion is ridden by the angel, and the bull is ridden by the eagle. They are crushing two

tions, and none in *Prudence*, *Fortitude*, or *Justice*, where God and his angels may be considered as being beyond time. Only *Charity* unites all three categories. But it is especially noteworthy that the Old Testament characters figure in the six known pieces and are found alone in *Hope*, if the three mythological winds are excepted. The biblical characters are also the only ones to appear more than once, consequently having different meanings (aside from the angels in two tapestries and God in three, all of which belong as much to the Old as to the New Testament). In fact, Abraham and Isaac, Jacob and Rachel, Moses, Gideon, and Judas Maccabaeus figure in two *Triumphs*, Esther figures in three, and Judith in four. David surpasses all, appearing five times (see Table 2). All of these figures were chosen, of course, because they shone with the virtue represented or, conversely, because they ridiculed it. In this case, they assume a vanquished position.

FAITH

Our knowledge of *Faith* is solely through a piece [15] (Fig. 4) kept with the *Triumphs* of *Charity* and of *Prudence* in Biltmore House, a castle built toward the end of the nineteenth century in Asheville, North Carolina, by George W. Vanderbilt. [16]

Fig. 4. *Triumph of Faith* in Biltmore House, Asheville. (Photograph courtesy of Biltmore House and Gardens, Asheville, North Carolina.)

enemies—on the left, in red, SIMON MAGVS, the Samarian magician who was baptized by the apostle Philip and stigmatized by Saint Peter because he had wanted to buy the power conferring the Holy Spirit (Acts 8:9–13 and 18–24); on the right, in blue, the founder of Islam, MAHVMETES. Their presence indicates that Faith triumphs not only over non-Christian religions but also over all those whose ''heart is not righteous before God.''

The other figures are divided into two groups that correspond to small images of the Church and the Synagogue that dominate them from either side on columns.

On the left is the ancient Law, indicated by the blindfolded woman who stands over the inscription VETVS TESTAMENTVM, the overturned tablets of the decalogue in her right hand and a broken banner in her left. Below appears one of the most common

scenes in medieval art:[17] ABRAAM, father of believers, in a green robe and red coat, leads to the place of sacrifice his son ISAAC, who is laden with wood for the blaze that will consume him, although he is the only son of the man to whom God had promised innumerable descendants (Gen. 17:15–19; 21:12 and 22). In the lower corner is the armored, decapitated body of GOLIAS, the head of whom DAVID, in a short, red tunic, stoops to retrieve, at the same time holding the enormous sword of his enemy in his left hand. Although he did not belong to Saul's army, David was not afraid to meet the giant in combat, for ''the Lord who delivered me from the lion and the bear, will deliver me also from the hand of the Philistine'' (1 Sam. 17:37).[18] Above him the presence of IVDAS MACHABEVS, in a light-colored tunic decorated with blue birds (the emblem found on the coat of arms he possessed as one of the Nine Valiant Men[19]), is a reminder that, in his constant battles against the generals of

Antiochus Epiphanes and later Antiochus Eupator and Demetrius Soter, this son of Matathias never lost his unshakable faith in the Lord even when enemy forces were superior in number: "for victory in war is not in the multitude of the combatants, but rather in the strength that cometh from Heaven" (1 Macc. 3:19; 2 Macc. 15:21 and passim). Next to this Jewish hero is a woman, and in front of a soldier IVDITH appears holding a sword and the head of Holofernes, over whom she triumphed because she had faith in God's protection and "believed it possible" that by Jehovah's "help" the Assyrian general who was threatening Bethuel would be "struck down by the hand of a woman" (Jth. 8:10–27; 13:7 and 9:15).

Further up is a series of tiny scenes. Near the border is the famous vision of Jacob's ladder at the time that God promised posterity and protection to Isaac's son (Gen. 28:10–22).[20] Toward the right, the ark tossed by the rolling sea probably shows that Noah (along with Isaac and Daniel,[21] one of the main symbols of the saved soul, while the ark symbolizes the Church) never doubted "the announcement of the flood, the salvation of his family, or Jehovah's covenant with him" (Gen. 6–7). Above, the chariot of fire drawn by two horses has been considered to be that of Elijah, the prophet who never questioned the divine orders (1 Kings 17–19 and 21; 2 Kings 1).[22] Finally, the drowning soldiers between Synagogue and Faith are the Egyptians over whom Moses—trusting in the Word of the Eternal God and represented here on the shore before a few Hebrews—caused the waters to flow, closing the gap that had opened in the night to allow safe passage for the Israelites escaping Pharaoh's tyranny (Exod. 14:15–31).

On the right, a crowned woman with a cross and, like Faith, carrying the chalice with the host (NOVVM TESTAMENTVM) presides over the assembly of those personages of the new Law who are particularly distinguished by the virtue honored here. In the foreground, wearing a yellow robe with blue folds and recognizable by his key, stands PETRVS, the "prince of the Apostles," who proclaimed Jesus "Christ, the Son of the living God" (Matt. 16:16). Further back, in a blue cloak over a red gown, appears HELENA, the mother of the Emperor Constantine, who converted to Christianity and discovered the true cross, thanks to Divine Grace.[23] Also

depicted are, in pink, the great Roman emperor THEODOSIUS, who eradicated paganism,[24] and SILVESTER, the fourth century holy pope, Constantine's contemporary, here holding a cross with two bars in his left hand.[25] In the background the pious king of France, LVDOVICVS (Louis IX), is wearing a red cape with a white collar. Finally, on the right, CONSTANT[IN]US is wearing the closed imperial crown and a sword. His clothing (a white dalmatic over a red tunic and breastplate) probably indicates his double role as victorious leader and introducer of Christianity as the official religion of the Roman Empire, the result of his vision of a fiery cross in the sky.[26] In the lower corner, in blue armor and with his chest pierced, lies IVLIANVS APOSTATA, the renegade emperor, mortally wounded while battling the Persians (363) and serving as counterpart to the also vanquished Goliath.

Above, one small scene corresponds to those on the left. CAROLVS MAGNVS, his armor covered by a blue tunic, kneels among a group of soldiers before the dead body of ROLANDUS, whose horn lies between him and OLIVERI, who is stretched on the ground, dressed only in a shirt and crucified. Above them, combat takes place on the edge of a body of water, over which shines a sun. In the upper corner clouds are parting to reveal a warrior in pink, who bounds forward, a sword in his right hand and a blue flag with a white cross in his left. This odd representation may be explained by an episode of the Charlemagne legend taken not from the *Song of Roland* but either from the illustrious book on the deeds and exploits of the "Holy Emperor" and his nephew[27]—the *Chronique du pseudo-Turpin*, which "enjoyed an astonishing success"—or from one of its numerous derivations.[28] In all versions Roland indeed dies, not by the hand of his enemy, but by bursting his veins in sounding his horn to call his uncle. In the poem, Oliver, on the other hand, is struck down from behind in a cowardly manner and does not face the same infamous fate, which, in the *pseudo-Turpin* and its later versions, made those Christians who had died at Roncevals veritable martyrs and Oliver himself an image of Christ. According to an edition of the *Chronique*, which is almost contemporary to our hanging, after Charlemagne had discovered

. . . Roland dead and lying on the ground, his arms crossed, [he found the following day] amongst others, Oliver, who had already died and gone to

Heaven, lying on the ground, his head turned facing the sky, his body spread out in the shape of a cross, bound and attached by four straps to four poles planted in the ground, and flayed from his neck down to the nails of his toes and fingers by sharp and cutting knives, and pierced with darts and arrows, lances and swords, and battered and beaten by great clubs. . . . Thus swore King Charlemagne that he would not cease in the pursuit of the Saracens and the enemies of God until he had found them. Straightaway he took off after them with his cavalry and the sun then ceased to move and the day was lengthened to three days: and Charles found the Saracens near the river named Ebra and camping near Saragossa. [He killed four thousand and returned to bury the] champions of the Faith.

The knight in the sky is consistent with one of the main types of representation of Saint James the Great, said to have appeared in the sky in 834 during the battle of Clavijo, riding a white horse and charging the Moors whom he caused to retreat by brandishing his standard. So we obviously have here the apostle of Spain who, at the beginning of the *Chronique*, appears to the weary emperor and tells him to take from the Saracens Galicia, where the archbishop Turpin will consecrate a church to him.[29]

HOPE

Three panels of *The Triumph of Hope* are still in existence. One is kept in the Moscow Fine Arts Museum, another in the Cluny Museum in Paris, and the last in the Carnegie Institute in Pittsburgh, Pennsylvania. Because my knowledge of the Moscow panel is limited to color photographs and the Cluny panel is seriously mutilated (the lower part has been cut), I was obliged to base my description on the Pittsburgh panel[30] (Fig. 6), even though it is of a later edition and is less distinct.

Bearing the Brussels mark and another (X), which we will discuss later, this panel has a continuous border identical (except for its upper part) to that of the Asheville *Faith*. Its inscription reads·

Irruat horribilis quamquam presentia mortis
Tuta tamen spes est in bonitate dei.
("Although the horrible presence of death may burst in
Sure, however, is Hope in the goodness of God.")

The presence of death is illustrated, upper right of center, by the shipwreck of a tiny boat and especially by the difficult situation of a ship whose occupants are panic-stricken (if they have not already fallen into the sea). The ship's masts are breaking under the force of the winds working their bellows. We see

VVLTVRNVS, the Southwest Wind, and BORCAS (for BOREAS), the titan, son of Astraeos and Aurora and the North Wind of the Greeks. Both are dressed in red and followed by AQVILO in a green robe with red sleeves and boots. Aquilo is the son of Aeolus and Aurora and is also the North Wind, but of the Latins.[31] A fourth wind's head appears among the clouds, farther to the right.

Should we see in this scene more than an ordinary shipwreck to clarify the distich and to illustrate the validity of hope in critical situations? Certainly, and for three reasons. First, this scene would be perhaps the only one in the hanging not associated with a definite character.[32] Second, *The Triumph of the Christian Virtues*, a Brussels set dating ca. 1550–1560 and belonging to the National Society of Industrial Credit (Belgium), has, as we shall see, an iconography almost entirely based on that of our series, and depicts on the bottom of its *Hope* panel (and much more distinctly than does ours) the story of Jonah. Jonah was thrown overboard to bring a calm to the tempest, which he caused by refusing to carry out among the Ninevites his mission assigned by God. Swallowed by a marine monster that spewed him out three days later (Jon. 1–2), Jonah symbolizes both the Resurrection and hope in God.[33] Third, although the subject is indistinct on the Pittsburgh panel, we do see fish tails in the Cluny work.[34] Therefore, one of the men in the sea is probably the prophet Jonah. Whatever the explanation, we do see, at the upper right, the bust of God the Father among the clouds. He is wearing a blue coat and his arms are open to receive those humans who turn to him. Hope moves forward from the center left. A scythe rests on her left shoulder, and with both hands she holds out to God a sickle, symbol of the harvest to be reaped in Heaven as well as on earth. The inscription reads SDES for SPES. Dressed in shades of green, Hope is seated at the stern of a vessel with its sails furled, one of her attributes. A cage containing a bird hangs from the mast and at the prow burns a fire from which is reborn a superb phoenix—an outstanding image of the Resurrection and thus of the hope of survival. The vessel is fettered to the metal collars of two men who pull it. Dressed in short robes (green for the man in the front, red for the other), their feet in water and soon to touch shore, their ankles chained to their belts and their hands held out imploringly and expectantly, these men, as I see it, sym-

Fig. 5. *Triumph of Trinity*. Christian Museum, Esztergom. (Photograph: Christian Museum, Esztergom.)

bolize the human condition.[35]

In the foreground and at the sides the characters turned toward God, almost all kneeling and praying, belong without exception to the Old Testament, an extraordinary circumstance in the hanging which emphasizes the importance of the second theological virtue for those men waiting for the fulfillment of the promise made to the patriarchs.

In the right half of the panel MOSES, in a red robe with a blue collar, raises his arms toward the celestial apparition just above him.[36]

Perhaps he is begging Jehovah to pardon the Hebrews for their worship of the golden calf (Exod. 32:30). It is true that the tablets of the Law appear at his side, although he has broken them in anger, but this is his usual portrayal.[37] Moses may also symbolize the quest for the Promised Land. Farther to the right, in a red miter and a blue brocade robe, AARON, guilty of having shaped an idol in his brother's absence (Exod. 32:4), is no doubt hoping for divine mercy for himself and his people.[38]

Farther down, a warrior in a red cloak draped over a rich breastplate (Fig. 7) bears an inscription on the orphrey of his short beige tunic. Here we distinguish merely the initial "G" and the last letters "EON." Comparison with the other two panels in which GEDEON is clearly legible leaves little doubt about his identity, as we discern, in front of the Judge of Israel (and more clearly in the Moscow and Paris tapestries), the sign of Gideon's future victory over the Midianites. The Hebrew liberator has in fact asked of God that a fleece be covered with dew during the night while the ground remained dry, then the following night that the opposite be made to happen (Judg. 6:36–40). This episode was to be retained by the medieval commentators as a prefiguration of the virginal conception of the long-awaited Redeemer and found accordingly in representations of the Annunciation. For example, it is found in a hanging of *The Life of Christ* at La Chaise-Dieu and also in a tapestry of the Annunciation dating from around 1480, conserved in the Gobelins Museum.[39] Behind Gideon, dressed in a blue cloak and recognizable by the harp on the

ground, we see King DAVI, whose psalms forever sing of his trust in the Lord. In the lower right-hand corner, the prophet and steadfast servant DANIEL appears from the waist up, dressed in a blue garment with a red collar. He stands behind the bars of the lion's pit in which he was twice thrown— first, when the ministers of Darius the Mede had extracted from this king an edict forbidding prayers to be addressed to anyone except himself for a period of thirty days (Dan. 6); second, during the reign of Cyrus the Persian, for having destroyed the idol Bel and killed a dragon that was venerated as a god. This time he was fed miraculously by the hand of the prophet Habakkuk, because of which he exclaimed: "You have remembered me, oh Lord, and You have not abandoned those who love You" (Dan. 14).[40]

In the left half of the tapestry, we find first a group of four women. The oldest in terms of Judaic history is on the left. If, in fact, only the first four letters of her name can be clearly made out on the orphrey of her chemise showing under the widely opened blue

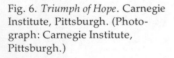

Fig. 6. *Triumph of Hope*. Carnegie Institute, Pittsburgh. (Photograph: Carnegie Institute, Pittsburgh.)

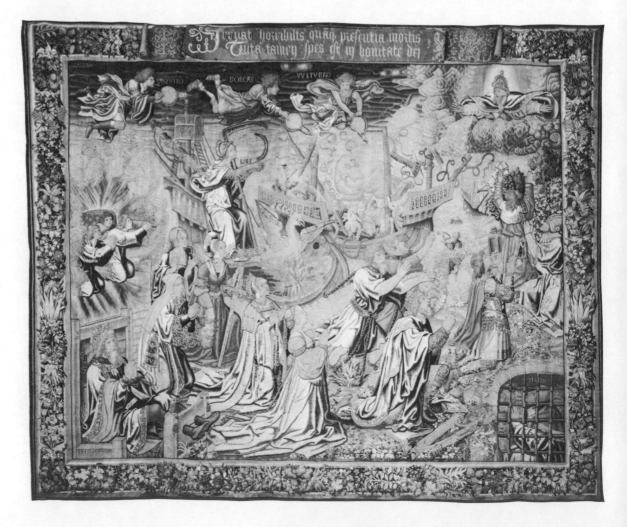

Fig. 7. Gideon, detail of *Hope* in Moscow. (Photograph: Pushkin Museum of Fine Arts, Moscow.)

dress, here again the inscription found on the Moscow and Paris panels, DELBORA, indicates that we have before us the prophetess Deborah, the Judge of Israel, who promised Barak that Jehovah would hand over to him the army of Sisera, general of King Jabin of Canaan (Judg. 4).[41] In front of her, Judith, dressed in red, holds the head of Holofernes. The inscription on the sword is more legible on the other *Triumphs of Hope*: IVDICH (Fig. 8). Not only did Judith believe in God, but she never doubted that he would raise his "arm as in times past," or that through a woman he would destroy an enemy who, however, had just crushed all the neighboring peoples west of Assyria; nor did she fear that he would ever abandon "those who place their hope in Him" (Jud. 9:11 and 15; 13:17).

Just in front is HESTER, wearing a crown and sumptuously dressed in a blue cloak with ermine collar over a blue dress with large beige designs. She is flanked on the left by her uncle MARDOCEVS, wearing a sort of beige-colored hood, the ends of which touch his fur-lined green tunic (Fig. 8). Together the two recall one of the biblical episodes most celebrated in the Middle Ages, namely, the rescue of the enslaved Jewish people from the death planned for them by King Ahasuerus' minister, Aman:[42] "O God, who surpasseth all in power, answer the prayers of those who have no other hope. . . ." So begged the young queen. And Mordecai: "Lord, Almighty King, . . . there is no one who can oppose You, if You have resolved to save Israel. . . . Change our grief into joy so that with our lives we may celebrate your name . . ." (Esth. 14:19; 13:9 and 17). As one of the principal foreshadowers of the Virgin Mary, Esther may also call to mind the hoped-for grace that the Savior's Mother will obtain for mankind at the Last Judgment.[43]

In the center, SVSANA, shown in profile, appears in a yellow-green dress with pink sleeves. Her hands are bound in preparation for her death, the result of being accused of adultery by two old men whose lust she has spurned. But "her heart had faith in the Lord," who raised up the young Daniel in order to confound the slanderers (Dan. 13).[44] In the left-hand corner, dressed in a wide-

sleeved blue tunic and red hose, MANSSES (Manasseh), King of Judah, wears a crown; but his feet are in a *carcan*, his hands are bound by a metal bracelet, and his neck is chained to his seat. He was punished by an Assyrian invasion for having raised altars to false gods and having spilled "much innocent blood": "They took Manasseh with hooks and bound him with bronze fetters and brought him to Babylon. And when he was in distress, he entreated the favor of Jehovah . . . and Jehovah received his entreaty and heard his supplication and brought him again to Jerusalem into his kingdom" (2 Kings 21:1–18, and especially 2 Chron. 33:1–20). Above Manasseh are three young Hebrews in a furnace (MISAEL in blue on the left, AZARIA behind him in beige, and ANANIA in green on the right). They also serve as symbols of the saved soul[45] and are equally examples of indefatigable hope: "If it be so, our God whom we serve is able to deliver us from the fiery furnace, and he will deliver us from your hand, O King," was their answer to Nebuchadnezzar who threatened them with death when they refused to adore his image (Dan. 3:17).

Except for the borders (here with compartments), the Moscow (Figs. 1–3 and 7–9)[46] and Paris tapestries (Fig. 10)[47] reproduce the same cartoon. We hardly notice some slight difference in dimensions; such difference is common and can be explained by the technique used as well as by the difference in borders. A few other details are also dissimilar—for example, the clouds surrounding God. But it is remarkable that the inscriptions are identical and the colors the same in all three versions, at least as far as the main figures are concerned, with variations in intensity of hue the result, possibly, of each panel's particular state of preservation. For example, Susannah's sleeves are of a deeper red in the Moscow and Paris tapestries, and in any case the Pittsburgh panel seems on the whole to have faded more. We have noted that its inscriptions are also less discernible, which may be explained by wear or by restorations, but also by the later weaving date of this tapestry (date displayed by the border). Its model was perhaps already slightly faded. Indeed, all facts prove that the three works were executed using the same pattern—not at all surprising since we know that in the low-warp process used in Brussels painted cartoons were placed under the warp. In the Cluny panel, however, Manasseh's eyes seem gouged out, which is hardly the case in the other two tapestries and represents a confusion with the story of Zedekiah, the last king of Judah who, like Manasseh, was taken in chains to Babylon after his defeat by Nebuchadnezzar (2 Kings 25:7). This is a minor difference, easily explained once again by the weaver's having mistaken for blood the brown-red tint of the iris on the Moscow tapestry. Aside from this detail and of course the above-mentioned defacements, the Moscow and Paris tapestries differ only in the inversion of motifs on the left border.

CHARITY

Three panels of *The Triumph of Charity* are also preserved. The first panel, restored, but in good condition, hangs in Biltmore House (Fig. 11) along with *Faith* and *Prudence*. The other two *Charities* (accompanied by a *Triumph of Fortitude*) are in a much more mediocre state of preservation, especially the Toledo piece. One is located in the Chenonceaux château and bears on the top the inscription from *Fortitude* (Fig. 12). The other is found in the Santa Cruz Museum in Toledo and is pieced out with large fragments of other tapestries, notably with a part of the inscription from *Temperance* (Fig. 13).

The Asheville panel (Fig. 11),[48] the lower guard of which is modern and therefore bears no distinguishing marks, presents a border with a continuous floral and fruit motif, of the same type as that of *Faith*, though not identical. Once again the scene is summarized by the inscription on the top:

Qui deamat toto celestia numina corde
omnia que pietas munera dictat obit
("He who cherishes with his whole heart the heavenly Powers
accomplishes all deeds that Piety dictates.")

Arriving from the upper right, a crowned CHARITA,[49] wearing a blue cloak over a bright damask gown, holds a heart in her left hand and stretches out her right arm to touch a sun with human features. At her feet a pelican pierces its breast to feed its young. Charity is seated in a chariot drawn by richly bedecked horses, on which ride two faithful

Fig. 9. Detail of the right border of *Hope* in Moscow. (Photograph: Pushkin Museum of Fine Arts, Moscow.)

Fig. 10. *Triumph of Hope*. Musée de Cluny, Paris. (Photograph: Réunion des Musées Nationaux.)

Fig. 11. *Triumph of Charity* in Biltmore House, Asheville. (Photograph courtesy of Biltmore House and Gardens, Asheville, North Carolina.)

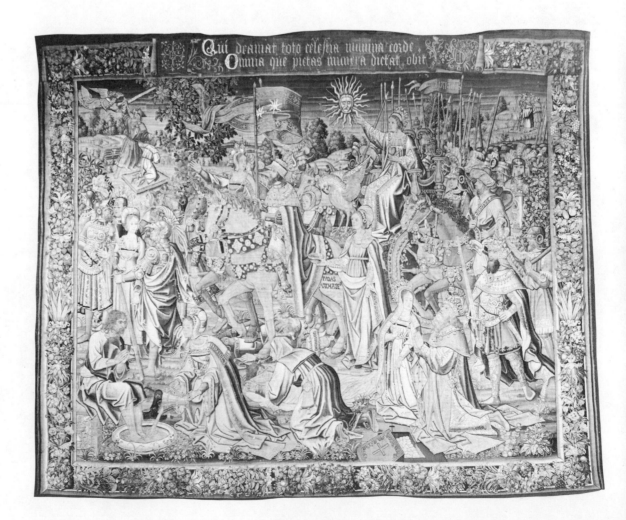

115

Fig. 12. *Triumph of Charity.*
Château de Chenonceaux.
(Photograph: Studio Henry,
Amboise.)

Fig. 13. *Triumph of Charity.*
Museo de Santa Cruz, Toledo.
(Photograph: Foto Rodriguez,
Toledo.)

servants of God who did not hesitate to offer their lives to save the Hebrew people. These are HESTER and IVDAS MACHABEUS. The latter is wearing a cloak in shades from blue to yellow, an odd hat, and is holding a red, sun-spangled banner. His presence here is explained perhaps less by his devotion to the Jewish cause than by the expiatory sacrifice which he ordered after a battle so as to atone for the wrongdoings of those soldiers who died in a state of sin and to insure their resurrection (2 Macc. 12:38–46).[50] These two figures trample the persecuting emperor NERO and a character named DIONISIVS, who is probably the tyrant Dionysius of Syracuse, infamous for his cruelty and mistrust. Following the chariot is a procession of warriors armed with pikes. One of them carries the banner of CHARITAS and in front we distinguish two horsemen. One bears the name BRVTVS, but as he is wearing a turban he is probably not one of the two Roman heroes, Lucius Brutus, who overthrew Tarquinius Superbus and set up the Republic, or Marcus Brutus, one of the conspirators against Caesar (both more celebrated for their rigor than for their "charity"). This figure more likely represents the grandson of Aeneas, that legendary Brutus who, forced to flee Italy after having killed his father during a hunt, arrived in Greece, where he freed the enslaved descendants of the Trojans and led them to Great Britain, and there founded a new Troy (the future city of London).[51]

At Charity's feet PIETAS, a cup in her right hand, inspires through the ages those deeds the love of God demands. The most ancient of these deeds of love is that of HABERAM, distinguishable in red on the hills in the upper left. An angel is withholding his sword which he has raised over ISAACH, kneeling dutifully in a blue tunic, for Abraham did not "refuse his only son" whom God demanded in sacrifice (Gen. 22:16) and Isaac showed the "greatest love" there is in "giving his life."[52] Below, with halberd in hand and a blue cloak draped over his breastplate, the valiant GODEFREDUS (Godfrey of Bouillon), liberator of the Holy Sepulchre, speaks to a woman and a group of warriors. In the lower left-hand corner, a woman dressed in green —who from the inscription ELISA-BETH.ELIS may be identified as Saint Elizabeth of Hungary, the wife of the landgrave of Thuringia—is pouring water into a basin on the feet of a pauper in blue, who clasps his hands as a sign of respect.[53] In

the center foreground old THOBIAS, also wearing a blue robe, draws a sheet over the face of a dead man, for, faithful unto the Lord, "he distributed his goods among all the people, as he was able; he would give bread to those who were hungry, clothes to those who were naked and showed great zeal in burying those who were dead or killed" (Tob. 1:19–20).[54]

The group kneeling on the right in front of DAVID is more enigmatic (Fig. 14). Once again we come across the cherished servant of God, David, here seen with a blue, tippet-style cloak draped over his breastplate and wearing a richly ornamented helmet and necklace. He holds his sword erect; a soldier follows him. A woman's figure, PLACELLA (whose name we see close by as PLACELL), is wearing a crown and a beautiful blue gown with patterns, over which is draped her red cloak. She is turning toward the emperor TIBERIVS, who himself is dressed in a damask robe half-concealed by a large green cloak. He is looking upward to heaven as if he were praying. Before him a chest of gold pieces, with the sign of the cross on its lid, lies embedded in the ground. The presence of these two figures in certain contemporaneous tapestries, in which they sometimes illustrate Prudence, other times Charity, allows us to clarify their significance in this particular panel. In a superb Brussels hanging, *The Twelve Ages of Man*, dating from around 1520 and kept at the Metropolitan Museum in New York (where an excellent study of it was done by Edith Standen),[55] human life is compared to the seasons and the months of the year. For October we find members of the same group just described, with their attendants. Over it an inscription tells how Tiberius was rewarded for his good works to the poor with a treasure hidden under a stone. The origin of this story is apparently to be found in Gregory of Tours.[56] In fact, according to the *Historia Francorum*,[57] the just emperor Tiberius II (578–582), who had given the poor much of the wealth amassed by his predecessor, the miser Justin, was one day scandalized to notice that a cross carved into the palace floor was being trampled under foot. Having commanded that the floor be taken up, he discovered a treasure of more than 100,000 gold pounds, which allowed him to indulge in even greater liberalities. In *The Twelve Ages of Man* the name of the queen represented is not indicated, and Miss Standen sees in that figure either Tiberius'

Fig. 14. Placella and Tiberius;
David; detail of *Charity* in
Chenonceaux. (Photograph:
Studio Henry, Amboise.)

wife or Justin's widow, but she states she knows of only one representation of this subject—in the New York series and its replicas. She points out that in the Dijon replica the emperor's *espeuse* is designated Placella, when in reality her name was Anastasia.[58] However, in a slightly earlier article on a remnant from a work commissioned by the Palatine Count Ottheinrich (the *Prudence* tapestry of the Heidelberg Museum, dating from 1531, which, while not belonging to our series, shares certain iconographic affinities, notably Placella herself), Anne-Lise Stemper had already necessarily turned to Gregory of Tours for an explanation of the discovery of Tiberius II; she indicates that the emperor was blamed by the widow of Justin for the distressing liberalities that compromised the existence of the state. Stemper was intrigued by the change of the real name of Justin's wife, Sophia, to Placella, and she raised the possibility of a corruption (but by what course?) of the name of Galla Placidia (392–450), who was the daughter of Theodosius the First and a much better known empress, although her piety was pretty much removed from the practical thriftiness that caused her in this tapestry to rebuke Tiberius for his generosity. Stating first that Placella appears in the same attitude in the *Justice* of the *Honors* of Madrid, A.-L. Stemper concluded that in the Ottheinrich *Prudence* Placella perhaps represents *Reason*.[59] However, the inscription of the Dijon panel—*Le . empereur . Thiberus . trouver . veult . ung . tresor . innestimable/dont . son . espeuse . en . veult . ouvrer . comme . femme . des . raissonable* ("The emperor Tiberius will find an inestimable treasure which his wife wants to use, as the unreasonable woman she is")—would tend to suggest the opposite. Therefore, from this freely adapted and mediocre replica, probably woven in Tournai, whose inscription is very different from that of the New York hanging in which Tiberius' charity is exalted,[60] I had thought that the author of these two verses was apparently unaware of the existence of Justin's widow, of the association of Prudence with Placella by his more educated Brabant confrères, and also of the contrast to the emperor's generosity which he does not seem to understand. He probably merely retained, from his examination of the scene, the material fact of the discovery of the treasure. However, Guy Delmarcel recently discovered that Placella was a Flemish corruption of the name of the wife of Emperor Theodosius I, "Flaccilla" or "Placilla," who

was praised by the Fathers of the Church and in particular by Saint Gregory of Nyssa for her generosity. Thus, we find her legend (communicated by the *Speculum historiale* by Vincent of Beauvais) contaminated with that of Tiberius II.[61]

On the hills, in the upper right-hand corner, stands a small group of men conversing. Several of them are wearing high, padded caps, but they are not identifiable because of the lack of inscriptions and typical details.

As in the different versions of *Hope*, here not only the same design appears throughout the other *Triumphs of Charity* but also the same colors, at least in the Chenonceaux tapestry (my knowledge of the Toledo hanging is limited to photographs). The color scale of the Chenonceaux *Charity* is subdued, owing to its state of preservation—the work has undergone considerable, but poorly done, restoration. The borders (besides the top, transposed with that of *Fortitude*) seem to have been mended, at least those at the sides. Yet they belong to the set classified in the group with a continuous band of fruit and flowers. The lower guard is preserved and on it to the left one can see an escutcheon between the two Bs of Brabant and Brussels and to the right the weaver's mark (X), similar to that of the Pittsburgh *Hope*.[62]

The Toledo panel, which is sadly disfigured, is also encircled with a continuous vegetal border and bears the arms of Brussels.[63]

PRUDENCE

At least four panels remain of *The Triumph of Prudence*. The first, in good present

Fig. 15. *Triumph of Prudence* in Biltmore House, Asheville. (Photograph courtesy of Biltmore House and Gardens, Asheville, North Carolina.)

condition, is in Asheville (Fig. 15),[64] along with the *Triumphs* of *Faith* and *Charity*. It has the same type of continuous vegetal border and includes the weaver's mark (4Ħ) and that of Brussels. But never before has it been remarked that its upper inscription is not appropriate and most certainly comes from one of the missing *Temperances*. The second panel, on the contrary, is in shameful condition but still retains its original border—a wide band of flowers and fruit—along with the marks of Brussels and of a different atelier (X). This panel is preserved in The Fine Arts Museums of San Francisco (Fig. 16).[65] Finally, the third panel, belonging to the series with a repeating design border (the upper edge is missing), figured in the Paul Eudel sale of 1898 and was purchased by the Royal Scottish Museum in Edinburgh (Fig. 17).[66] This panel was probably exhibited in Rome in 1870 and, according to Barbier de Montault, was perhaps part of the "Vatican's Warehouse." In fact, its flower and fruit border included "birds enclosed within medallions,"[67] and Rachel's inscription was missing, as is also the case with the Edinburgh panel. The fourth is in Vienna.

An examination of the first two panels, as well as the information kindly sent me on the third, establishes once again that the color distribution is basically the same in the three tapestries. Their descriptions will therefore be regrouped and those names which seem missing on certain panels will be indicated.

The upper inscription, which appears only in the Fine Arts Museums piece (Fig. 16), reads:

Provida metitur rerum Prudentia fines
Discernens certo fasque nefasque modo.
("Far-sighted Prudence measures the limits of things,
distinguishing clearly between good and evil.")

Enthroned in a formidable red chariot with baluster wheels and advancing toward the right, PRVDENTIA[68] is wearing a blue gown and a green and red cape. Her head is crowned with laurel; she holds a great staff in her right hand and in her left her usual symbols, a mirror and a snake biting its tail (Fig. 16). She is flanked by cranes, birds usually associated with her. Each crane grasps a stone with one of its lifted feet because, as the Bestiaries tell us,[69] " if she falls asleep, their stones will drop." The bird, whose duty it is

119

Fig. 16. *Triumph of Prudence* in The Fine Arts Museums of San Francisco. Gift of the Crocker Family to the M. H. de Young Memorial Museum, 62.19.3.

Fig. 17. *Triumph of Prudence* in the Royal Scottish Museum, Edinburgh. (Photograph: Tom Scott, Edinburgh.)

120

to keep watch for the others, can thus keep awake and not be surprised. The chariot is drawn by two blue and red speckled dragons, attentive guardians of treasures. They are held in rein by a woman in red (whom Barbier de Montault, probably mistakenly, saw as Philosophy)[70] and by a warrior in a blue breastplate and plumed helmet. He proudly carries a two-forked red banner bearing the initial of Prudence, "P." An inscription on his right knee, CARNEADES (barely legible on the San Francisco panel), permits his identification as the Greek philosopher Carneades (219–126 B.C.), who taught that man cannot know what is true with certainty and therefore must be satisfied with approving that which appears to be the most likely. As in *The Triumph of Charity*, the chariot is followed by a crowd of warriors; the first of them is the wise Roman emperor TITVS. His name is inscribed both on his hatband and on his horse's harness. In the center of the tapestry CASSANDRA, in a green dress and carrying a book, gives Prudence the benefit of her advice, as Pietas did for Charity.[71]

Figures from mythology and the Old Testament surround the cortege. In the sky PALLAS, goddess of wisdom, is seen twice, armored and wearing a long flowing gown in shades of yellow to blue.[72] In the left-hand corner she grasps the arm of PROMETHEVS, showing him the zodiacal group in the sky—Cancer, Leo, and the bottom of the next sign. Dressed in red this Titan, whose name signifies "foresighted," flies in the company of the helpful goddess. He carries a wand in the right hand, a basin in the left. Wiser than the gods themselves, he is shown ascending into the celestial regions, up to the chariot of the Sun whence, with a torch, he will steal the fire to be brought back to earth for the purpose of putting life into the man he created from mud. This man now lies lifeless on the hill below.[73] On the right, PALLAS is depicted, carrying a staff or lance in her right hand. She is giving PERSEVS[74] her shield of polished bronze to use as a mirror to look at the Gorgons, since a direct gaze would turn him to stone. In fact, MEDVSA, the only mortal of the three sisters, is already lying on the ground, decapitated, wearing a brown breastplate and a red skirt;[75] Pegasus, born from her blood, takes off on the right. Another mythological character, CADMVS, seen in the lower left in a blue breastplate over a red robe and a feathered helmet, raises his spiked club over a three-headed dragon,

pustular like those pulling the chariot. This beast is trampling two men dressed in blue or red in front of a beautiful, Renaissance-accented fountain on top of which stands the statue of a warrior. The Phoenician, having received from Apollo the advice to found Thebes, was first obliged to destroy a dragon that guarded a nearby fountain and killed all Cadmus' companions when they went to fetch water.[76]

Meanwhile, above this combat, IVDITH appears (for the third time) in a champagne-blue gown with vivid accents over a red skirt. She is turned toward a bearded old man in a pointed cap and an enveloping red cloak. He could be identified as Ozias, the chief of Bethuel, who, were it not for Judith, would have resigned himself to surrendering over to Holofernes the besieged city, which was dying of thirst. After his victory, he would declare Judith to be "blessed by the Lord, the almighty God, more than all the women on earth" (Jth. 6:11; 7:10–25; 8:28–34; 13:23–25). Or this figure may represent the Ammonite prince Achior, who was delivered over to the Israelites by the Assyrian general, furious at Achior's declaration of this people as invincible, "except when they stray from the service of the Lord their God." When Achior regains consciousness, after having fainted from horror at the sight of Holofernes' head, he too declares Judith blessed by God, and he abandons heathen worship and converts (Jth. 5, 6, 13:27–31 and 14:6).

The fact that Judith was chosen to illustrate the virtue of Prudence can obviously be explained by the cleverness of her plan.[77] Without confiding in anyone, she left the city accompanied solely by a servant carrying food; she asked only that they pray for her until her return. In adorning herself so that her exceptional beauty "shone before the eyes of all with an incomparable brilliance," she already excited the admiration of the Assyrian soldiers guarding the outer gates. She declared to them her belief that the Hebrews would be defeated and that therefore she wished to show their chief an entry by which "they could be taken without losing a single man." She was then led to Holofernes, to whom she announced that the Jews must be punished for their sins. This leader received her so favorably that she obtained "the permission to go out from sundown to sunup in order to pray." This she did for three nights. On the fourth, Holofernes, smitten by her beauty, invited Judith to a feast. Taking advantage of her enemy's drunkenness, she cut off his head and, placing it in the servant's sack, easily made her way through the camp (Jth. 8:30–34; 9–12; 13:1–12). When she arrived in Bethuel she wisely instructed her people to hang this trophy from the walls and to feign an attack so that the Assyrians would run to awaken their leader and, finding him decapitated, would flee in terror. She then instructed, "Pursue them hardily, for the Lord will crush them." And this is exactly what came to pass (Jth. 14 and 15:1–8).

Between Cadmus and Cassandra we find RACHEL in a red dress, seated, with her hands clasped. Is this because not yet having conceived a child by Jacob, whereas her sister Leah had already had several, she gave her husband "Bilhah, her maid, for wife.... That she may bear upon my knees, and even I may have children through her" (Gen. 30:1–4)? And Bilhah bore Jacob two sons before Rachel herself became mother of Joseph and Benjamin. Or rather is there not here an allusion to her behavior when Jacob and all his household fled before Laban who pursued them? Rachel had in fact stolen her father's household gods without her husband's knowledge, and when Laban came to search her tent she sat upon them and said she could not get up (Gen. 31:17–35).[78]

The episode illustrated in the center foreground by the kneeling GEDEON, dressed in blue breastplate and tunic and holding a bottle in his left hand, does not enjoy at all the same popularity as the one in *The Triumph of Hope*. It appears to me that the flail in the hero's right hand is to remind us that "he was beating out wheat in a wine press to hide it from Midian," the oppressor of the Hebrews, at the moment when an angel of the Lord appeared to him, telling him to deliver Israel. A prudent man, Gideon excused himself as being too poor, but when God insisted, he said, "Give me a sign that it is thou who speakest with me." Gideon then prepared a kid "and unleavened cakes; the meat he put in a basket, and the broth he put in a pot, he ... offered them unto Him. And the angel of God said to him: 'Take the meat and the unleavened cakes, and put them on this rock, and pour the broth over them.' And he did so." The angel touched the offering with his staff and it was consumed (Judg. 6:11–21). Therefore, it is probably this "broth" that fills Gideon's raised bottle. For this container is not the broken jar also associated with him by reason of his strategy later in defeating the

Midianites,[79] when he encircled his adversary's camp with 300 men carrying torches in jars that they broke when the trumpets were sounded, thus spreading terror among Gideon's enemies, who slaughtered each other (Judg. 7:15–22).

In the lower right-hand corner we meet DAVID for the fourth time. He is standing, haughtily grasping a halberd and wearing a helmet and brown breastplate with a green tunic and red cloak. On this occasion it is not he who is being praised for his prudence, but rather the woman kneeling before him in a green gown, ABIGAEL. When she learned that her husband, the rich and "evil" Nabal, had refused David's emissaries food (David had been forced to seek refuge from Saul's animosity in the desert, but nevertheless he had protected his shepherds), this good wife, possessor of "great wisdom," supplied the troops with provisions so that they would not swoop down upon the house of Nabal. And so she said to a placated David, "When the Lord ... has appointed you prince over Israel, my lord shall have no cause for grief, or pangs of conscience for having shed blood without cause or for my lord taking vengeance himself" (1 Sam. 25:2–35).[80]

Above, behind the dragons, the bearded character in a yellow-green coat can only be King Solomon, for the crowned woman turned toward him, magnificently dressed in a blue gown with red motifs and an ermine-collared robe, bears on her breast the inscription SABA.[81] Solomon's wisdom, which the Queen of Sheba put to the test through riddles and found to be greater than she had expected, certainly needs no further amplification (1 Kings 10:1–10).[82]

A heroine even more popular than Judith during the Middle Ages was Esther, whom we see here for the third time, a bit farther up in the little scene adjacent to the right-hand border. Her name is not indicated, but that of ASSVERVS on the figure in the blue robe, cloak, and crowned red hat seated facing her leaves no room for doubt. Even if his name were missing we would recognize the scene by the king's appearance of touching the young woman with his scepter, thereby signifying that the terrible law that punished by death anyone who appeared before him without a summons did not apply to her (Esther 5:1–3 and 15:4–19). Esther demonstrated the virtue of prudence by inviting Ahasuerus to a series of feasts after she had tested his feelings for her. On the second day of festivities she begged his mercy on her life and on that of her people, revealing her membership in the race condemned by Haman (Esther 5:4–8 and 7:1–7).[83]

JUSTICE

As is the case for *Faith*, our knowledge of *The Triumph of Justice* is limited to a single tapestry. This work is found in The Fine Arts Museums of San Francisco (Fig. 18), along with a *Triumph of Fortitude*[84] and a *Prudence* (of different origin).

Justice has a continuous fruit and flower border; in addition to the Brussels mark, a sort of double "4" (⚹), almost identical to that found on the Asheville *Prudence*, appears on the lower guard. Its inscription can be understood only when the first word has been identified as Astraea or Aestraea, the goddess of Justice, daughter of Zeus and Themis (divine Justice). Her name signifies Virgin Star, and during the Golden Age she lived on earth, doing good works for the benefit of mankind. She later became the constellation Virgo.[85]

Estrea utilibus rectum preponere suadens
Cuique suum iusta ius dare lance iubet
("Astraea, advising that what is righteous be placed before what is useful,
orders that each man's right be rendered with a just balance.")

As in *Hope*, God the Father appears in the heavens, but this time he is flanked by two angels and dressed in a red cloak. With the orb in his left hand and his right hand raised in blessing, he is turned toward IVSTICIA. A scale hangs from her little finger, and in her left hand she holds a raised sword on which her name is written, while in her right hand she grasps another sword by the tip, its hilt resting on the clouds. In the *Virtues* set of later date (of which we have already spoken several times) Justice is depicted exactly as above, but God is absent. Miss Calberg saw the second sword as that of the Lord, the "Judge of judges," and she quoted from Emile Mâle,[86] "the first two verses from an inscription accompanying a Justice similarly possessing two swords in an illuminated manuscript for the duke of Nemours around 1470: 'The Sword of the Sovereign Judge / Is above him who doth others judge.'" This interpretation is certainly very sound. Nevertheless, given the frequent appearance of another concept in the Brussels allegorical tapestries of the late fifteenth and early sixteenth centuries, in which God the Father is

flanked by Mercy on his right (the place of honor) and Justice on his left, we may question if there does not enter here, however subtly, the idea that God will not allow himself to be swayed in his judgments, as is often the case, by Mercy.[87] Crowned Justice, like Charity, arrives from the right, dressed in blue; Prudence's crane is, strangely, placed before her, perhaps a reminder of the vigilance that she must constantly observe.[88]

Justice sits on a chariot, the back of which is decorated with a man riding a dolphin. The vehicle is drawn by two great unicorns resembling bearded horses, here perhaps as much for their reputation for indomitable strength, a very necessary ingredient of justice, as for their suggestion of purity. They are ridden by a woman in red, her hands joined in prayer, and by a gracious young man dressed in blue and carrying a staff. If we were to refer once again to *The Triumph of Christian Virtues* (1550–1560), in which we find inscriptions that probably figured in other editions of our *Justice* (the man seated on the unicorn in that series is bearded, but this is of no significant difference), we should know that we have here Sarah, Abraham's wife (Sarah was also the prefiguration of Mary, the "sinner's intercessor" on Judgment Day, "because she conceived her son Isaac contrary to all expectations, by the will of God"[89]) and "Joseph, the son of Jacob, whose whole life heralds the principal events of the Savior's life."[90] More precisely, Joseph could be glorified here by reason of his praiseworthy actions in Egypt and the pardon he accorded his brothers, despite their having rid themselves of him. A ribbed column bearing the inscription CATILINA (referring to Cicero's criminal enemy) lies beneath the hind legs of the unicorns, who trample the bodies of two Roman generals, infamous for their partisan vengeance and the cruelty of their proscriptions. They are MARIUS, who is wearing a sort of crown over his helmet,[91] and SCILLA.

Behind the chariot advances a troop of knights, one of whom carries a banner with a the word JVSTICIA. In the foreground, wearing a breastplate over a red tunic and riding a richly caparisoned horse, we find FABRICIVS, the ideal of ancient Roman virtue. Not only did he keep nothing of the enormous booty from the conquest of the Samnites, the Brutians, and Lucanians, and refuse to accept any gift from either the Samnites or Pyrrhus, but he warned this king that

Fig. 18. *Triumph of Justice* in The Fine Arts Museums of San Francisco. Gift of The William Randolph Hearst Foundation to The California Palace of the Legion of Honor, 1957.125.

his doctor was ready to poison him for a fee. Pyrrhus exclaimed, "It would be easier to divert the sun than this Roman from his sense of justice and honor." Fabricius was so unselfish that he died leaving nothing, and the Senate was obliged to marry off his daughter at public expense.

The figures surrounding the procession are taken, as in *Prudence*, from pagan and biblical antiquity.

In the upper left, near a boat above which appears the word NOE, a small group of tiny figures on shore are kneeling in prayer. This is the patriarch's family, which alone was saved from the flood, for as Jehovah declared to Noah when the latter entered the ark, "I have seen that you are righteous before me in this corrupt generation" (Gen. 7:1). Below are gathered a few warriors among whom we may distinguish the young CATO, his red cape draped over his breastplate. He may represent integrity, in contrast to the brilliant general SCIPION AFFRICAN<u>US</u>, who, although very talented, was not overly scrupulous where legality was concerned. Shocked by the ostentation and the haughty

manners of the future conqueror of Carthage, for whom he was the questor in Africa, Cato had in fact returned to Rome, where he did not cease to discredit him. However, assuming this to be the case, Scipio would figure as a sort of "antihero," when, on the contrary, it is by reason of his merits that he stands next to the throne of *Justice* in the Madrid *Honors*, while in *The Triumph of the Christian Virtues*[92] in which Cato has disappeared, Scipio stands as the champion of a quality in which he might at first be said here to be lacking. Does the idea illustrated in our tapestry therefore differ from that of the *Honors*; and, being too subtle, was it forgotten because of Scipio's glory in other domains, thus explaining the complete reversal of meaning in the hanging of 1550–60? Or do these two Romans coexist here merely as illustrious contemporaries? According to Guy Delmarcel, Scipio always appears in the hangings of the period as a positive example.[93]

A little farther down, standing before a soldier in profile, REBECCA, dressed in blue, is speaking to a woman who lifts her red dress with both hands. Should the trick by which she obtained for her younger son Jacob the blessing of Isaac reserved for the eldest (Gen. 27) be considered justified, since at an earlier date Esau "overwhelmed with fatigue" had sold his birthright to his brother for a "potage of lentils" (25:29–34)[94]? In the lower corner the woman in the green cloak kneeling before the emperor TRAIANUS and showing him a dead child in red lying on the ground calls to mind the episode of the legend of Trajan, celebrated during the Middle Ages and painted by Roger van der Weyden for the Brussels City Hall, as well as represented in a very important tapestry of the mid-fifteenth century in the Berne Historical Museum.[95] When one of his soldiers kills a widow's son, Trajan promises her that if he, Trajan, should die, his successor would see that justice is done. But at her insistence Trajan changes this dilatory sentence and condemns the guilty man on the spot.

In the foreground CHARVNDE, dressed in a red tunic, his spread arms causing his cloak to billow, runs through his own chest a sword that he has unsheathed and the pommel of which he has stuck in the ground. According to Diodoros, in fact, Charondas, the seventh-century B.C. Greek legislator born in Catania, killed himself because he had come armed to the Assembly, having forgotten one of his own prohibitions. Farther to the right the couple RACHEL and IACOB the patriarch, dressed in green, perhaps recalls Laban's iniquity. Jacob served him seven years because he loved Laban's daughter. On their wedding night, Laban substituted his elder daughter Leah for the younger and relinquished Rachel only in exchange for seven more years of service (Gen. 29:15–30). Behind them CORNELIA, her name woven on the orphrey of her red gown, is speaking to a hooded man. She is probably neither the mother of the Gracchi nor Caesar's first wife nor Pompey's wife nor the fourth-century B.C. Roman woman accused of poisoning during a time of plague; rather she is the great Vestal who was buried alive during the reign of Domitian for having broken her vows. Along with her presumed accomplice, the knight Celer, she protested her innocence and died with the greatest dignity.[96] Lastly, the SELEVCHVS in a green cloak, whose right eye is being wiped by a servant in blue, is not the Syrian king Seleucus II Callinicus, who was defeated by the Egyptian king Ptolemy III, then taken prisoner while fighting the Parthians and was later believed to have died in captivity; nor is this his grandson, Seleucus IV Philopator (186–174 B.C.)—"Seleucus the very Bad," as he was called in the twelfth century by Petrus Comestor (Pierre Le Mangeur), who authored a History of the People of God, the *Bible historiale*, which enjoyed extraordinary success for several centuries.[97] Rather, as Guy Delmarcel pointed out to me, we have here king Zaleucus of Locris. His son had committed rape and therefore was to have his eyes gouged out, but the King offered one of his own eyes so that his child could keep one.[98]

FORTITUDE

Fortitude is the panel of which we possess the greatest number of versions. Aside from one fragment at the Langeais Castle (Fig. 19),[99] there are a total of four complete tapestries, the first of which is found at Chenonceaux (Fig. 20). As has been explained, the inscription of this tapestry has been exchanged with that of *Charity*.[100] Its border consists of a continuous band of flowers and fruit, found on two other panels. One belongs to the Santa Cruz Museum in Toledo (Fig. 21) and bears the Brussels arms, but it is in a deplorable state and is pieced out with fragments of other tapestries,[101] as is the case for *The Triumph of Charity*. The other is in The Fine Arts Museums of San Francisco (Fig. 22).[102] The fourth is located in the Walker Art Gallery in Liverpool (Fig. 23),[103] and its border is of the repeating motif design already mentioned in connection with the Moscow and Cluny *Hopes* and the Edinburgh *Prudence*. Not having examined the Liverpool tapestry (and the Chenonceaux work having been badly repaired), I base my description once again on the San Francisco version, which is not in very good condition either but has not been extensively restored. It is also interesting in that it still retains its marks on the lower guard: the double B of Brussels on the left and, opposite, a weaver's mark (⼄) almost identical to the ones found on *Justice* of the same museum and the Asheville *Prudence*.

The scroll (Fig. 22) reminds us, albeit rather darkly, that fortitude is necessary not only in earthly affairs, but that the prospect of eternal life should prevent us from fearing death, which offers access thereto:

Obiicit adversis interrita corda periculis
Virtus, eque iuvat morte recepta salus

("Valor matches intrepid hearts against adverse
perils.
Likewise, the salvation received from death is useful.")

FORTITUDO, wearing armor and a green
skirt, her helmet visor raised, supports a
column on her right shoulder and with her
left hand strangles a dragon, a classical
portrayal. The most powerful bird, the eagle,
is at her feet. She arrives from the right in a
chariot drawn by two lions ridden by two
now-forgotten characters wearing helmets:
DENTAT<u>US</u> and CINOPE.

The warrior carrying a bundle of spikes in his
right hand and five crowns encircling his left
arm is certainly Lucius Sicinius (or Siccius)
Dentatus, assassinated by order of the
decemvirate in 450 B.C., whom Pliny cites in
his *Natural History* as an example of courage:

He was present at 120 military engagements,
won eight single combats and received forty-five
wounds in the front but none in the back. This
same man had taken thirty-four spoils of enemies,
received as gifts eighteen pike staffs without tips,
twenty-five military decorations, eighty-three
necklaces, 160 bracelets, twenty-six crowns of

which fourteen were civic, eight gold, three mural,
and one obsidional.[104]

However, in the Brussels hanging of *The
Twelve Ages of Man*, which we already
mentioned, more particularly in connection
with Tiberius and Placella, it is the other
Dentatus appearing in the *History*: "Curius"
who is quoted in the inscription over a warrior carrying, as above, a number of pikes
(including a few broken ones) and surrounded by several men and women presenting him with many crowns, bracelets,
and a necklace.[105] Therefore, it is tempting
to see in this particular character Manius
Curius Dentatus, the ideal of the old Roman
who, as consul in 290 B.C., ended the war
against the Samnites, refused the gold with
which they tried to appease his severity, and
finally punished the Sabines and defeated
Pyrrhus and the Lucanians, accepting only
seven acres of the vast lands offered him by
the Senate. But it is not so, despite the name
"Curius" woven into the New York tapestry,
surely an error for "Siccius," whom the
scene suits much better.[106] Besides, in the
above-mentioned replica (in Dijon) of *The*

Fig. 20. *Triumph of Fortitude.*
Château de Chenonceaux.
(Photograph: Studio Henry,
Amboise.)

Fig. 21. *Triumph of Fortitude.*
Museo de Santa Cruz, Toledo.
(Photograph: Foto Rodriguez,
Toledo.)

Fig. 22. *Triumph of Fortitude* in The Fine Arts Museums of San Francisco. Gift of The William Randolph Hearst Foundation to the California Palace of The Legion of Honor 1957.126.

Fig. 23. *Triumph of Fortitude*. Walker Art Gallery, Liverpool. (Photograph: John Mills, Liverpool.)

Twelve Ages of Man, the warrior laden with pikes and offered crowns is named "Lucius Sisinius Dentatus."[107]

As for Cinope, the female warrior in a red gown and carrying a shield, it is hard to believe her to be (as Miss Calberg has said with regard to the *Christian Virtues* where Cinope is riding, along with Dentatus, the *Fortitude* lions) "the eponymous heroine" of the city of Sinop on the Asian coast of the Black Sea. According to legend, Zeus had become enamored of her and promised to grant her whatever she wished. The young maiden dared to request that he respect her virginity—which he was obliged to do, having given his word. She took the same line later with Apollo, as well as with the River-god Halys, and "she allowed no mortal to take what the gods could not obtain."[108] The figure here is more probably one of those nine Valiant Women whom the ending Middle Ages had paired off with the nine Valiant Men. Except for Semiramis and Penthesilea, they have not been extensively studied[109] and therefore are nearly unknown today. But the *Fortitude* tapestry includes two other of these women, Thamaris and, justly, Penthesilea. Many of these valiant women had been chosen from among the Amazons. Such is the case for Cinope, whose career is outlined in a beautiful unpublished manuscript belonging to the Vienna National Library, written in Troyes in 1472 by Robert Briart and illustrated by Jean Colombe. Its title is *L'Histoire et faits des neuf Preux et des neuf Preues* (which will be referred to as *The Story of the Nine Valiant Men and the Nine Valiant Women*). It was composed in 1460, by order of Louis de Laval, lord of Châtillon, by his chaplain, Sébastien Mamerot.[110] Cinope's career is described as follows:

"Seneppe, called by some Synope, daughter of Queen Marpecia, often called Marsepia, was a queen of great constance, sense and valor, who remained forever a virgin. She was made queen of the Amazons around 1300 B.C." Sinope's mother had been killed in a surprise attack by her adversaries, whom she "scorned," having many times defeated them. Once Sinope was "elected" queen, she ended the mourning period, fearing that their enemies might take advantage of their "discouragement" and attack them. Desirous also of avenging Marpecia and her companions, she raised a great army, "shed much blood, and won innumerable treasures. There was not a people among whom they entered that

they did not bring into subjection by force of arms." The news of these conquests reached "mighty Hercules and Theseus his companion." The two "knightly heroes were much terrified, fearful lest the Amazons undertake the conquest of Greece." So, desiring "to see to the remedy . . . before ravage of fire and also . . . to gain glory," Hercules and Theseus assembled their troops, set "sail towards those lands" where the "Amazons were" and attacked them "by night, for they dared not by day." . . . "The very valiant queen Sinope," who had just prepared "with her sister, the noble Hippolyte," an expedition "to enter Greece and to bring it into subjection," regrouped her surprised warriors. A hand-to-hand combat between "Menaloppe" and Hercules, Hippolyte and Theseus ensued which lasted until evening. Finally, the two Greeks, "very much ashamed that these two women resisted them so well, exerted themselves . . . until they had finally conquered and taken them." Sinope, "very much distressed," had "to render her arms" in order to ransom her sisters and "peace was declared . . . except that, once Menaloppe was returned, Theseus took Hippolyte as his wife, with the consent of Queen Sinope." Everyone returned home and the Amazon "reigned very peacefully ever after until she was old and died famous, much bemoaned and regretted by all her subjects, who greatly praised her most noble and valiant feats of arms."

S. Mamerot was apparently desirous of placating the male pride of the two Greek heroes, for in *Le Chevalier errant*, composed in about 1394 by Thomas III, marquis of Saluces, we read that "Hippolyte and Menalippe . . . with Hercules did combat/Until they had beaten him to the ground/And Theseus his good friend" did not come away any better. "And hear the great marvel/Those whom no man could defeat/As if they were of iron/So strong and brave were they/Were defeated and beaten" and the Greeks were "wounded, slaughtered and killed."[111]

Behind the chariot march two warriors. One of them, PHINEES, is certainly not the famous king of Thrace—who was struck sightless by Boreas for having blinded his sons and afterward tormented by the Harpies, but delivered by the Argonauts—although this character figures in one of the panels of the *Honors*, whose relationship to ours we have already indicated.[112] Nor do we have here the son of Lycao, struck down along with his brothers, nor Andromeda's uncle who, in love with his niece and despondent at seeing her abducted by Perseus, went to massacre those in the festive banquet hall, but was turned to stone by Medusa's head. Rather we have here Phinehas, "the son of Eleazar, grandson of Aaron, the priest." When a Hebrew had brought a Medianite woman to his brothers for purposes of debauchery, while the people were camped on the plains of Moab, Phinehas "rose and left the congregation and took a spear in his hand and went after the man of Israel into the inner room, and pierced both of them, the man and the woman, through the belly. Thus the plague was stayed from the people of Israel," and Jehovah granted to Phinehas, and to "all his descendants after him, the covenant of a perpetual priesthood, because he had been zealous for the cause of God" (Num. 25:6–13).[113] It is not surprising to see him with halberd, shield, and helmet, because at the head of the troop that follows,[114] in the upper right, carrying pikes and a banner, we meet his contemporary IOSVE. He is in modern garb, his red robe covering his blue armor. The presence of Moses' successor is explained by his valor during the long conquest of the Promised Land. As Jehovah repeated three times before having him cross the Jordan, "Be strong and of good courage" (Josh., 1:1–9).[115]

Above, a scene with tiny characters matches two others of the same format located on the left. Beneath the word NEEMIAS, the scene on the right shows four warriors keeping watch from the towers of HIERVSALEM, while a man bent beneath a heavy load climbs a ladder toward them. This is the reconstruction of the Holy City by Nehemiah, cupbearer of Artaxerxes, king of Persia, in the fifth century B.C. Having learned that the Jews, escaped from captivity, were now living "in great misery and infamy," that the walls of Jerusalem were "demolished and its gates destroyed by fire," he obtained authority to rebuild them. Upon his arrival in the city he began work with the aid of his compatriots. This was such a considerable enterprise that it occasioned discouragement ("The burden carriers' strength is giving out and there is much rubble. We will not be able to build the wall") and, above all, such hostility on the part of the neighbors that he had to arm half of his men to ward off a possible attack while the other half finished the work (Neh. or 2 Ezra, 1–6). Toward the left the warrior in blue armor and red clothing slaying an elephant

that bears on its back a tower in which two threatening warriors are perched is obviously Eleazar. During the battle of Bethzacharias waged by Judas Maccabaeus against Antiochus V Eupator (164–162 B.C.), Eleazar "saw one of the elephants wearing the royal harness and surpassing all in height. Believing the king to be riding the beast, he lay down his life in order to deliver his people. . . . He slid underneath the elephant, drove his sword in [his belly] and killed it. The elephant fell down on top of him and Eleazar died there" (1 Macc. 6:43–46). Finally, in the upper left-hand corner, climbing the walls of a besieged citadel, appears the conqueror of the Persian empire, ALEXANDER, whose exploits had so struck the medieval imagination that he was made one of the nine Valiant Men.[116]

Below, IVDICH, dressed in green, is once again represented, but this time at the entrance of Holofernes' red tent. She is about to behead the general, who lies in a drunken stupor, while her maid, dressed in blue, opens their provision sack ready to receive his head (Jth. 13:8–11). No virtue was of greater value than *Fortitude* in carrying out, step by step, such an audacious plan, and it was for this virtue that the Jewish heroine prayed above all others: "Pray that God gives me the strength to realize my plan," she had said to the elders in the very beginning (VIII, 31), before addressing the same entreaty to Jehovah: "Put in my heart enough constancy to scorn him (Holofernes), enough strength to destroy him. . .give power to the plan which is in my heart" (9:14 and 18). Then, immediately after taking from above his bed "the sword which was hung there" and with which she was to accomplish her plan, she repeated twice, "Lord God, strengthen me" (13:7 and 9). Finally, upon her return the people of Israel exclaimed, "The Lord has blessed you in His strength" (13:22).[117] The three characters below Judith are taken from the war waged against Rome by the Etruscan king Porsenna (ca. 507 B.C.). First of all, CHLOELIA, dressed in a red gown, holding a stick and mounted on a half-immersed horse, is the famous Cloelia who was immortalized as an equestrian statue in Rome. As Porsenna's hostage, she had escaped and reached Rome by swimming across the Tiber. The consul delivered her to the king, who released her along with several of her companions, showering her with gifts.[118] Beneath the horse, we see Horatius COCLES in armor and helmet, only his torso visible above the water. He single-handedly defended the Sublicius bridge, thus giving his men time to cut the way down, then made his escape swimming, yet without abandoning his arms. As for MVTIVS SCEVOLA, he had infiltrated the enemy camp in order to kill Porsenna but mistook his victim and was immediately arrested. He placed his hand on live coals to punish it for that error and declared to the king that 300 young Romans had vowed to kill him. Terrified, the Etruscan chief engineered a peace. This hero is seen in the foreground, a blue cloak draped around his opulent red breastplate, a plumed helmet on his head, a dagger in his right hand, and his left hand thrust into the flames of a splendid standing brazier.[119]

Farther to the right the warrior SCEVA is falling to his knees, pierced by arrows, javelins, and a dagger, yet without dropping his sword. He is the centurion of Caesar's army, Marcus Cassius Scaeva, who, in charge of the defense of a fort, withstood the attacks of four legions of Pompey's party for several hours, even though severely wounded.[120] Next come two Valiant Women. The first is PENTHESIEEA (for Penthesilea), said to be the most famous of the nine along with Semiramis, in a blue breastplate and red skirt, a spear in her right hand, a shield on her left arm, and her hand on the hilt of her sword. Queen of the Amazons, she lent support to Priam during the Trojan war, in which she perished after several heroic deeds.[121] The second is THAMARIS, a warrior in a reddish breastplate and a blue skirt, who, sword in hand, is holding a bearded head over a stone tank full of a red liquid. She cannot be identified either as Thamar, the queen of Georgia in the twelfth century, or as the Canaanite of the same name who seduced her father-in-law Juda (Jacob's fourth son) after having married his two eldest sons, nor as David's daughter, raped by her half brother, Amnon. Rather it is Thomyris, the queen of the Scythians, who, in order to avenge her son, slain by order of Cyrus the Persian king, lured her enemy into an ambush and had him brought to her. Then, when Cyrus' speech displeased her, she had his head cut off and threw it into a goatskin full of blood. In the Middle Ages she is found under the name of Thamaris, be it in illuminations of the *Chevalier errant* (Wandering Knight);[122] in the inventory of the tapestries of Charles VI, in which a set of Valiant

Women appear bearing the duke of Berry's arms[123] and which seems to be composed like the group of Valiant Men in the Cloisters; in the above-mentioned *Story of the Nine Valiant Men...* by S. Mamerot;[124] or again in *La Nef des dames vertueuses* by Simphorien Champier.[125] Yet she is named THOMIRIS in the *Justice* of the *Honors* of Madrid, in which she holds one side of a canopy while Scipio holds the other.[126] To the right and a bit farther back stands a warrior dressed in red garments and blue armor, whose bust alone is visible, seemingly as a result of his being in a ditch with the lion that he is facing and menacing with a stick. He may be Milo of Crotone, his left hand apparently stuck in a tree trunk.[127]

With the two right-hand groups we return to the Bible. In the lower corner a woman dressed in blue, IAHEL, lifts a mallet over a huge spike placed on the temple of a warrior, asleep with his head on his helmet. He is stretched out on a red cloak draped in such a way that a green tunic and breastplate can be seen, of which the left shoulder piece bears the letters "SIS," the right one only "S"; a bottle is conspicuously placed before a section of the tent. It is the depiction of Deborah's prophecy. After having sent Barak out against the army of the Canaanite king, Jabin, led by Sisera, she predicted to Barak that glory would not be his, for "Jehovah shall deliver Sisera into the hands of a woman." Indeed, the enemy leader, defeated by Barak and having taken refuge in the tent of Jael, the wife of Eber the Cinean, had fallen asleep. His thirst was quenched and he believed himself in safety. But, "she took a stake of the tent and having taken a hammer into her hand, she went to him stealthily and drove the stake into his temples and beat it into the earth while he was fast asleep and weary, and he died" (Judg. 4:9 and 15–21).[128] Above, three soldiers respectfully present a small cask and two bottles to DAVID, who, standing beneath Fortitude, turns to them, a red cloak draped over his breastplate. Yet, though the king of Judah appears in the hanging for the fifth time, it is his servants who here demonstrate their courage. During a war their master, having voiced his desire

... to drink of the water in the cistern at the gate of Bethlehem, ... the three mighty men forced their way into the camp of the Philistines and drew water from the cistern and carried it to David; and he did not consent to drink it, but poured it out to Jehovah. And he went on to say: "It is unthinkable on my part, O Jehovah, that I should drink this water! Is it not the blood of the men going there at the risk of their souls?" and he did not consent to drink it [2 Sam. 23:13–17].[129]

Here the virtue of *Fortitude* is illustrated by heroes once again borrowed from the Bible and antiquity.

TEMPERANCE

As stated above, no panel of *The Triumph of Temperance* has been preserved. However, the inscription now sewn onto the top of the Asheville *Prudence* does *not* belong to this piece, as comparison with the San Francisco *Prudence* has demonstrated. It is not found in the *Triumphs* of the other virtues either, but bears exactly the same lettering; without a doubt it belongs to the *Temperance* that it suits perfectly. Its existence is therefore proof, if necessary, that a piece was devoted to this virtue in the set. This proof is further substantiated by the presence of the left half of this same inscription across the Toledo *Charity*.

It is true that the word MODERATIA[130] can be seen in the place of TEMPERANTIA, but they are virtually synonymous, and the name CARITAS does not appear in the inscription of the *Charity*, nor does JUSTICIA in the *Justice*, nor FORTITUDO in the *Fortitude*. The terms, especially, are convincing:

Illicitos animi moderatia comprimit estus
Teque metro stringit Plute, Lyee, Venus.
("Moderation of the soul restrains illicit ardors and restricts you, Plutus, Lyaeus, Venus.").

Plutus being the god of riches and Lyaeus one of the names for Bacchus,[131] the inscription therefore advises restraint of the passion for money, drunkenness, and debauchery. One may assume that these three gods of ancient mythology appeared on the tapestry, as did the winds on the *Hope* and Pallas with Prometheus and Perseus on the *Prudence*.

A clue as to the rest of the iconography is provided by the *Temperance* of *The Triumph of the Christian Virtues*, a set of eight Brussels tapestries dating from mid-century. We have already discussed this set which, though offering a quite different style, is from the standpoint of iconography merely a simplification of our own.[132] Consequently, we cannot be certain as to which characters were present in the hanging of 1520–35, but it appears more than likely that it contained at least all those of the other.[133] Therefore, Temperance was pouring water into wine and a fox sat at her feet, contemplating its image in a mirror, to signify that one must take care not to be deceived by false appearances. Her chariot arrived from the left side, drawn by two elephants, symbols of chastity,[134] led by two men, one of whom is Socrates. It is trampling two other men, probably Epicurius and Tarquinius Superbus, the last king of Rome, and he was accompanied by a troop led by Boetius, whose *De consolatione Philosophiae* had so greatly influenced medieval thought. Athena no doubt appeared behind, at the head of a small group, probably that of the ancient adepts of Wisdom. Last of all came Diogenes.

Our series being much richer in figures than the *Virtues* of the Brussels bank, we deplore the disappearance of this seventh piece and hope that the publication of this essay will lead to discovery of some fragment thereof.

Having elucidated this iconography, we must now ask what highly cultured individual was able to compose for the cartoonist—such artists "inventing" little at that time—this subtle and in some ways disconcerting grouping of figures. Such an assortment belongs generally to medieval iconography, but not in all cases, as we can see from the exceptional episode of Gideon with the flail and the bottle, or Judith's presence as an illustration of such varied virtues, or, better yet, the presence of ancient characters such as Carneades, Charondas, Dentatus, Fabricius, or Scaeva. Unlike Alexander and Trajan, these characters had been little used in the common imagery of the preceding centuries. At first, we might well reply that only a humanist familiar with the Bible and the ancient authors could make such choices and, without limiting himself to the habitual representations, extract from his readings certain characters, retained for their intrinsic qualities and not merely on the basis of the significance attributed to them by the commentators. However, as Mr. Delmarcel has pointed out to me, the heroes just mentioned as well as many others, though they do not belong to the customary repertory of illustrations, are found in Valerius Maximus, one of the Latin authors most widely read at the end of the Middle Ages. (For instance, he gives Fabricius, Zaleucus, and Charondas as models of just men, and Horatius Cocles, Clelia, Scaeva, and Dentatus as examples of courage. He also writes of Alexander, Catilina, Cato and Scipio, Marius and Sylla, and, outside of Rome, Tomyris, Carneades, Milo of Crotone, and Denys of Syracuse). But many of the characters in the hanging are also found in the Summa, as it were, for the Gothic period, the *Speculum historiale* of Vincent de Beauvais. (Among them are Moses, Joshua, Deborah, Jael and Sisera, Gideon, Zaleucus, Manasseh, Milo, Constantine and Sylvester, and Theodosius and Placella.) Thus, we must wonder upon exactly which sources this scholar drew.

Although he may have had direct recourse to texts, especially the Bible—and the importance given the Old Testament suggests the design might well have been elaborated by a cleric, one concerned with reform of the Church—the author may also have used (or even primarily used) the medieval works that transmitted knowledge of Jewish and pagan antiquity. In this he would be typical of those early sixteenth-century literati, not Italian, who had been nourished on tradition yet remained open to the novelties of their times; they would obviously be quite unaware of our too sharply drawn distinction between the "Middle Ages" and the "Renaissance." Though I have explained the presence of many of the figures here depicted with the help of biblical and other texts, I have done so fully realizing that many may have been learned of through compilations, but the sources also have a good chance of being multiple, for the iconography of these tapestries seem to reflect the culture of one man much more than the direct illustration of one particular work.[135] In addition to identifying sources, we should investigate, if not the reasons behind this mixture of tradition and innovation, readily explicable in the beginning of the Renaissance, then at least the reasons behind the choice of characters.

This research is being done by Guy Delmarcel, who is studying *The Honors*, the iconography of which is richer. He has pointed out the presence of several characters of *The Virtues* in that hanging (for instance, Simon the Magician, Mohammed, and Julian the Apostate), as well as a number in *The Moralities* also kept at the Patrimonio Nacional in Madrid[136] (the group of saints in the *Faith* panel—Helen, Constantine, and others). I shall not, therefore, pursue this topic but merely note that the two Madrid hangings contain inscriptions in the same vein as ours and a similar mixture of biblical and ancient characters, along with a few figures from Christian history. For example, in the *Justice* panel of *The Honors* appear Abraham, Sarah, Isaac, Rebecca, David and Judith; several Olympian gods, Thomiris,

Scipio and Nero, and finally Placella. Because *The Honors* predate the *Seven Virtues* and are more important, they influenced our hanging; hence the originality of thought lies more with *The Honors* than with *The Virtues*, and the iconography of these may turn out to be similar to that of tapestries of ca. 1520.

For instance, in the four panels of *The Twelve Ages of Man* (in which, as I stated above, the stages of life parallel the seasons of the year), the Latin inscriptions are also of the same type, and Placella and Tiberius appear together with "Tobias" and "Jacob blessing Joseph's sons" to illustrate Winter, whereas the three other seasons juxtapose Jews and pagans. And Edith Standen, rejecting Jean Lemaire de Belges as the source for the Madrid *Honors*, as Emile Mâle had thought,[137] suggests as a possible author the Dutch humanist Jerome van Busleyden (ca. 1470–1517), an ecclesiastical member of Margaret of Austria's Grand Council.[138] Other tapestries could also be mentioned: the *Fortune* panel found at Narbonne Cathedral, the *Prudence* in The Art Institute of Chicago (though they are merely more or less simplified replicas of one or another of *The Honors*), *The Triumph of the Faith* and of *Divine Wisdom* of the Burrell collection in Glasgow,[139] the above mentioned *Prudence* in Heidelberg (1531), and a panel in the Germanisches Nationalmuseum in Nuremberg most likely belonging to the same series.[140]

However, representations of the theological or cardinal virtues were a common occurrence in Christian art at the end of the Middle Ages and during the sixteenth century,[141] and in many tapestries one or another virtue is accompanied by many others in a context very different from that of the *Honors*. Examples are, at the beginning of the century, in the *paños de oro* of the Madrid Patrimonio Nacional, purchased in 1502 by Juana la Loca from Peter van Aelst;[142] in the immense hanging, *The Redemption of Man*, in which these virtues contend for the sinner with the vices they combat;[143] and in the panels related to this theme, like those of *The Prodigal Son*,[144] the handsome *Allegory of the Vices and Virtues* of the erstwhile Stroganoff collection;[145] the curious tapestry of New York's Metropolitan Museum in which *Temperancia* is associated with the Coronation of the Virgin,[146] and the set of the Detroit Institute of the Arts.[147] Or we find the virtues in a ship guided by Prudence seated in the crow's nest, helping Man to win the crown proffered by

Perseverance (*Allegory*, perhaps from Tournai, of about 1515, in the Minneapolis Institute of Arts).[148] Or we see them again in front of the "Virtuous King" and the "Princess of Peace," where they surround the little - "Prince of Peace," in a mediocre but interesting panel from about 1530 in the Isabella Stewart Gardner Museum of Boston.[149] This panel is preceded by another, which, in 1923, was preserved in a private German collection and in which "Loyalty" hands the newly born "Prince of Peace" to his mother.[150]

In the *Virtues* hanging herein discussed, there is hybridism between the theme of the Virtues and that of the Triumphs, which, born in Italy in the fifteenth century, spread into the sixteenth—the Triumphs of the Romans; the Triumph of the Emperor Maximilian; the Triumph of Jesus Christ and the Virgin; the triumphs of the gods, seasons, and arts.[151] In tapestry we are above all familiar with the celebrated *Triumphs of Petrarch*, of the early sixteenth century, either the Brussels panels of the Rijksmuseum in Amsterdam, Hampton Court, and Victoria and Albert Museum in London,[152] or the magnificent Vienna series of a totally different style.[153] In those hangings, as in ours, the main character, accompanied by men and women having served him well, is seated in a chariot crushing his enemies. The influence of these *Triumphs of Petrarch* on those of *The Seven Virtues* is also indicated by specific details—for instance, the animals. However deeply rooted the beliefs originating from the *Bestiaries* may have been with regard to the animals, it is perhaps not altogether coincidental that *Faith*'s chariot is drawn by the four Gospel symbols, like that of *Eternity*, and that unicorns draw *Justice* as well as *Chastity*.[154] We know of other *Triumphs* in tapestry—that of Trajan, for instance, of the former Friedel collection (ca. 1530);[155] or, under the name of *The Seven Deadly Sins*, that true *Triumph of the Vices*, which is the splendid set of 1540–1550 kept in the Patrimonio Nacional of Spain.[156]

Our *Triumph of the Virtues* quite naturally takes its place in this mainstream, and the survival of vestiges of at least five editions proves its success, which is also manifested by the existence of hangings derived from it. There is one, a bit later, of which one panel, *The Triumph of Fortitude*, before World War II was to be found in the museum of Industrial Arts in Berlin. Less cluttered, it contained fewer characters than does ours, but none that are not in ours and grouped in a some-

time very similar manner.[157] The other example is that *Triumph of the Christian Virtues* already mentioned, in an outright Renaissance style and more ordinary in any case; but Calberg points out that the analogies with ours are "highly conspicuous," despite a "basically different style," and "prove an obvious filiation." Yet, since of the scattered set she knew only of the reproductions by Pinchart of *Faith* and *Charity* today in Biltmore House, she believed her hanging to have been primarily influenced, at least with respect to the iconography of *Hope*, by the superb series of *The Seven Virtues* of Vienna, woven in the mid-sixteenth century, based on cartoons by Michael Coxcie and from which the style of the tapestries of the Belgian bank also derive.[158]

Actually, both sets borrow from ours, the Brussels one much more exclusively than the Austrian.[159] Yet in both cases the new style in the Italian manner fully triumphed, whereas just as our set still largely depends on medieval thought for its iconography, so too it perpetuated in its style an outlook that is in many respects of the waning Gothic, even if certain elements, such as the decor of the chariots or the breastplates, are Renaissance. One need only compare it with a nearly contemporaneous hanging, *The Months* (today scattered), which is attributed to Bernard van Orley.[160] In this tapestry the scenes unfold in an oval embellished with the signs of the zodiac and are surrounded with figures (some of which, such as the Winds armed with bellows, offer many analogies to those of our *Hope*—as well as to those of *The Twelve Ages of Man*, incidentally). More modern on the whole than that of *The Virtues*, the style of these *Months* is very similar to that of the set in New York, a work from about 1520 also attributed to Bernard van Orley.[161] The slight differences between the two series can be explained by the fact that a few years separate them. On the other hand, if *The Seven Virtues* offer a unified space, whereas *The Twelve Ages* retain the juxtaposition of scenes popular in the late fifteenth century, they contain more archaic characters. Noble and solemn, enveloped in clothes of rich material that ripple in abundant folds, they are akin to those calm and pensive characters of the group of tapestries attributed to Margaret of Austria's decorator Jean of Brussels or Jean van Roome. They are especially close to the famous *Herkinbald's Miraculous Communion*, in the Royal Museums of Art and History of Brussels, the petit patron of which he was paid for in 1513.[162] Of course, differences exist between the two works, but they pertain primarily to the composition, which is less cluttered in *The Virtues* and devoid of architectural elements. These differences can be explained as resulting from the development of the painter, who was quite capable of going through transformations, if he was, as has been suggested, the author of the *paños de oro* and other works from around 1500. In the latter works the strict organization of Gothic retables distinguishes itself from the more adaptable *Herkinbald* in which the Renaissance already dominates the architecture. Since there is no further mention in the documents of Jean van Roome beyond 1521, *The Triumph of the Seven Virtues* would be, if his, among his last works. We must not forget, however, that many of the works attributed to his "school" were probably done by imitators of the style in fashion; he himself probably supplied only the little patterns and could have maintained a studio in which Bernard van Orley might have begun his career. This theory would explain the analogies that are also found between this *Triumph* and *The Legend of Our Lady of the Sablon* (1518), attributed to the latter artist and in which the spatial disposition approaches that of *The Virtues*, even though the architectural division is present.

However, Raphael had just had woven in Brussels cartoons that were to revolutionize the art of tapestry—namely, those of *The Acts of the Apostles*, which Pope Leo X commissioned for the Sistine Chapel. *The Triumph of the Seven Virtues* illustrates at the same time a conception of art no longer that of, for instance, *The Battle of Pavia* offered to Charles V in 1531, or of *The Story of Jacob* at the Royal Museums of Art and History of Brussels, the cartoons of which, probably painted around 1525, were woven after the establishment of the city mark in 1528, but before 1539.[163] These observations, together with our remarks concerning first the borders and then the iconography and its filiation with respect to *The Honors*, lead us to wonder whether the cartoons for these *Virtues*, so obviously steeped in the same current of thought and art of the years 1510–1525, were not executed at approximately the same time as *The Twelve Ages of Man*, or rather around 1525—the pieces preceding 1528 being less numerous than those bearing marks—by an artist of great talent, certainly, but who did not belong to that small phalanx of truly great renovators and, perhaps old or busy and not very anxious to employ his imagination, contented himself with the pre-existing commonplaces, perhaps not even allowing a new designer to intervene. Or the latter believed he had done enough by drawing on the repertory of *The Honors* and other recent hangings. The cartoonist was nevertheless able to organize this multitude of beautiful yet somewhat outmoded figures into vast compositions of indisputable monumental grandeur, clear though somewhat encumbered. Moreover, whenever the panel has not been overly damaged, it is endowed with a bright color scheme in which blues, reds, and yellow-greens enhance the beige-browns.

A point often overlooked by art historians, who are always mindful of the emergence of new forms, is that perhaps the touch of archaism was such as to assure the success of the series. Contemporaries, sometimes disconcerted by marked changes, perhaps preferred works that, while conforming in some degree to the tastes of the day, did not overly upset their traditions. This may have been the case during the era in which Italianism was being introduced. In any event, this work met with approval since, before inspiring other hangings, it went through several editions.

Other questions should now be posed so that the remaining problem regarding origin may be addressed. Who owned these various editions? Especially, for whom was the first weaving carried out? Who commissioned the cartoons? I have not the space to elucidate these points, but let me simply say that the quality and scope of the work demonstrate that it was no doubt conceived for some influential figure.

Because of the subject matter and because we know that the *Prudence* in Edinburgh (which belongs to one of the oldest sets) may have come from the Vatican, we may ask whether the *oeuvre* was ordered by a pope—perhaps Leo X (1513–1521) or Adrian VI (elected in 1522 but indifferent to the arts) or Clement VII (1523–1534). Yet the commission to Raphael, a bit earlier, of *The Acts of the Apostles*, shows that the sovereign pontiffs did not hesitate to turn to Italian painters most in vogue, probably what would happen in this instance. Nevertheless, some potentate may have had the hanging done in order to offer it to a pope.

We might also consider whether it was commissioned by Margaret of Austria, daughter of Emperor Maximilian and Mary of Burgundy and regent of the Netherlands during the infancy of her nephew Charles V. We know how strongly this princess supported letters and arts. Unfortunately, the inventory of her holdings made in her palace at Malines in July 1523 and supplemented by the acquisitions she made prior to her death in 1530 fails to mention any tapestries called *Virtues*.[164] Nevertheless, her great "library" included several works on this subject[165] and on both Jewish and pagan antiquity. Thus, it is quite possible that the designer was one of the many humanists in her entourage— Busleyden, Lemaire de Belges, Molinet, and others among whom it is reasonable to search for the creator of the plan for the great Brussels hangings of the period.

Nor is there any *Triumph of the Virtues* in the recently published inventory of François I's Paris warehouse. It is true, however, that it does not include all the king's collections.[166] Yet it is perhaps not unreasonable to consider Henry VIII of England, no doubt one of the greatest patrons of tapestry of all time, since at his death he held over 2,000 hangings. This king inherited many works already collected by Cardinal Wolsey and, in addition to many *Triumphs*, had at Westminster "7 peces of tapestrie of the *VII Virtues*." To verify that these are indeed our tapestries, we would have to consult the manuscript of his inventory, only excerpts of which have been published.[167]

To help hasten the discovery of the first owners of *The Triumph of the Seven Virtues*, it is necessary to evaluate, with the help of a table listing the physical characteristics of the set (Table 1), the feasibility of reclassifying the panels extant; that is, to reconstitute their editions. That is the purpose of my conclusion.

To begin with, we can easily state that the *Hopes* in Moscow and Cluny, the *Prudence* in Edinburgh (Fig. 24), and the *Fortitude* in Liverpool belong to earlier sets than do the other virtues, since their repeating-design border was in use prior to the plant border. Moreover, we have already established that these unmarked panels were probably woven before 1528. However, it is difficult to go any further.

As far as the panels with repeating-design borders are concerned, it is clear that there were at least two editions, since there are two

Hopes. However, the extant *Prudence* and *Fortitude* were not necessarily part of these editions. With the facts now available, we can only advance conjectures. The workmanship of the tapestries appears comparable.[168] The differences in size can be explained not only by greater or lesser tension on the threads during the weaving process, but also by later modifications.[169] The origins of all these tapestries are unknown, since none can be traced beyond the nineteenth century. *Prudence*, however, may have belonged to the Popes (but since when?), and *Fortitude* seems to have come from Spain. Yet perhaps the tapestry in Cluny is older than that in Moscow. The Jonah episode (which is incomprehensible in the panel in Pittsburgh, with a continuous design border) indeed appears clearer in the first one. Manasseh's apparently gouged eyes indicate—if they are not an old, inaccurate restoration—an error later corrected.[170] May we therefore presume that the Paris *Hope* was part of the princeps edition of the hanging? It is impossible to give a definite answer. In any case, we find in this first group vestiges of two, three, or four weavings, and even five if the *Fortitude* in Langeais also had repeating-design borders.

There are many more in the second group with continuous plant borders. In this group we have already seen three *Charities*—at Asheville, Chenonceaux, and Toledo—and three *Fortitudes*, at Chenonceaux, Toledo, and San Francisco. But here as well we can arrive at no definite conclusions. The workmanship is truly equal, as are the dimensions, a similarity that can be accounted for by the fact that different editions of the same panel were woven from the same cartoon. As for the borders, the side ones all have about the same design. On the other hand, the bottom ones all appear different, except in the *Faith* in Asheville and the *Hope* in Pittsburgh. The same is true of the top borders, except for those in *Charity* and *Prudence* in Asheville[171] on the one hand, and *Justice* and *Fortitude* in San Francisco on the other (with the obvious exception of the phylacteries). The border factor is, in consequence, hardly significant.

Because the origins of all the panels are equally unknown (except to a certain extent those in Toledo, which come from the cathedral), the marks at first seem to be of some help. As far as the Brussels mark is concerned, the first "B" is backwards (ᗺ) on the *Charity* in Chenonceaux, the *Prudence* in Asheville, the *Justice* and the *Fortitude* in San

Prudence in Asheville (⚌) and of the *Justice* (⚌) and the *Fortitude* in San Francisco (⚌)? Miss Calberg has pointed out [173] that if this mark contained "the famous number 'four,' whose importance in the [variegated] old marks was stressed by Léon Gruel," then according to the historian of Brussels tapestry, Alphonse Wauters, it could be, she says, "a double merchant's sign, the indication of the carrying out of a commission for a leading citizen giving business to his less fortunate colleagues, or again by a weaver who was also involved in the selling of tapestries." For Göbel this mark remains an enigma. [174] But once again, the owner of this insignia could have woven several series and, inversely, the panels from one edition could have been made in more than one workshop. [175]

Thus it is not certain that the *Justice* and *Fortitude* in San Francisco belonged to the same set as the *Prudence* in Asheville and, consequently, as *Faith* and *Charity*, which seem to have had the same background. [176] If such were the case, these last three panels also would be of Spanish origin. Be that as it may, there are at least three hangings with continuous plant borders whose basis is the series in Asheville, Chenonceaux, and Toledo, which each have a *Charity*. We have then to assume that, for instance, the *Fortitude* in Langeais had a border with compartments and that, for instance, the *Hope* in Pittsburgh and the *Prudence* in San Francisco were part of the same edition as the *Charity* and *Fortitude* in Chenonceaux, just as the *Justice* and *Fortitude* in San Francisco were part of the series in Asheville, the panels in Toledo constituting the third set. [177] There were seven sets if we presume that the series in Asheville, Chenonceaux, Toledo, and San Francisco, the isolated pieces in Pittsburgh and San Francisco, and perhaps that in Langeais, were distinct—other assumptions (intermediate) are also possible of course.

In addition to the series with the compartmented borders, there were a minimum of five editions and (though unlikely) a maximum of eleven, not counting those that have disappeared altogether. The number of editions, as well as the influence of the series, demonstrates the extraordinary success enjoyed by the hanging. Indeed, it can be compared to the success of one of the most famous sets of the last third of the fifteenth century, *The Trojan War*. [178] Nevertheless, *The Seven Virtues* was of limited duration,

Francisco. It was the same way on the Asheville *Faith*. It is not on the *Hope* in Pittsburgh, the *Prudence* in San Francisco, nor, it seems, on the *Charity* and *Fortitude* in Toledo. This fact does not seem to be a significant factor either. The *Charity* in Chenonceaux, for instance, cannot belong to the series of the *Faith* and *Prudence* in Asheville, which are already accompanied by a panel on this subject, the guard of which was redone.

Weavers' marks can be assigned to two groups. The first includes the *Hope* in Pittsburgh (χ), the *Charity* in Chenonceaux (χ), and the *Prudence* in San Francisco (χ). In the second the bottom is worn away, which may explain the slight difference in design, and the first can have been modified. The three panels, along with the *Fortitude* in Chenonceaux, the guard of which is modern but already accompanies *Charity*, could then possibly have been part of one series, which would have originated in Spain, since that seems to be the case for *Hope*. However, this is not at all certain, for the same master may well have woven the hanging several times. In any case, the mark is unknown. [172] Is it the weaver's personal sign or has it a signification analogous to that which, for lack of a more precise identification, is attributed to the ⚌ of *The Triumph of the Christian Virtues*, in which the oblique line sometimes crosses the right vertical and consequently looks much like the marks of the

whereas that of *The Acts of the Apostles*, a bit older, persisted for several centuries. This was doubtless because, even though the cartoons in *The Acts* signaled the beginning of a new concept that eventually proved fatal to the art of tapestry making, they are the work of an artist of much greater renown.

Even so, *The Triumph of the Seven Virtues* constitutes, by its scope, the loftiness of subject matter, subtle richness of treatment, and the powerful beauty of design and execution, an exceptionally interesting set. It is a notable illustration of the outlook of an age at that exquisite and moving moment when, embued with the Gothic spirit, imaginations were already drifting toward a new world, that of the Renaissance. Its high level of art warrants that it be recovered from undeserved oblivion and classed among the great hangings woven in Brussels while at its zenith as tapestry capital of the world.

ACKNOWLEDGMENTS

The author wishes to acknowledge the help of Jean-Paul Asselberghs, Curator in charge of Textiles at the Royal Museums of Art and History of Brussels, who identified the present place of conservation of many of the tapestries discussed here. His untimely demise is a great loss. This paper, written in 1974, is dedicated to his memory.

TABLE 1

Physical Characteristics of Sixteen Tapestries

VIRTUE	LOCATION	DIMENSIONS (m)	BORDER TYPE	WARP THREADS (cm)	MARKS PLACE	ATELIER
Faith	Asheville	4.57×5.74	Continuous vegetation	6	ex [mark]	
Hope	Pittsburgh	4.47×5.64	"	6 to 7	[mark] B	[mark]
	Moscow	4.42×5.25	Repeating			
	Cluny	3.20×5.45	"	7	Cut	Cut
Charity	Asheville	4.57×5.74	Continuous vegetation	7	Modern guard	Modern guard
	Chenonceaux	4.50×5.50	"	7	[mark]	Lower worn [mark]
	Toledo	4.55×5.70	"	6	From Brussels	
Prudence	Asheville	4.57×5.74	"	6 to 7	[mark]	[mark]
	San Francisco	4.50×5.59	"	7	[mark]	(Lower left-hand corner worn) [mark]
	Edinburgh	4.135×5.135	Repeating	7	Without	Without
Justice	San Francisco	4.37×5.49	Continuous vegetation	7 to 8	[mark]	[mark]
Fortitude	Langeais	2.90×3.30	Without	7	Cut	Cut
	Chenonceaux	4.50×5.50	Continuous vegetation	7	Modern guard	Modern guard
	Toledo	4.52×5.60	"	6	From Brussels	
	San Francisco	4.40×5.56	"	7 to 8	[mark]	[mark]
	Liverpool	4.11×5.33	Repeating	8	Without	Without
Temperance	Inscription in Asheville *Prudence* (complete); in Toledo *Charity* (fragment).					

TABLE 2 **List of Characters in Hanging**
(Virtues and anonymous figurants excepted)

The names of the characters represented
without inscription, but identified, are within
parentheses; the names of the three gods
mentioned for *Temperance* are in italics.

	FAITH	HOPE	CHARITY	PRUDENCE	JUSTICE	FORTITUDE	TEMPERANCE
Aaron		•					
Abigail				•			
Abraham	•		•				
Alexander						•	
Ananias		•					
(Angels)	•	•			•		
Aquilon (No. Wind)		•					
Ahasuerus				•			
Azariah		•					
Bacchus (=Lyaeus)							
Boreas		•					
Brutus			•				
Cadmus				•			
Carneades				•			
Cassandra				•			
Catilina					•		
Cato					•		
(Celer)					•		
Charlemagne	•						
Charondas					•		
Cinope (see Sinope)							
Clelia						•	
Constantine	•						
Cornelia					•		
Daniel		•					
David	•	•	•	•		•	
Deborah		•					
Dentatus						•	
(God)	•	•			•		
Dionysus			•				
(Church)	•						
(Eleazar)						•	
(Elias)	•						
Elizabeth			•				
Esther		•	•	(•)			
Fabricius					•		
Gideon		•		•			
Godfrey de Bouillon			•				
Goliath	•						
Helen	•						
Holofernes						•	
Horatius Cocles						•	
Isaac	•		•				
Jacob	(•)				•		
James (Saint)	•						
Jael						•	
(Jonas ?)		•					
(Joseph ?)					•		
Joshua						•	
Judas Maccabaeus	•		•				

139

	FAITH	HOPE	CHARITY	PRUDENCE	JUSTICE	FORTITUDE	TEMPERANCE
Judith	•	•		•		•	
Julian the Apostate	•	•					
Louis (Saint)	•						
Lyaeus (see *Bacchus*)							•
Mohammed	•						
Manasseh		•					
Mordecai		•					
Marius					•		
Medusa				•			
(Milo)					•		
Michael		•					
Moses	(•)	•					
Mutius Scaevola					•		
Nehemiah					•		
Nero			•				
Noah	(•)				•		
Oliver	•						
Pallas				•			
Penthesilea						•	
Perseus				•			
Phinehas						•	
Peter (Saint)	•						
Pietas			•				
Placella			•				
Plutus							•
Prometheus				•			
Rachel				•	•		
Rebekah					•		
Roland	•						
Sheba				•			
(Solomon)				•			
(Sarah ?)					(•)		
Scaeva (M. Cassius)						•	
Scipio Africanus					•		
Seleucus					•		
Simon the Magician	•						
Sinope						•	
Sisera						•	
Susanna		•					
Sylla					•		
Sylvester	•						
(Synagogue)	•						
Thamaris						•	
Theodosius	•						
Tiberius			•				
Titus				•			
Tobias			•				
Trajan					•		
Venus							•
Vulturnus		•					

NOTES

1. Except as far as its inscription is concerned (see discussion of *Temperance*). A letter dated 18 May 1955 from American tapestry scholar Ella S. Siple shows that she, too, had no knowledge of any *Triumph of Temperance*, in spite of having recorded the remnants of at least four editions of the hangings.

2. The ones published were usually done so in a very brief manner and without knowledge of the whole. Madeleine Jarry mentioned seven other tapestries of the series in her short account of the *Fortitude* of Langeais (see discussion of *Fortitude*), and yet the *Triumphs* of *Faith* and *Charity* are cited in reference to the former Lowengard collection. It is significant that, about fifteen years ago, while studying a set of the same subject, albeit of later date, the former curator of textiles of the Royal Museums of Art and History of Brussels drew a comparison between the Lowengard series and this set, describing it as "known only for two pieces of rare nobility of expression—the *Triumphs of Faith* and *Charity*—reproduced without comments by A. Pinchart in the volume "L'Histoire générale de la tapisserie' devoted to the Netherlands." See M. Calberg, "Le *Triomphe des Vertus Chrétiennes*. Suite de huit Tapisseries de Bruxelles du XVIe siècle," in *Revue Belge d'Archéologie et d'Histoire de l'Art 29* (1960): 36. In the volume of plates devoted to the Netherlands in his monumental story of tapestry, Heinrich Göbel does not reproduce a single one. See *Wandteppiche* I, *Die Niederlande* II (Leipzig: Klinkhardt & Biermann, 1923).

3. Alphonse Wauters, *Les Tapisseries Bruxelloises, Essai historique sur les tapisseries et les tapissiers de haute et de basse-lice de Bruxelles* (Brussels: Baertsoen, 1878), pp. 143–49. However, according to Prof. Jan-Karel Steppe, the mark could have been added to already woven tapestries or affixed in a sporadic fashion, "already a little before 1528." See "Inscriptions décoratives concernant des signatures et des mentions du lieu d'origine sur des tapisseries bruxelloises de la fin du XVe et du début du XVIe siècle," in *Tapisseries Bruxelloises de la Pré-Renaissance, Exposition . . . 22 janvier–7 mars 1976, Musées Royaux d'Art et d'Histoire, Bruxelles*, p. 195. But even if this were the case, and nothing here allows us to believe so, our dating would not be modified because of the other elements on which it is based.

4. Mr. E. Morris specified that there was no mark on the Liverpool piece, as did Mr. R. Oddy concerning the Edinburgh piece before its restoration; nor does it appear on the Moscow piece. (See my Table 1, "Physical Characteristics of Tapestries.")

5. *Tapisseries flamandes d'Espagne, Musée des Beaux-Arts, Gand, 19 juillet–20 septembre 1959*, catalogued by Eric Duverger (Ledeberg/Gand: Erasmus, n.d.), nos. and pl. 11–12, pp. 32–34. *The Pentecost* of the Patrimonio Nacional in Madrid, also with large fruit and flowers, its central stem twisting more visibly, thus evoking the continuous, narrow plant border of the beginning of the century, is probably slightly older. [See J. Crooke y Navarrot, count Valencia de Don Juan, *Tapices de la corona de España* (Madrid: Hauser y Menet, 1903), no. 67; and Paulina Junquera, "Colección del Patrimonio nacional, Tapices de los reyes catolicos y de su epoca," in *Reales sitios, Revista del Patrimonio nacional* 7, no. 26 (1970, 4th quarter): 22, color pl., p. 23.] *The Passion*, commissioned in 1520 by Marguerite of Austria from Pieter de Pannemaker in the presence of Bernard van Orley already contains fruit and flowers of rather considerable dimensions, and may be said to have opened the way to this particular type (Valencia de Don Juan, nos. 28-31; P. Junquera, in *Reales Sitios* III, no. 7 (1966): 54f, pl. p. 52. The same may be said for a work such as the "dais of Charles V": *Christ bids Farewell to the Holy Women*, which is today found in the Patrimonio Nacional and figures in the inventory of M. of Austria in 1523 (Valencia de Don Juan, nos. 25–27; and *Carlos V y su ambiente, Exposicion Homenaje en el IV centenario de su muerte* [1558–1958], exhib. Toledo. Oct.–Nov. 1958. [Madrid: Artes graficas, 1958] no. 646, pp. 245–46).

6. Göbel, pl. 375. See also the *Triumph of Love* with its slightly more Renaissance characters, in the Patrimonio Nacional of Madrid (ibid., pl. 80), and, of a slightly different type, the *Story of Jacob* dated c. 1528–1539, possession of the Royal Museums of Art and History, Brussels (Roger-A. d'Hulst, *Tapisseries flamandes du XIVe au XVIIIe siècle* [Brussels: L'Arcade, 1960], no. 21, pp. 183–92, illus. A *Triumph of Trajan*, also dating from c.1530, which appeared in 1923 in the Berlin Art Trade, has a border of the same type but without inscription, bearing masks in the upper corners and fragmented by the frame (Göbel, pl. 377). A little later, the fruit and flowers were to be grafted onto a thick central stem with overlapping leaves. Perhaps ushered in by the *Battle of Pavia*, a set given to Charles V in 1531 (ibid., pl. 376; and d'Hulst, no. 18, pp. 147–56, illus.), we find this type in:

—a *Story of Cyrus* which Ella Siple dates ca. 1535 in "Some recently Identified Tapestries in the Gardner Museum in Boston", *Burlington Magazine* 57 (Nov. 1930): 241–42, fig.) and which passed from its original owners, the Barberini family, into the Ffoulke collection under the name of the series of the Archdukes Albert and Isabella [see *The Ffoulke Collection of Tapestries Arranged by Charles M. Ffoulke* (New York: private printing, 1913) pp. 88–91] before its acquisition by the Gardner Museum of Boston [*The Isabella Stewart Gardner Museum, General Catalogue*, by Gilbert Wendel Longstreet (Boston: University Press, 1935), pp. 150–52];

—*A Life of Saint Paul*, ca. 1540, embellished with cupids (Göbel, pl. 384a);

—in tapestries with flowers and the arms of Charles V, from the same epoch (d'Hulst, no. 22, pp. 193–202, blk and col. fig.) and in several works of the middle of the sixteenth century, as:

—*The Story of Joshua*, of the Austrian national collections (Göbel, pl. 322);
—*Leaving for the Hunt*, of the Galleria degli Arazzi of Florence (ibid., pl. 394);
—the magnificent *Apocalypsis* of the Patrimonio Nacional of Madrid, woven before 1562 by Willem de Pannemaker, most likely from older cartoons by B. van Orley (ibid., pl. 128; d'Hulst, no. 19, pp. 157–70; black and colored fig.; and P. Junquera, "Tapices en nuevos salones del Palacio de Oriente," in *Reales Sitios* . . . 5, no. 16 (1968²): 58-60 and color pl., pp. 45–46).
Other varieties of this border of large fruit and flowers can be found still, for example, in the *Genealogy of Ottheinrich, the Palatine Elector*, 1540, in the Bayerisches Nationalmuseum of Munich, from the Neuburg a.d. Donau castle (a piece reported in Göbel, pl. 69), or in the Vatican's pearl-gallooned *Procris and Cephalus*, dating from the second third of the century (ibid., pl. 392), and elsewhere.
7. This is found on a piece in a private collection which depicts a woman seated on a throne, holding a book and surrounded by people. She was believed to be *Faith* (Archives photo from Monuments Historiques, photo 45–F, 4363).
8. Marthe Crick-Kuntziger, *Musées Royaux d'Art et d'Histoire de Bruxelles, Catal. des Tapisseries (XIVe au XVIIIe s.)*, n.d. (1956), no. 12, pp. 27–28 and pl. 16.
9. For *Saint Jerome* see especially Valencia de Don Juan, no. 24, and P. Junquera (1970), p. 22 and color pl. p. 16. For *Turnus* see Valencia de Don Juan, no. 23, and Junquera, p. 22 and fig. p. 20).
10. At least two, since both the *Charities* of Chenonceaux and Toledo, both the *Prudences* of Asheville and San Francisco, and finally the *Fortitude* of San Francisco and of Toledo bear the mark of Brussels. More likely there are three, since the *Charity* of Asheville, whose edge has been redone, accompanies a *Faith* which had the arms of Brussels and a *Prudence* that still possesses these markings. And since the *Fortitude* of Chenonceaux, with a modern edge, goes with a marked *Charity*, perhaps even four are possible if the *Fortitude* of Langeais, the borders of which today are lacking, is added to the list. There may even be more if those existing pieces with an unbroken band of vegetation originated in different sets. (See my Table 1, which attempts to reconstruct the various tapestry editions.)
11. Valencia de Don Juan, pl. 32–40, and chiefly a soon-to-be-published thesis by Guy Delmarcel, which will save me the necessity of giving a more extensive bibliography. On this subject he has already published "De structuur van de Brusselse tapijtreeks *Los Honores*," in *Annales du XLIe Congrès (Malines, 1970) de la Fédération archéologique et historique de Belgique*, pp. 352–56.
12. For example, in those cited previously, *The Salve Regina, The Story of Jacob, The Life of Saint Paul, The Story of Joshua*, and *The Apocalypsis*. On the other hand, the inscriptions found on *The Legend of Our Lady of Sablon*, most probably completed in 1518, are still in Gothic lettering. [See essential bib-

liography in *Chefs-d'oeuvre de la Tapisserie du XIVe au XVIe siècle, Grand Palais, 26 oct. 1973–7 jan. 1974, Catal.* by Geneviève Souchal (Paris: edn des Musées Nationaux, 1973), nos. 85–86, pp. 200–207, fig; and nos. 90–91 of the American edition.] The same is true for four pieces, ca. 1520, *The Twelve Ages of Man* (in New York), of which more later. This is also the case for *The Honors* and *The Moralities* of Madrid in which, however, the names of the characters are, as we have here, in Roman capitals.
13. It measures about 28cm in width (Cluny and Liverpool pieces) by about 40cm for the continuous border of vegetation. The small differences in size among tapestries are also explained as being the result of varying degrees of tension in the threads during the weaving process and the result of shrinkage of the central scene along the edges, most probably owing to alterations. In addition, we know that the size of tapestries varies from one measuring to another. We shall see that the pieces have nevertheless been woven on the same very precise cartoons called for by the low-warp technique employed in Brussels.
14. Emile Mâle, *L'Art religieux de la fin du Moyen Age en France, Etude sur l'iconographie du Moyen Age et sur ses sources d'inspiration* (Paris: A. Colin, 1908), pp. 319–20, 1969 edition. Believing my study sufficiently comprehensive, I shall not go into detail concerning this question of attributes but shall leave this task to Mr. Delmarcel in his work on *The Honors*.
15. The photographic portfolios of the Musée des Arts décoratifs in Paris include a *Triumph of Faith* bearing the inscription LONDRES (?), but, as it presents the same borders and particularities as the *Triumph* of Biltmore House, we may very well have here the same piece and an erroneous legend, unless the work was conveyed by way of the English capital. I should also like to point out a fragment of tapestry conserved in the Christian Museum of Esztergom, Hungary—inv. 58.4.1, 2.60m high by 3m wide—whose photograph Mr. J. Guillaume kindly forwarded (Fig. 5). In this photograph the Trinity is frontally seated in a chariot pulled by the four Evangelic symbols: the angel on the bull and the eagle on the lion. This chariot is framed by two groups of men; in the first row on the left we recognize Saint Peter. At the top runs the bell-lined border apparently typical of the Tournai production. We have here, in fact, one of those mediocre interpretations of the great Brussels tapestries which Tournai, already on the decline, was weaving about 1525–30, of which another example later (see p. 655 and n. 58).
16. *Biltmore House and Gardens*, Asheville, N.C. (Biltmore Estate, 1965) pp. 12 and 31. It is more than likely *The Triumph of Faith* shown in Paris in 1866 along with *The Triumph of Charity* and *The Triumph of Prudence*. At that time the three pieces belonged to M. Bourouet. [See Alfred Darcel, "Union centrale des Beaux-Arts appliqués à l'Industrie, Musée Rétrospectif, Le Moyen Age et la

Renaissance," *Gazette des Beaux-Arts*, 20 (1866): 74–75. Mr. Darcel calls our attention to the mark of Brussels on the blue edge of the *Prudence* as well as on that of the *Faith* (ᛒ�figures), but with a slightly different design. In Asheville the said mark exists on the *Prudence* but has been left out on the *Faith*.] The *Triumph of Faith*, the borders being identical, is certainly also the tapestry reproduced without comments by A. Pinchart in the volume devoted to the Netherlands in *Histoire générale de la tapisserie*, vol. 3, "Tapisseries flamandes" (Paris: Soc. an. de publ. périodiques, 1880), pl. Along with this tapestry appears a *Triumph of Charity* mentioned as belonging then to the Lowengard collection. Such was surely the case for the *Faith*. But these pieces are not to be found in the catalogues from the sale of this famous Lowengard collection (*Catalogue des Tapisseries . . . Paris, Galerie Georges Petit . . . Vendredi 10 juin 1910 . . .* ; small copy, Louvre Library no. 11336; large illustrated copy, ibid, no. 34852. Second sale: *Catalogue des objets d'art et de haute curiosité . . . Paris, Hôtel Drouot . . . vendredi 3 et samedi 4 mars 1911*). Since G.W. Vanderbilt traveled all over Europe to furnish his castle during its construction (the land was bought in 1888 and the opening of the residence took place in 1895; see *Biltmore House . . . ,* p. 2), he doubtless acquired at that time the three *Triumphs* still probably grouped together as they were in 1866, even if Pinchart reproduced only two in 1880. Lowengard must have therefore possessed all three. My thanks go to Mr. W. A. V. Cecil, the castle's present owner, who provided me with photographs and allowed me to study the tapestries of the Biltmore House. (Description: 4.57m by 5.74m; present state good; restorations. About six warp threads per centimeter. No marks; edge redone.)

17. See, for example Louis Réau, *Iconographie de l'Art chrétien*, (Paris: PUF, 1956–59), t. 2, *Iconographie de la Bible*, vol. I, "Ancien Testament," pp. 125–38.

18. In Christian iconography the victory of David over Goliath generally prefigures that of Christ over Satan (ibid., pp. 260–63).

19. See X. Barbier de Montault, *La Tapisserie des Preux à Saint-Maixent (Deux-Sèvres)* (Saint-Maixent: Ch. Reversé, 1893), pp. 21, 26, 48, 51, 55, 71, and 121–22; and Robert L. Wyss, "Die neuen Helden, Eine ikonographische Studie," *Z. für schweizerische Archäologie und Kunstgeschichte* 17 (1957): 98–100.

20. On Jacob see Réau, t. 2, vol. 1, pp. 142–55.

21. Ibid., pp. 104–15.

22. He usually symbolizes hope in the Resurrection and prefigures the Ascension of Christ (ibid., pp. 356–58).

23. Réau, t. 3, *Iconographie des Saints*, vol. 2, pp. 633–36.

24. Vincent de Beauvais, the "encyclopedist" of the thirteenth century, whose *Speculum historiale* was indicated by Mr. Delmarcel as one of the great sources of the *Honors*, discussed at length a celebrated event, the repentance of Theodosius after the massacre of the Thessalonians, which had led

Saint Ambrose to bar him from entering the Church of Milan (edn. Bénédictins de Saint-Vaast, Douai, 1624, vol. 17, ch. 53–54, pp. 672–73). But this emperor more probably figures here because of his role in spreading Christianity for:

ante eum enim Imperator Maximus Constantinus qui primus pietate morum ornavit Imperium, sacrificare daemonibus interdixit, non tamen eorum templa evertit . . . Itaque usque ad tempora huius magni Theodosii, & ad Idolorum aras ignis ascendebatur, & libamina ac sacrificia offerebantur . . . Sed haec omnia Theodosius catholicus imperator extirpare radicitus imperavit, & evulsit, corripuit & condemnavit" (ibid., ch. 55, p. 674). Vincent de Beauvais also writes later that it was prayer that enabled the emperor to vanquish the tyrant Eugenius (ch. 107, p. 692).

25. Similarly, vol. 13, ch. 46, p. 520; and Réau (1959), t. 3, vol. 3, pp. 1217–30.

26. Concerning him, see Vincent de Beauvais, pp. 507–40; and Réau, t. 3 (1958), vol. 1, pp. 341–44.

27. Rita Lejeune and Jacques Stiennon, *La Légende de Roland dans l'Art du Moyen Age*, (Brussels; L'Arcade, 1966) t. 1: 270.

28. Jules Horrent, *La Chanson de Roland dans les littératures française et espagnole au Moyen Age* (Paris: Les Belles-Lettres, 1951), pp. 79–95; 334–42 (esp. 341) and passim. See also Raoul Mortier, ed., *Les Textes de la "Chanson de Roland"* (Paris, La Geste francor): t. 1, "La Version d'Oxford," 1940; t. 2, "La Version de Venise IV," 1941; t. 3, "La Chronique de Turpin et les Grandes Chroniques de France. Carmen de prodicione Guenonis. Ronsasvals," 1941.

29. *Cronique et histoire faicte et composee par reverend pere en dieu Turpin archevesque de Reims l'ung des pairs de fra*n*ce Contenant es prouesses et faictz d'armes advenuz en son temps du tres magnanime Roy Charles le gra*n*t, autrement dit Charlemaigne: & de son nepveu Raoula*n*d . . .* (Paris: printed for Regnauld Chauldiere, 1527), fol. XXXIV vᵒ, XL vᵒ–XLI vᵒ, I vᵒ–II vᵒ et XXXII vᵒ. For the latin text of *Turpin* and that of the *Grandes Chroniques de France*, see Mortier, t. 3, pp. 76–79. The chapter devoted to Charlemagne in the famous *Triomphe des Neuf Preux*, published 30 May 1487 by Pierre Gérard in Abbeville and republished by Michel Le Noir in Paris, 3 December 1507 (with gaps), follows the same tradition. Also in *Ly myreur des histors, Chronique de Jean des Preis dit d'Outremeuse* [published by Ad. Borgnet (Brussels: F. Hayez, 1873), t. 3, pp. 144 and 152] which, along with the *Chronique saintongeaise*, that of Philippe Mousquet, that attributed to Daniel Aubert, and many other texts, an adaptation of the pseudo-Turpin, we find, for example, that the Saracens have dragged Oliver "into a wood and tied him to a tree with three ropes from the saddle straps of his own steed, then they cut him up into straps from head to foot. So was Oliver murdered, and they left him dead." The same story is in Vincent de Beauvais, vol. 24, ch. 20, p. 969. Nevertheless, the reproductions of Oliver's martyrdom and that of his companions in the important illustration of Lejeune and Stiennon are scanty (vol. 2, figs. 483 and 509). Sometimes Oliver is represented tied to a

tree (see Vol. 1, pl. LX and p. 380, which is a page from *L'Histoire et faits des Neuf Preux et des Neuf Preues* by Sébastien Mamerot, Cod. 2577–78 of the Österreichische Nationalbibliothek of Vienna, which we encounter again when dealing with Sinope in the *Fortitude* tapestry); or else his hands are attached to his feet (vol. 2, fig. 380). The illustration of Roland's death or the discovery of his dead body by Charlemagne are much more numerous (vol. 1, pl. XXV, XLII, L, LII, LVI; vol. 2, fig. 288, 293, 331, 332, 487, and 490). On Charlemagne and Roland's iconography see also Réau, t. 3, vol. 1, pp. 292–98, and t. 3, vol. 3, pp. 1162–64. On Saint James's, ibid. t. 3, vol. 2, pp. 690–702.

30. Purchased about 1926 from Symons Inc. of London and New York by French & Co., it was restored in 1927 by Luigi Orselli of Florence and sold 24 October 1928 to William Randolph Hearst, who, according to Ella Siple's letter, owned two other pieces of the set—the *Triumph of Justice* and *Triumph of Fortitude*, which are today in the California Palace of the Legion of Honor, San Francisco (see discussion of *Justice*). Toward the end of 1953 it was given by the Hearst foundation to the Carnegie Institute, which received it on 4 March 1954 (inv.54.6.1). Delmarcel explained that according to Marillier's handwritten catalogue (in the Victoria and Albert Museum, London) which has the *Fortitude* coming "from Marques de dos Aguas" and then passing into Hearst's possession "with two others," the Spanish origin of the three pieces is probable. This piece was briefly studied in "A Gift of Tapestries," *Carnegie Magazine* (April 1954), pp. 123–24 and 129, fig., and by Helen Comstock, "Tapestries from the Hearst Collection in American Museums," *The Connoisseur Yearbook* (1956), pp. 41 and 43, fig. p. 44. My greatest thanks to Mr. David T. Owsley, curator of the Carnegie Institute, who facilitated the study of this tapestry. (Description: 4.47m high by 5.64m wide. Present state good; restorations; less distinct than the two others; 6–7 warp threads per centimeter. Marks: coat of arms between two Bs on the left side of the lower edge; X on the right.)

31 Victor Verger, *Dictionnaire de la fable . . .* (Limoges: Barbou, 1852), pp. 55 and 93; Pierre Chompré, *Dictionnaire abrégé de la fable . . .* (Paris: Delalain, 1885), pp. 34, 50, and 277; Pierre Grimal, *Dictionnaire de la mythologie grecque et romaine* (Paris: PUF, 1951), pp. 66–67. It should especially be noted that there are three of those winds appearing also with bellows in the upper part of a Brussels hanging that in many aspects is related to the *Seven Virtues: The Twelve Ages of Man*, studied by Edith Standen and to which we shall return. [See "The Twelve Ages of Man," *Metropolitan Museum of Art Bulletin* 12, no. 8 (April 1954): 241–48, 8 figs. See especially "The Twelve Ages of Man: A Further Study of a Set of Early Sixteenth-Century Flemish Tapestries," *Metropolitan Museum Journal* 2 (1969): 127–68; 23 figs.]

32. Aside from the retinues following the chariots, one or two members of which are identified by name, only the small scene in the upper right-hand side of the *Charity* may be mentioned.

33. Calberg, pp. 11–12 and fig. 3, p. 10. See also Réau, t. 2, vol. 1, pp. 410–19.

34. The photographs of the Moscow tapestry hardly permit a decisive statement on what is merely a small background scene.

35. N. I. Romanov saw here an image of *Penitence*; see p. 223 of his article on the Moscow Museum's similar piece ["The Flemish Tapestry *Spes* in the Moscow Museum of Fine Arts," *Art in America* 17, no. 5 (August 1929): 223–34, 3 figs.] For Calberg (p. 9) "they represent the souls held captive on earth, and their aspiration to eternal bliss."

36. The inscription is repeated on his alms-purse.

37. Romanov saw his slippers there (p. 223)! In medieval iconography Moses' actions herald those of Christ (Réau, t. 2, vol. 1, 175–212).

38. As high priest he normally prefigures Christ. After Korah's revolt his was the only staff among the twelve tribes of Israel that flowered—a miracle to be considered as symbol of Mary's virginal motherhood (ibid., pp. 213–16).

39. G. Souchal, no. 71, pp. 167–70, fig. (no. 76 of the American edition). Concerning Gideon, see also Réau, t. 2, vol. 1, pp. 230–34.

40. This well-known episode was considered to be the prefiguration of both the Resurrection of Christ and the soul's salvation (ibid, pp. 401–06).

41. Deborah appears in the folio f.l.v°-f II of "La Fleur des Dames," the first book of *La Nef des Dames Vertueuses*, a flattering collection dedicated by the physician Simphorien Champier to the duchess of Bourbon, Anne de Beaujeu, eldest daughter of King Louis XI of France, and published by Jehan de Lagarde in Paris 3 May 1515: Deborah, wife of Lapidoth and prophetess, had to find room in the crow's nest of our ship. God had revealed to her things to come and all the Hebrew people came unto her on the mountain of Ephraim to ask her judgment. That Deborah urged war against Jabin's city of Azeroth, and she being in prayer on Mount Tabor, and Barak fighting, the city was completely overcome. From that she composed a hymn in which she exhorted the victorious to thank our Lord, and that she and Barak sang after the victory.

Although Champier mentions many of the women found in our *Triumph of the Seven Virtues* (Penthasilea, Thamiris, Minerva, Cassandra, Medusa, Cloelia, Rebecca, Rachel, Jahel, Esther, Judith, Abigail, and Susanna), considering his comments on Medusa and Jahel (refer to our subsequent discussions of *Prudence* and *Fortitude*), this compiler cannot possibly be the designer of our tapestries' master plan. But his work having appeared at about the same time as the formulation of this theme, it provides evidence that heroines were popular and on what score. That is why he is quoted here as a witness of the "intellectual tenor" of the minds of his time.

42. Concerning the popularity of the story of Esther reproduced on tapestries, see G. Souchal's *Catalog*, no. 70 (*Les Trois Couronnements* de Sens), pp. 165–67, fig.; no. 74 (*Tapisserie Mazarine*, at the Washington National Gallery), pp. 174–80, fig.;

and no. 76 (*Scènes de l'Histoire d'Esther*, at the Victoria and Albert Museum, London), pp. 182–83, fig. (nos. 75, 79 and 81 of the American edition). Also see G. Souchal, "*Les Paños de Oro* ou *La Dévotion de Notre-Dame* du Patrimonio nacional de Madrid," *Bulletin de la Société Nationale des Antiquaires de France*, 1975, pp. 142–43.

43. Réau, t. 2, vol. 1, pp. 335–42.

44. Along with Noah, Isaac, Daniel, and the three young Hebrews in the furnace Susanna is one of the main symbols of the saved soul. She also represents the persecuted Church (Réau, pp. 393–98), which accounts for her success, further evidenced by the slightly earlier tapestries of the Marmottan Museum. Like Judith and Esther (fol.f IIVº), Susanna is placed by Simphorien Champier among the "virtuous women" because she "preferred to die rather than commit adultery with the two evil old men . . . . But because she still placed her hope in God and loved and feared Him in the extreme, she was delivered by Daniel the prophet from their hands." (fol. g II).

45. They are also symbols of the grace of God, which protects his chosen people; in the same way they prefigure the descent of Christ into Limbo and the virgin motherhood of Mary (Réau, t. 2, vol. 1, pp. 398–401).

46. Given by M. Zoubaloff of Moscow to the Roumjantsoff Gallery of the same city, *The Triumph of Hope* entered the Moscow Fine Arts Museum in 1924. Totally unaware of the other pieces of the series, N. I. Romanov examined *The Triumph of Hope* in his article chiefly from the standpoint of the conception of its design and style. He believed it to be the work of Jean Lemaire de Belges, though he claimed the style belonged to the same Philippe to whom Joseph Destrée [*Maître Philippe, auteur de cartons de tapisserie . . .* , (Brussels: Vromant, 1904)] attributed the large group of early sixteenth century Brussels tapestries— associated by some with Jean van Roome (question summed up in G. Souchal's *Catalog*, nos. 73–75, pp. 173–74 and 180–82; nos. 78–80 in American edition). Romanov thought that PHILE for Philippe could be discerned on Gideon's sleeve, but this is very doubtful. A reproduction of the Moscow tapestry may be found in "Izobrazitel'noe iskusstvo," *Gosudarstvennyj Muzej Izobrazitel'nyx Iskusstv Im. A. Puškina*, Moscow, album in-fol., no page numbers, pl. 8–11 color and black and white, color cover. I wish to thank Mrs. Galina Jesipowa, Curator of tapestries for the Museum of Fine Arts, Moscow, who kindly provided me with this album, photographs and information. (Description: 4.42m high by 5.25m wide.)

47. No. 1237 of the inventory. This piece belongs to the most ancient collection of the Cluny Museum, works collected by Alexandre du Sommerard before his death in 1842. It was simply described by F. de Guilhermy, "Musée de l'Hôtel de Cluny," *Annales Archéologiques* 1 (1844): 45; and by Edmond du Sommerard in A. du Sommerard, *Les Arts au Moyen âge en ce qui concerne principalement le Palais romain de Paris, l'Hôtel de Cluny issu de ses ruines et les objets d'art de la collection classée dans cet hôtel*, vol. 5 (Paris: 1846), p. 262. It was engraved in vol. 3 of the *Album* appended to the latter work (pl. XXXIV) and announced as being from the end of the fifteenth century in several catalogues of the museum by E. du Sommerard (no. 1691 in the editions of 1847, 1855, 1858, 1864, 1869, 1873, and 1874; and no. 6323 of 1881 and of the last edition, *Musée des Thermes et d l'Hôtel de Cluny, Catalogue et des cription des objets d'art de l'Antiquité, du Moyen Âge et de la Renaissance exposés au Musée* [Paris: Hôtel de Cluny, 1883], pp. 501–2). Reproduced in one of the albums published by Guérinet, *Tapisseries des Gobelins, de Beauvais et de Flandre*, it was mentioned recently in the controversial book by G. T. Van Ysselsteyn, *Tapestry, the Most Expensive Industry of the 15th and 16th Centuries: A Renewed Research into Technique, Origin and Iconography* (La Haye/ Brussels: Van Goor Zonen, 1969), pp. 111–12 and pl. 93, with a faulty reading of the inscription, an erroneous interpretation ("allegory based on the four winds"!), and an unsupported attribution to Van Orley and Pieter de Pannemaker's atelier. (Description: The lower portion cut off, it now measures only about 3.20 m high by 5.45 m wide. Its condition is very poor; large parts are missing, notably in the inscription, the ships [almost all of the phoenix and the dismasted vessel above], the face of the man in red pulling Hope's ship, finally Manassah's neck, Mordecai's chest, and David's arm. Also in the lower part, to Esther's right, a major gap does away with a large portion of Susanna. This sad condition seems relatively new, because the line engraving, dated 1840, from du Sommerard's *Album* of the *Arts au Moyen Âge*, represents the complete scene. Only the lower border is missing and parts that are now destroyed— such as Susanna's right arm or the head of the phoenix—present a design that conforms with the pieces of Pittsburgh and Moscow. Also, the inscription is written down in its entirety. [An error: "Irritat" for "Irruat" and the abbreviations of *quamquam* are not solved]. About seven warp threads per centimeter.)

48. Same bibliography as that for *The Triumph of Faith* (see discussion of *Faith*). This piece, reproduced in the portfolios of photographs in the Musée des Arts Décoratifs in Paris, with a border identical to the one in the old Lowengard collection, is certainly the tapestry from Asheville. (Description: 4.57m high by 5.74m wide. Present state good; repairs. About seven warp threads per centimeter. No mark; edge has been rewoven.)

49. In Chenonceaux we read CHARITAS.

50. Calberg, p. 13. Nevertheless it is "mostly at the time of the Counter-Reformation [that] Judas Macchabaeus enriched Christian Art," because the redemption of the sins of the dead by the prayers and sacrifices of the living testified in favor of the dogma of Purgatory over the teachings of the Protestants (Réau, t. 2, vol. 1, pp. 303–4).

51 His exploits—narrated in the twelfth century by Geoffrey of Monmouth in the first book of his *Historia regum Britanniae*, adapted in verse by Robert Wace under the title of *Brut*—were illustrated in a most beautiful wall hanging made about 1460, of which only a piece remains in the Saragossa cathedral [E. Bertaux, "Les Tapisseries Flamandes de Saragosse," *Gazette des Beaux-Arts* (1909): 226–28, fig.].

52 Gospel according to Saint John, 15:13. It is why he has been compared to the Savior (Réau, t. 2, vol. 1, pp. 138–42).

53. Daughter of King Andrew II of Hungary. Married in 1221 to the margrave of Thuringia, she devoted her short life (1207–31) to the poor, the sick, and the lepers. Canonized as early as 1235, she is represented either as a princess or as a Franciscan of the Third Order and then often with a beggar at her feet, whom she nurses or to whom she gives alms [Réau, t. 3, vol. 1 (1958), pp. 417–21].

54. The burial of the corpses by Tobia, secretly by night, in spite of Sennacherib's interdiction, was taken as an illustration of the seventh of the "Works of Mercy" (Réau, t. 2, vol. 1, pp. 318–27).

55. In the articles cited. Refer here particularly to the second (1969).

56. According to M. J. Milne (Standen, p. 155, n. 84).

57. Georges Florent Grégoire, Bishop of Tours, *Histoire Ecclésiastique des Francs*, 10 vols. trans. and edited by J. Guadet and N.R. Taranne (Paris: J. Renouard, 1837), vol. 2, pp. 111 and 251–53.

58. Pp. 157 and 162, n. 98. For the Dijon hanging, of which only two pieces are kept since 1952 in the Musée des Beaux Arts, see J. -P. Asselberghs, *La Tapisserie Tournaisienne au XVIe siècle* (Tournai: 1968), no. 15, pp. 22 and 24 and pl. 15.

59. Anne-Lise Stemper, "Der Prudentia-Teppich des Pfalzgrafen Ottheinrich im Kurpfälzischen Museum zu Heidelberg," *Heidelberger Jahrbücher* 2 (1958): 68–95 and notably 86–87.

60. Pauperibus dederas Tyberi pia munera Cesar/Sub saxo Tyberi reddita gaza fuit.

61. I am grateful to Guy Delmarcel, who, very obligingly, informed me of a discovery he made, after lengthy research. See in his text the detailed exposé of the Placella question covered by Vincent de Beauvais, vol. 17, ch. 55, 673b.

62. My thanks to Bernard Voisin, Curator of the Chenonceaux château, and Mr. de la Morandière, manager of the estate, for their kind cooperation in my research. (Description: Approximately 4.50m high by 5.50m wide. Poor condition, with many faulty restorations. Approximately seven warp threads per centimeter. Marks in the lower border: on the left a shield between two B's; on the right X̄ , the bottom part worn out.)

63. From the cathedral that still owns this piece. I am very grateful to Matilde Revuelta Tubino, Curator of the Santa Cruz Museum in Toledo, for the information and photographs she gave me. (Description: 4.55m high by 5.70m wide. Extremely poor condition; pieces inlaid especially in the center part and in the pauper on the left; more than the left half of the inscription of *Temperance* is placed vertically, to the right of Tiberius. Approximately six warp threads per centimeter. Mark of Brussels on the left of the lower edge.)

64. *Biltmore House . . .* , pp. 30–31. It is very likely one of the three pieces exhibited in 1866 in Paris (Darcel, pp. 74–75), probably located also at Lowengard's (see discussion of *Faith*). (Description: 4.57m high by 5.74m wide. In good condition, many small repairs; 6–7 warp threads per centimeter. Marks in the lower border, on the left: a shield between two B's. On the right: ⚕ .)

65. Gift of the Provident Securities Co., inv. no. 62.19.3. Mentioned in Ella Siple's letter of 18 May 1955, as being located "in the estate left by the late William H. Crocker of San Francisco." It has therefore an origin different from that of the *Justice* and *Fortitude* in the California Palace of the Legion of Honor in San Francisco. I express here my gratitude to D. Graeme Keith, former Curator of Decorative Arts at The Fine Arts Museums of San Francisco for his kind welcome and generous help and I also thank Anna G. Bennett, Curator of Textiles. (Description: 4.50m high by 5.59m wide. Poor condition: torn parts, bared threads, in spite of many restorations. Approximately seven warp threads per centimeter. Marks on the lower border: on the left a shield between two B's, on the right X , with lower left corner worn out.)

66. *Catalogue des Tableaux . . . , gravures, objets d'art et d'ameublement . . . , Tapisseries composant la collection de M. Paul Eudel . . . Vente . . . 9 . . . 12 mai 1898 . . .* (Dijon: Impr. Darantière, n.d.) p. 8 and 67, no. 361 and fig. The lower border was sewn, then, in the place of the missing upper part. At the time of its acquisition by the Royal Scottish Museum, 1898, it was placed again at the bottom, and an upper border, painted, was executed at the museum in its image without any inscription; the medallions in the lower corners were rewoven (which explains why we find birds in the four corners instead of the faces that appear in the rest of the series). Inv. no. 1898.324. My thanks to Mr. R. Oddy, Keeper of the Art Department, for the information and photographs he sent me with endless courtesy. (Description: 4.135m high by 5.135m wide. Cleaned and relined in 1973; lower galloon then was rewoven. Seven warp threads per centimeter. No marks on the blue lower galloon before its restoration.)

67. X. Barbier de Montault, *Inventaire descriptif des Tapisseries de Haute-lisse se trouvant à Rome* (Arras: Rohard-Courtin, 1879), pp. 55–58. Yet no mention is made of the absence of one of the borders, but it may be that the tapestry, described as being in a state of "perfect conservation," was then complete and mutilated later by the collector in order that it fit the wall section receiving it—an operation, alas, not uncommon.

68. Its name is badly restored as PRVDENCIM in Asheville and DRVDENVA in San Francisco.

69. For example, C. Hippeau, *Le Bestiaire d'Amour*

de Richard de Fournival, suivi de la Réponse de la Dame (Paris: 1860), p. 73.

70. In *The Triumph of the Christian Virtues* from the mid-century, this figure is inscribed above with the name OTHEA, which, for Calberg (p. 25) is "likely . . . Orthaea, one of the four Hyacinthides, daughters of Hyacinthos the Lacedemonian, who, in obedience to an ancient oracle, were offered in sacrifice on the tomb of the cyclop Geraestos to save the city of Athens laid waste by plague and famine during the war waged against Attica by Minos." But Delmarcel points out that in this suite OTHEA is the name of the Athena placed above, who gives her shield to Perseus.

71. She was also extolled by Simphorien Champier (fol c.5) who explains "that Apollo, being greatly inflamed with love, begged her to do his will, which she, after several requests, granted on condition that, before he had his pleasure, he would confer on her the gift of predicting future events. This condition once granted, she mocked him and refused herself to him. That is why Apollo ensured that nobody would believe her."

72. Her name, woven on the fringe of her skirt, is no longer decipherable in the left-hand figure of the San Francisco piece; for the figure on the right in the three tapestries, the beginning of the name disappears into the folds. Jupiter's daughter is mentioned also by Champier (fol. c IIII v⁰) among "five Minervas."

73. According to some it was his absent-minded brother, Epimetheus, who had created men without either a protective casing or the qualities required to assure them mastery over animals, and the fire brought back by Prometheus was to be their best protection. According to another tradition Jupiter had deprived men of fire, angry that Prometheus had assisted them at the time of a sacrifice; the Titan went then "to the wheel of the sun" to snatch fire for men. For this deed he was tied down on the Caucasus, where an eagle was to devour his liver eternally. But here, as Delmarcel indicated to me, it is the version given by Boccaccio in his *Genealogia deorum gentilium* ("the great source for the mythology in the *Honors* hanging"), which is evidently followed. On the authority of "Servius and Fulgentius" (the latter an eminent Christian mythograph of the sixth century), Boccaccio recounts in fact:

> . . . that, when Prometheus had created man without soul from mud and earth, Minerva marvelled at the excellence of his work. She offered all that he would want from the wealth of heaven to perfect his work. And when Prometheus answered her that he did not know how he could go about it if he could not see the things that were needed, as they were in heaven, she raised him to Olympus. Upon arriving there, as he saw that all celestial beings were animated by flames, he secretly put a little branch to the wheels of Phoebus. And with that flaming twig he stole fire and took it down to earth. He applied this fire to the breast of the man he had created and thus gave him a soul and called him "Pandora." Because of that, the gods, extremely angry, had Mercury tie him up on the Caucasus mountain. . . .

vol. 4, ch. 44, trans. (Paris: Anthoine Vérard, 9

February 1498), fol. Lxx. On this first man, represented in the *Honors* piece entitled *Virtue* with the name PANDORA—a name for which the author of *Genealogia* gives a strange etymology—see ibid., ch. 45, fol. lxxi v⁰. See also Dora and Erwin Panofsky, *Pandora's Box: The Changing Aspects of a Mythical Symbol* (London: Routledge & Kegan Paul, 1956), ch. 1, pp. 3–13. For Boccaccio, Epimetheus, "the first, created an image of man from mud or earth," but Jupiter, in great anger, changed him into a monkey (ch. 42, fol. lxix v⁰).

74. Her name has been woven incompletely a second time: PER—EV.

75. It is strange to see what happens to her legend in *La Nef des Dames Vertueuses*, in which S. Champier describes her as being "of such marvelous beauty that she inflamed all who saw her . . . . Into her land came Perseus, a noble and courageous knight from the kingdom of the Argins, in a ship with a winged horse as an ensign. Thanks to her wise and prudent conversation, he took home a magnificent booty" (fol. d 4 v⁰). Moreover, the beauty of Medusa before her metamorphosis was sung by ancient poets such as Pausanias and Ovid.

76. Again according to Delmarcel it is the dragon and not Cadmus who would symbolize prudence here, referring to Boccaccio, who states that when the hero "looked at the said snake, he comprehended that the snake knew someone was looking at him" (vol. 2, ch. 63, fol. xxxix).

77. It is precisely for her prudence that Champier praises her (fol. f II v⁰).

78. According to Réau, the possession of the theraphim implied the privileges of primogeniture and Rachel thus despoiled her brother of the inheritance of their father Laban for Jacob's profit (according to the code of Hammurabi). Rachel also symbolizes the contemplative life, Leah the active life (t. 2, vol. 1, pp. 148–50). Nor has she been forgotten by Champier, for "she was a most beautiful and charming lady, but sterile, so she prayed God to give her a child. God having hearkened to her, she had Benjamin" (fol. e 7 v⁰).

79. Réau, t. 2, vol. 1, p. 230.

80. She is justly celebrated by Champier for "her wisdom and soft speech," thanks to which she "curbed and appeased David's anger against her house" (fol. fiii v⁰-f 4). Often placed facing the Virgin, as a companion piece to the Queen of Sheba offering presents to Solomon or with Esther before Ahasuerus, this paragon of prudence and diplomacy is considered as a prefiguration of Mary the mediator (Réau, t. 2, vol. 1, pp. 271–72).

81. Changed into SADA in the piece of Asheville.

82. Wise and pacific, Solomon was held to be a prefiguration of Christ; the visit of the Queen of Sheba (herself a representative of the Gentile church) announcing the visit of the Magi (ibid., pp. 287 and 294–96).

83. She is presented to Ahasuerus by a young man similar to the one apparently bringing her a message in the enigmatic little scene in the upper right-hand corner of the Mazarine tapestry (in Washington, D.C.). And, as in the two scenes below, in the same tapestry (Ahasuerus pardons Esther and gives her his ring), a counselor, older here, is standing at Ahasuerus' right. This counselor is found again near the throne in the *Glorifications of Christ* in Saragossa, in the New York Cloisters, and in Brussels. There is here evidently a direct illustration of some literary text, which came between, as I believe was generally the case, the Bible and the cartoonists. [See G. Souchal's *Catalog*, no. 74, pp. 177–78 (no. 79 of the American edition) and the *Paños de Oro . . .* , passim.]

84. Gift of the Hearst Foundation, as the *Triumph of Fortitude* (see discussion of *Fortitude*). These two pieces are therefore the ones seen by Ella Siple "some years" before 1955, "in the New York warehouse where the Hearst things were stored" (see her letter cited in n. 1 and 30). Yet they are not mentioned in Helen Comstock's article on the tapestries of the Hearst collection. According to Delmarcel they would come from Spain, as did the *Hope* in Pittsburgh (see n. 30)—but do they belong to the same hanging as the latter? We cannot be sure and they have different atelier marks. Inv. 1957.125. (Description: 4.37m high by 5.49m wide. Poor condition: holes, torn edges. Approximately 7–8 warp threads per centimeter. Marks in the lower border: on the left, a shield between two B's; on the right ⚓ .)

85. According to Ovid, whose popularity in the Middle Ages is well known, the virgin Astraea abandons a blood-drenched earth when all the gods have already left it (*Metamorphoses*, I, ch. ii). See also F.A. Yates, *Astraea, The Imperial Theme in the Sixteenth Century* (London: Routledge, 1974).

86. P. 314 and fig. 169.

87. G. Souchal's *Catalog*, pp. 176 and 209; M. Calberg, p. 16, fig. 5, and p. 17.

88. Ibid. Calberg's opinion.

89. Ibid. and p. 18. This interpretation explains the presence of Sarah, who chased away Ishmael, the son that her servant Agar had by Abraham, so that he would not be heir with Isaac (Gen. 21:9-14). This action, to our modern eyes, does not seem particularly marked with the stamp of Justice. See also Champier on Sarah; he praises her "great constance when she saw Ishmael, the son of Agar her chambermaid, who took away her son Isaac to worship idols. Then, without doing him any harm, she told Abraham to throw out the servant and the son" (fol. e 7 v⁰)

90. Calberg's article, p. 17, Réau, t. 2, vol. 1, pp. 156–71.

91. The inscription NARIS on *The Triumph of the Christian Virtues* is not thus to be read as NERON (Calberg, p. 18); it is a bad spelling for MARIVS. Here Marius wears also a diadem.

92. Ibid., p. 16, fig. 5, and p. 18.

93. Marius, Fabricius, Cato, and Scipio Africanus are among the characters dedicated a few verses in the famous *Anthologia veterum latinorum Epigrammatum et Poematum*, published by Pieter Burman

(Amsterdam; 1759–73), revised by Heinrich Meyer (Leipzig, 1835), and republished by Alexander Reise (Leipzig: Teubner): *Anthologia latina . . .* , I, "Carmina in codicibus scripta": fasc. I, "Libri Salmasiani aliorumque carmina," 1894; fasc. II, "Reliquorum librorum carmina," 1906. This is also the case for Trajan, except for the episode of the widow; for Boreas, Vulturnus, and Aquilo (*Hope*); for Nero (*Charity*), and many characters in *Fortitude*: Thomyris and Cyrus, Alexander, Penthesilea, Mucius Scaevola and M. Cassius Scaeva; while Bacchus is mentioned, under the name of Lyaeus, as in *Temperance*. It is noteworthy that, except for the poems on Scaevola, Bacchus and the Winds, the others, according to Reise, probably do not predate the fifteenth century; several (nos. 831 to 854) being likely "e libro quodam iconographico, quales adamaverunt librarii Romani, . . . collecta" (pp. 300–301). One might then ask if our author knew of, not a manuscript of this *Anthologia* which identifies Dentatus as Curius and not Sicinius (see our n. 107), but perhaps a similar text. As Pierre Laurens reminds us ("L'épigramme latine et le thème des hommes illustres au seizième siècle: 'Icones' et 'imagines'" in *Influence de la Grèce et de Rome sur l'Occident moderne, Actes du Colloque des 14, 15, 19 Décembre 1975 [Paris E.N.S., Tours]*, Paris: Les Belles Lettres, 1977, p. 130 and n. 20), many of these stanzas are among those composed at the beginning of the Quattrocento, by the Roman humanist Francesco da Fiano, to accompany the figures of illustrious men painted in the Sala degli Imperatori, in the Foligno Palace (Ludwig Bertalot, "Humanistisches in der Anthologia latina" in *Rheinisches Museum für Philologie*, n.s. 66 (1911): 64–77; and Angelo Messini, "Documenti per la storia del palazzo Trinci di Foligno, 1: Gli epigrammi latini nella Sala degli Imperatori" in *Rivista d'Arte* 24 (1942): 74–98, 2 fig.). We immerse ourselves in this environment of neo-Latin culture, the importance of which Pierre Laurens has also reminded us in a vast *Anthologie (Musae reduces, . . .* in collaboration with Claude Balavoine, Leiden: E. J. Brill, 1975, 2 vols.). On Marius, see Reise, no. 843, fasc. ii, p. 305; on Fabricius, ibid., no. 838, p. 303; on Cato, no. 846, p. 306; and on Scipio, no. 842, p. 304, where six lines praise his conquests, but not his righteousness:

Ille ego sum, patriam Poeno qui Marte cadentem
Sustinui rapuique feris ex hostibus urbes
Hispanas, Hannonisque acies magnumque Syphacem
Perdomui et fractum totiens armisque repulsum
Hannibalem, victorque ferox mihi regna subegi
Punica et excelsas altae Carthaginis arces.

Delmarcel also pointed out that many of the characters of the *Triumph of Justice*, and of *Fortitude*, are found in the *Factorum et dictorum memorabilium libri novem* by Valerius Maximus, Latin author of first century A.D., greatly appreciated in the fifteenth century, who assembles ("De justitia," vol. 6, ch. 5) the examples of Fabricius (Rom. 1). just discussed; of Charondas (Foreign 4); and of Zaleucus (Foreign 3), on which we will comment shortly. In the course of his work he names Cato, Scipio in a laudatory way, Marius with mixed appreciation, Catilina and Sylla critically (see, for instance, Pierre Constant's translated edition (Paris: Garnier, no. d.), 2 vols., passim.

94. About her Champier says only: "Rebecca, virgin of marvellous beauty, comes to our ship. She had been, by divine will confirmed by her brothers, brought up to become Isaac's wife. She was sterile but God gave an ear to Isaac's prayers for children" (fol. e 7 v⁰).

95. D'Hulst (no. 8, pp. 59–60); and Anna-Maria Cetto, "Der Berner Traian- und Herkinbald-Teppich" (Bern: 1966), 230 pp., figs., extract from *Jahrbuch des Bernischen Historischen Museums* 43/44, 1963-64. Miss Cetto made a comprehensive study of the Trajan legend and classifies therein two more tapestries from Brussels, one from the early sixteenth century, kept in a private collection in Paris, the other from ca. 1530, formerly belonging to Mr. Friedel (figs. 12 and 14, the latter reproduced in the portfolios of the Arts Décoratifs, no. 294, 11).

96. *La Nef des Dames Vertueuses* (fol. d I v⁰) makes a mention of Cornelia, wife of Scipio Africanus, but as an erudite; evidently it is not the same.

97. Fol. ccclii v⁰ of Anthoine Vérard's edition, ca. 1498.

98. Told by Valerius Maximus (see n. 93), this story was taken up again by Vincent de Beauvais in his *Speculum historiale*, vol. 2, ch. 4, 81 a.

99. *Catalogue des objets d'art et de haute curiosité du Moyen Âge et de la Renaissance . . . composant la collection de feu M. Desmottes . . . Vente . . . à Paris, hôtel Drouot . . . 19 . . . 23 mars 1900 . . .* (Paris: Imprim. de l'Art E. Moreau, no. d., p. 63, no. 417). Bought for FF.3,960. at this auction, on 23 March, by Mr. Siegfried for Langeais through Sarlins. Only mentioned by F. Lesueur, "Le Château de Langeais," in *Congrès archéologique de France, CVIe session, Tours, 1948* (Paris: Société Française d'Archéologie, 1949), p. 398, it was published briefly by M. Jarry ("La Collection de Tapisseries du château de Langeais, *"Bulletin de la Société de l'Histoire de l'Art français*, 1972: 49–50, fig.) My thanks to Mme Régnier who offered every opportunity for study of this tapestry, owned, like the castle itself, by the Institut de France. (Description: H. 2.90m by 3.03m wide. On the left are Horatius Cocles, Cloelia, and a large portion of the beheading of Holofernes; on the right are Scaeva, Thamaris, and above, Cinopes and Dentatus riding the lions of *Fortitude* whose lower part only remains; the entire border is gone. Present condition good, but numerous restorations; it was repaired early at Pluyette, then at Aubry in 1972. Approximately 7 warp threads per centimeter.)

100. See *Triumph of Charity*. (Description: about 4.50m high by 5.50m wide. Poor condition, many faulty restorations, borders rewoven in places, inscriptions missing completely or partially; the one on top is that of *Charity*. Approximately 7 warp threads per centimeter. No marks,

the lower guard being new.)

101. Same characteristics as *Triumph of Charity*. *The Triumph of Fortitude* was published under the title "Alexander's Story" (!) in the catalogue *Carlos V y su ambiente . . .* (no. 672, p. 262). (Description: 4.52m high by 5.60m wide. Very poor condition. Approximately 6 warp threads per centimeter. Brussels mark in the lower left-hand border.)

102. It is located there with *The Triumph of Justice* and seems to have met the same fate (n. 84): Inv. 1957.126. See also *The Triumph of Prudence* in The Fine Arts Museums of San Francisco (our n. 65). (Description: 4.40m high by 5.56m wide.). Rather poor condition but few repairs; shortened slightly on top under the border: cut and sewn again. Approximately 7–8 warp threads per centimeter. Marks in the lower border: left, a shield between two B's, right ⊞ .

103. M. de Soler, Sir Ronald Storrs, and Lady Storrs Collections. Offered by the Martins Bank to the Walker Art Gallery in 1953. Summary description found in *Loan Exhibition, Selected Acquisitions of the Walker Art Gallery, Liverpool, 1945–1955*, [catalogue by Ralph Fastnedge], p. 39. According to Edward Morris, Keeper of Foreign Art, who is entitled to my gratitude, this tapestry may come from Spain. A note from the museum's files would indicate, without other details, that it "or another version of it, was listed in the inventory of Don Berenguer Torres y Aguilar." (Description: 4.11m high by 5.33m wide. Poor condition. Cleaning at the Victoria and Albert Museum in 1961. Approximately 8 warp threads per centimeter. No marks.)

104. Vol. 7, no. 28, trans. E. Littré (Paris: J.J. Dubochet, Le Chevalier & Co, 1848); vol. 1, p. 295. He is called there "Siccius," but "Sicinius" is the usual form of the family name. On the authority of Varron (116–27 B.C.) Valerius Maximus had already reported in chap. 2 of bk. III (Rom. 24, I, 222), the fabulous deeds of this Dentatus, different from the M. Curius Dentatus whom he mentions in bks. IV (iii, Rom. 5) and VI (iii, Rom. 4): ibid. I, pp. 320–323, and II, pp. 32–35. Calberg also identifies with this "Roman Achilles" the Dentatus burdened with lances and crowns who rides one of the *Fortitude*'s lions, next to Sinope, in the Brussels tapestry of the mid-sixteenth century which she studied (p. 21).

105. E. Standen (p. 146 and p. 147, fig. 12). Inscription: *Quamvis innumeras Curius devicerat Urbes / Munera despexit. Gloria sola satis.*

106. Moreover Standen has remarked on the divorce between the representation and the story of Curius Dentatus:

The designer of the tapestry had clearly not the slightest knowledge of the story he was to illustrate beyond the fact that a victorious hero was to be shown refusing rich gifts. It seems unlikely that he even understood the Latin; the lances held by Curius, some broken, may represent the enemies he had conquered, but they are hardly appropriate symbols for cities, and the Samnite delegation would scarcely have included women. The same error is perpetuated in a tapestry from the old Fflouke collection, dealing exclusively with Dentatus, and largely inspired by the scene from *The Twelve Ages of Man*, but it is of a somewhat later date. The inscription is the same as the one in New York. It therefore cites Curius (see n. 105), while the warrior who grasps a sheaf of lances and to whom women and men respectfully offer piles of crowns is evidently Sicinius (*The Ffoulke Collection . . .* , p. 44 and pl.).

107. Asselberghs (no. 14, p. 23 and pl. 14). My gratitude to Mr. Pierre Quarré, Chief Curator of the Dijon Museums, who checked the details of this study and forwarded photographs. We can see, by inverse example, how the mistake could occur. The *Anthologia* already quoted devotes a few lines to Dentatus:

Quid iuvat imperio populos rexisse potenti,
Fulvaque Mygdoniis ornasse palatia gemmis ?
Quamquam civis inops, toto notissimus orbe
Hic fuit, egregio domuit qui Marte Sabinos
Fregerit ipse licet fulgentis robora Pyrrhi,
Pauperiem lato Samnitum praetulit auro.

(Reise, no. 837, fasc. II, p. 303, where the hero is mistakenly called "Denatus.") So we deal here with Manius Curius. But on p. 189 of the *Annotationes*, Burman-Meyer edition, which reads on the fifth line "ingentis" instead of "fulgentis" (no. 716, p. 235), it is stated: "*Inscribitur Marcus Curius Dentatus, sed legendum est Manius Curius Dentatus. In ms. goth. Cirenius pro Curius est.*" From "Cirenius" to "Sicinius" it is but a step in Gothic script. If we add an error in the first name (it was generally shortened), just as in the manuscript of the *Anthologia* Curius was close to being called Cicinius, in the same fashion the author of the set of *The Twelve Ages of Man* may have had in his hands a text in which the name of the Dentatus who received so many lances, necklaces, bracelets, and crowns, L. Siccius or Sicinius, had been corrupted; he would have called him "Curius" in error. What is curious is to see the error corrected on the mediocre Dijon version.

108. P. 21 and fig. 6. Identification according to Grimal, p. 424.

109. Some have been briefly identified by Jules Guiffrey relevant to the tapestries of the *Valiant Women* owned by Charles VI: "Inventaire des Tapisseries du Roi Charles VI vendues par les Anglais en 1422," *Bibliothèque de l'École des Chartes* 48 (1887): 90–91 and 93. The series of mural paintings in the castle of La Manta in Piedmont, however, is well known. See also details in Wyss's article on the *Valiant Men*.

110. Österreichische Nationalbibliothek, Cod. 2577–2578. Bibliography in the recent catalogue by Otto Pächt and Dagmar Thoss, *Französische Schule I* (Vienna: Österreichische Akademie der Wissenschaften, 1974), p. 79. Also see Marcel Lecourt's "Notice sur *L'Histoire des Neuf preux et des Neuf Preues . . .*, de Sébastien Mamerot," *Romania* 37, (1908): 529–37; and Antoine Thomas, "Note biographiques et bibliographiques sur Sébastien Mamerot," ibid, pp. 537–39. The story of Sinope

fills folios 239 v⁰-242 v⁰ of Cod. 2578. Dr. Otto Mazal, Director of the Manuscripts Cabinet, was kind enough to send me reproductions.

111. Paris: Bibl. Nat., French manuscript 12559, fol. 124. Sinope is represented on fol. 125 v⁰, with the other *Valiant Women*, in a blue houppelande lined with white, with gloves and a white banner, a crown, and a shield de *gueules à trois têtes couronnées, 2 and 1*.

112. *Justice*. On Phineas, see the dictionaries quoted, by Verger, p. 399; by Chompré, p. 214; and by Grimal, pp. 369–70.

113. See also the Book of Joshua 22:30–32 and 24:33. The Liverpool piece shows PHNEES, error corrected in the later editions.

114. Calberg saw the nine *Valiant Men* in the corresponding group of the *Christian Virtues* (p. 22), but in addition to Joshua there are two more in the rest of the tapestry (Alexander and David), and the crowds who follow the carriage are anonymous in the other *Triumphs*.

115. Joshua is usually a prefiguration of the Messiah, the capture of Jericho that of the Last Judgment, the introduction of the Hebrews into the Promised Land that of the leading of men into Heaven by Jesus (Réau, t. 2, vol. 1, pp. 219–27).

116. He is also celebrated in the *Anthologia veterum latinorum Epigrammatum et Poematum* (Burman-Meyer edition, nos. 701–3, p. 232; Reise edition, no 862, fasc. ii, p. 313).

117. It is for her strength that she is generally praised. The Middle Ages saw in her a prefiguration of the Virgin victorious over Satan. The *Speculum humanae salvationis* associates her with Jael and Thomyris immersing Cyrus' head in blood (see below, note 122). She was also a symbol of chastity and humility (Réau, t. 2, vol. 1, 329–35).

118. She figures also in *La Nef des Dames . . .* (Champier, fol. e Iv⁰-e II) and, especially, in Valerius Maximus (III, ii, Rom. 2, I, 202–03) and so do the following: Horatius Cocles (III, ii, Rom. 1, and IV, vii, Rom. 2, I, 200–201 and 364–65), Mucius Scaevola (III, iii, Rom. 1, I, 230–33) and Caesius Scaeva (III, ii, Rom. 23, I, 218–23).

119. A poem is dedicated to him in the *Anthologia latina* (Burman-Meyer edition, no. 712, p. 234; Reise edition, no. 155, fasc. i, p. 146).

120. He too survives in the *Anthologia . . .* (Burman-Meyer edition, no. 729, p. 238; Reise edition, no. 844, fasc. ii, p. 305):

Igne calens belli mediaque in caede cruentus,
Pompeiana phalanx patulis exire ruinis
Dum furit, et properat claustrorum frangere turres,
Scaeva ego Caesarei defendi culmina valli.
Dum timet Oceanus praeclari Caesaris arma,
Textum pampineae gessi sublime coronae.

One cannot indeed accept the identification proposed by Calberg for the SCENA of the *Christian Virtues* who also falls "his flanks pierced with two arrows, a lance, and a sword. . . . The hero in question is the invincible Caeneus of Greek mythology, who, under the name of Caenis, was first a woman, daughter of the Lapithe Elatos.

Loved by Poseidon, she obtained from the god her metamorphosis into an invulnerable man. He participated brilliantly in the struggle against the Centaurs who, unable to kill him, buried him alive under trees" (p. 22). To the episode of the fort, Valerius Maximus (see above n. 118) adds one occurring at the time of Caesar's conquest of Great Britain. Scaeva, who had reached by raft a rock near an island occupied by the Barbarians, was attacked at ebb tide; he pushed them back, but, stabbed through and through, he escaped by swimming and begged Caesar's pardon. Caesar made him a centurion!

121. Except on the Chenonceaux piece, where a bad restoration had the word HESILEA woven, the form PENTHESIEEA is to be found everywhere, which shows that the replacement of the "L" by an "E" is an error not of the weaver but of the painter and that, once more, all the suites were woven from the same cartoons. Penthesilea figures also in Boccaccio's *De mulieribus claris* (chap. xxxii), in the *Anthologia* . . . (Burman-Meyer edition, no. 705, p. 233; Reise edition, no. 861, fasc. I, p. 313), and among "La Fleur des Dames" in the first volume of *La Nef des Dames Vertueuses* by S. Champier (fol. c, iiii). She is represented on a famous "millefleurs" of the end of the fifteenth century, kept in the Angers castle. She was also present in the ninth and tenth pieces of the great *Story of Troy*, woven several times in the last third of the fifteenth century [See Jean-Paul Asselberghs, "Charles VIII's Trojan War Tapestry," in *Victoria and Albert Museum Yearbook* (1969), pp. 80–84; and "Les Tapisseries Tournaisiennes de la Guerre de Troie," in *Artes belgicae* (Brussels: Musées Royaux d'Art et d'Histoire, 1972), pp. 5–94; G. Souchal's *Catalog*, nos. 7–10, pp. 46–60; nos. 7–11, American edition.]

122. Where she is represented with Sinope, Penthesilea, and the other *Valiant Women* (fol. 125 v⁰). Yet she is called "Tameramis" in the text where she addresses herself to Cyrus after having put "his head in a heap of blood and said: 'Now drink plenty / Of the blood you were never tired of!'" (fol. 124 v⁰).

123. Guiffrey (pp. 90 and 411). On the *Valiant Men*, see G. Souchal's *Catalog*, nos. 3–4, pp. 39–43; same nos. in American edition.

124. Vienna, Nationalbibliothek, Cod. 2578, fol. 260–68.

125. Fol. c, iiii and v⁰.

126. She is also called "Tomyris" in the Burman-Meyer edition of the *Anthologia* (no. 699, p. 232), but "Tamyris" in the Reise edition (no. 859, fasc. ii, p. 312). Cyrus is extolled in the preceding number (Burman-Meyer, no. 698, p. 232; Reise, no. 858, fasc. II, p. 312). Valerius Maximus speaks of Thomyris in chap. x of vol. IX (Foreign I, in II, 338–39) and Boccaccio in chap. xlix of his *De mulieribus claris*.

127. The tragic end of the athlete, torn by wild beasts when he could not free himself from the crack he had tried to enlarge in a tree, is also narrated by Valerius Maximus (IX, xii, Foreign 9, in II, 358–61), and utilized again by Vincent de Beauvais (II, cxii, 83b).

128. Jael is also mentioned by Vincent de Beauvais (II, 1vii, 65b). As in the case of Medusa it is interesting to see how this story is transformed in *La Nef des Dames Vertueuses* (fol. f ii):

Of our flowers we must not deprive Jael, wife of Abner Caeneus. By her wisdom and prudence, she kept her house in tranquillity and in the grace of Jabin, king of Asur. So when Sisera, prince of the army of Jabin, king of Asur, was driven away by Barak, she left her house and came to him, saying: "Enter with me, my good Lord, and have no fear." And when he asked for water, she gave him milk. And she covered him with her cloak and stayed at the door of the tabernacle to see that nobody came to take him.

Was Anne de France's extoller fearful of shocking the austere princess by going further into the story? Or was it that Jael's action seemed to him more blameworthy than commendable? Less well known than Judith, Jael is also a symbol of the Virgin victorious over Satan (Réau, t. II, vol. I, 327–28).

129. According to Réau (p. 270), this "caprice" of David evokes the temptation over which Jesus triumphs; it was popularized by the *Speculum humanae salvationis* as prefiguring the offerings of the Magi to Jesus.

130. We find this form in both cases; is it an error for MODERATIO or has the scribe ventured a MODERANTIA whose tilde of abbreviation was omitted?

131. He figures in the poem no. 573 dedicated to Bacchus in the *Anthologia* . . . (Burman-Meyer edition, p. 204): "Huc ades Lyaee, Bassareu, bicornis / Nycteli, bimater, crine nitidus . . . ."

132. Here is the case: Faith arrives facing front in a chariot drawn by the symbols of the four Evangelists. She is accompanied by Abraham and Isaac, possibly by Judas Maccabaeus, and by Saint Peter. The background scenes represent the passage through the Red Sea and Charlemagne's discovery of Roland and Oliver's bodies. The only differences are that Virtue holds a book and a blossoming palm, and Paul the Apostle accompanies Saint Peter. Hope arrives from the left, a sickle in hand, a phoenix in front, on a vessel (but with wheels) towed by two men in chains, as we find here. David with his harp and Esther and Mordecai are kneeling on the left; the stories of Jonas and Gideon's Fleece are represented in the background. In the *Charity* piece Virtue comes from the right, followed by a throng. She raises her hand to the sun, holds also a heart, and is escorted by a pelican. The horses that draw her chariot are ridden by Esther and Judas Maccabaeus and they trample on two men, one of whom only is named, but he is Nero. Isaac's sacrifice is also represented on the upper left-hand side. Prudence, coming from the left with staff and mirror, a crane at her feet, is pulled by two dragons ridden by a woman and by Carneades. In the upper right-hand corner Pallas Athena presents a shield to a warrior whom

Calberg could not identify but who is now specified as Perseus. In *Justice* Virtue, preceded by a crane, holds in the same way a sword and a scale, while holding out her right arm towards another sword. Her chariot, arriving from the right, is drawn by two unicorns straddled by a couple, Sarah and Joseph, and it runs over Marius (and not Nero, see n. 91). It is followed by a group that includes Fabricius. In the foreground appears Scipio and the episode of Trajan's Justice, while in the back Noah's ark alone escapes the Flood. Fortitude, finally, comes also from the right, with column, dragon, and eagle, in a chariot pulled by lions, guided by Sinope and Dentatus, and followed by a troup including Joshua. Scaeva (and not Caeneus, see n. 120) falls down in the foreground, while in back Eleazar strikes an elephant and Judith gets ready to decapitate Holophernes (per Calberg). This hanging contains one piece more than ours—not counting *Temperance*, of course—for the figure of a young girl, "personification of all the Virtues melted into one to realize Christian perfection," precedes the others (Calberg, pp. 5–6 and p. 4, fig. 1).

133. Ibid., pp. 25–29 and fig. 8.

134. According to Brunet Latin, for example:

. . . the nature of the elephant is such that the female, before she is thirteen, and the male before fifteen, are ignorant of lust. And so they are so chaste that between them there are no quarrels over females, because every one has his own, for whom the male cares every day of his life . . . . And because lust is not compelling them in such a way that they know each other as do the other beasts, it occurs by guidance of Nature that the couple go towards the East near the Garden of Eden, until the female finds an herb called mandrake; and she eats some and entices her male to eat some also, now they become so enflamed that they make love and engender one child only, and this happens once in their lifetime. . . . ("Le Livre du Trésor," in *Jeux et Sapience du Moyen âge*, Paris: Gallimard, Bibl. de la Pléiade, 1951), p. 817.)

135. He does not seem to have used the *exempla*, those anecdotes or short stories, fables or parables, morality plays or descriptions "used for supporting doctrinal, religious, or moral exposés," of which the Middle Ages made such great use, but "definitely waning in the fifteenth century." This decline was due to lack of renovation, abusive usage of the profane *exemplum*, and opposition from the humanists and the Church councils alike (in the second half of the fifteenth century and in the sixteenth century) to utilization in the pulpit of these fabulous and apocryphal tales (J. Th. Welter, *L'Exemplum dans la littérature religieuse et didactique du Moyen Age* (Paris/Toulouse: E. H. Guitard, 1927), index and pp. 1, 377, and 449–51). Moreover our hanging reflects a loftier biblical and classical culture. Its inspiration is rather comparable to that of the short Latin poems (some have been mentioned above), devoted to ancient heroes, not written before the fifteenth century (see n. 93), which indicate the same knowledge of the pagan world.

136. Valencia de Don Juan, nos. 20–22.

137. Pp. 342–45.

138. Notably pp. 163–65.

139. Acquired in 1958 (inv. 46/129 and 46/130). Former Prince d'Arenberg collection. See J. K. Steppe, "Vlaams Tapijtwerk van de 16.eeuw in Spaans Koninklijk bezit," *Miscellanea Josef Duverger, Bijdragen tot de Kunstgeschiedenis der Nederlanden* 2 (1968): 719–65; and *Carpets and Tapestries from the Burrell collection, June 23rd–August 16th, 1969, Glasgow Art Gallery and Museum, Kelvingrove*, typewritten catalogue, nos. 144–45, p. 15. I wish to thank W. Wells, Curator of the Burrell collection, who kindly forwarded photographs of these works.

140. Stemper, pp. 68–95.

141. Mâle, II, i, 295–346, fig.

142. G. Souchal, "Les Paños de Oro . . .," pp. 139, 145–46, and 151.

143. G. Souchal, *Catalogue*, nos. 87–88, pp. 208–13, fig. (nos. 92/93 of the American edition.)

144. Philippe Verdier, "The Tapestry of the Prodigal Son," *The Journal of the Walters Art Gallery* 18 (Baltimore: 1955): 9–58, fig.

145. Sold 25 March 1972 by the Cranbrook Academy of Art of Bloomfield Hills (Michigan), Sotheby, Parke-Bernet in New York, sale 3336, no. 201, color pl.

146. Inv. 25.177.3. See J. B[reck], "A Loan of Tapestries," *Metropolitan Museum of Art Bulletin* 17 (March 1922): 58; (January 1926), 21.

147. A. Coulin Weibel and F. Waring Robinson, *Four Late Gothic Flemish Tapestries of Virtues and Vices, from the Collection of William Randolph Hearst, Given by the Hearst Foundation to the Detroit Institute of Arts, 1955*, no. d., no. p., fig.

148. "A Gothic Tapestry Based on a Morality Play," *The Connoisseur*, April 1937, pp. 212–13, fig.; and "A Gothic Tapestry Based on the Moralities," *Bulletin of the Minneapolis Institute of Arts* 31 (3 October 1942): 84–89, 5 figs.

149. *Catalogue.*, pp. 272–73.

150. Göbel, t. I, vol. II, pl. 92. Let us mention the beautiful *Prudence* of a later date, but apparently unknown, of the University of Virginia, Charlottesville, Va.

151. Mâle, 278–91.

152. H. C. Marillier, *The Tapestries at Hampton Court Palace* (London: H. M.'s Stationery Office, 1962), pp. 20–23, pl. 15–17. C. Nordenfalk, "Queen Christina's Roman collection of Tapestries," *Queen Christina of Sweden, Documents and Studies* no. 12 (Stockholm: Nationalmuseum, Nationalmusei Skriftserie, 1966), pp. 266–95.

153. Bibliography in Elizabeth Scheicher, "Die Trionfi. Eine Tapisserienfolge des kunsthistorischen Museums in Wien," extract from *Jahrbuch des kunsthistorischen Sammlungen in Wien* 67 (1971: 7–46, 39 figs.

154. And we have seen that elephants probably guided our Temperance, just as in Petrarch's *Triumph of Fame*.

155. Cetto, pp. 42–44 and fig. 14.

156. D'Hulst, no. 23, pp. 203–12, fig.

157. Photograph in the portfolios of the Arts Décoratifs, no. 294, 10. In the center, Fortitude, hold-

ing column and dragon, is drawn in a chariot by two lions, one of which is mounted by a woman, behind whom a knight holds a banner. Standing on the left Alexander is apparently showing to Penthesilea the group formed in the lower right-hand corner by Jael killing Sisera. Above on the left Judith brandishes her sword at Holofernes, while on the right a soldier climbs a ladder leaning against a tower defended by another warrior. The border is of laurel stems, punctuated by decorative motifs alternating with bunches of fruit and flowers.

158. Calberg, pp. 31–36. On the *Virtues* from the National Austrian collections, see L. Baldass, *Die Wiener Gobelinsammlung* (Vienna: Hölzel, 1920), fasc. iii, nos and pl. 46–52.

159. Where we can cite the presence, in *Faith*, of Abraham, Isaac, and David with Goliath; in *Charity*, that of David, and Saint Elizabeth washing the feet of a pauper; in *Fortitude*, of Jael killing Sisera, and Judith beheading Holofernes. The front of *Hope*'s chariot is in the shape of a prow, where a phoenix raises its head.

160. Two pieces are kept in the Palazzo Doria in Rome (*January* and *February*), two at The Art Institute of Chicago (*February* and *July*), one in the collection of Dumbarton Oaks in Washington (*April*), one at the Rijksmuseum in Amsterdam (another *April*), two at The Metropolitan Museum of Art in New York (*August* and *October*), one at the Minneapolis Institute of Arts (*September*). Göbel has published the month of *July* found in the Seligmann collection (pl. 146, and I, 166). An *April* was sold a few years ago at Dario Boccara's; the latter reproduced it in his *Belles Heures de la Tapisserie* (Milan: Les Clefs du Temps, 1971), p. 61 (bibliography, p. 225). The presumed date of this hanging is 1525–28.

161. Standen, p. 167.

162. G. Souchal, *Catalogue*, nos.73–75 and 82–86 (78–80, 87–91, and 94–97 in the American edition.) See also n. 46.

163. M. Crick-Kuntziger, *La Tenture de l'Histoire de Jacob, d'après Bernard van Orley* (Anvers: Lloyd anversois, 1954), 47 pp., 32 pl., and D'Hulst, no. 21.

164. Henri-Victor Michelant, "Inventaire des vaisselles, joyaux, tapisseries, peintures, livres et manuscrits de Marguerite d'Autriche, régente et gouvernante des Pays-Bas (1523)," extract from *Bulletins de la Commission royale de Belgique*, 3d ser. 12 (Brussels: F. Hayez, 1870): nos. 1–2. See also Paul Saintenoy, "Le Palais des ducs de Bourgogne sur le Coudenberg à Bruxelles du règne d'Antoine de Bourgogne à celui de Charles-Quint," *Les Arts et Les Artistes à la Cour de Bruxelles* 2 (Brussels: Palais des Académies, 1934), pp. 166–68 ("Les Tapisseries du Palais sous Marguerite d'Autriche"). For the tapestries brought back from Spain by Marguerite after the death of her husband, Don Juan, see Rudolph Beer, "Acten, Regesten und Inventare aus dem Archivo general zu Simancas," *Jahrbuch der Kunsthistorischen Sammlungen des allerhöchsten Kaiserhauses . . . 12,*

pt. 2 (Vienna, 1891), p. cxviii; text republished by Jose Ferrandis, "Inventarios Reales (Juan II a Juana la Loca)," *Datos documentos inéditos para la historia del Arte Español* 3 (Madrid: Graficas Uguina, 1943), document V, pp. 48–49, and document IV, pp. 26–27. In 1543 the tapestries of the court of Brussels were to be repaired, among them, *The Seven Virtues*, *The Seven Vices*, and *The Seven Ages* (Paul Saintenoy, "Les Tapisseries de la Cour de Bruxelles sous Charles V," extract from the *Annales de la Société royale d'archéologie de Bruxelles* 30 (Wetteren: J. de Meester, 1921):7). But in all likelihood it is not question here of our hanging, which is probably the one appearing again in the 1598 inventory, No. 7: "a large tapestry for drawing-room, also with gold, of *The Seven Virtues and Seven Vices*, measuring 6½ aulnes high and 14 aulnes wide (p. 23)."

165. Also, another of medium size, covered with blue velvet, with gold nails, which is called *Book of the Three Virtues to teach Ladies and Maidens* [from Christine de Pisan's *Livre des Trois Vertus à l'Enseignement des Dames et Damoiselles*];
also, another of medium size, covered with black velvet, which is called the *Rosary of the Virtues*; also, another large, covered with blue velvet, with gold nails, which is called *Book of Virtues*; also, another of medium size, covered with blue velvet, with gold nails, which is called *Table of Rubrics in the Book of the Three Virtues* [from Christine de Pisan's *Cy commance la table des rubriches du Livre des Trois Vertus*];also, another large, which is called the *Treatise of the Vices and Virtues*; also, another small, which is called *The Life of the Fathers, The Debate of Body and Soul, The Doctrinal to Simple People containing the Truth of the Virtues* (Michelant, pp. 37, 41, 42, 45, and 46).

166. Sophie Schneebalg-Perelman, "Richesses du Garde-Meuble parisien de François Ier, Inventaires inédits de 1542 et 1551," *Gazette des Beaux-Arts*, November 1971, pp. 253–304, esp. 264 and n. 36.

167. W. G. Thomson, *A History of Tapestry from the earliest Times until the present Day* (London: Hodder & Stoughton, 1930, 2nd ed.), p. 248 (for the *Triumphs*, see also pp. 249, 253, and 259). Could it be that one of the pieces with the repeated design border comes from Henry VIII?

168. Seven warp threads per centimeter at Cluny and Edinburgh, 8 at Liverpool; but it is well known that the difference can easily be two threads, depending on where the measurement is made. For the piece in Moscow, no information.

169. In the *Prudence* of Edinburgh, for instance, where borders have been transferred and restored, the upper part of the sky is missing, thus cutting off the upper part of Pallas; under the upper border of *Fortitude* in Liverpool, a woven band, which exists in other versions, is also missing.

170. In the same way, Rachel's name is missing in the *Prudence* of Edinburgh, which is seen in subsequent series.

171. This border of *Prudence* belongs in reality, as has been said, to *Temperance*.

172. Göbel (t. I, vol. I, pl. 4 for the marks) gives indeed $\overline{X}$ as the mark of the Brussels tapestry maker Leo van den Hecke, but about 1575; it is then difficult to attribute it to this weaver, who in any case had two other marks.

173. Pp. 29-30.

174. He was wondering if it were not a merchant's mark (t. I, vol. I, pl. 7).

175. Evidence of this is found for the tapestries offered by the city of Tournai to Jean de Daillon, Lord of Le Lude, shortly before his death circa 1481 (see G. Souchal, *Catalogue*, no. 44, pp. 122-124; no. 47 of the American edition). Further proof: many Brussels sets carry two different marks—for instance, *The Acts of the Apostles* of the Patrimonio Nacional in Madrid (D'Hulst, no. 16, p. 136), *The Apocalypsis* and *The Seven Deadly Sins* in the same collection (ibid., no. 19, p. 168, and no. 23, p. 212), or again *The Months with Grotesques* at the Kunsthistorisches, Museum in Vienna (ibid., no. 27, p. 244). The eighteen pieces of the magnificent biblical series of the Wawel Castle in Cracovia are "the collective work of six Brussels ateliers" (S. Schneebalg-Perelman, "La Tapisserie flamande et le grand témoignage du Wawel," *Les Tapisseries flamandes au château du Wawel à Cracovie. Trésors du roi Sigismond II Auguste Jagellon*, ed. by Jerzy Szablowski (Anvers: Mercator, 1972), p. 416.

176. We saw that the San Francisco *Prudence* has an origin different from that of the *Justice* or *Fortitude* from that city, at least judging from the little known of it.

177. The Pittsburgh *Hope* and the San Francisco *Prudence* could also come from the Toledo series, although the *Charity* and *Fortitude* of that city are in much poorer condition. But the absence of an atelier mark on the latter pieces deprives us of the frail clue that would permit us to match, for possible reconstitution of the original series, the two American tapestries with those in Chenonceaux. Finally, the Pittsburgh *Hope* which was in Hearst's collection, as were the *Justice* and *Fortitude* of San Francisco, may have belonged to the same hanging as these two latter, in spite of the fact that they bear a different atelier mark; yet the fact that they were given to different museums is evidence in favor of diverse origins (even if the three come from Spain, where we know the Brussels tapestries were imported in great numbers).

178. Recent bibliography mentioned earlier in regard to Penthesilea in our n. 121, *Fortitude*.

APPENDIX   *POSSIBLE GROUPINGS OF PIECES WITH CONTINUOUS VEGETAL BORDERS*

ASHEVILLE	FAITH / CHARITY / PRUDENCE	PITTSBURGH:	HOPE	TOLEDO	CHARITY / FORTITUDE
CHENONCEAUX	CHARITY / FORTITUDE / PRUDENCE	SAN FRANCISCO			
SAN FRANCISCO	JUSTICE / FORTITUDE				

... or should Pittsburgh *Hope* be placed with the San Francisco pieces? ...

THE TRIUMPH OF THE SEVEN VIRTUES AND RELATED BRUSSELS TAPESTRIES OF THE EARLY RENAISSANCE

Guy Delmarcel

Several museums throughout the world still today preserve isolated pieces of a tapestry series illustrating *The Triumph of the Seven Virtues*. At least five editions were woven in Brussels around 1535, and three of these Triumphs—those of *Prudence, Justice*, and *Fortitude*—now belong to the collections of The Fine Arts Museums in San Francisco.[1]

These pieces, and those representing the other cardinal and theological virtues, are worked out as allegorical processions. The female personification of each virtue is seated on a chariot, carried by different animals through crowds of various people— worshippers or examples of the represented virtue. These exemplary figures, identified by their actions or by their woven names, are borrowed from many literary sources (see in this volume Geneviève Souchal's analysis of these numerous and sometimes complicated *exempla* as well as of the several editions of the series).

At first sight, the composition of these tapestries is rather confused. The several exemplary figures shown around the personified virtues seem to be acting in their own way, and the design of the whole seems to lack coherence. Nevertheless, all these figures are acting in the spirit of the celebrated virtue, and the internal relationship between them is not established so much by the design or by their formal location in the woven picture as by the intellectual links provided by common literary sources, such as the Bible and books of ancient history and mythology.

A fine example of this iconographic relationship between the figures is provided by *The Triumph of Fortitide*. Arranged in front of the personified virtue, who is clasping a column in her right hand, are several Roman warriors—Dentatus, holding a sheaf of spears; the girl Cloelia, crossing the water on horseback; Cocles swimming beside her; Mucius Scaevola, holding his right hand in the fire; and Scaeva, kneeling at his left. All these figures, though apparently very dispersed and independently composed, are in fact closely related, because their acts are described in the chapter devoted to examples of Roman fortitude in Valerius Maximus' *Facta et dicta memorabilia*.[2]

This literary and scholarly character of the set links up with a tradition already existing in tapestry. Many figures, even entire groups of *The Triumph of the Seven Virtues*, can be found on at least four contemporary or slightly older Brussels tapestry series. Two of them, belonging today to the Spanish royal collection, were created by the same generation of scholars and artists that invented the *Triumphs*. They may be considered as important iconographic forerunners of the pieces discussed here. The largest set consists of nine tapestries called *Los Honores* ("The Rewards of Honor"). They were most likely designed for the young emperor Charles V in 1520, the year of his coronation, and delivered to him in Seville in 1526.[3] The other set, consisting of only three tapestries, is called *Las Moralidades* ("The Moralities"), or sometimes *Los caminos de los Honores* ("The Ways Leading to Honor"). Belonging stylistically to the same period as *Los Honores*, or *The Honors*, they became part of the Spanish royal collection at an unknown date.[4] Both tapestry series were conceived as being instruments of secular and dynastic morality, for teaching rulers how to live and act correctly. They are therefore mainly devoted to the seven principal virtues—the four cardinal (Prudence, Temperance, Fortitude, and Justice) and the three theological (Faith, Hope, and Charity)—just as happens in the set discussed here.

The literary compilers and the artistic designers of the *Triumph* tapestries made several borrowings, mainly from these two sets and also from two other tapestries. The figures copied on these weavings can be divided into three categories: (1) a figure can be adapted both in its form (design) and in its sense (iconography); (2) it can be copied for its design but changed in its iconographic function; (3) it can be taken for its name only but designed in a different way, thus preserving only its iconographic meaning. Some examples taken from three weavings of the *Triumph* set—those of *Prudence* (San Francisco), *Faith*, and *Charity* (Asheville, Biltmore House and Gardens)—may illustrate these three types of adaptation.

In the *Triumph of Prudence* (Fig. 1) the personification of Wisdom is carried in a chariot going from left to right. The snake and the mirror, Wisdom's common attributes, can also be found in two *Honors* tapestries and in the middle piece of *The Moralities*.[5] Three mythological scenes fill the upper corners and the lower left—Prometheus stealing the fire from heaven, Perseus receiving the

156

Fig. 1. *Triumph of Prudence*. The Fine Arts Museums of San Francisco. Gift of the Crocker Family to the M.H. de Young Memorial Museum, 62.19.3.

shield from Athena, and Cadmus slaying the dragon. These episodes from classical mythology could have been derived from the tapestry makers' most common source, the *Ovid Moralized*, but in this case we believe they relied upon the handbook of mythology most widely used from the fourteenth-century on, Boccaccio's *Genealogy of the Gods*. All three scenes illustrate an activity related to Prudence or Wisdom (Sapientia). The goddess Pallas Athena, helping both Prometheus and Perseus, is clearly delineated by Boccaccio as being an outstanding personification of Wisdom. The Cadmus story is included here because of the dragon, also considered by Boccaccio as being a symbol of Prudence in this case.[6]

Moreover, the two upper groups are borrowed from contemporary weavings, where they were explicitly used in the same iconographic sense. Prometheus stealing the fire with Pallas' help is already represented in the upper right corner of the third *Honors* tapestry, devoted to *Sapientia divina*, Heavenly Wisdom (Fig. 3).[7] Taking the fire

from the Lion, the zodiacal sign of the sun, he acts here as a symbol of mankind, trying to find wisdom by himself. The design of this group is much more detailed and refined on the *Honors* tapestry, while the rather stiff and clumsy representation on the *Prudence* piece of the *Triumph* clearly indicates it is a copy or at least a derivative composition.

This is also true for the episode of Pallas Athena giving a shield and a weapon to Perseus, represented in full detail on an older Brussels tapestry belonging to a set with the *Story of Perseus* (Fig. 4).[8] In this piece Athena hands a sword and shield over to the hero, who afterwards, in the upper right corner, kills Medusa, while from Medusa's blood the flying horse Pegasus is born. Athena's shield, considered by Boccaccio as a symbol of wisdom, is used as a mirror by Perseus in order to be able to look indirectly at Medusa and behead her without being transformed into stone. This donation of arms, both on the *Perseus* and the *Prudence* tapestry, was surely inspired from a miniature appearing in almost every manuscript of Christine de Pisan's

Epître d'Othéa à Hector (1401). Here Othéa, a variant name for Athena, is giving weapons to Hector and to his companions (Fig. 5).[9] It can be deduced from a later edition of *The Triumph of Prudence*, a very reduced variant woven around 1560, that this Athena-Hector scene was borrowed for the Athena-Perseus group on the two tapestries (Fig. 8).[10] Almost all the examples are omitted around Prudence's chariot, except for the upper right scene of Athena giving the shield to Perseus. It is remarkable that Athena is called here OTHEA, a peculiar form of her name used only by Christine de Pisan. This clearly proves that the visual model of this scene was provided by the illustrations in the French narration.

After these explicit borrowings of both design and iconography, numerous figures of the *Triumph* are closely related only by their design to examples shown in the *Honors* set. Compare, for example, Carneades, the warrior holding Prudence's banner in front of her chariot, and the standard-bearer Scipio in *The*

Apotheosis of the Seven Virtues, the fourth piece of the *Honors* series (Figs. 1 and 6).[11] Many similar cases can be indicated in *The Triumph of Faith* (Fig. 2). The beheaded body of Goliath, at the lower left, is almost identical to that of Holofernes in the *Honor* tapestry; the creeping Mahumetus is similar to the emperor Valerianus on the *Fortune* weaving; Julian the Apostate, lying dead with a fragment of a spear in his chest, appears in a similar attitude on both the *Honor* and *Infamy* tapestries.[12] The prophet Elijah flying in his chariot to heaven in the upper left corner of *Faith* can be related by his location and composition to Prudence driving to Divine Wisdom, the counterpart of the Prometheus group on the third *Honors* piece.[13]

A fine example of a whole group borrowed from an older piece mainly for its iconography can also be shown on the *Faith* tapestry. Beneath the statue of the New Law (*Novum Testamentum*) Pope Sylvester, the empress Helen, and the emperor Constantine are represented, followed by the emperor

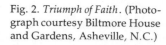

Fig. 2. *Triumph of Faith*. (Photograph courtesy Biltmore House and Gardens, Asheville, N.C.)

Theodosius and the saint King Louis of France (*Ludovicus*). This group was already introduced, although in a different design, in the left foreground of the allegory of *Glory and the Seven Virtues*, the central piece of the *Moralidades* set (Fig. 7).[14] Together with other Christian heroes, such as Godfrey of Bouillon and Charlemagne, they represent those who reach Honor by means of *virtus infusa*, the theological virtues given by God. On the *Faith* tapestry they fulfill an identical role and they emphasize the general idea of Christian faith placed under the sign of the cross. The holy cross, borne by Faith and also held by the New Testament, and repeated by Oliver bound on the hill in a cross shape, is also the main theme in the lives of several of these figures. The empress Helen was said to have found the True Cross, and her son Constantine acquired his victory over his rival thanks to this sign. The cross-bearing Pope Sylvester was said to have received the pontifical states from Constantine because he cured the emperor of leprosy.[15] According to the medieval *Golden Legend*, Constantine called him after having been ordered to do so in a dream by the Apostles Peter and Paul, also present in this group on the tapestry.[16] The slain Julian the Apostate, lying in the foreground, is an

example of a heretic opponent of the True Cross, as it is explained by the same *Golden Legend*.[17]

A last instance of these relations with other sets can be seen in *The Triumph of Charity*.[18] In the right foreground an emperor TIBERIVS and an empress PLACELLA are kneeling beside a treasure they have found under a marble slab. This group is borrowed from the last piece of the Brussels set of the *The Twelve Ages of Man*, woven before 1528 and now in The Metropolitan Museum of Art, New York. In her analysis of this set Edith A. Standen suggests that this scene should represent an episode from the life of the emperor Tiberius II (A.D. 578–582), as told by Gregory of Tours.[19] This emperor gave all his wealth to the poor, and so was rewarded with finding an even greater treasure under a marble slab in his palace's pavement; this gold allowed him even to increase his liberality, thus becoming a fine example of Christian charity. The wife of Tiberius II, however—not named on the New York tapestry—was called Anastasia. The Placella here represented is, in fact, the wife of the emperor Theodosius (represented on the *Faith* tapestry), and like Tiberius II she

Fig. 3. *Prometheus Stealing the Fire from Heaven*. Detail from the third tapestry of *The Honors* set. Patrimonio Nacional, La Granja de San Ildefonso, Spain. (Courtesy of the Patrimonio Nacional.)

Fig. 4. *Athena Giving Weapons to Perseus*. Brussels tapestry, around 1520. Actual location unknown.

Fig. 5. *Othéa Giving Weapons to Hector*. Miniature from Christine de Pisan, *Epître d'Othéa*. Flemish, around 1460. Brussels, Albert I Royal Library, ms. 9392, fol. 16 v° (Photograph courtesy Royal Library, Brussels.)

was also renowned for her great generosity toward the poor. Her original Latin name was Flacilla or Placilla, and her story is told by Gregory of Nyssa and is repeated in Vincent of Beauvais's enormous *Speculum historiale*.[20] Jacob van Maerlant translated large parts of this encyclopedia in Flemish, and on this occasion the name Flacilla was transformed into Placella.[21] Since Flemish was the language spoken in Brabant, where the tapestries were made, this name naturally appeared on them. The composers of the tapestries thus joined two parallel legends of imperial liberality— that of Theodosius's wife Flacilla/Placella (about A.D. 386) and that of Tiberius II (A.D. 578–582)—into one scene. This group is repeated in a later variant of the *Twelve Ages*, and Placella alone is shown as an example of liberality in the *Justice* tapestry of the *Honors*.[22]

From these few examples one may deduce that the *Triumph* set refers to models of composition and of iconography already present in some older series, each of them also related to the virtues and to allegories of exemplary life. There are, however, closer links between the *Triumph* tapestries and their related models; these refer to the manner in which they are composed and ordered.

Notice first that several virtues are riding in chariots going in different directions. *Faith* is moving from the background to the foreground (Fig. 2); *Prudence* (Fig. 1) and *Hope* (in her ship) are moving from left to right; *Charity*, *Justice*, and *Fortitude* are moving from right to left.[23] From the numerous editions of around 1535 no *Triumph of Temperance*, the missing cardinal virtue in this set of seven, is preserved. However, Mrs. Souchal points out that an inscription referring to a lost *Temperance* piece is now fixed on top of the *Prudence* in Asheville; and from the later, very reduced edition of around 1560 now in Brussels, we may deduce that Temperance's chariot initially drove from left to right (Fig. 9).[24] With these various movements in mind, we may look at this tapestry set not as a successive story, with a beginning and an end and from left to right, but rather as a converging to a central panel, that of *Faith*, from the left (*Prudence*, *Temperance*, and *Hope*) and from the right (*Justice*, *Fortitude*, and *Charity*).[25]

The exact location of each separate tapestry within the set can be determined in even more detail. From its frontal position we see that *Faith* is normally placed in the center. It thus becomes the focal point of the set, with

Fig. 6. *The Apotheosis of the Seven Virtues*, fourth tapestry of *The Honors* series. Patrimonio Nacional, La Granja de San Ildefonso. (Courtesy of the Patrimonio Nacional.)

three other virtues on each side. This position fits in with the peculiar value of Faith in medieval Christian ethics: Faith is the most important of all virtues; she leads and dominates the others.[26]

The next distinction to be established is that between the theological and the cardinal virtues. The theological virtues have priority over the others: they are immediately infused in mankind by God, given by divine right, whereas the cardinal virtues are acquired by man in a natural way.[27] Hope and Charity might therefore be grouped with Faith in the center of the set, and since each of these virtues is moving from a different direction it seems acceptable to place *Hope* at the left and *Charity* at the right, directing them toward *Faith*.

Even a proper place for the cardinal (or natural) virtues, more removed from *Faith* and her theological companions, can be suggested. From the two pieces preceding the central group, we can assert that *Prudence* (Fig. 1) was surely placed first, the virtue of Wisdom being considered by all ancient and medieval authors as the first and introductory one to the others, their *conditio sine qua non*.[28]

Temperance is then located between *Prudence* and *Hope*. It is harder to define a precise order for the last two tapestries, *Fortitude* and *Justice*. Because of her particular value as a royal virtue, perhaps *Justice* could have taken the last position, acting as an organ point and closing the set.[29]

Summarizing these compositional movements, we obtain the following scheme:

SCHEME 1. *Triumph of the Seven Virtues:*

Prudence Temperance Hope Faith Charity Justice Fortitude
Fortitude Justice

Based only on the composition of the procession and our knowledge of medieval ethics, this ideal reconstruction of the order of the *Triumphs* might remain purely hypothetical. We think, however, that this order may be seen to be even more practicable when it is compared to the sequence in *The Honors* and *The Moralities*.

Considering first the *Honors*, one may notice that the tapestry with the *Apotheosis of the Seven Virtues* (Fig. 6) celebrates in fact the same personifications as those who form the procession of the *Triumphs* set. On this weaving Faith is also located in the central axis and she is flanked by Hope and Charity, standing on pedestals next to her throne; Prudence and Temperance are located on the left of this central group, and Justice and Fortitude on the right. When we confront the sequence in the set of the seven *Triumph* tapestries with the location of these seven virtues on a single tapestry, belonging to a series that has apparently served as a model, the obvious spatial relationship between both cannot be denied:

SCHEME 2. *Triumph of the Seven Virtues:*

Prudence   Temperance   Hope   Faith   Charity   Justice   Fortitude
                                                       Fortitude Justice
$\rightarrow$ $\rightarrow$ $\rightarrow$ $\downarrow$ $\leftarrow$ $\leftarrow$ $\leftarrow$

Apotheosis (The Honors):
Prudence   Temperance   Hope   Faith   Charity   Justice   Fortitude
$\rightarrow$ $\rightarrow$ $\rightarrow$ $\downarrow$ $\rightarrow$ $\rightarrow$ $\rightarrow$

One gets the impression that the seven capital virtues, seated on their thrones and worshipped in their temple on the *Honors* piece, stepped down from their pedestals to mount their chariots and to move to each other, converging to *Faith*, the most essential of all virtues.

Since precise information is lacking as to who composed both sets and who ordered the first edition of the *Triumphs*, the internal order of the *Triumphs* cannot be deduced from the *Apotheosis* tapestry in a conclusive way. However, the parallel is evident and this is even confirmed when the *Honors* set is examined as a whole. One main conclusion in our research about this great "woven morality," is precisely the fact that the entire *Honors* series was also conceived as being a converging and not to be read as successive tapestries.[30] In this set of nine weavings the fifth and central piece is that of *Honor*, the most coveted reward of every ruler. Staircases at the right border of the *Apotheosis of the Seven Virtues* (Fig. 6), the fourth piece, and at the left of the sixth, representing the *Temple of Fame*, lead to the central theater stage of *Honor*.[31] The first half of the set is further devoted to the virtues the ruler should practice in his private life. It opens with the dynastic image of Fortune, afterwards overcome by the seven virtues. The second half relates to the ruler's public behavior, ending in the procession of Infamy, opposed to Honor and Fame.

Such a convergence to a central moral theme, climax of a whole allegorical set, can also be found in the smaller series of *The Moralities*. The three tapestries of this set can be perceived as a woven triptych. The central piece illustrates the apotheosis of *Glory and the Seven Virtues* (Fig. 7). The crowned personification of Glory, bearing a sword and a golden globe, sits on a throne under a canopy in the center of the theater stage; she is represented according to the description of Fame or Worldly Glory *(fama e gloria mundana)* in Boccaccio's *Amorosa Visione*.[32] Glory is surrounded by the three theological virtues on the left and by the cardinal four on the right. In the foreground, Christian figures are shown coming from the left and biblical characters from the right to receive a crown as rewards for their virtuous life. The tapestry on the left, the first to be read in the sequence of these three, is devoted to *Natura*, that is, to those who are naturally virtuous, the ancient and pagan heroes, walking from the left to the right toward the central panel. Their procession is vainly held up by three of the seven deadly sins: Pride, Envy, and Avarice. The third piece, on the right of *Glory*, shows the Worthies led by *Scriptura*, the Ancient Law. They come from right to left, and here also four other deadly sins vainly try to stop them: Luxury, Gluttony, Anger, and Sloth.[33]

The iconographic links between the *Moralities* and both the *Honors* and the *Triumph* are particularly close. In all three sets the seven principal virtues play the major role. According to the inscriptions on the *Moralities*, the virtuous men led by Nature, by Scripture, or by Divine Grace, are directed to Honor, the same final point as in the *Honors*.[34] Finally, all three sets are conceived of as converging to a central piece, where the main theme, the apex of the entire allegory is shown: Honor in the *Honors*, Glory and the seven virtues in the *Moralities*, and Faith in the *Triumph*. These powers gather their companions around them in a moral harmony, expressed by the visual symmetry. Instead of the normal order we find here a polarization to a central point. This system seems to have been adopted as a compositional principle for "woven moralities" belonging to the period 1520–1535.

The sequence of the *Triumph of the Seven Virtues*, chronologically the youngest of the three, goes back to the former two, the *Honors* and the *Moralities*, but in doing so, it greatly alters the other compositional type to which it belongs, namely, the Triumphal Procession. The idea of putting personifications on chariots in a procession, driving suc-

Fig. 8. *Triumph of Prudence*, Brussels tapestry, around 1560. Société Nationale de Crédit à l'Industrie, Brussels. (Photograph: A.C.L., Brussels.)

cessively over the bodies of the vanquished and opposed forces, originated in the late Middle Ages in the representation of the *Trionfi* according to Petrarch, where Love is overcome by Chastity, Chastity by Death, Death by Fame, Fame by Time, and Time by Eternity. This allegorical march had already been worked out on tapestry several times before the *Triumph* set discussed here, and it was used again in later series such as the *Triumph of the Seven Deadly Sins* (Brussels, around 1545; now in Madrid and in Vienna, series XXXV) or Rubens' *Triumph of the Eucharist* (Brussels, around 1625–1628; first

edition now in the Descalzas Reales, Madrid).[35] The initial dynamism of this procession, with successive powers overcoming their predecessors, is given up here in favor of a converging symmetry: we could almost say that the chariots of the virtues, no longer in a cortege, lead nowhere except to a very harmonious but finally static gathering around the central allegory.

This compositional contradiction must have been appreciated by the following generation of Flemish weavers and tapestry designers when they had to work out a new series of the *Seven Virtues* in the third quarter of the sixteenth century. This set, woven by Frans Geubels before 1572 and of which editions are now preserved in Vienna (series XVII) and in Burgos, was surely inspired by the *Triumph* of around 1535 discussed here.[36] Almost all the iconographic attributes of the virtues in the 1535 set are used again, and the composers of the later series adopted also the main exemplary scenes of each tapestry, taking up again only the biblical episodes and leaving out the classical and pagan stories.[37] However, only two virtues are still shown as moving in a vehicle: Hope, in her boat floating from left to right, and Faith in her chariot driving from right to left. They seem to converge on Charity, who is no longer riding but standing now frontally on a socle. Also the four cardinal virtues are now seated on socles or on thrones, thus repeating the the representation in the *Apotheosis* tapestry of the *Honors* (Fig. 6).

We believe that a late echo of the original sequence of the *Triumph* set (scheme 1) and even of the *Apotheosis* tapestry cited (scheme 2) is present in these later *Seven Virtues* of

around 1570. The faces of Prudence and of Temperance are turned to the right, those of Fortitude and of Justice to the left. If we assume that this orientation is directed toward a central panel (which should be Charity amidst the two other theological virtues), we may imagine that this set could have been ordered as following[38]:

SCHEME 3. Seven Virtues, around 1570

Prudence Temperance Hope Charity Faith Justice Fortitude
→　　　→　　　→　　↓　　←　　←　　←

This scheme is similar to the preceding two, except that Charity and Faith are in an inverted order. If this hypothesis is correct, the order of this later *Seven Virtues* series gives evidence of the lasting influence of the 1535 *Triumph*.

Next to this indirect influence, we should remember the more direct and already cited later edition of the *Triumph* of around 1560, now preserved in Brussels.[39] This later and abbreviated set was copied in its turn on a painting of a *Nocturnal Banquet*, now in the Kunsthistorisches Museum in Vienna, dated

Fig. 9. *Triumph of Temperance*, Brussels tapestry, around 1560. Société Nationale de Crédit à l'Industrie, Brussels. (Photograph: A.C.L., Brussels.)

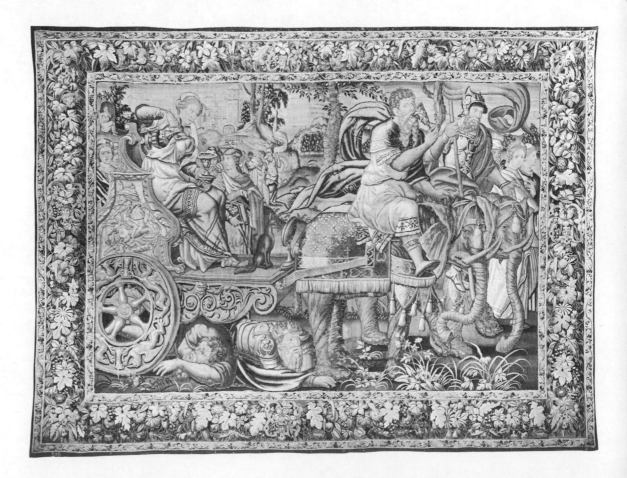

1640 and signed by the German painter
Wolfgang Heimbach (d. 1678). Five tapestries
hang on the wall between the windows; the
two pieces on the left are *The Triumph of Charity* and *The Triumph of Temperance* from the
1560 edition (Fig. 10).[40] Since the former history of the series of around 1560 is unknown,
we are still ignorant as to where and under
what circumstances the painter could have
copied these tapestries.

A final major problem that remains unre-
solved about the *Triumph of the Seven Virtues*
is that of its origin: by whom were the cartoons initially ordered, and for whom was
the first edition woven? No documentary
evidence has been found to answer these
questions. We believe, however, that the iconographic and compositional links between
the *Triumph* and the related contemporary
tapestries discussed in this article may
suggest an appropriate solution. All these
morality sets, so closely alike in their form
and their program, surely originated in the
same cultural and artistic entourage: the

court of the Hapsburgs in the southern
Netherlands. *The Twelve Ages of Man* were
almost surely made for the court of Margaret
of Austria, since her portrait appeared in the
figure cited as Tiberius's wife.[41] This set,
which dates between 1525 and 1528, borrowed elements from the *Honors*, finished in
1525, a series that we know was conceived as
a dynastic morality for the emperor Charles V
and was delivered to him in 1526, on the occasion of his wedding to Isabel of Portugal.[42]
The three *Moralities* tapestries, reflecting an
almost identical program and belonging to a
same style as the *Honors*, must also have been
ordered by the imperial court.[43]

The Triumph of the Seven Virtues relies strongly
on these series both for its internal order and
for many figures and groups. No series of this
subject is indicated in the partially preserved
inventories of the emperor, but when the
empress Isabel died in 1539 a set of six tapestries with the *Ystoria de las syete virtudes* is
cited in the inventories of her art treasures.[44]
These six tapestries were transmitted to

166

Charles's youngest daughter, Doña Juana, in whose inventory they appear again in 1573.[45] Perhaps they were shown at the historical encounter of Philip II of Spain and Sebastian of Portugal at Guadalupe Abbey in 1576; an indefinite number of tapestries of the *Seven Virtues*, belonging "to the emperor" and thus referring to pieces of the first half of the century, is cited by the chroniclers as being hung for the decoration of the monastery.[46] No such tapestries are preserved today in the Spanish royal collection. Possibly they were given to some church or some noble family in later times; several pieces of *Triumph* sets, now in the United States, apparently came from Spain, and two of them are still preserved in Toledo.[47] Perhaps the first edition of *The Triumph of the Seven Virtues* was ordered by Isabel of Portugal or by the emperor who gave them to her. Since both knew the *Honors* series very well, they could have asked the same composers and weavers to make a similar woven morality to serve as an example at their imperial court.

ACKNOWLEDGMENTS

The author wishes to express his most sincere thanks to Madame Geneviève Souchal for having given him access to her manuscript while her study was still unpublished. He also expresses gratitude to Brian Williams for editing the English version of his article.

NOTES

1. Anna G. Bennett, *Five Centuries of Tapestry from The Fine Arts Museums of San Francisco* (San Francisco: The Fine Arts Museums of San Francisco and Charles E. Tuttle Co., 1976), pp. 93–101.

2. Bennett, p. 98, and plate, p. 99; Valerius Maximus, *Facta et dicta memorabilia*, Bk. III, ch. II (*de fortitudine romana*), para. 1: Cocles; 2: Cloelia; 23: Scaeva; 24: Siccius Dentatus; ch. III (*de patientia romana*), pt. 1: Mucius Scaevola.

3. Guy Delmarcel, "De structuur van de Brusselse tapijtreeks 'Los Honores,'" in *Annales du XLIe Congrès (Malines 1970) de la Fédération archéologique de Belgique*, vol. 2 (Mechelen: Kon. Kring voor Oudheidkunde, 1971), pp. 352–56; idem, "The Dynastic Iconography of the Brussels Tapestries Los Honores (1520–1525)," in *Actas del XXIII Congreso Internacional de Historia del Arte, Granada 1973*, vol. II (Granada: Universidad de Granada, 1977), pp. 250–59. The *Honors* set is fully reproduced in Conde de Valencia de don Juan, *Tapices de la Corona de España*, vol. I (Madrid; 1903) pl. 32–40 (further cited as: Valencia), and in Albert F. Calvert, *The Spanish Royal Tapestries* (London and New York: John Lane, 1921), pl. 15–24.

4. Valencia, vol. I, pl. 20–22; Calvert, pl. 195–197; Elias Tormo Monzo and Francisco J. Sánchez Cantón, *Los tapices de la Casa del Rey N.S.* (Madrid: Artes Gráficas "Mateu", 1919), pp. 41–42, pl. XV–XVI; since Valencia de don Juan, vol. I, p. 15, it is accepted everywhere in art literature that *The Moralities* were brought to Spain by Mary of Portugal, on her wedding to Philip II in 1543. However, no such tapestries can be traced in her inventory of 1545 (Archivo General de Simancas, Casa y Sitios Reales, legajo 73). They are first mentioned in the inventory of 1598, made after Philip's death and used again in 1617 and 1621 (Archivo del Palacio Real de Madrid, legajo 919-I, pliego 104, fol. 1 r°).

5. Valencia, I, pl. 22 (our Fig. 7), pl. 32 (our Fig 6), and pl. 38 (Prudence in the middle of the stage). Most of the attributes of the other virtues in the *Triumph* set are also represented on the *Apotheosis* tapestry of *The Honors* (Fig. 6) and on the *Glory* piece of *The Moralities* (Fig. 7). For this iconography see Rosemond Tuve, "Notes on the Virtues and Vices. I. Two XVth Century Lines of Dependence on the XIIIth and XIVth Century," *Journal of the Warburg and Courtauld Institutes* 26, (1963): 264–94.

6. Giovanni Boccaccio, *Genealogie deorum gentilium libri*, ed. by Vincenzo Romano, *Scrittori d'Italia*, 200–201 (Bari: G. Laterza, 1951), p. 199 (Bk. IV, ch. 44, Prometheus), "Minerva, scilicet sapientem virum . . ."; p. 595 (Bk. XII, ch. 25, Perseus), "scutum Palladis accipiendum reor pro prudentia . . ."; p. 110 (Bk. II, ch. 63, Cadmus), "serpentem . . . senem hominem atque prudentem . . . intelligo." See also Bennett, p. 96, and Guy Delmarcel, "Présence de Boccace dans la tapisserie flamande des XVe et XVIe siècles," in *Boccaccio in Europe*, edited by Gilbert Tournoy [*Symbolae Facultatis Litterarum et Philosophiae Lovaniensis*, sers. A, vol. 4

(Leuven: University Press, 1977)], p. 83–85, for a further analysis of this tapestry.

7. Valencia, I, pl. 39; Calvert, pl. 16.

8. Former collection Heilbronner, actual whereabouts unknown; it appeared last at the Sotheby's sale, London, 26 October 1973 (catalogue p. 8, no. 2, color pl.). See G. Demotte, *La tapisserie gothique* (Paris and New York: Demotte, 1924), pl. 88, and Marguerite Calberg, "La Pluie d'Or, Première pièce d'une tenture de Persée," *Revue belge d'archéologie et d'histoire de l'art* 38 (1969): 65.

9. Albert I Royal Library, Brussels, ms. 9392, fol. 16 v°. Cf. also Lucie Schaefer, "Die Illustrationen zu den Handschriften der Christine de Pizan," *Marburger Jahrbuch für Kunstwissenschaft* 10 (1937): 119–208; for example, pl. 13, British Museum, London, Harley ms. 4431, fol. 102 v°.

10. Brussels, Société Nationale de Crédit à l'Industrie. Marguerite Calberg, "Le triomphe des vertus chrétiennes. Suite de huit tapisseries de Bruxelles du XVIe siècle," *Revue belge d'archéologie et d'histoire de l'art*, 29 (1960): 3–36 (this piece is on p. 23, fig. 7; Calberg's identification of Othéa as Orthaea, p. 25, can no longer be accepted).

11. Scipio stands between the two columns at the left part.

12. Holofernes lies at the lower right side of Valencia, I, pl. 33, and Calvert, pl. 20; Valerianus also in the lower right corner of *Fortune* tapestry, Valencia, I, pl. 36, and Calvert pl. 17; for Julian on *Honor* and *Infamy*, see Valencia, I, pl. 33 and 37, and Calvert, pl. 20 and 23. Moreover, Muhammet as a symbol of Heresy lies under Faith's feet on the *Apotheosis* panel; see our Fig. 6.

13. Valencia, I, pl. 39, and Calvert, pl. 16. Elijah, considered as the founder of the Carmelites, wears their habit, a brown robe and a white mantle; see Cécile Emond, *L'Iconographie Carmélitaine dans les anciens Pays-Bas méridionaux* [*Académie royale de Belgique. Classe des Beaux-Arts, Mémoires in-8°, 2e série, tome XII, fasc. 5* (Brussels: Académie Royale de Belgique, 1961)], pp. 70–71, 265, 269.

14. Valencia, I, pl. 22.

15. *Encyclopaedia Britannica*, (1957), s.v. *Donation of Constantine*, Nicolas Huyghebaert, "La Donation de Constantin ramenée à ses véritables dimensions," *Revue d'Histoire Ecclésiastique*, vol. 71 (Louvain, 1976), pp. 45–68.

16. We consulted Jacques de Voragine, *La légende dorée*, vol. I transl. into French by J. M. Roze, *Garnier-Flammarion*, no. 132 (Paris, 1967), p. 97: Saint Sylvester.

17. Voragine, I, pp. 172–173: St. Julien du Mans.

18. Biltmore House and Gardens, Asheville, N.C. See Bennett, p. 95, fig. 47.

19. Edith A. Standen, "The Twelve Ages of Man: A Further Study of a Set of Early Sixteenth-Century Flemish Tapestries," *Metropolitan Museum Journal* 2 (1969): 154–155; the story is cited from Gregory of Tours, *Historia Francorum*, V, 19.

20. Bk. XVII, ch. 60: "Quod Flacilla imperatrix intendebat pauperibus sustentandis, ipse vero Theodosius idolis evertendis" [*Bibliotheca mundi*

seu Speculi maioris Vincentii Burgundi praesulis Bellovacensis ... Tomus Quartus. Qui Speculum historiale inscribitur, Duaci (Douai), 1624, p. 673]. About the historical Flacilla see A. Pauly and G. Wissowa, *Realencyclopaedie der klassischen Altertumswissenschaft, 11. Halbband* (Stuttgart: J. B. Metzlersche Buchhandlung, 1907), col. 2431–33.

21. Jacob van Maerlant, *Spiegel Historiael*, pt. III, Bk, II, ch. 8: "Van Placella der keyserinnen," edited by M. de Vries and E. Verwijs, (Leyden, 1863), vol. II, p. 97. Vincent's encyclopedia was finished around 1264; Maerlant's translation was written in 1282–90.

22. For a variant of the *Twelve Ages* in Dijon Museum, see Standen, p. 162, note 98. Placella on the *Honors*, see Valencia, I, pl. 40, and Calvert, pl. 15 (lower right side).

23. Bennett, pl. on pp. 94–101.

24. See the article by Geneviève Souchal in this book. The first half of each of these verses is also sewn into the panel of *The Triumph of Charity* at the Museo de Santa Cruz, Toledo, Spain. The small fox looking at himself in a mirror, at Virtue's feet on this *Temperance* panel, proves that this later edition reflects the original composition of around 1535, now lost. The group of the fox covered in a monk's cape and unmasked by a mirror appeared before only on the knees of Cautio on the second panel of *The Honors* (Valencia, I, pl. 38; Calvert, pl. 21), the major source for the examples of the *Triumph* set. This image of Cautiousness goes back to Isidorus of Sevilla.

25. Both Geneviève Souchal and the author came independently to this conclusion during our preliminary study of the *Triumph* series. See also Bennett, p. 93.

26. Thomas Aquinas, *Summa theologiae*, IIa IIae, qu. 4, art. 4: "Utrum Fides sit prima inter virtutes"; Hugo Ripelinus, *Compendium theologiae veritatis*, Bk. V, ch. XX: "De effectu Fidei"; "Alios habet effectus voluntarios et secundarios, ut est credere, et dirigere opera aliarum virtutum, et imperare omnibus suo modo," in *Alberti magni Opera Omnia*, edited by S. Borgnet, vol. 34, (Paris, 1895), p. 169.

27. Ripelinus, Bk. V, ch. XVII: "De differentia virtutum cardinalium et theologicarum"; "Virtutes theologicae habentur per infusionem, cardinales vero per acquisitionem. Virtutes theologicae movent ad opera ex rationibus sumptis a iure divino, sed cardinales a iure naturali (cited ed., p. 166). On the *Glory* tapestry of *The Moralities* (our Fig. 7) the angels distributing the crowns are called *virtus infusa* and *acquisita*; they correspond to the theological and cardinal virtues seated on the platform.

28. J. Pieper, *Traktat über die Klugheit* (Munich: Kösel Verlag, 1960), pp. 12 and 23.

29. We consider primarily the *Triumphs* as a dynastic morality, as well as the already cited *Honors*; see the end of this article. For a discussion of Justice as the outstanding royal virtue, see J. Balogh, "Rex a recte regendo," *Speculum* 3 (1928): 580–82, and Dora M. Bell, *L'idéal éthique de la royauté en France au Moyen Age, d'après quelques moralistes de ce temps* (Geneva and Paris: Droz-Minard, 1962), pp. 19, 30, 59, 102.

30. See our articles cited in note 3.

31. Valencia, I, pl. 32, 33, 34; the entire sequence of *The Honors* must be read as follows: Valencia, I, pl. 36–38–39–32–33–34–40–35–37, and Calvert, pl. 17–21–16–19–20–22–15–18–23.

32. See Delmarcel, "Présence de Boccace," pp. 72–74, for more details about Boccaccio and this tapestry series.

33. The exact sequence of *The Moralities* is Valencia, I, pl. 21–22–20, and Calvert, pl. 196–195–197.

34. The banderoles in the upper borders can be read as follows (we underline): *Natura*, "Omnes inclynat Natura homynes *ad honores* Quos virtus praeclara viris insignibus affert"; *Glory*, "Gracia divinos evangelizat *honores* Et dat perpetuas magna cum laude coronas"; *Scriptura*, "Sacra Dei Scriptura vocat *veros ad honores* Quos tantum dignis virtus dispensat alumnis."

35. A brief account of the *Trionfi* in tapestry is given in Jan-Karel Steppe and Guy Delmarcel, "Les tapisseries du cardinal Erard de la Marck, prince-évêque de Liège," *Revue de l'Art* no. 25 (1974): 52, note 78. See also Bennett, pp. 86–89, no. 17.

36. Ludwig Baldass, *Die Wiener Gobelinssammlung* (Vienna: Ed. Hölzel & Co., 1920), pl. 46–52; Erik Duverger, "Tapijtwerk uit het atelier van Frans Geubels," in *L'Age d'Or de la tapisserie flamande. Colloque international 23–25 mai 1961* (Brussels: Kon. Vlaamse Akademie voor Wetenschappen, 1969), pp. 143–154.

37. The following examples may be mentioned: *Prudence*, David and Abigail; *Fortitude*, Jael and Sisara, Samson, Judith and Holofernes; *Justice*, Solomon; *Temperance*, no comparison with a 1535 piece possible; *Faith*, David and Goliath, Abraham and Isaac, Peter and Paul; *Hope*, Daniel and the lions, three men in the oven; *Charity*, Tobiah burying the dead, David, Sarah washing the feet of the angel (similar to the Elisabeth group of 1535).

38. Baldass, pl. 49–51–47–48–46—50–52, or Vienna, inventory no. XVII, 4–6–2–3–1–5–7.

39. See Calberg, "Le triomphe ...," cited in note 10.

40. Vienna, Kunsthistorisches Museum, Gemäldesammlung, inventory no. 599, oil painting on copper, 62 cm×114 cm. Klaus Demus, *Kunsthistorisches Museum Wien. Verzeichnis der Gemälde* (Vienna: A. Schroll, 1973), p. 84, pl. 135. Compare with Calberg, "Le triomphe," figs. 4 and 8. These tapestries, however, are apparently a repaint, and they may have been added after 1640. The other three tapestries on the right belong to a hitherto unidentified series.

41. Standen, p. 157. The same figure is used as Queen Esther on the foreground right of David's unction in the *Nobilitas* tapestry of *The Honors*, where the dynastic references to Charles V are obvious. See Valencia, I, pl. 35, and Calvert, pl. 18, also Delmarcel, *The Dynastic Iconography*, p. 254, fig. 3.

42. Delmarcel, cited article, and J. K. Steppe, "Vlaams tapijtwerk van de 16de eeuw in Spaans koninklijk bezit," *Miscellanea Jozef Duverger*, vol. II (Ghent: Vereniging voor de Geschiedenis der Textielkunsten, 1968), pp. 725–726.

43. See note 4.

44. Archivo General de Simancas, Casa y Sitios Reales, legajo 67, fol. 26 r°. The six mentioned tapestries offer an odd coincidence with the now preserved editions, all of them lacking the Temperance triumph. The mentioned height of six *anas* corresponds to the actual size of about 440 cm in the preserved copies.

45. Cristobal Perez Pastor, *Noticias y documentos relativos a la historia y literaturas españolas, 2. Memorias de la Real Academia española*, vol. 11 (Madrid, 1914), p. 358, no. 88.

46. Steppe, p. 728, note 41, first made this relation. See F. de Uhagon, *Relaciones históricas de los siglos XVI y XVII. Sociedad de Bibliofilos españoles*, vol. 32 (Madrid, 1896), p. 116: "unos paños de lana y seda, que fueron del emperador, la historia eran las siete virtudes."

47. H. C. Marillier (manuscript *Subject Catalogue of Tapestries*, vol. *Arts & Sciences*, T 37, p. 75, now in the department of Textiles, Victoria and Albert Museum, London) alleged that *The Triumph of Fortitude* belonging to W. R. Hearst, now in San Francisco (Bennett, p. 98, no. 20), came from the "Marques de dos Aguas," apparently a Spanish family, "with two others" (*Justice*, now San Francisco, and *Hope*, now Pittsburgh ?). The legend of Saint James of Compostela (*Santiago Matamoro*) shown in the upper right corner of the *Triumph of Faith* (Fig. 2) might also refer to an original command of a court related to Spain, thus to Charles and Isabel, monarchs of the Spanish territories around 1535.

From the beginning of the seventeenth century, when French tapestry making began to emerge from obscurity, it took brilliant flight and occupied prominent place among the luxury industries, first in France, then in the whole of Europe. Under the reign of Louis XIV both the Gobelins and Beauvais tapestry manufactories were created, and the workshops of the small town of Aubusson received permission to call themselves royal tapestry manufactories. Beautiful weavings were produced by these ateliers, and even today one speaks of "a Gobelins," "a Beauvais," or "an Aubusson" to designate a tapestry.

Although the Gobelins Manufactory is so illustrious that its name is synonymous with "tapestry" in several foreign languages, it was not created overnight; in fact, its origin goes back to 1608. It took nearly fifty years to establish the royal workshops from which were to come the series of immense tapestries destined to furnish the palaces of the king. The story of those early Parisian workshops that preceded the founding of the Gobelins Manufactory will be unfolded in this study.

THE ATELIERS

The blossoming of the art of tapestry in France was the result of economic reorganization measures taken by French sovereigns, beginning with Henri IV, who favored creating tapestry ateliers and grouping them into factories. For Henri IV (1553–1610), the aim was to liberate France from an important yearly tribute paid to foreign countries in exchange for manufactured goods. In 1583, when he was still only king of Navarre, Henri had shown interest in a plan presented by one of his advisors, Duplessis-Mornay, which stressed the possible advantages to Béarn offered in establishing a colony of Flemish weavers then fleeing the religious persecutions of their native country.

In Paris at the time there were two principal ateliers of tapestry, one founded by Henri II and established in the *maison professe* of the Jesuits, faubourg Saint Antoine, and the other organized at the Hôpital de la Trinité, rue Saint Denis. Henri IV decided to enlarge the scope of these workshops. By a charter dated January 4, 1608, he granted to the weaver Girard Laurent, trained at the Trinité workshop, a lodging located under the recently constructed Grande Galerie of the Louvre. In December 22 of that year, letters patent established at the same place Maurice

Dubout, also an alumnus of the Trinité workshop and an associate of Laurent at the *maison professe* of the Jesuits, rue Saint Antoine. But Henri IV's real accomplishment was in calling Flemish weavers to Paris and getting them established there.

In 1601 Henri's emissaries succeeded in attracting to France a Flemish weaver, François Vernier or Versier. Nothing is known of his life, but his arrival preceded that of several of his countrymen, among them Francis van den Planken (François de la Planche), originally from Oudenaarde, and his brother-in-law, Marc de Comans, born in Antwerp. A deed of association was signed by the brothers-in-law, and in January 1607 they obtained letters patent for the opening of a manufactory. A reading of the document reveals the cleverness of the essential arrangements, which reconcile the interests of the king of France with the benefits offered those concerned.

The king recognizes the weavers' pretensions to nobility, which permits them to enjoy the privileges attached to this rank. Moreover, he accords them the exclusive right to make tapestries for fifteen years, forbidding anyone else from opening up a similar workshop. He also forbids the importation of tapestries under penalty of confiscation and fine. Free lodgings are accorded to the two associates in Paris and in the province. The workers are exempted from dues and taxes on the raw materials necessary to weaving. Each entrepreneur is awarded a yearly income of 1,500 livres, in addition to a lump sum of 100,000 livres to cover the expenses of setting up the workshop. And finally a special clause: the weavers are permitted to brew beer for themselves and their collaborators.

In exchange for these advantages, the Flemings pledge to maintain eighty looms active, sixty in Paris and twenty in Amiens or any French town of their choice. They also promise to train twenty-five apprentices the first year, which number is reduced to twenty the following years. They agree not to sell their products at a higher price than that of the Flemish tapestries which are prohibited. They are assured of royal subsidy but remain an independent enterprise, free to fill the orders of any private party as well as those of the king.

The looms were first installed in the annexes of the Palace of Tournelles, but the location was not favorable and the weavers moved out shortly afterwards. They chose the Gobelins district because of its good light and the proximity of running water in the Bièvre, tributary stream to the Seine. The Gobelins were an old Parisian family to which La Planche may have been related. Around 1440, the Gobelins brothers, coming from Reims, had founded a scarlet dye shop in the faubourg Saint Marcel. This first dye shop on the Bièvre became very famous, and the name of Gobelins remained attached to the district itself.

The establishment of François de la Planche and Marc de Comans was to thrive in spite of inevitable financial difficulties and problems caused by the magistrates of Paris, and when their concession expired on 18 April 1625, they were able to obtain an eight-year extension.

The death of François de la Planche in 1627 proved a blow to the harmonious relationship between the two families, and the association dissolved in 1638. Marc de Comans remained in the faubourg Saint Marcel and was succeeded by a son and then by another son. Raphael, son of François de la Planche, opened another workshop in the faubourg Saint Germain, and was in turn succeeded by his son, Sébastien François. The small street, "de la Planche," recalls the memory of this manufactory. The ateliers closed for good in 1667–68. The reputation of the looms in the faubourg Saint Germain surpassed that of all other Parisian workshops, a fact that is borne out by the inventories established for the estates of François in 1627 and by those of Raphaël's wife in 1661, where the quantities of tapestries manufactured are recorded.

Great difficulties arise when one attempts to trace the origin of tapestry looms, as inventories and documents are not always precise, and often even obscure. The similarity of the marks—a "P" accompanied by a fleur-de-lys used by different ateliers—does not facilitate the task of the historian. Sometimes, also, several compositions were based on the same paintings but woven on looms in different workshops.

THE CARTOONS: TAPESTRY AND PAINTING

The first half of the seventeenth century is one of the most brilliant and creative periods in the history of tapestry. Perhaps never has it been so closely tied to the work of the great painters. Indeed, at that time there existed no profound difference between the two arts of painting and tapestry: the great artists exercised their talents as much in one field as in the other. This tradition probably came from the sixteenth-century Italy, where tapestry was considered to be among the "fine arts" and all worthy artists tried their skill at painting cartoons.

The first of these artists was Raphael, who at the beginning of the sixteenth century drew for the ateliers of Brussels (Peter d'Alost) the famous cartoons of *The Acts of the Apostles*. Later, Pontormo, Bronzino, Salviati, Bacchiaca, and Stradano made cartoons for the prosperous Italian tapestry manufactories. Here one must mention that universal man, Vasari. From 1555 on he was in charge of decorating with tapestries the Palazzo Vecchio in Florence. In his writings, Vasari emphasized the role of the painter who made the cartoon and considered the weaver merely the executor of the design. Thus, he would praise the way a tapestry would render "the hairs of a beard drawn with a brush." This was the beginning of the idea of the art of tapestry as a reflection of the art of painting. In any case, Vasari believed that tapestries should complement frescoes and that, rather than be mobile and temporary decorations, they should be fixed, permanent ornamentation.[1]

By the seventeenth century in France, tapestries, as well as paintings, were being used to embellish churches and castles. When Rubens was called to the French court, the queen mother, Marie de Médicis, commissioned him to do paintings for the two galleries of the Luxembourg Palace in Paris, and King Louis XIII ordered the twelve cartoons which would form the series of *The Story of Constantine*. Simon Vouet's paintings in the gallery of the Hôtel de Bullion in Paris served as models for the cartoons of *The Story of Ulysses* series. Not only did Louis XIII ask Poussin to decorate the Grande Galerie of the Louvre, but he also requested a series of cartoons representing *The Seven Sacraments*. Even at the end of the century, after the downfall of Lebrun, this tradition was upheld and Mignard drew for the gallery of the castle of Saint-Cloud the great paintings after which was patterned one of the most famous tapestries woven at the royal Gobelins workshops, *The Gallery of Saint-Cloud*.

Thus, tapestry weaving was not considered to be a minor art. Quite the contrary, the greatest masters of painting devoted them-selves to it—not only Rubens but also Simon Vouet, La Hyre, Philippe de Champagne, Claude Vignon, Sébastien Bourdon, and the refined Baugin. Indeed, as Jacques Thuillier has remarked, in the seventeenth century at times "tapestry takes the lead."[2] The *Suite of the Old Testament*, which Vouet designed just for the tapestry, may even surpass in rich-ness of invention the best painted decors of the time. Nevertheless, at that time tapestry and painting were kept distinct.

Two sources of inspiration may be discerned for that period: lyric exaltation and analysis of the human heart. Tapestry did not follow painting in these two themes, however. Its primary mission was decorative, and this aim hindered the representation of psycho-logical complexities. On the other hand, lyricism suited the medium. It represented heroes who sacrificed everything to glory: the mythological heroes such as Ulysses, as well as the Christian emperor Constantine, or the saints such as Saint Gervais and Saint Protais, and finally fictional heroes on the order of Theagenes in the novel by Heliodorus, all found exaltation in the woven image. All that had color, rhythm, or powerful effect was magnificently repre-sented. Thanks to the art of tapestry, as Thuillier states, "one discovers that this period counts in French art as one of the great epochs of lyric expression."[3]

Since that time all the painted galleries have been destroyed, and only scattered represen-tations of such painting are left. Tapestries, to some extent, replace them.

THE TAPESTRIES[4]
To best appreciate the activity of the seventeenth-century ateliers and their bril-liant production, let us look at eleven tapes-tries. These are taken from among the thirty-six hangings studied by Fenaille in the first volume of his authoritative history of the Gobelins factory, which volume is devoted to the *"ateliers parisiens au dix-septième siècle de-puis l'installation de Marc de Comans et de Fran-çois de la Planche au faubourg Saint Marcel en 1601 jusqu'à la fondation de la Manufacture royale des meubles de la couronne en 1662."*

THE STORY OF PSYCHE
Michel Coxcie (Mechlin, 1499–1592) origi-nated the series depicting *The Story of Psyche*, which apparently came into being initially in Brussels for Francis I, king of France. The first set was destroyed in 1797, when the Directoire had the most beautiful tapestries from the Royal Furniture Warehouse burned in order to retrieve their gold and silver. Probably in-spired by the Raphaelesque motifs and the frescoes attributed to Perino del Vaga in the Castel Sant'Angelo in Rome, the compo-sitions of Michel Coxcie are found again in a series of engravings executed by the Maître au Dé and also in the stained-glass windows from Ecouen now at Chantilly.

In the seventeenth century this series met with tremendous success and was woven by the ateliers of the Louvre as well as the rue de la Chaise factory. The Royal Furniture Ware-house preserved several versions in addition to Francis I's set. One is exhibited in part in the Pau Museum; another, complete, belongs to the Mobilier National. Several are found in miscellaneous collections; the one shown here belongs to the Los Angeles County Museum of Art (Fig. 1). In this tapestry, *Psyche Carried on the Mountain*, four men carry Psyche, who is reclining on a litter. Trumpet players, torch carriers, and children holding candles accompany her. The father, mother, and friends of Psyche bring up the rear. A painted version representing the same tab-leau and attributed to Michel Coxcie is kept in a collection in Paris.

If we compare the Los Angeles tapestry with the one in the Mobilier National, some differ-ences are apparent. First, it will be noticed that the scenes are mirror images of each other and that the children in the Los Angeles tapestry are clothed. There are also minor variations in the landscape, trees, and plants. In addition, the borders of the two, though both are decorated with grotesques, differ in design. The Los Angeles version does not carry a coat of arms.

THE HUNTS OF KING FRANCIS
The inventories of the seventeenth century record in several instances the existence of the hangings of *The Hunts of King Francis*,[5] the drawings for which were probably executed by Laurent Guyot, who lived at the begin-ning of the century. But this painter was most likely copying other models or basing the car-toons for the tapestries on pictures or engrav-ings of the sixteenth century, because the characters appear in costumes dating from the reign of Francis I.

Fig. 1. *The Story of Psyche. Psyche Carried on the Mountain.* H: 3.10m. W: 5.87m. Los Angeles County Museum of Art, gift of Mr. and Mrs. Richard Weininger.

In the inventory drawn up at the death of François de la Planche in 1627, two of these hangings are mentioned. A complete set, kept in the royal collection, existed in Versailles in 1789, but it is now lost.

The Mobilier National does not own today a version of *The Hunts of King Francis*. We know of several hangings woven in the seventeenth century. Those from the old collection of the Forest Divonne, which now belongs to the Monuments Historiques de France, included eight pieces. The scenes depicted are completely different from those among the tapestries in the Gaston Menier collection published by Fenaille. In both sets the details of the hunt are presented with a precision worthy of illustrating the treatises on venery and falconry.

In *The Woodcock Hunt* (Fig. 2), on the right, in a thickly wooded landscape, we see a lord presenting a richly dressed lady with a pair of dead woodcocks. She holds out her hands toward an already captured bird in the bushes. The border is decorated with foliage; in the center of each side there is a grotesque figure, in each corner a nosegay.

THE STORY OF ARTEMISIA[6]

The series of *The Story of Artemisia* had its origin in a manuscript by Nicolas Houel, Parisian apothecary, art patron, and philanthropist. Inspired by the story of Artemisia—the disconsolate widow of King Mausolus and regent of the kingdom of Caria—Houel had the idea of glorifying in a long poem the reign of Marie de Médicis. Houel's 1562 manuscript, kept today in the Bibliothèque Nationale, consists of four books. Only the first two were illustrated, with seventy-four subjects that Fenaille was able to reconstruct; fifty-nine original drawings are presently known.

Of these fifty-nine drawings kept in the Louvre and the Bibliothèque Nationale, Jean Ehrmann attributes forty-four to Antoine Caron, the rest to artists in Fontainebleau. Some are by Niccolo dell'Abbate and his son Giulio Camillo. Six original drawings, depicting the procession of King Mausolus, could be by Henri Lerambert; certainly Lerambert, appointed by Henri IV as "painter for the tapestry weavers of the King," created some of the large-scale cartoons for the Louvre atelier, where it seems the first tapestries of *The Story of Artemisia* were created. It is likely that some of the cartoons were made by Laurent Guyot, who succeeded Lerambert in his position. We may also surmise that Guyot was appointed by Marc de Comans and François de la Planche, who in 1601 were associates in managing the first Gobelins atelier.

The success of the *Artemisia* series was immense. In 1627 the inventory made after the death of François de la Planche records that there were seventy-eight pieces of this hanging in storage as well as on the looms. Seventy-nine were to be found in the General Inventory of the Furniture of the Crown under Louis XIV. The Mobilier National has twenty-eight of them today. Several are hanging in various museums in Europe and in the United States. The Minneapolis Institute of Art owns the suite offered in 1625 by Louis XIII to the cardinal legate François Barberini. The Art Institute of Chicago has two "entre-fenêtres" (tapestry panel to hang between two windows). The Metropolitan Museum of Art in New York has recently acquired a tapestry of that suite, *The Two Statues.* [7]

In *Soldier Carrying a Vase on a Litter* (Fig. 3) we see on the right two soldiers carrying a big vase and two small cups full of gold pieces on a litter. They are followed by four soldiers, each holding a vase. This subject does not exist in the collections of the Mobilier National. The border is adorned with cartouches, flowers, and ribbons. At the center of the top border are the armorial bearings of

France and Navarre; on the bottom is the monogram of Louis XIII, a beribboned L between two scepters crossed in an X.

The drawing corresponding to the subject represented is at the Cabinet des Estampes in the Bibliothèque Nationale.

The Story of Constantine

The *Constantine* series was commissioned by Louis XIII from Rubens at the beginning of 1622, when the latter was in Paris to submit to Marie de Médicis his plans for the decoration of the Grande Galerie of the Palais de Luxembourg in Paris, the construction of which had been completed in 1620. Louis XIII felt the need to renovate the antiquated models, whose multiple repetitions had exhausted their appeal. This set comprises twelve tapestries.

Fig. 2. *The Hunts of King Francis: The Woodcock Hunt,* wool and silk. H: 3.32m. W: 3.10m. Monuments Historiques de France. (Photograph: Caisse Nationale des Monuments Historiques et des Sites)

176

Back in Antwerp, Rubens settled to work on the project. In the last days of November 1622 he forwarded to François de la Planche four rough drawings painted with oil on wood. It seems likely that Laurent Guyot, following sketches, executed the cartoons and the borders.

The Story of Constantine met with considerable acclaim, and five sets are recorded in the Inventory of the Crown Furniture in 1663. We know that in 1625 Louis XIII presented the cardinal legate François Barberini with a seven-piece set woven in gold, which was completed in Rome by seven other pieces executed in accordance with the drawings of Pietro da Cortona. Today this set is preserved in Philadelphia.

If we look at *The Building of Constantinople*[8] (Fig. 4) we see on the right the emperor Constantine draped in a toga and crowned

with laurels. He is accompanied by a bearded old man and he supervises the activity of two workers who, kneeling, present him with a plan (that of the Pantheon). In the background men are building a town. An eagle flies over the scene, carrying in its beak a crown of laurels. The Rubens sketch that is the source of this composition is kept in the Maxwell Macdonald collection in Glasgow.

THE LIFE OF THE VIRGIN [9]

This group of fourteen tapestries was manufactured from 1638 to 1657 for the benefit of Michel le Masle, prior of the Roches, canon and cantor of Notre Dame of Paris, who gave them to the cathedral to adorn the choir on holy days. Cardinal Richelieu apparently had a hand in the project, for his monogram and armorial bearings are found on the upper part of all the borders, while the

Fig. 3. *The Story of Artemisia: Soldier Carrying a Vase on a Litter.* H: 4.06m. W: 4.22m. Monograms of Philippe Maecht and Hans Taye. Mark of Paris. Atelier of Saint Marcel. The Minneapolis Institute of Arts. The Ethel Morrison Van Derlip Fund.

Fig. 4. *The Story of Constantine: The Building of Constantinople.* H: 4.84m. W: 4.79m. Monograms of Philippe Maecht and Hans Taye. Mark: P and fleur de lys. Atelier of Saint Marcel. Philadelphia Museum of Art.

coat of arms of Abbot Le Masle, his intendant, are visible in the lower corners.

The year 1638, it should be noted, is the date of the vow of Louis XIII and of the subsequent consecration of France to the Virgin. The execution of these tapestries took about twenty years. One of them was woven in an atelier in Brussels. Seven others bear the signature of the tapestry weaver Pierre Damour, who worked in Rheims until 1650 and later in Paris; his workshop was probably located close to Notre Dame.

The series of *The Life of the Virgin* is the work of several artists. The earliest, and the favorite artist of the cardinal, was Philippe de Champagne, but it is certain also that Le Masle requested cartoons from two other

painters of great renown, Charles Poerson and Jacques Stella.

The tapestries were exhibited at Notre Dame Cathedral until 1699, at which time the architect, Robert de Cotte, undertook to renovate the choir. The hangings were then banished to a storeroom and later exhibited in other churches in Paris. In 1739 they were given to the chapter of Notre Dame of Strasbourg. The inscription of the cartouche in the center of the lower border was replaced by a new inscription in Latin bearing the date 1739.

In *The Flight into Egypt* (Fig. 5) we see that the action takes place in a wooded countryside. The Virgin is seated in the foreground on what looks like an antique tomb in ruins.

Fig. 5. *The Life of the Virgin: The Flight into Egypt.* H: 4.85m. W: 5.45m. Mark: PAR AMOUR. Notre Dame de Strasbourg. (Photograph: Caisse Nationale des Monuments Historiques et des Sites)

She is holding the Child Jesus on her lap and Saint Joseph stands behind her. Two kneeling angels offer doves and fruit to the Child. In the background two cherubs are playing with a donkey; another is flying away. The border is decorated with cartouches and cherubs. In the upper border are armorial bearings and monograms of Cardinal Richelieu. In the lower border is the coat of arms of Michel Le Masle. The sketch of this composition, a pen drawing by Poerson, is kept in the Cabinet des Dessins in the Louvre.

THE LIFE OF SAINT GERVAIS AND SAINT PROTAIS [10]

On 2 December 1651, the council of the churchwardens and former churchwardens of the church of Saint Gervais decided to commission a tapestry representing the martyrdom of their patrons, Saint Gervais and Saint Protais. This hanging was executed by the tapestry weaver Girard Laurent after the paintings of several artists: Eustache Lesueur, Thomas Goussé, Sébastien Bourdon, and Philippe de Champagne. The first four tapestries were delivered 31 January 1661. Sold in 1874 by the church, they were recovered by the City of Paris in 1880.

Saint Gervais and Saint Protais, the sons of Saint Vital and Saint Valerie, suffered martyrdom in Milan in A.D. 64 under the reign of Nero. Their relics were miraculously found in 386 by Saint Ambrose in Milan.

In *The Discovery of the Relics* (central part, Fig. 6) we see that Saint Ambrose, assisted by prelates and surrounded by a great multitude, has the corpses of both saints, miraculously preserved, pulled from their tombs. In the foreground the sarcophagus has just been elevated by a hand-winch. The drawing of Philippe of Champagne, which is the source of this composition, is kept in the Cabinet des Dessins at the Louvre.

THE SIMON VOUET TAPESTRIES[11]

In 1627 King Louis XIII sent for Simon Vouet, then in Italy to request him to attend to "the ornamentation of the royal houses and of the new tapestry manufactories which His Majesty had the intention of bringing to fruition" (Lépicié, *Vie des premiers peintres du Roi . . . .* Paris, 1752).

Vouet returned to Paris on 15 November 1627, accompanied by his Italian wife, Virginia da Vezzo, who served often as his model. He established himself in the galleries of the Louvre. Simon Vouet had a determining influence not only on the aesthetics of the art of tapestry, but also on the organization of the work of the cartoonist. As his pupil Charles Lebrun was to do later in the Gobelins, Vouet employed many French and Flemish assistants who drew the cartoons after his own designs.

His woven compositions reveal an extraordinary range and sumptuously beautiful colors. Their decorative value is enhanced by opulent borders, which reproduce *en camaieu* the frames of the artist's pictures. These frames had been worked in stucco, under the supervision of the painter himself, by the sculptor Jacques Sarrazin.

These borders (Fig. 7), often very wide, constitute one of the distinctive characteristics of the hangings of that time. They represent garlands of flowers and foliage linking medallions held high by children, satyrs, or divinities. Michel Faré, [12] writing about their models, mentions the name of the painter Lubin Baugin, Simon Vouet's disciple, who at the end of his life was residing in the rue de la Chaise, near the ateliers of Raphael de la Planche.

THE OLD TESTAMENT

The Old Testament series, which comprises eight pieces, was manufactured after models ordered by Louis XIII from Simon Vouet, shortly after his return in 1627. This set was meant to decorate the Palace of the Louvre,

as is indicated by the Tortebat engravings of Samson at the feast of the Philistines. Some of these pieces were woven in the ateliers of the Louvre, as is shown by the General Inventory of the Crown Furniture. From the atelier of Raphael de la Planche were also delivered tapestries in the same series, woven as well in the ateliers of Amiens.

In the detail from *Solomon's Judgment* (Fig. 8) we see the lower part of Solomon's throne and, in the foreground, a superb canine. On the right the executioner is raising his arm to cleave the living child with his sword. On the ground the dead child is being shown to

Fig. 6. *Saint Gervais and Saint Protais: The Discovery of the Relics* (central part). Dimensions of the entire tapestry: H: 4.85m. W: 7.25m. Atelier of Girard Laurent. City of Paris. (Photograph: Caisse Nationale des Monuments Historiques et des Sites)

Fig. 7. *The Story of Theagenes and Chariclea: The Shepherd Finds the Infant Chariclea,* detail of the border. The Fine Arts Museums of San Francisco, Gift of H. K. S. Williams to the California Palace of the Legion of Honor, 1929.9.1.

Fig. 8. *The Old Testament: Solomon's Judgment* (detail). Dimensions of the entire tapestry: H: 3.20m. W: 3.30m. Monuments Historiques de France. (Photograph: Caisse Nationale des Monuments Historiques et des Sites)

Fig. 9. *The Old Testament: Moses Saved from the Waters.* H: 3.20m. W: 1.40m. Monuments Historiques de France. (Photograph: Caisse Nationale des Monuments Historiques et des Sites)

Solomon (not shown in the scene) by his mother, who is standing nearby.

In *Moses Saved from the Waters* (Fig. 9), a very narrow tapestry, we see only the central part of Simon Vouet's composition. The Pharaoh's daughter, surrounded by her women, is lifting the little Moses from his basket. The border is of flowers and vases of flowers.

RINALDO AND ARMIDA [13]

The subjects of the eight pieces that comprise the *Rinaldo and Armida* series were inspired by the French novel *La Jérusalem délivrée*. They were modeled on the paintings of Simon Vouet for the Hôtel de Bullion and woven by both the atelier of the Louvre and the atelier of the faubourg Saint Marcel. The General Inventory of the Crown Furniture records three sets of this hanging, two of which were woven in gold. None are to be found in the collections of the Mobilier National. Numerous other tapestries, in public or private collections, bear witness to the success of the theme.

Besides the pieces mentioned by Fenaille, we must add the tapestry in the museum in Detroit representing the *Garden of Armida*, woven by Alexandre de Comans; the hanging of the Haras du Pin; the piece in the Musée des Arts Décoratifs; one in the château of Bourdeilles (Dordogne);and miscellaneous panels belonging to the Monuments Historiques.

In *Armida about to Stab Rinaldo* (Fig. 10) we see Rinaldo lying at the foot of a tree. He has been put to sleep by the song of a siren, who can be seen on the right, bathing in a lake. Armida is rushing on from the left, dagger in hand, while a little cupid is letting fly an arrow in her direction. The cartoonist added to Vouet's composition two genies riding on the clouds and protecting Rinaldo with their wands. The border is decorated with small cupids *en camaïeu*.

THE STORY OF ULYSSES

Shortly after his return to France in 1634–35, Vouet decorated the upper gallery of the *hôtel* of Bullion, the Superintendent of Finances, with paintings representing the trials of Ulysses. According to Piganiol de la Force, "It cannot be said that these paintings are the artist's best, so they are not listed with his works" (Lépicié, *Vie* . . . . . Paris, 1752).

It is likely that the cartoons made from these paintings were the models for *The Story of Ulysses*. This series is mentioned in the General Inventory of the Crown Furniture drawn up by Gédéon du Metz and preserved in the Archives de l'Oise (mentioned by Fenaille, p. 330). A complete set of hangings showing *The Story of Ulysses* (eight pieces) belongs to the marquis of Vibraye, in the château of Cheverny (Loir-et-Cher). Miscellaneous pieces belong to the Monuments Historiques, others to the museum of Besançon, the museum of Caen, and to the Palais de Justice in Riom.

Fig. 10. *Rinaldo and Armida: Armida about to Stab Rinaldo.* H: 3m. W: 3.60m. Monuments Historiques de France. (Photograph: Caisse Nationale des Monuments Historiques et des Sites)

Ulysses and the Sirens (Fig. 11) is an illustration of canto XII from the *Odyssey*. In the foreground we see three sirens holding each other's hands. In the background a ship is departing, bearing Ulysses and his friends. Acting on the advice of Circe, Ulysses has succeeded in escaping the songs of the Sirens by filling his and his companions' ears with wax and having himself tied to the mast of his vessel. The border is ornamented with cartouches and beribboned garlands of flowers and fruit. In the center of the upper top border is a trophy of flags.

THE STORY OF THEAGENES AND CHARICLEA [14]

The scenes of this series are borrowed from the novel by Heliodorus, translated into French in 1547 by Jacques Amyot, bishop of Auxerre. The vogue of the pastoral novel was just starting. To illustrate this story two sets of tapestries were woven by the Parisian ateliers. The first one was made according to the cartoons of Ambroise Dubois; the second was based on compositions of a different style made by Simon Vouet. There are several pieces to this set, and The Fine Arts Museums of San Francisco own a very beautiful series.

In *Chariclea Led away by the Pirates* (Fig. 12) we see on the right a weeping Chariclea being carried away by pirates, while on the left a ship has run aground and its crew, killed, left lying on the shore. This tapestry may be compared to the one belonging to The Fine Arts Museums of San Francisco, which is smaller but has an identical subject. The borders, decorated with putti, are not similar. A tapestry representing the same subject, and also with a different border, may be found at the Museo de Arte, in Saõ Paulo.

CREATION OF THE GOBELINS ROYAL FACTORY

The troubles of the Fronde (1648–1653) slowed down the activities of the ateliers of

Fig. 12. *The Story of Theagenes and Chariclea: Chariclea Led away by the Pirates.* H: 3.20m. W: 4m. Monuments Historiques de France. (Photograph: Caisse Nationale des Monuments Historiques et des Sites)

Paris. The professional skills that they had developed were turned to best advantage when the Maincy Manufactory was created at the behest of Nicolas Fouquet, Superintendent of Finances for Louis XIV. However, when Fouquet was arrested, Colbert prevented Louis XIV from scattering the looms of Maincy and had them transported to a building in Paris, where he also added the looms of the Louvre as well as those of the last Comans and La Planche. "Thus," to quote Roger-Armand Weigert, "the royal factory of the Gobelins came to birth, fortified by the lessons of the past."[15]

In 1662 the first four tapestry ateliers were established in the Gobelins, under the management of the painter Charles Lebrun, to continue weaving tapestries for Louis XIV and his successors. From that time on, France gained an international reputation in the field of tapestry making.

Discussion of the "Parisian workshops" on pages 171–72 and 182–83 is adapted from material that originally appeared in Roger-Armand Weigert, *La Tapisserie,* Paris, 1956 (*French Tapestry,* English translation, © 1962 by Faber and Faber Limited, pp. 100–101, 104–105).

NOTES

1. Mercedes and Vittorio Viale, *Arazzi e tappetti antichi*, memorial exhibition catalogue, Turin, 1948 (Turin: 1952).

2. Jacques Thuillier, *Chefs-d'oeuvre de la tapisserie parisienne, 1597–1662*, exposition catalogue (Orangerie de Versailles, 1967), p. 11.

3. Ibid., p. 11.

4. Ibid. Refer to this exhibition catalogue for a more comprehensive bibliography of these hangings.

5. Name in *L'Inventaire général des meubles de la Couronne: Le Vol du héron* ou *Les Chasses de François Ier*.

6. Jean Ehrmann, *Antoine Caron, peintre à la cour de Valois, 1521–1599* (Geneva, 1955); Jean Ehrman, "Tapisseries et tableaux inédits dans la série de la reine Artémise," *Bulletin de la Société de l'histoire de l'art français* (Paris), 1965; *Minneapolis Institute of Art Bulletin*, October 2, 1948; Madeleine Jarry, "Tapisseries inédites de la tenture d'Artémise," *L'Oeil* (Paris), November 1973.

7. Information graciously given by Edith Standen.

8. John Coolidge, "Louis XIII and Rubens. The Story of the Constantine Tapestries," *Gazette des Beaux Arts*, May-June 1966, pp. 271–292; Daniel Du Bon, *Tapestries from the Samuel H. Kress Collection at the Philadelphia Museum of Art: The History of Constantine the Great designed by Peter Paul Rubens and Pietro da Cortona* (London, 1964).

9. Strasbourg Exhibition, 1966, *Tapisseries du Moyen Âge à nos jours* (Strasbourg: Anc. Douane, 1966).

10. Louis Brochard, *Les Tapisseries de l'église de Saint Gervais d'après des documents inédits* (Aurillac, 1933).

11. William R. Crelly, *The Painting of Simon Vouet* (New Haven, Conn., and London: Yale University Press, 1962).

12. Michel Faré, *Le Grand Siècle de la nature morte en France: Le XVIIe siècle* (Office du Livre, 1974).

13. Louis Demonts, "Les amours de Renaud et Armide, décoration peinte par Simon Vouet pour Claude de Bullion" in *Bulletin de la Société de l'histoire de l'art français* (1913).

14. Anna G. Bennett, *Five Centuries of Tapestry from The Fine Arts Museums of San Francisco* (San Francisco: The Fine Arts Museums of San Francisco and Charles E. Tuttle, Co., 1976), pp. 203–11.

15. Roger–Armand Weigert, *La Tapisserie* (Paris, 1956), p. 113.

SELECTED BIBLIOGRAPHY

Coural, Jean. "Notes documentaires sur les ateliers parisiens de 1597 à 1662." *Chefs d'oeuvre de la tapisserie parisienne, 1597–1662*. Exhibition catalogue. Orangerie de Versailles, 1967.

Fenaille, Maurice. *Etat général des tapisseries de la manufacture des Gobelins, depuis son origine jusqu'à nos jours, 1600–1900*. Vol. I (1601–62). Paris, 1923.

Göbel, Heinrich. *Wandteppiche:* Pt. II *Die romanischen Länder*, Vol. I. Leipzig, 1928.

Guiffrey, Jules. *Comptes des bâtiments du Roi sous le règne de Louis XIV*. Vol. I. Paris, 1881.

———*Inventaire général du mobilier de la Couronne sous Louis XIV*. Pt. I. Paris, 1885.

———"Les Manufactures parisiennes de tapisserie au XVIIe siècle." *Mémoires de la Société de l'histoire de Paris et l'Ile de France*. Vol. XIX. Paris, 1892.

Janneau, Guillaume. *Evolution de la tapisserie*. Paris, 1947.

Jarry, Madeleine. *La Tapisserie des origines à nos jours*. Paris, 1968.

Salet, Francis. *La Tapisserie française du moyen-âge à nos jours*. Paris, 1946.

Standen, Edith. "Mythological Scenes: A Tapestry Series after Laurent de La Hire." *The Museum of Fine Arts, Houston, Bulletin* 4, no. 1 (Spring 1973): 10-21.

Weigert, Roger-Armand. *La Tapisserie et le tapis*. Paris, 1964.

The Beauvais Manufactory in 1690

Bertrand Jestaz

Very little is known about the Beauvais Manufactory at the time of Louis XIV, since the establishment's archives of this period no longer exist. Fabrication records were kept only from 1724 on, and production prior to that date may be ascertained only through later documents, such as a list of cartoons kept in 1723 and two lists of tapestries for sale in 1724 and 1731.[1] This break in the documentation explains why a history of the Beauvais work, like the one by Maurice Fenaille on the Gobelins production, has not yet been established. Information may be gleaned only from notary acts, essentially order contracts or tapestry sales. Roger-Armand Weigert, who discovered a great number of such documents, has outlined what little we know of the history of the manufactory during the time of Louis XIV, and he summed it up in a recent study.[2]

The Beauvais Manufactory was created by letters patent on 5 August 1664, which granted to director Louis Hinart, a tapestry merchant established in Paris but native of Beauvais, a concession of thirty years and an advance capital of 60,000 livres on condition that he put one hundred weavers to work immediately and that he recruit one hundred more each year for six years. Nevertheless, until the French Revolution the manufactory was a private enterprise, which explains the pecuniary embarrassments its management suffered most of the time.

The first production was modest, if we are to judge by the mentions of tapestries produced then: many "verdures" (greenery), "jeux d'enfants" (children playing),[3] and "Ténières" (popular scenes in the manner of David Teniers II). The royal commissions were not enough to support the establishment, and after the death of Colbert, its main protector, Louis Hinart had to retire. On 21 February 1684, a contract was signed for its "reestablishment," on the same terms as those set forth in the original charter of 1664, with a new director, Philippe Béhagle, originally from Oudenaarde. Beginning June 13th, for fifteen years Béhagle associated himself with two other tapestry makers, Jean Baert, also from Oudenaarde, and Georges Blommaert, who had exercised his trade in Lille. Nothing is known of the results of this association, only that the financial situation grew rapidly worse. Béhagle succeeded in keeping the enterprise together as long as he lived, but at his death in 1705 he was employing only fifty-three workers and his debts amounted to 176,000 livres.

Yet the production of that period was not negligible, and important tapestries were made,[4] among them *The Conquests of Louis XIV,* based on the cartoons of J. B. Martin; *The Acts of the Apostles,* from the famous compositions of Raphael; *The Elements,* from the same cartoons that Lebrun conceived for the Gobelins but which, in Beauvais, were woven on the low-warp looms, thus presenting a mirror image; *The Birds of the Menagerie,* which may have been designed by a certain Firens; the "tenture chinoise," after L. de Vernansal and J. B. Blain de Fontenay, a very popular series at the beginning of the eighteenth century; *The Sea Ports,* from the cartoons by Kerchove and Campion; and, finally, the famous *Grotesques à fond jaune,* usually attributed to Berain but in fact designed by J. B. Monnoyer. Other sets are also vaguely mentioned in various documents but have not been identified. Thus, on the whole it was a limited *oeuvre,* especially since some sets were woven only once or twice, such as *The Conquests of Louis XIV* or *The Acts of the Apostles.* No doubt many other tapestries of that period could be attributed to Beauvais, which would give us a better appreciation of Béhagle's leadership, but signed or marked pieces are as rare as documents and no new attribution has appeared recently that would enlarge the catalogue established at great pains by Weigert.

The discovery of a few unpublished notary acts[5] permits me to contribute new information to the history of the manufactory and to identify a number of tapestries which greatly enrich the list of its production. From these acts which Béhagle deposited with his notary in 1690, one can see the extent of the debts he contracted with two businessmen—and there were others, for we know of creditors he was trying to appease by the same means.[6] As early as 1684, he owed 63,000 livres; then 9,000; then, in 1688, more than 45,000; in 1689, more than 40,000; until finally, in August 1690, the establishment was in debt by a sum of 122,747 livres. The association, meanwhile, had dissolved, probably because of the financial problems: Jean Baert left as early as 1685,[7] and Blommaert at the end of 1688. On 13 May 1690 Béhagle and Blommaert put their business in order by listing the assets they had shared until the end of 1688, and Béhagle agreed to buy back his former

188

associate's share and remain the lone proprietor. Unfortunately, this list does not describe the stock of tapestries for sale but only the materials, tools, and supplies of the manufactory. For instance, the wool stocks represented only 5,850 livres, the silk stocks 11,906, the cartoons 6,418—a relatively high sum, which indicates their great number. Yet there were only forty-nine looms equipped. The assets, not counting the tapestries, amounted to 56,062 livres, a paltry sum compared to the enormous capital invested and the loans contracted during the last years.

As sole director and owner on 1 January 1689, Béhagle was confronted with a difficult situation. Short on liquid assets, he was obliged to deliver to his creditors the products of his manufactory. It was, of course, a very expensive arrangement, since presumably the tapestries were disposed of for a sum far below their actual value; in a memorandum left by Béhagle he complains bitterly of often having sold his tapestries at a loss.[8] But historians may rejoice at this occurrence since the arrangement contracted by Béhagle with one of his creditors on 19 August 1690 constitutes probably the most valuable document we have in research pertaining to the Beauvais production at that date.

To pay part of his debt, Béhagle agreed in fact to deliver nine sets of tapestries, described as follows:

the first, numbered 129, including six pieces, Metamorphoses in large figures, for the sum of 4,200 livres;
the second, numbered 149, including six pieces, Cephalus and Procris, for 2,400 livres;
the third, numbered 152, in six pieces, Verdure, for 1,900 livres;
the fourth, numbered 164, six pieces, small figures, Metamorphoses, for 2,400 livres;
the fifth, numbered 188, including six pieces, representing Psyche, for 2,100 livres;
the sixth, numbered 207, including six pieces, Metamorphoses, large figures, from the design of Sieur Houasse, for 6,000 livres;
the seventh, numbered 157, in six pieces, Metamorphoses, small figures, for 2,200 livres;
the eighth, numbered 187, six pieces, Metamorphoses, small figures, for 2,200 livres;
and the ninth, numbered 192, six pieces, Verdure, for 1,600 livres.

Moreover, he promised to furnish, "within the next eight months at the latest,[9] a tapestry set numbered 167, in eight pieces, large figures, Metamorphoses, from the design of Messrs. Sève and Houasse," for the equivalent of 7,400 livres.

It is not our intention to evaluate the obvious loss suffered by Béhagle in this operation; the main interest of this document remains for us in the enumeration of a certain number of Beauvais tapestry sets from which may be deduced entirely new information on the manufactory's production, useful not only in its identification, but also in its quantitative evaluation.

In fact, the sets mentioned are all carefully numbered, most likely in the order of their entrance into the warehouse, hence denoting their rank in the manufactory's production. The highest number is 207, so we may conclude that the manufactory, by August 1690, had produced already *at least* 207 sets—and probably even more, since it is not proven that set number 207 was the last produced at the time. If we suppose that each set included an average of six pieces—which is the usual number of the Beauvais series, and Béhagle's agreement with his creditors confirms it—these 207 sets represent a total of 1,242 tapestries. It is evident that such a considerable production could not have been realized during the first six years of the Béhagle leadership: there was no reason for beginning a new numeration in 1684, since the preceding works could not all have been sold by then. The numeration must then cover the production of the manufactory since its creation in 1664, and the figure of 1,242 tapestries may be considered a *minimal* estimation of the production between 1664 and 1690. Let us evaluate it at 1,300 pieces or more.

I will not elaborate further on this figure, except to underline the fact that up to now we possessed no data to appraise quantatively the production possible in the ateliers of old. While the art of tapestry has always yielded masterpieces, it has been first and foremost a mass-production operation. As approximate as this evaluation is, it is the first to furnish proof of that fact.

Furthermore, the indication of the subject and number of pieces of each series permits new attributions[10] which would considerably enrich the presumed Beauvais output before 1690. I shall make only brief reference to the Verdure tapestries. This type of piece was very common and evidently represented the most simple level of production —the estimated price confirms that deduction. The director apparently did not wish to claim as his own these pieces by having his mark woven on them, so no Verdure bears a mark permitting its attribution to Beauvais. Yet we may easily imagine a work on a slightly higher level that we could designate "improved Verdure," the landscape being enhanced by the presence of small figures or animals. In the first case, these figures may be either hunters, as in two pieces kept in the Azay-le-Rideau castle on which all the letters of the name "Béhagle" are woven,[11] or else various creatures apparently borrowed from other tapestries, particularly Grotesques, as seen on a piece framed in acanthus, with the name of Beauvais in the border.[12] In the case of animals, one must refer to the series called *The Birds of the Menagerie*, because they were, in fact, Verdures with birds from the Versailles menagerie in the foreground. The best of this kind of "improved Verdure" is probably the set in four pieces belonging to the city of Lausanne and kept at the villa Mon Repos, inscribed also with the name Béhagle on three of its pieces.[13] Plain as they are in conception, these greenery tapestries are handsomely executed, rich in bright, solid colors, and often adorned with beautiful borders of foliage, typical of the Beauvais production. But though they represent the lowest level of the Beauvais output, they were at the same time the best Verdures executed in France then and eminently superior to those of Aubusson.

The story of Cephalus and Procris had been a popular theme in tapestry since the sixteenth century. We have already known that a series with this subject was produced in Beauvais in the eighteenth century, supposedly designed by the painter Florentin Damoiselet from Brussels, and that in 1728 it was woven in four pieces, though it could comprise eight.[14] We know now that this series was made even prior to 1690 and that it then consisted of six pieces. Until now only one set of four pieces has been identified; it was shown in 1946 at the French Tapestry Exhibition but since then has disappeared without a trace except for three photographs published in Fr. Salet's work following the exhibit.[15] According to the exhibition catalogue, the hanging carried Béhagle's mark, but in the reproductions published it did not bear the name of Béhagle as ordinarily found but rather a simple fleur-de-lis woven in the galloon. Yet there is no doubt concerning its Beauvais origin, for the border is typical of that produced by this manufactory. It is characterized by an alter-

nating of foliage and palms; by the presence of shells and baskets of fruit in the horizontal parts; and by the "candelabra" in the vertical border made of flowers, foliage, shells, and motifs in the shape of a lyre resting on a doe's feet and a marble socle.[16]

The four pieces of this set represented *The Return of Cephalus*, *The Gift of the Javelin* (which, unfortunately, was not reproduced), *The Departure for the Hunt*, and *Cephalus Moaning the Death of Procris*. Familiarity with the traditional iconography of this fable will help us over any difficulty in imagining the subjects of the two missing panels, which, with the others, would comprise a six-piece set. One missing panel was probably *The Abduction of Cephalus by Aurora*, which would come first; the other was probably *Procris's Death*, which showed Cephalus throwing his javelin toward the bush behind which his beloved was hiding. The large-figured series of the Metamorphoses develops the latter subject, and the same cartoon was possibly utilized also for the *Cephalus and Procris* series.

As to the *Abduction*, it is recognizable in an isolated piece sold in Paris in 1958 as a Beauvais tapestry from this same set of Métamorphoses.[17] It represents indeed *Aurora and Cephalus* at the moment of the abduction, and in spite of a certain ambiguity in the rendition of the faces and attitudes, there cannot be any doubt as to the subject (Fig. 1). But as we will see, this subject does not belong to the Houasse *Metamorphoses* series. On the other hand, this tapestry had the same border[18] as the known pieces in the set of *Cephalus and Procris* and the same height, 3.10m; thus, it is logical to see it as the first episode in the series, even if the style seems at first somewhat more developed.

In any case, it is necessary to wait for the definitive identification of the missing subjects before we can define the style of the *Cephalus and Procris* story in its entirety and appreciate its unity. Already, judging from the three pieces published by Fr. Salet, the following features deserve our attention: a certain naiveté in the drawing of figures and in the conception of the landscape, the static character of the compositions, the parallelism of the attitudes of Cephalus and Procris when they depart for the hunt, and the great number of right angles. All these particularities follow strictly the classical tendencies of French painting in the mid-seventeenth cen-

tury. It may be that Florentin Damoiselet, a minor and little-known painter born in 1644, whose name is given in the statement of 1731, had been following his master's style. His cartoons of Cephalus and Procris may be an early work created for Hinart in the first days of the manufactory. But since he and Houasse were in contact, we must wonder again if the style of *Aurora and Cephalus* does not betray a later addition to the early series,[19] made under Houasse's influence.

The story of Psyche was made fashionable in the early sixteenth century by the set of engravings by the Master of the Die, and it remained one of the most popular themes in the arts. We know that tapestries with the same subject were woven in Paris, first in the workshop of Raphael de la Planche, rue de la Chaise, and later at the Gobelins.

So the mention of a set of *Psyche* produced by Beauvais is not surprising, but the work still had to be identified. The late H. Delesalle had remarked upon two sets in which he detected the style of the manufactory, and thanks to his research I am now able to present a reconstitution of the *Psyche* series.

One of these sets is kept at the Bowes Museum at Barnard Castle. It carries no mark and no signature, but its border assumes their function, for it is of a very particular pattern called "à la carte de France," from the

motif so called in the center of the lower border; and H. Delesalle, by reference to the description of a set in the inventory of the royal furniture in 1673, recognized in the pattern a specialty of Beauvais.[20]

The other set is kept at the Troyes Museum and has no mark either, but its border is typical of Beauvais, with foliage in Vitruvian scrolls on the horizontal parts, candelabra of flowers on lyre-shaped lions' feet on the sides, all on an ochre background, as on the Verdures of Lausanne signed by Béhagle already mentioned, or as on the *Acts of the Apostles* at the Beauvais Cathedral.

The two sets each contain five pieces, with different subjects. By rearranging them, we can reconstruct a series comprising more than six pieces. The first piece (Bowes Museum), according to tradition, represents *The Old Woman Telling the Story of Psyche* (Fig. 2). The second (Bowes Museum and Troyes) was sometimes recognized as *Psyche Going to the Sacrifice*,[21] but one should rather see in it the *Homage Rendered by the Crowd to the Beauty of Psyche*. Indeed, it is said that Psyche was even more beautiful than her sisters and inspired so much admiration that no man dared pretend to her hand. That is probably what this tapestry is relating by placing the heroine in front of her sisters, in the center of a plaza, surrounded by a crowd that expresses, with different gestures, admiration and respect (Fig. 3).

The third piece (Bowes Museum and Troyes) shows *The Father of Psyche Sacrificing to the God* in order to learn from the oracle how to thwart Fate and find a husband for his daughter (Fig. 4). The fourth (Bowes

Museum) represents *Psyche Taking Leave of Her Family* before going to the mountain where she must be abducted by the expected monster (Fig. 5). Then we find *Psyche Carried by the Winds,* who leave her at the Palace of Cupid. One version is at Troyes and another appeared in a sale in 1926 (Fig. 6).[22] The sixth (Troyes) is *Psyche Recognizing Cupid* by the light of her lamp (Fig. 7).

Fig. 2. *The Old Woman Telling the Story of Psyche*. The Bowes Museum, County Council of Durham, England.

Fig. 3. *Homage Rendered by the Crowd to Psyche's Beauty (Psyche Advancing to the Sacrifice)*. The Bowes Museum, County Council of Durham, England.

Fig. 4. *The Father of Psyche Sacrificing to the God*. The Bowes Museum, County Council of Durham, England.

Fig. 5. *Psyche Taking Leave of Her Family*. The Bowes Museum, County Council of Durham, England.

Fig. 6. *Psyche Carried by the Winds*. Present location unknown. (Reproduced from 1926 sales catalogue.)

Fig. 7. *Psyche Recognizing Cupid.*
Musée des Beaux-Arts, Troyes.

The seventh scene would be an episode of the trials suffered by Psyche after being abandoned by Cupid, possibly *Psyche Saved from Suicide* by Cupid's intervention (Fig. 8); versions of it are in the Bowes Museum, at Troyes, and also in a collection in Norway.[23] Finally, this series should probably include that tapestry which Göbel claimed earlier was a part of the series of *Theagenes and Chariclea*, woven by the workshop of the faubourg Saint Marcel,[24] a claim that is untenable. The eighth piece we consider here has the "à la carte de France" border and appears to represent *Psyche Returning from Hell with the Water of Youth* (Fig. 9).

Thus, we obtain a set of eight pieces, yet it is still probably incomplete since a traditional subject, *Psyche Carried on the Mountain,* is lacking, as is also the necessary denouement of the story, *The Banquet of the Gods for the Wedding of Psyche and Cupid.* It may be surmised that the Beauvais Manufactory owned a fairly extensive set of cartoons that included at least ten subjects[25] and that, following commissions, it made from them more or less complete sets, since the one produced in 1690 had only six pieces.

We now know enough to study this *Psyche* series, and the first thing we can be sure of is that it has no relation to the well-known set of Raphael de la Planche and the Gobelins. Most of its subjects are not the same and in any case the cartoons are altogether different. The Beauvais series is thus a special *oeuvre,* and the more original for its complete freedom from the iconographic tradition inherited from the Master of the Die.

To define its style, one might call it an example of naïve classicism. The most characteristic composition in this respect is *Psyche Admired by the Crowd,* with its emphasis on simple, orthogonal forms, its statism, and the naïveté of the figures and of the Roman setting, as though a Poussin had been copied by a child. One may find traces of all this in the *Sacrifice* and in *Psyche Carried by the Winds,* and again in *The Old Woman Telling the Story.* However, the last piece shows an almost mannerist style in the drawing of Psyche and Charon. Nevertheless, it is the classical feeling that pervades the most elaborate panel, *Psyche Taking Leave of her Family,* where one can perceive another echo of Poussin's art in the design of the stretcher-bearers and in the strength of the lighting which gives relief to the central group.

It may seem audacious to speak of Poussin in connection with works as naïve as these, but his influence must not be measured by the quality of the result obtained, and without that influence a style so particular could not be explained. Taking for granted that probably not all the cartoons of this series were drawn by the same hand, we must believe that the most typical ones were from a painter of the school of Poussin. Just as with the story of *Cephalus and Procris,* we are dealing here with a work which was conceived during the third quarter of the seventeenth century (at the beginning of the manufactory) and which must have had a short-lived production.

Apart from these rare sets, which appear in a single version in the document of 1690, the *Metamorphoses*[26] probably represented an important production at Beauvais, because they comprised, in the form of two different series, six of the sets granted by Béhagle. The distinction made in the size of the figures was then usual, and easily understandable, since figures were the parts most difficult to weave and for which the quality of the cartoon mattered the most. That is why the tapestry prices differed, from 2,200 livres for the small-figured ones up to 6,000 for the large, for the same number of pieces. Thus, we must distinguish carefully, as they did of old, between these series, of which the quality and price varied so greatly. The identification of the tapestry sets is that much more difficult.

The small-figured *Metamorphoses* pose a nearly insolvable problem, as they belong to a type very common at the time, but not a piece bears marks to permit identification. Such tapestries were woven in Paris, but also in the Netherlands in the centers with which Beauvais had connections owing to the origins of its workers and of Béhagle himself, places such as Oudenaarde and Brussels.[27] The possibility of confusion is particularly strong and only a text more precise than the covenant of 1690 would allow identification of the works from Beauvais. H. Delesalle seems to have found such a text in the Inventory of the Furniture of the Crown, having discovered the description of a "tapestry set of verdure and landscape with small figures, low warp, wool and silk, design by La Hire, Beauvais workshop, manufactory of Béhagle, representing four subjects of Metamorphoses, to wit: the nine Muses and the Pierides metamorphosed into

Fig. 8. *Psyche Saved from Suicide (Cupid Appearing to Psyche by a Stream)*. The Bowes Museum, County Council of Durham, England.

Fig. 9. *Psyche Returning from Hell with the Water of Youth*. Present location unknown. (Reproduced from Göbel.)

magpies, Cephalus and Procris, Hercules and Omphale and the Education of Bacchus . . . ."[28] The author of the cartoons, the ateliers, the subject of four pieces—we seem to know almost everything. But for all that, this text does not permit complete identification.

First, the mention of La Hire is somewhat surprising, because we now know that a series of the *Metamorphoses* with large figures, patterned on his paintings,[29] was woven in Paris, probably at the Gobelins, and that the subjects of these paintings do not coincide with those of the Beauvais set, except for *Cephalus and Procris*. This last one,[30] on the other hand, at Beauvais could belong to the series of the same name as well as to the *Metamorphoses* with large figures. Finally the existing works fit only partially with the document, since H. Delesalle has been able to discover only three tapestries that agree with it:[31] three pieces kept in Orleans, at the prefecture of Loiret, which represent *Apollo and the Muses* (with flying magpies), *The Childhood of Bacchus*, and *Theseus Discovering His Father's Sword and Sandals*, with a border similar to that of the *Cephalus and Procris* series. But this last piece is purported to derive directly from the Poussin painting on the same topic, and it is difficult to see how this subject could fit into a set illustrating if not specifically *Metamorphoses*, at least Ovidian mythology, and especially *The Loves of the Gods*, as they were called then. As things stand now, and keeping in mind Delesalle's interpretation, we must confess that we cannot offer a coherent list of the subjects of that series. It would be sensible to wait for more information before dealing with the topic.

The large-figured *Metamorphoses* are fortunately known on the basis of other documents. The statement of 1731 mentions three sets on the subject, in six pieces, the cartoons of which are attributed to Houasse and the title of one piece specified as *The Abduction of Orithyia by Boreas*.[32] A certain number of tapestries with the same subject still exists; they carry an identifying mark or a typical border. The existence of other pieces belonging to the same set allowed H. Delesalle to determine the first five subjects of this series, and at the same time to confirm their identity through the record of manufacture for the years 1724–28.[33]

This identification is confirmed by the composition of three groups of tapestries. The first group numbers three pieces and belonged formerly to French and Co. of New York: a *Pan and Syrinx* signed by Béhagle, *Vertumnus and Pomona*, and *Cephalus and Procris*. The second group consists of other pieces[34] sold in 1934, with no marks but with a border as explicit as a signature, picturing the same three subjects just mentioned. The third consists of three more pieces, with the arms of Versainville,[35] marked "Beauvais"; that is, *Boreas and Orithyia, Pan and Syrinx*, and *Alpheius and Arethusa*. These three groups permit identification of five subjects.

A complete set in six pieces, sold recently in Paris,[36] has afforded confirmation and completion of this identification. It carried no mark either, and its border was a simple frame of acanthus, but the fact that it included the first five subjects of the story was sufficent to place it. And the sixth subject was revealed: a narrow composition, as indicated in the records of manufacture,[37] in which Diana leans toward a young woman. This could be called *Diana and an Attendant*, but I would rather call it *Diana* (that is, Jupiter) *and Callisto*.

The result, then, is that it is possible to reconstitute this series in its entirety. Its subjects will be presented in the order in which they appear in the fabrication records—that is, in decreasing order of widths, from 8 to 3 aunes (the Beauvais aune=70 cm)—and illustrated with pieces of diverse origins which show different types of borders.

The first piece, 8 aunes wide, *The Abduction of Orithyia by Boreas* (Fig. 10), was probably popular, since we can count at least seven versions of it.[38] One of them, with the arms of Versainville, was marked "Beauvais" and had a border of the type most often used characterized by a shell between two quivers in the middle of the horizontal borders, and by torches, a shell, and palm leaves in the candelabra on the sides. The piece at The Fine Arts Museums of San Francisco bears the name of Béhagle and presents, it seems, the composition in its maximum width, but its border of flowers mixed with cross-motifs is more rare and probably older.[39] The piece in the National Collections of Bavaria, which since 1976 has been exhibited in the Neue Residenz of Bamberg, probably comes from the collections of the Wittelsbach, and one wonders if it is not part of that set which Béhagle was so proud of having sold to the duke of Bavaria when he was governor of

Fig. 10. *The Abduction of Orithyia by Boreas*. The Fine Arts Museums of San Francisco, Gift of Mrs. Bruce Kelham and Mrs. Peter Lewis to the California Palace of the Legion of Honor, 1948.4.

the Netherlands and settled in Brussels.[40] The composition was bereft of its clump of trees on the extreme right, but the panel possesses a beautiful border of the type already mentioned, with quivers and torches.

The second piece, 7 aunes wide, represents *Pan and Syrinx* (Fig. 11). There are at least seven versions,[41] one of which is signed Béhagle and another marked "Beauvais," both with the same border of quivers and torches. Of the complete set sold in 1974, the panel reproduced here has a border of a simple picture frame enhanced with acanthus, usually thought to be an invention of the eighteenth century, but actually typical of the end of the seventeenth century.

The third piece, 6 aunes wide, was *Vertumnus and Pomona* (Fig. 12), of which eight versions are known.[42] Several of them carry the border with the quivers; others carry the border with the Chinese men, which is equally typical of Beauvais. The piece reproduced here has been exhibited since 1976 at the Neues Schloss in Bayreuth and belongs to the Bavarian National Collections. I believe this panel

to be part of the same set as the *Boreas and Orithyia* of Bamberg, and it probably also belongs to the set bought from Béhagle by the governor of the Netherlands; in any case, it has the same border and height.

The fourth piece, 5 aunes wide, represented *Alpheius and Arethusa* (Fig. 13). I could not detect more than six versions,[43] and only the one in the Versainville set bears the mark "Beauvais."

The fifth piece, 4 aunes wide, was devoted to *Cephalus and Procris*, showing Cephalus preparing to throw his javelin at Procris, who is hiding in the bushes (Fig. 14). It seems to have been seldom executed since only three versions may be cited.[44] The one sold in 1934 unfortunately lost its right-hand border, which was of the quiver and torch type; but until now it was the only one reproduced.

Finally, the sixth piece, 3 aunes wide, showed a meeting of Diana with another female figure; I believe it may be titled *Diana and Callisto* (Fig. 15). It must have been rare, judging by the small number of versions known,

Fig. 11. *Pan and Syrinx*. Present location unknown. (Reproduced from 1974 sales catalogue.)

Fig. 12. *Vertumnus and Pomona*. Neues Schloss, Bayreuth.

200

Fig. 13. *Alpheius and Arethusa*.
Badisches Landesmuseum,
Karlsruhe.

Fig. 14. *Cephalus and Procris*.
Present location unknown.
(Reproduced from 1934 sales
catalogue.)

Fig. 15. *Diana and Callisto*. Present
location unknown. (Reproduced
from 1914 sales catalogue.)

probably because its narrow size limited its use to hanging between windows. Only two versions can be cited with certitude—one I have seen in the complete set sold in 1974 (unfortunately not reproduced in the catalogue) and the one reproduced here,[45] whose border of flowers framed by convoluting ribbons is noteworthy.

The covenant of 1690, as well as the statement of 1731, certify that this series was drawn by Houasse, that is René-Antoine Houasse, a minor painter and disciple of Lebrun known for his tapestry cartoons made for the Gobelins and also for the twenty-one pictures he painted for the Trianon. Curiously enough, the subject of the first piece of the series, *Boreas and Orithyia,* seems inspired by a painting in the Trianon by François Verdier.[46] It is a vertical composition, and the attitudes of the figures differ; but the conception of the two figures in flight—required by the subject—and of the attendants kneeling in the foreground to gather flowers is comparable. On the other hand, the *Alpheius and Arethusa* tapestry derives directly from the Houasse painting at the Trianon (Fig. 16). Its composition is identical and the attitudes of the figures very close, the main difference being that, in the tapestry, the figure of Alpheius is set slightly apart from those of the two women in order to adapt the scene to the composition in width.

The other subjects of the set were not painted in the Trianon, and the *oeuvre* of Houasse is still too little known for us to compare it with the tapestries. Perhaps eventually, the *Metamorphoses* tapestries will assist in identifying Houasse's paintings. Actually, there is no reason to doubt the attribution made by the documents, not only because of the clear connection between the painting and the *Alpheius and Arethusa* tapestry, but also because of the unquestionable uniformity of style in the different scenes of the set, found also in the Houasse pictures at the Trianon. Despite the peculiarities of weaving and framing which differentiate the tapestries, their similarities are striking: the importance placed on foliage, the scale of the figures and their tiered position in the landscape, and the constancy of the female types and of their attitudes—notably the women kneeling or squatting away from the viewer and the arm positions and the designs of the hands. All these features are found in the paintings of Houasse, as witness Iris who appears to Morpheus, Narcissus, or even Cyana and

Proserpina holding a garland among figures languidly reposing in the landscape.[47] Houasse, then, is clearly the author of the cartoons for the large-figured *Metamorphoses.* We must remember that if the tapestries existed already in 1690, the cartoons could have been designed even *before* the Trianon paintings, which were commissioned only after 1688.

One point that must be clarified is the composition of the last set mentioned in 1690, having the same subject but eight pieces, made from the cartoons of Houasse and Sève. According to its description, we may be dealing with an extension of the preceding set, and both adjunct tapestries may have been drawn by either Gilbert or Pierre Sève, both minor painters known only for having designed, after Lebrun, tapestry cartoons for the Gobelins. It was probably not an ordinary production, because the fabrication registers of the eighteenth century record only the six pieces already mentioned. The chance of identification, in the absence of any mention of subject, is practically nil, yet an assumption can be made.

A set of five pieces,[48] some of which bear the name of Béhagle, with mythological subjects, permitting their integration into the *Metamorphoses,* was sold in Paris in 1919. Only two of the pieces were reproduced in the catalogue, *The Abduction of Europa* (Fig. 17) and *Diana and Endymion* (Fig. 18). Except for *Diana's Repose,* the other subjects could not be described with enough precision to be recognized. However, since the set had exactly the same border (foliage and candelabra of flowers on lions' feet, framed with convoluted ribbons) as that on the sixth piece of the *Metamorphoses* (Fig. 15), one may wonder if the narrow piece (2.25 m) designated then as "Diana and an Attendant" is not another version of the composition I have called *Diana and Callisto.* If so, it would constitute a decisive link between the *Metamorphoses* set and this five-piece set from which we may subtract *Diana and Callisto,* a basic element of the main series.

The four other pieces could have been optional extensions, and since one was certainly meant to be hung between windows as a companion piece to *Diana and Callisto,* they could be taken as three horizontal panels to complete the Houasse hanging. We would thus have, at the most, a series of ten pieces made up of eight horizontal and two

Fig. 16. *Alpheius and Arethusa*, by
René-Antoine Houasse.
Château de Trianon, Versailles.
(Photograph: Cliché Musées
Nationaux.)

Fig. 17. *The Abduction of Europa*.
Collection of Mrs. Sheldon
Whitehouse, New York.

Fig. 18. *Diana and Endymion*.
Present location unknown.
(Reproduced from 1914 sales
catalogue.)

entrefenêtre panels. This hypothesis is supported by two important considerations: first, the fact that at least two of these subjects are extremely rare[49] and, second, the fact that the five pieces signed by Béhagle cannot be associated with any other Beauvais set (their subjects are linked together only by the theme of *Metamorphoses;* that is, mythological inspiration).

To sum up, I propose that among them are the two pieces added by Sève to the Houasse series. No opposition is found in the style, for *Diana's Repose, Diana and Endymion* and *The Abduction of Europa* are perfectly related to the preceding pieces as far as general conception and inspiration are concerned. However, they differ in some details, as is natural since we are dealing with the compositions of another painter; in particular, they show a rounder and more compact drawing of the figures, an off-center composition filling one side of the panel and leaving the other empty, and an inclination to include unnecessary Cupids.

Even if positive identification of the two additional pieces of the *Metamorphoses* series were not possible, the covenant of 1690 would still have thrown considerable light on the Beauvais production at the end of the seventeenth century. The identification of these sets indeed permits a complete view of the style of the manufactory at that time. The first thought that comes to mind is that all the sets listed in that document were nearly unknown to us, as none of the famous sets are found there. Since they must have represented the current production, which was always available, it means that until now we have appreciated seventeenth-century Beauvais tapestry through works which were not its most representative (excepting the *Grotesques* which were extremely popular at the end of the reign of Louis XIV). We must now correct this view in accordance with the new facts.

If we consider all tapestries listed above, we notice that, except for the Verdures, which have no subject, all the sets dealt with themes borrowed from mythology and chosen for their poetic and fabulous flavor. There is nothing heroic or solemn. Psyche, Cephalus and Procris, or various themes of the *Metamorphoses* are all occasions for telling fables that unfold in pleasant groves where the marvelous always embellishes reality. If we add to the production discussed the popular series—that is, the attractive landscapes of the *Birds of the Menagerie,* or the *Sea Ports,* the *Chinese* set with its dazzling exoticism, and above all the *Grotesques,* in which were concentrated the charm of ephemeral surroundings and the merriment of festivals—we see that the work of Beauvais represented the flourishing of a particular taste that was opposed to the noble style said to have dominated all French art during the Age of Louis XIV.

The essential characteristics of Beauvais tapestry were fantasy, a taste for the marvelous, sensitivity to landscape, that is, a tender and trustful feeling for nature, all of which largely anticipated the eighteenth century. It was the opposite of the "academic" style, and we could say that Beauvais was to the Gobelins what Trianon was to Versailles: neither a rival nor an equal, but a vital counterpart.[50] Indeed, Houasse was not Lebrun, and the Beauvais repertory was limited to a special genre that did not pretend to rival the grand style. Nevertheless, without Beauvais, as without Trianon, something essential to French art at the end of the seventeenth century would be lacking. It would be like a palace without a garden.

NOTES

1. These documents are published *in extenso* in J. Badin's still fundamental work, *La Manufacture de tapisseries de Beauvais . . .* (Paris: Société de propagation des livres d'art, 1909), pp. 20–26.

2. R.-A. Weigert, "Les Commencements de la manufacture royale de Beauvais, 1664–1705," *Gazette des Beaux-Arts* 2 (1964): 331–46.

3. From the *Children Playing* series: two pieces could be identified by H. Delesalle, "Tapisseries exposées à Beauvais . . .," *Revue du Louvre* (1965), pp. 201–208.

4. On the *Acts of the Apostles, Sea Ports,* and *Birds of the Menagerie,* see Delesalle; on the *Grotesques,* see R.-A. Weigert, "Les Grotesques de Beauvais," *Hyphé* 1, no. 2 (1946): 66–78.

5. These acts are to be published in the *Bulletin de la Société de l'histoire de l'art français.* They are essentially three statements, dated 7 November 1684, 20 March 1685, and 17 June 1690, pinpointing the origin of the funds borrowed by Béhagle, deposited on 17 June 1690 at his notary's; an agreement drawn up on 19 August 1690 between Béhagle and his creditor Gilles Thomas, sieur de la Chapelle, to which is attached Joris Blommaert's autographed act of abandonment dated 13 May 1690 showing estimated common assets.

6. To free himself of his indebtedness to Jean Talon, Béhagle had to turn over to him on 2 April 1689 a group of tapestries by means of an act that makes known the existence at that date of *Grotesques* and *Birds of the Menagerie.* See *Nouvelles archives de l'art français,* 3rd ser., 8 (1892): 62–64. Béhagle was able to nullify these proceedings shortly afterward.

7. On 20 March 1685 Béhagle and Blommaert were recognized as sole debtors, "seeing that Sieur Bart and his wife have left the said society."

8. "It can easily be understood . . . how great the profit of the manufactory would have been if all the goods . . . had been sold under the same conditions, which would have happened if I had had enough funds to keep them in my warehouse and sell them for what they are worth" (ed. Badin, p. 13).

9. The foreseen delay does not mean that the set was in the process of fabrication (its order number is the proof) but is explained by the fact that it had been pawned with a Sieur Grosseilles, "master of the warehouse of the Brussels tapestries," who had to be reimbursed before its return.

10. In this search for identification, I found valuable information in the documentation assembled by the late Hubert Delesalle.

11. The detail of a similar piece belonging to the Mobilier National was reproduced by R.-A. Weigert, 1964, p. 338, fig. 3. It just happens that a set of this type was described in the inventory of the Crown Furniture, as "a set . . . Beauvais workshop, Béhagle's manufactory, representing landscape and verdure and a hunt with small figures . . .," (see J. Guiffrey, ed., *Inventaire général du mobilier de la Couronne* 1, (Paris, 1885: 363, no. 176.

12. This piece (2.50 m×4.40 m), which belonged to the Paris merchant Dario Boccara, was reproduced in color in the review *Connaissance des arts,* no. 255 (May 1973): 3. Another, with a much richer foliage border, was sold in New York at Parke Bernet, on 10–11 November 1972, no. 226, repr.

13. See J. Niclausse, "Notes sur quelques tapisseries françaises conservées en Suisse," *Hyphé* 1 (1946): 236–39. Also see H. Delesalle's article (note 3). A lone piece belonging to M. Ragnar Moltzau in Oslo was published by R.-A. Weigert (1964), p. 341, fig. 5, and H. Delesalle, p. 205, fig. 3. Another was sold in Versailles by maître Martin on 6 July 1976.

14. Badin, pp. 22, 23, and 57.

15. *La Tapisserie française du moyen âge à nos jours: Catalogue* (Paris: Musée d'art moderne 1946), pp. 66–67, nos. 147–50. Also Fr. Salet, *La Tapisserie française du moyen âge à nos jours* (Paris: ed. Vincent et Fréal, 1946), pl. 80–81.

16. *L'Inventaire général du mobilier de la Couronne* 1, 349–51 and 363, describes similar motifs on the borders of several Beauvais sets, also "foliage of large red and blue leaves in the manner of panaches . . ." (no. 95), "the festoon of leaves and flowers ornamented with large red and blue leaves in the middle of which, at top and bottom, are baskets full of fruit" (nos. 102, 104) and, at the base of the vertical borders, "claws . . . supported by a marble-colored socle" (nos. 176, 177).

17. Hôtel Drouot, maître Bondu, estate of Mlle Colombier de Dion (fourth sale), 3 February 1958, no. 141, repr. pl. V (3.10 m×5.20 m).

18. In the photograph only one difference of detail is evident: there is no wicker basket under the fruit in the middle of the horizontal border. Consequently, the *Aurora and Cephalus* tapestry did not belong to the same set as the four pieces in the exhibition of 1946. Although by its style it seems to be more closely related to the large-figured *Metamorphoses,* this resemblance may be due more to the time of the weaving than to the style of the cartoon.

19. Badin (p. 57) has indeed established that the *Cephalus and Procris* series could comprise eight pieces, but not all the subjects may have existed from inception, nor even in 1690. The usual number of pieces was six, as attested in 1690. Then it is possible that the subject of Aurora and Cephalus was added later as a prelude to the set.

20. "A set . . . Beauvais manufactory, representing *Children Playing,* in a border with a ground color of bronze with foliage, eagles, and festoons of flowers; in the middle of the upper border is a world map in a cartouche; at either end of this border, the King's motto, and in the middle of the lower one, a map of France" (*Inventaire général . . .,* 1, p. 304, no. 56). W. G. Thomson already recognized this border and attributed the *Psyche* set of the Bowes Museum to Beauvais.

21. See W. G. Thomson, *A History of Tapestry,* 3d ed. (Wakefield: E P Publishing Limited, 1973), p. 438, repr. p. 441; and *Encyclopaedia Britannica* 21

(1961), s. v. "Tapestry," pl. VIII, p. 1. The Troyes piece, on the other hand, was already accepted as the *Hommage rendered to Psyche's Beauty* by Louis Le Clert, *Musée de Troyes, Art décoratif, Catalogue* (Troyes: 1897), p. 25.

22. Hôtel Drouot, salle 1, maître Lair-Dubreuil, 14–15 May 1926, no. 248, repr. (3 m×2.75 m).

23. *Fransk Kunstindustri og Kunst i norsk eie*, Kunstindustrimuseet Exhibition, Oslo, 1952, p. 46, repr.

24. H. Göbel, *Die Wandteppiche . . . in Frankreich . . .* (Leipzig: Verlag Klinkhardt & Biermann, 1928), p. 77, repr. pl. 52. It was part of a set of four pieces seen by Göbel for sale at Munich, but unfortunately he did not indicate the subject of the others. The error on the subject was noticed by Marillier in his recension of Göbel's book, *The Burlington Magazine* 52 (1928): 150. He proposed to see in it "Psyche interviewing Charon," which was better, and an Aubusson work, which was worse.

25. One could also imagine other traditional subjects in the iconography of the fable, notably *Psyche Visited by Her Sisters* and *The Flight of Cupid*, in which Cupid is awakened by a drop of oil falling from the lamp.

26. H. Delesalle had written out an article entitled "Les Métamorphoses d'Ovide dans la tapisserie de Beauvais," unfortunately not published, which I have read with profit although I do not accept some of his arguments. With no knowledge of the document of 1690, he had succeeded in distinguishing the two successive series and in reconstituting almost entirely the second one; however, in following the documents published by Badin, he dated it 1725.

27. See, for instance, a large Verdure with small figures, in a border of flowers that could be taken as a Beauvais (except that the central bunch of flowers on the lower border runs over the picture, which does not occur any more at that date in France) but which carries in the galloon a Brussels mark and Jakob van der Borcht's initials (Parke Bernet, New York, 2 March 1974, no. 95, repr.).

28. *Inventaire général . . .* 1, no. 178, 364. Thomson (p. 439) was aware of this text.

29. This hanging has been masterfully reconstituted by E. Standen, "Mythological Scenes: A Tapestry Series after Laurent de la Hire," *The Museum of Fine Arts, Houston, Bulletin* n.s. 4 (1973): 10–21.

30. H. Delesalle intended to recognize this subject of the small-figured *Metamorphoses* in the *Aurora and Cephalus* tapestry sold in 1958 (Fig. 1), because it had the same border as the three Orléans tapestries. On the contrary, I prefer to integrate this tapestry in the series of *Cephalus and Procris*, which has the same border and the same dimensions, the reason being that it does not seem likely that a piece that shows in fact *Aurora and Cephalus*, and in which Procris does not appear, could be designated under the title of *Cephalus and Procris*.

31. P. M. Auzas, in *Les Monuments historiques de la France* 5 (1959): 122–23, where the piece *Apollo and the Muses* is reproduced, had already published the opinion of Jean Dautzenberg according to which we dealt with Beauvais tapestries; and he signaled another version of *Apollo and the Muses* already sold (Hôtel Drouot, 20 June 1952, no. 153, pl. XV) under Beauvais attribution.

32. Badin, p. 21.

33. This book of the "prices of works and accounts of workers" gives the details of payments effected for the execution of every vertical band of the cartoons and cites occasionally characteristic features of panels—for instance, the figures of Boreas and Orithyia in the first piece, of Pan and Syrinx in the second, of Pomona in the third, of Diana in the fourth *(Alpheius and Arethusa)*. In the fifth piece the details are more vague (foliage of light oak, "little Cupid in the trees") but coincide with the composition of *Cephalus and Procris*. For the sixth, they did not allow any identification, owing to their obscurity, but they take on meaning when the tapestry is in full view (cf. note 37).

34. Hôtel Drouot, room 1, maître Boisgirard, 28 May 1934, nos. 145–47, repr.

35. London, Sotheby, 13 December 1957, no. 89 *(Boreas and Orithyia)* and no. 90 *(Pan and Syrinx)*, and 28 February 1958, no. 77 *(Alpheius and Arethusa)*. These tapestries must be considered along with an account by the painter Lepape (or De Pape), who mentioned improvements and arms he had added to the cartoons of the *Metamorphoses* for the President de Versainville's set (Badin, p. 15).

36. Hôtel Drouot, room 10, maître Morelle, 6 May 1974, no. 116, 3 repr.

37. The last piece was only 3 aunes wide. The vague notations of the register are verified in this composition. The figure on the left is directly under the median motifs of the border, the one on the right is under a "light foliage," and the "blue mantle" is on the ground at the figure's feet.

38. One with the arms of Versainville (note 35), 3.68m×5.64m; one in San Francisco, signed Béhagle, Anna G. Bennett, *Five Centuries of Tapestry from The Fine Arts Museums of San Francisco* (San Francisco: The Fine Arts Museums of San Francisco and Charles E. Tuttle, Co., 1976), p. 222, no. 67, repr. 3.10m×5.28m; one in Bamberg, Neue Residenz, formerly in Munich, in a border with quivers and torches (3.90m×5.30m); one now in New York in the Kellogg collection, from the Earl of Abington's sale, Sotheby, 15 June 1928, no. 163 (3.50m×4.20m), with the same border; one in a frame border, sold at the galerie Charpentier on 15 March 1937, no. 154, repr. pl. XIV (3m×4.70m); one in the Leonino's sale at the galerie Charpentier, 24 March 1939, no. 134, repr. (3m×5.20m) in a border with acanthus bands twining around a stem; one sold by Sotheby on 13 December 1963; not counting a fragment exported from France in 1969.

39. It is tempting to identify it with the border described on a Beauvais Verdure in the Crown furniture already catalogued in 1681: "a festoon of flowers entwined with an ornament in the shape of an 'S' . . .'' (*Inventaire général* . . . 1, p. 353, no. 114).

40. ''Another, finer kind [of tapestry], *Story of Metamorphose:* sold a set in Brussels to the Lord Duke of Bavaria, then Governor of the Netherlands, and he preferred my fabrication to that of Brussels'' (Badin, p. 12). The duke became governor of the Netherlands in 1692.

41. In addition to those of French's (3.28m×4.57m); of the 1934 sales (3.40m×4.70m); 1957, Versainville (3.68m×4.44m); and 1974 (3.25m×3.40m), these following may be cited: Victorien Sardou's sale, galerie G. Petit, 27 April 1909, no. 334, in a frame border (2.85m×4.05m); for sale at Palais Galliéra, 2 December 1968, no. 122, repr., in a border with rectangular motifs and fleurons (3.10m×3.74m). In addition, J. Dautzenberg had also seen one in 1878 in the Dalseme collection in Paris, with a border of Chinese grotesques, bearing the mark MR and a shield with the arms of France.

42. Besides the French's version (3.25m×3.96m) and those at the sales of 1934 (3.38m×3.60m) and 1974 (3.25m×3.35m), there are the Bayreuth version reproduced here, which M. Lorenz Seelig kindly pointed out to me (3.90m×4.06m); one in a Paris sale, galerie Charpentier, 12 June 1936, no. 93, repr., in an interesting border with ornaments spiraling around a stem and interlaced with olive foliage (3m×3.80m); one in the Lewisohn collection, sold by Parke Bernet, 16 May 1939, no. 298, with the Chinese border (3.37m×3.91m); another (?) with the Chinese border, seen by J. Dautzenberg in 1878 in the Dalseme collection; and one more, sold at Hôtel Drouot by Me Lemée, 31 March 1965, no. 169, repr. pl. VI, in a border of foliage and flowers (3m×3.88m).

43. In addition to the Versainville version (3.66m×2.49m) and to the one sold 6 May 1974, no. 116F, not repr. (3.25m×2.35m), there are a piece at the J. Charles-Roux sale, 5 December 1918, no. 287, in a border similar to that of the *Vertumnus and Pomona* sold (see note 42) on 31 March 1965 (2.95m×3.20m); another sold in New York by Parke Bernet, 31 May 1974, no. 67, repr., in a frame border, which shows on the right an exceptional expanse of landscape (2.37m with a fold at the head×3.66 m); the Karlsruhe tapestry reproduced here (I am grateful to Miss E. Zimmerman for the photograph), which has lost its border and been provided instead with a frame of embroidery (2.88m×2.87m without border); and finally a piece listed in a sale at the galerie van Diemen by Paul Graupe, in Berlin, 25–26 January 1935, no. 532, reproduced in mirror image, pl. 94, in a border with foliage coiling round stems and with corner ornaments (3.21m×3.15m).

44. They are a piece formerly at French's (3.23m×2.82m); another in the 1934 sale (3.33m×2.41m) reproduced here; another in the 6 May 1974 sale, no. 116D, not repr. (3.25m×3.35m).

45. The one sold 6 May 1974, no. 116E, was missing all its borders (3.25m×1.45m). The other one, reproduced here, was for sale at Hôtel Drouot, room 6, 31 March 1914, no. 135, repr., and again 14 December 1938, room 1, no. 117, repr., with indications of dimensions slightly different (3.20m or 3.30m×2.10m or 2.26m).

46. A. Schnapper, *Tableaux pour le Trianon de marbre* (Paris, 1967), no. I, 1, repr. fig. 3.

47. Ibid., figs. 7, 15, and 18.

48. Galerie G. Petit, 30 May 1919, nos. 42 and 46, *Diana's Repose* (3.35m×5.05m); *The Abduction of Europa* (3.35m×4.60m); *Diana and Endymion* (3.35m×4m); *Diana and an Attendant* (3.35m×2.25m); *Meeting of Two Figures* (3.40m×2.05m).

49. The *Diana's Repose* tapestry is known in two versions only, one at the 1919 sale, another at the Bucharest Museum, in a border with quivers and torches (3.45m×5.20m) (see *Catalogul Expozitiei de tapiserii franceze* . . ., text by Viorica Dene [Bucharest, 1964], § *Beauvais,* no. 1, reproduced inverted). The *Abduction of Europa* is so far a *unicum:* that of the 1919 sale went to New York for the Whitehouse collection (located by Edith Standen). *Diana and Endymion* exists in four versions: the one at the 1919 sale, resold at Versailles by maître Chapelle on 27 May 1973, no. 148, repr.; another one, in a border with foliage characterized by eagles in the upper corners and vases in the lower corners, in a sale at Hôtel Drouot, room 1, 9 June 1952, no. 34, repr., pl. VI (3.25m×4m); another at Bucharest, in a set with *Diana's Repose* already mentioned (3.40m×3.84m), see *Catalogul* . . ., no. 2, repr.; another, mutilated, was seen by H. Delesalle at the merchant Dario Boccara's in 1965.

50. This necessity was particularly felt in the last years of the century; not only did it bring about the realization of the *Trianon de Marbre,* but it affected even the Gobelins, where a series of the *Metamorphoses* (Fenaille, *Etat général des tapisseries . . . des Gobelins,* vol. 3 [Paris, 1904], pp. 121–32) was woven, partially inspired by the Trianon paintings. This series could be considered, on the part of the state manufactory, as a concession to the ''Beauvais style.''

Some Beauvais Tapestries Related to Berain

Edith A. Standen

It has been known for nearly fifty years that the Beauvais series still often called the *Grotesques de Berain* was designed by the flower-painter, Jean Baptiste Monnoyer—"Baptiste" to his contemporaries. Roger Armand Weigert wrote in 1931 that he had identified the artist; in 1933 he named him, quoting a documentary source, and in 1946 he attributed the information to "une correspondance manuscrite inédite, conservée ailleurs qu'en France."[1] Finally, in 1964, he and Carl Hernmarck published this correspondence, the letters exchanged by the Swedish architect Nicodemus Tessin the Younger in Stockholm with the Baron Daniel Cronström in Paris between 1693 and 1718.[2] A set of the *Grotesques*, with furniture upholstery to match, made for the Swedish Chancellor Carl Piper, was an important topic of this correspondence from 1694 to 1697 and Cronström mentioned in his letter of January 18, 1695, that the designer was "Baptiste, excellent peintre et dessignateur d'ornement icy." Monnoyer, in fact, had actually been in London since 1690, but there was presumably no reason why Cronström should know this.

The designs of this tapestry series, however, though they are rich indeed with the flowers of Monnoyer's specialty, have much in common with Berain's prints. The three panels that are usually wide—the *Camel* (Fig. 1),[3] the *Elephant* (Fig. 11) and the *Animal Tamers*—have the tripartite division of such a Berain print as *Feasting Nymphs and Cupids* (Fig. 2); here, too, are the latticed arbors, though less

flowery than those of the tapestries, and, on the far left, little dancers very like several figures on the hangings. The enthroned dignitaries at either side of the *Camel* are like those on another print (Fig. 3), and the statue in the rear center of the *Feasting Nymphs* is like the *Bacchus* (Fig. 4) and the *Pan* (Fig. 5) of the tapestry series. The latter has a girl with a tambourine on the right who is close to a figure on another print (Fig. 6),[4] but the other characters have, as has been pointed out by Anna G. Bennett, a much more unusual source: the statue of the god, the girl kneeling on a goat, the small boy who offers her a basket, and the girl with a tambourine on the left are all from Poussin's *Triumph of Pan* (compare Figs. 7 and 8), painted for Cardinal Richelieu in 1635–36, and now owned by the Walter Morrison Picture Settlement, Sudeley Castle, Gloucestershire.[5]

The tapestries must have been designed before 1689, when the then head of the manufactory, Philippe Béhagle, used several pieces as security for a loan.[6] The series was woven for more than forty years; an inventory of 1731 lists a 1730 weaving of "une autre tenture du dessein de *Grotesques* avec petites figures chinoises par Batiste et Vernensal, de 3 aunes de France de hauteur [about 12 feet] sur 16 aunes de cours en six pièces."[7] The small figures of the *Grotesques de Berain* are certainly not Chinese, but no chinoiserie grotesques made at Beauvais are known; the compiler of the inventory may have been thinking of the border sometimes found on

Fig. 1. *Grotesques with a Camel*, wool and silk tapestry, French (Beauvais), late seventeenth to early eighteenth century. The Metropolitan Museum of Art, New York, gift of John M. Schiff, 1977.

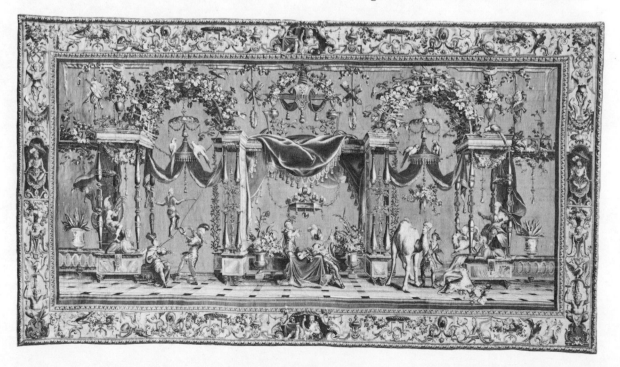

210

sets of this series (Figs. 1 and 4). It contains two chinoiserie figures, of which the one in the vertical borders is reminiscent of the emperor in the *Audience* of the Beauvais *Story of the Emperor of China* (Fig. 9); Guy Vernansal is known to have been one of the designers of this series, and pieces of it have been found with the inscription "Vernansal invenit et pinxit," suggesting that he was the principal one. The figures of the *Grotesques* borders are markedly better designed than those of the central fields. A single piece of the *Grotesques* is listed as ordered in 1732.[8] Several sets of six pieces, presumably complete, are known, and more than 150 individual tapestries have been located.[9] The *Animal Tamers* is the rarest of the usual subjects with only about twelve examples recorded; some, such as that in The Fine Arts Museums of San Francisco, include only one of the usual three motifs. There are, however, some even less frequently found pairs of musicians, such as the seated man playing a cello-like viol and a woman with a triangle found in San Francisco, Aix-en-Provence and Námest Castle, Czechoslova-

kia. Two other pairs have been published. The six well-known embroidered copies, or imitations, were last seen when they were sold at Christie's, 10 July 1975, no. 153.

The Tessin-Cronström correspondence, which provides a wealth of information about interior decoration in Paris at the end of the seventeenth century, tells the story of how one set of the *Grotesques* was commissioned and supplied. Louis XIV had dismissed all the workers at the Gobelins manufactory in April 1694 because he needed money for his wars; as a result, Cronström wrote on May 7, "la misère et le manque de travail est général. . . . Tous les tapissiers des Gobelins, Janse etc., demandent quasy l'aumône." Jans was the head of an *haute-lisse* workshop and, according to Cronström in a later letter, "d'un degré meilleur que les autres des Gobelins." If the king of Sweden wanted furnishings or tapestries, said Cronström, he could buy them at half price. By February 24, of the next year, twenty Gobelins weavers had asked Cronström if they could emigrate to Sweden.

Fig. 2. *Feasting Nymphs and Cupids*, engraving by Scottin the Elder after Jean Berain. The Metropolitan Museum of Art, New York, Rogers Fund, 1921.

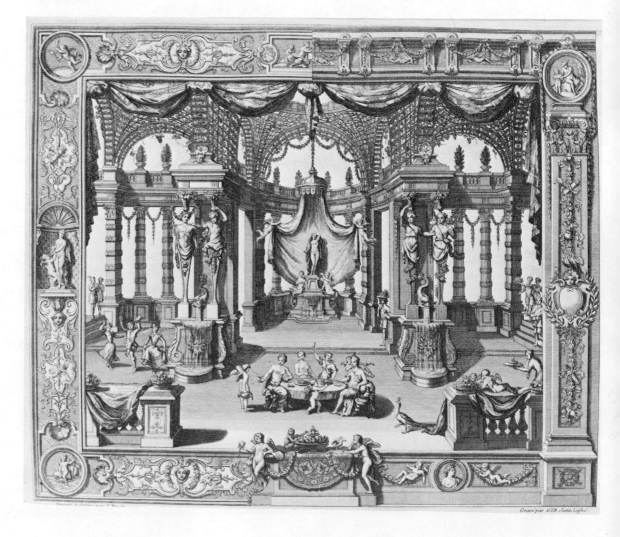

Fig. 3. *Grotesques*, engraving by Le Pautre after Jean Berain. The Metropolitan Museum of Art, New York, Rogers Fund, 1921.

Fig. 4. *Grotesques with a Statue of Bacchus*, wool and silk tapestry, French (Beauvais), late seventeenth to early eighteenth century. The Metropolitan Museum of Art, New York, gift of John M. Schiff, 1977.

But when it was not the Swedish king but a nobleman who was asking advice about furnishing a house, Cronström did not recommend the Gobelins. On 29 November 1694, knowing that Piper wanted "du bon goust plus tost que du magnifique," he was lavish with suggestions. He wrote that damask was more fashionable than brocatelle or gilt leather and that it was essential to have "plusieurs Sophas ou Canapés, licts de repos, cabinets, estudiolles, etc." Sofas were, he said, very much the thing and he showed himself to be a good prophet when he wrote on 24 February 1695 that this fashion, "la plus nouvelle et la plus agréable et la plus commode, . . . sera apparement de durée." Both he and Tessin were very conscious of changes in fashion and what changed most, wrote Cronström on 15 April 1695, were "les meubles et les habits."

By 18 January 1695, Cronström was ready to go into details for Piper, especially about "tapisserie de haute-lisse."[10] Except for the very best Gobelins, he wrote, there was nothing so well designed and made as the two Beauvais sets he had found, a *Grotesque* and a *Ports de Mer*, "les plus jolies tentures qu'on puisse jamais voir de ces prix la," each of six pieces amounting to 19 running French *aunes* (about 76 ft.). But Piper needed eight or nine

pieces making up only 10 or 14 running *aunes*; these, Cronström had ascertained, could be made to measure in three months, or the second-hand set could be cut up, "ce qui se peut faire dans la Grotesque sans quasy gatter le dessein." An example of a made-to-measure *Grotesques* design that has been drastically curtailed in both height and width is the *Camel* in the Victoria and Albert Museum (Fig. 10). If the finished set was cut up, Cronström continued, the old borders could be used again or new ones woven: "Comme tous ces adjoutages de bordeures seront faites sur les métiers des tapisseries mesme, il ne faut pas craindre que cela soit bousillé et mal accomodé." Both the *Grotesques* and the *Ports* were fine enough to be hung in bedrooms rather than relegated to anterooms. Cronström advised that the *portières* also be of grotesque tapestry to make "une uniformité charmante"; this would be in very good taste and *portières* prevent the smell of food from spreading. Corridors and dining-rooms were not usual in French houses at this date.[11] Later, however, Cronström would write (14/4[12] February 1698) that "les portières ne sont quasy jamais tirées et qu'aincy l'on ne laisse de voir les tableaux [the overdoor paintings] souvent; au bout de quoy je ne veux pas entièrement justifier cette manière, mais c'est la mode."

Fig. 5. *Grotesques with a Statue of Pan*, wool and silk tapestry, French (Beauvais), late seventeenth to early eighteenth century. The Metropolitan Museum of Art, New York, gift of Mrs. Guy Fairfax Gary, 1950.

Fig. 6. *Winter*, engraving after Jean Berain. The Metropolitan Museum of Art, New York, Rogers Fund, 1921.

Fig. 7. *Grotesques with a Statue of Pan*, detail, wool and silk tapestry, French (Beauvais), late seventeenth to early eighteenth century. Formerly in the Clarence H. Mackay Collection.

Going off on another tack, Cronström recommended, as an alternative to tapestry, white woodwork "à filets d'or," with "portières de hautelisse magnifiques," such as the half-finished ones then on the abandoned looms of the Gobelins; the arms of the Swedish king or of Piper himself could be substituted for those of Louis XIV. These *portières* must be some of the sets after Le Brun, recorded as begun early in 1694, but which were not finished until much later;[13] it is interesting that they were apparently available for purchase. Cronström's description is helpful in imagining the appearance of a suite of rooms with these *portières* at each succeeding doorway; vast quantities of armorial *portières* were woven at the Gobelins for Louis XIV in the late seventeenth and early eighteenth centuries. It was not until 2 January 1699 that Cronström could report that "Le Roy a fait des fonds pour faire achever tous les ouvrages de tapisserie qui estoient commencés aux Gobelins avant la guerre."

Piper evidently decided to have new tapestries woven rather than to cut up old ones, and at some point he sent a plan of the rooms he was furnishing; it is mentioned in a letter of 8/18 July 1695. There seem to have been seven rooms, a "salle," and for Piper and for his wife each an "anti-chambre," "chambre," and "cabinet." Cronström accordingly provides many ideas for wall-coverings, since, as he wrote on 24 February 1695, "on ne peut guerre faire deux chambres de mesme." Cronström was waiting for the definitive tapestry order and money for a deposit when he wrote on April 15/5 and by May 10/20 sixteen looms at the Beauvais manufactory were at work on the 28 running *aunes* of the *Grotesques* and the *Ports de Mer*; the former were to be a third and the latter a quarter less high than usual. There would be about 16 *aunes* of the *Grotesques* and 12 of the *Ports*. Cronström then wrote the sentence that associates Berain with this set of the *Grotesques*: "Je fais mettre à la grotesque, une bordeure d'un goust grotesque du dessein de Berain, à bastons rompus rouges sur un fond bleu [Fig. 11], au lieu d'une bordeure ordinaire de feuilles de persil tournantes sur un fond bleu."[14] One large set with this border is known, that formerly owned by Clarence Mackay;[15] all the pieces are small, showing one motif each instead of the three that appear on the wide tapestries of the series (Figs. 1, 10, and 11). Two are signed by Béhagle. It is not impossible that this is Piper's set, though

the border was used on other pieces.[16] The height, under 9 feet, might be considered as a third less than the 3 or 3¼ *aunes* (12 or 13 ft.) of the pieces pledged in 1689.

The Beauvais weavers had said that the work would take three months. Cronström's contract with them had set the date of completion at September 8, but he offered a large tip to the workers if they could deliver the tapestries by August 15. To speed things up, he wrote on July 29, he had cancelled his instructions to put Piper's initials and coronet on the cartouches of the borders, "car un rien est capable de retarder et embarrasser ces animaux de tapissiers, ou, du moins, de donner pretexte de retardement." But it was August 28/18 before he could write that he had seen the finished tapestries, having spent an afternoon looking at them, even though it was Sunday. They were "fort belles et bonnes" and the weavers had very nearly earned their tips. There is no record of the actual shipment, but on December 11 Tessin wrote that Mr. Piper was "charmé de ses tentures qu'on ne scauroit l'estre d'avantage. Elles sont touttes deux parfaitement belles et rien ne scauroit estre plus gentil pour un petit appartement que ces grottesques." Tessin added that, if it were not for the veneration in which he held Mr. Piper, he would envy him: ". . . je ne scaurois m'imaginer de trouver quelque chose de plus jolie pour meubler une petite salle dans la maison que je fais batir présentement." There is no evidence that Tessin ever did commission a set of Beauvais *Grotesques* for his own house, but there is one in the Stockholm City Hall, five rather small pieces that came from the Bielke family; perhaps they were ordered because the Bielkes admired the Piper tapestries. Count Nilo Bielke had been the Swedish ambassador in Paris, but from 1679 to 1682, too early for him to have bought them there.

The story of the upholstered furniture that Cronström ordered for Piper is a good deal longer and a great deal more complicated. Though the wall-hangings have disappeared (unless, indeed, they are the Mackay set), Carl Hernmarck has identified four tapestry chair-seats and three backs in the National Museum, Stockholm, as coming from Piper's furniture.[17] A chair with similar upholstery is in the Metropolitan Museum (Fig. 12); the monogram on back and seat is C.P. for Carl Piper (or Comte Piper), and the yellow grounds are the same as those of the *Grotesques*.

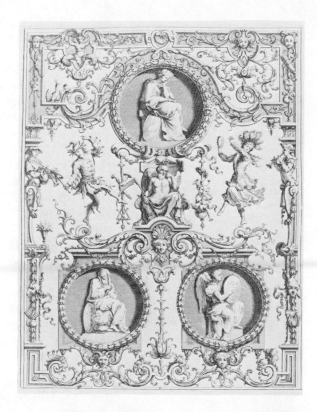

But from the correspondence it is clear that Cronström's first idea was to have Piper's upholstery embroidered, rather than woven, after designs by Berain. He spoke of this in his first letter about Piper on 29 November 1694. On 18 January 1695, he wrote that, if Mme Piper's antechamber was to have "hautelisse" hangings, the chairs could be covered with "tapisserie des desseins de Mr. Berain" and the chairs in her cabinet could also be "de tapisserie du dernier dessein de Mr. Berain." "Je fais preséntèment faire une chaise par Mad.^{e} Berain sur le dessein dernier de son mary car il n'y a qu'elle qui les puisse d'abord bien executer." This suggests that Berain's designs could be so sketchy that only his wife could make the first interpretation of those for embroidery; Cronström wrote on 16 April 1694 that they were always in Chinese ink and not colored. Cronström went on to say that he was having six chaircovers made.

By April 15/5 it had been decided that the chairs would be placed in Mme Piper's antechamber. The wooden frames were ready to be shipped by May 27/June 6, but since only one person was working on the embroidery, the upholstery was not finished. On June 4/May 25, Cronström wrote that he hoped to have eight chairs ready in July; he added, "Les chaises de Mr. Piper se font aux Gobelins. . . . Elles seront toutes de laines d'Angleterre. La tapisserie est de laine de pays." This must refer to embroidered upholstery, worked in French wool on English wool grounds; embroidery as well as tapestry was made at the Gobelins manufactory. By July 8/18 six "chaises de tapisserie" were ready and Cronström was sending twelve frames, which "ne coutent guerre," but on July 29 he was still speaking of work being done on the chaircovers: "mais comme cela se fait à l'éguille et qu'il n'y a qu'une personne qui puisse travailler à chaque morceau, cela va plus lentement." On August 19 Cronström said that the order consisted of six armchairs and six sidechairs. "L'on met icy une chaise et un fauteuil, l'un près de l'autre, et, aincy en continuant," so that the twelve pieces would not take up as much space as twelve armchairs, which Piper had said his room could not hold. It was customary to stand chairs against the walls round a room at this time. By 26/16 January 1696 the chairs were almost ready, but some had to be remade because they were not exactly like the others.

Finally, by 4 May–24 April 1696, a full year after work had begun on the embroidery,

Fig. 8. *Triumph of Pan* by Nicolas Poussin, detail, oil on canvas. Walter Morrison Picture Settlement, Sudeley Castle, Winchcombe, Cheltenham, England.

Fig. 9. *The Audience of the Emperor*, detail, wool and silk tapestry, French (Beauvais), late seventeenth to early eighteenth century. The Metropolitan Museum of Art, New York, gift of Mrs. J. Insley Blair, 1948.

Fig. 10. *Grotesques with a Camel*, wool and silk tapestry, French (Beauvais), late seventeenth to early eighteenth century. The Victoria and Albert Museum, London (T53–1955).

Cronström had decided to have the upholstery made of "hautelisse." Piper could have "quelques chaises ou fauteuil de commodité faits à l'eguille sur le premier dessein de Berain," which were "assez jolys," but the twenty-four pieces were not really good enough: "l'on ne peut pas empêcher qu'il ne s'y trouve quelques difference de couleur et de travail n'estans pas faits de la mesme main."[18] Tapestry covers, Cronström said, would even be a little cheaper. By July 20/10, eight were finished, and he wrote, "Je feroy faire les bois incessament," but it was October 26/16 before the upholstery and the frames were ready to go. Piper was evidently pleased with them, for Cronström had to explain on 21/11 June 1697 that though he had had "chaises de tapisserie de hautelisse . . . rapportant à la tenture des Grotesques" made for Piper, he could not order anything comparable for Piper's other set, the *Ports de Mer*: "il est impossible de mettre un paysage ou veue dans un dossier de chaise, à moins que d'estropier les objets ou faire un travaille d'une finesse et d'une cherté excessive." Cronström said that he owned the "six tableaux que j'ay fait faire exprés pour lesdites chaises" and could have other pieces woven from them. The six designs were presumably the cartoons from which the tapestries were woven; all the surviving specimens of upholstery are alike, so that three identical designs for a chair back and three for a seat would have enabled six looms to work from them at the same time. Tessin did, in fact, order some chairs for himself, which were

sent as "douze morceaux de tapisserie de basselisse, grotesques, dessein pareil à celluy des chaises de Mr. Le C. Piper, le fond un peu différant," with Tessin's initials, when Cronström wrote on 9/19 June 1699.

It will have been noted that Cronström never names the designer of the tapestry upholstery nor the manufactory at which it was woven. The latter was presumably Beauvais, as Piper's wall hangings had been made there, though a Paris workshop is not impossible; Cronström wrote on 8/18 July 1695 that many people were having tapestries made "chez eux" "à cause de la désoccupation des tapissiers," but "il faudroit que la chose valust la peine de faire un hastelier exprès." This would hardly have been the case for a set of chair covers. The designer could not have been Monnoyer, who was in England, and is unlikely to have been Berain; Cronström, knowing how much Tessin admired this artist,[19] would surely have mentioned his name.

As the early records of the Beauvais manufactory have been lost, the first mention of tapestry upholstery comes from 1725, a "canapé à pavots."[20] Cronström, however, does not indicate that he is doing anything unusual when he orders Piper's furniture coverings to be woven; it seems probable that such productions, which were to be a mainstay of the manufactory for 200 years, were already being made there. Other early pieces have not, however, been identified, and Piper's chair coverings remain the first documented set of tapestry upholstery made to harmonize with wall hangings.

A very different set of tapestries, known only from a single weaving, can also be said to reflect the style of Berain. It consists of armorials: two with landscape backgrounds in the Metropolitan Museum (Fig. 13) and one with a plain ground in the Nelson Gallery of Art, Kansas City. They are probably all from the sale of the Marquise de Y. (Landolfo-Carcano), Hôtel Drouot, Paris, 28 November–2 December 1921, nos. 603–606; of these four pieces, two had "fonds de paysage" and two "fonds verts." Three pieces with the same arms were in the Mme X sale, Hôtel Drouot, 20–23 April 1892, nos. 410–42; all are said to have "fonds de parcs" and the one illustrated shows a formal garden in the background. A piece with this background was in the Lefortier sale, American Art Association, 28–29 November 1924, no. 513. Four pieces, said to have landscape backgrounds, were in the Prince Paul Galitzin sale, Hôtel Drouot, 10–11 March 1875, no. 180. As many of these tapestries are not illustrated in the sale catalogues, it is not possible to reconstitute the original set. It might have been made up of eight pieces: four with garden backgrounds, two with country landscapes (in the Metropolitan Museum), and two with plain

backgrounds (one in Kansas City). As always, it is hard to visualize a room entirely hung with these monotonous but vivid and somewhat overwhelming tapestries and harder still to understand the frame of mind that would consider such an effect desirable.

The relationship of the design with Berain can be seen by comparing the tapestry with a print from his *Ornemens Inventez* (Fig. 14). The borders of both are similar and not unlike the *bastons rompus* of the *Grotesques* (Fig. 11). The heads in profile under plumed headdresses at the top of the tapestry appear lower down on the print, flanking the supports of the two winged herms. The vases of flowers at the top of the print can be compared to those on either side of the tapestry and the semi-circle of stiff drapery under the swans with the two similar pieces at the foot of the print.

The arms were identified when the tapestries were acquired by the Metropolitan Museum.[21] They are those of the Swiss family Greder, whose initial G appears in the borders, and Blumenstein.[22] The latter is not a family name, but an estate that belonged to the Greder family of Solothurn. The tapestries must have been commissioned by the head of the house and in all probability by François Laurent Greder (1658–1716), who inherited Blumenstein on the death of his father in

Fig. 11. *Grotesques with an Elephant*, wool and silk tapestry, French (Beauvais), late seventeenth to early eighteenth century. Courtesy of The Art Institute of Chicago.

Fig. 12. Armchair with tapestry upholstery, French, 1696. The Metropolitan Museum of Art, New York, bequest of Benjamin Altman, 1913.

1691. This was the year in which he was promoted to the rank of brigadier in the French army; the pieces of armor at the foot of the tapestries must refer to his military career. The tapestries were presumably commissioned between 1691 and 1694, when Greder was made a knight of the order of Saint Louis,[23] an honor he would surely have included in the design as soon as he was entitled to it. He was the last Greder to own Blumenstein, as he bequeathed it to his sister, Maria Franziska Molodin, who named the house "Laurentin" after him.[24] It is rare to find tapestries of this period, other than Gobelins, that can be so precisely dated.

It is, however, not possible to say where the set was woven. The tapestries in New York and Kansas City have all been woven in two pieces and are joined vertically down the middle. There are inept variations in the background colors. Both these facts suggest a smaller and less well organized manufactory than Beauvais. The Bacor workshop in Paris is a possibility. The *Great Gods* series, inspired by Berain engravings, were woven there;[25] the designs and coloring are comparable to those of the Greder armorials. But as these have no marks or documentation, this possibility must remain pure speculation.

Fig. 13. Armorial, wool and silk tapestry, French, 1691–94. The Metropolitan Museum of Art, New York, bequest of Lucy Hewitt, 1935.

Fig. 14. *Grotesques*, engraving by Dolinart after Jean Berain. The Metropolitan Museum of Art, New York, transferred from the Library, 1921.

NOTES

1. Roger-Armand Weigert, "Un atelier de tapissiers français à Berlin au début du XVIIIe siècle," *Revue de l'Art*, 60 (1931): 205; "Les Grotesques de Beauvais et les tapisseries de Chevening (Kent)," *Bulletin de la Société de l'Histoire de l'Art français*, 1933, pp. 12, 13; "Les Grotesques de Beauvais," *Hyphé* 1 (1946): 71. The author said little about tapestries in his *Jean I Berain*, 2 vols. (Paris: Les Editions d'Art et d'Histoire, 1937), but he gave a brief summary of the artist's connection with tapestry manufactories in his *La Tapisserie et le Tapis en France* ["Le lys d'Or," Histoire de l'Art français (Paris: Presses Universitaire de France, 1964)], pp. 126, 127. Other details can be found in his "Les commencements de la Manufacture Royale de Beauvais," *Gazette des Beaux-Arts* ser. 6, 64 (1964): 342–46.

2. *Les Relations artistiques entre la France et la Suède*, 1693–1718, Nationalmusei Skriftserie no 10 (Stockholm: no pub., 1964).

3. The example of the *Camel* illustrated has the *Musicians* as its central motif instead of the more usual peacock and vase (Fig. 10).

4. The tiny peacock, so unexpectedly perched in the upper left corner of this print, resembles the birds in the upper areas of many of the tapestries.

5. Anna G. Bennett, *Five Centuries of Tapestry from the Fine Arts Museums of San Francisco* (San Francisco: The Fine Arts Museums of San Francisco and Charles E. Tuttle Co., 1976), p. 226, fig. 73.

6. Heinrich Göbel, *Wandteppiche, II, Teil, Die romanischen Länder*, 2 vols. (Leipzig: Klinkhardt & Biermann, 1928), vol. 1, p. 213. The tapestries are described as "grotesques à petits personnages" and, unusually for Beauvais, contained gold thread.

7. Jules Badin, *La Manufacture de Tapisseries de Beauvais depuis ses Origines jusqu'a à nos Jours* (Paris: Société de Propagation des Livres d'Art, 1909), p. 21.

8. Badin, p. 56.

9. Weigert, "Grotesques," *Hyphé*, p. 69.

10. In a letter of 10 June 1696 Cronström explained that "selon la langage ordinaire tout ce qui est fait sur des metiers s'appelle hautelisse qui est le mot générique; la terme de basse lisse n'est proprement conneu que des ouvriers." He uses "tapisserie" to mean textile wall hangings of any kind; writing on 22 May 1693 about Versailles, he said, "Les tapisseries, qui sont d'estoffes, règnent par tous, mesmes sur les cheminées et portes, nonobstant les tableaux dessus les cheminées et portes." On 10 October 1694 he spoke of "tapisseries de gros point, comme on les appelle, et que les Dames elles-mesmes peuvent aisement travailler."

11. Tessin on 27 January 1697 described "un petit appartement que je voudrois réserver pour la parade" in the house he was building for himself; it consisted, he wrote, of "une Salle, Antichambre, Chambre du lict et Cabinet dans un enfilade, d'une grandeur assez raissonable et prez de vingt pieds d'hauteur."

12. France adopted the Gregorian calendar in 1582, Sweden not until 1700. The difference between the two at this period was ten days.

13. Maurice Fenaille, *Etat général des Tapisseries de la Manufacture des Gobelins depuis son Origine jusqu'á nos Jours 1660–1900*, 6 vols. (Paris: Maurice Fenaille, 1903–23), vol. 2 (1662–99), pp. 4, 11, 12, 18, 19.

14. Cronström did not mention the chinoiserie border (Fig. 1 and 4); perhaps it had not yet been designed or was not available, or it may have been merely more expensive.

15. George Leland Hunter, *Tapestries of Clarence H. Mackay* (New York: privately printed, 1925), pp. 68–76. Six pieces are illustrated and what is said to be "the seventh of the original set of eight" is described as given by Mrs. John Mackay to the Victoria and Albert Museum in 1909: (A.F. Kendrick, *Catalogue of Tapestries*, no. 46 (London: Board of Education, 1924). The *Dancing Piper* of this set (usually found as the right-side motif of the *Elephant*, Fig. 10) is in the Museo Lázaro Galdiano, Madrid (Paulina Junquera, "Tapices del Museo Lázaro Galdiano," *Goya*, no. 103, July–August 1971, p. 6, illus.). Four piece of the set were sold at Christie's, 27 July 1939, no. 114, of which *Pan* and one motif of the *Camel* (called *Les Funambules*) were exhibited at the Musée des Arts décoratifs, Paris, *Louis XIV, Faste et Décors*, 1960, catalogue nos. 761, 762, without the name of the owner.

16. As well as on the *Elephant* in The Art Institute of Chicago (Fig. 11), the *bastons rompus* border is found on a *Musicians* in Kronborg Castle, Denmark, signed Béhagle, and on examples sold at auction of all the usual subjects.

17. Carl Hernmarck, "Avdelningen för konsthantverk," *Nationalmusei Årsbok*, n.s. 4 (1934): 140, fig. 95.

18. Embroidered upholstery for an armchair in Gripsholm Castle, Sweden, has been identified as from Piper's set (*Relations artistiques*, p. 100, note 6).

19. Tessin, in his notes on his visit to Paris in 1687, described Berain as "fort mon ami" (Roger-Armand Weigert, "Notes de Nicodème Tessin le Jeune relatives à son séjour à Paris en 1687," *Bulletin de la Société de l'Histoire de l'Art français*, 1932, p. 268). A Berain drawing sent by Cronström to Tessin is illustrated in Carl Hernmarck, "Korrespondensen mellan Tessin och Cronström," *Kontakt med Nationalmuseum*, 1963, p. 23. It includes the Swedish royal arms and is inscribed "Le dosier."

20. Badin, p. 65.

21. Harry B. Wehle and John Goldsmith Phillips, "Bequest of Lucy Work Hewitt," *Metropolitan Museum Bulletin* 30, no. 4 (1935): 91, 92.

22. Greder: Ecartelé d'azur à une patte et cuisse de cygne argent, accostées de deux fleurs de lys d'or. Blumenstein: D'or à la fasce d'azur accompagnée de cinq roses de gueules, 3 et 2. Jean Tricon and D.L. Galbreath, "Les documents héraldiques du Musée des Tissus de Lyon," *Archives Heraldiques*

Suisse 45 (1931): 153, showing similar arms with swans as the supporters on an embroidery. Three large wool embroideries in the National Museum, Stockholm, have the same arms.

23. F.A.J.D. Béat, Baron de la Tour Châtillon de Zur-Lauben, *Histoire Militaire des Suisses au Service de France* (Paris, 1751), vol. 3, pp. 16–18, 78–81.

24. E. Schlatter, *Kanton Solothurn* [*Das Burgerhaus in der Schweiz*, no. 21, 30 vols. (Zürich and Leipzig: Schweizerischen Ingenieur und Architekten-verein, 1910–37)], vol. 21 (1929), p. XLI.

25. Michel Antoine, *Les Manufactures de Tapisseries des Ducs de Lorraine au XVIIIe Siècle* [*Annuales de l'Est*, no. 26 (Nancy: Faculté des Lettres et des Sciences humaines de l'Université de Nancy, 1965)], pp. 51–53, gives an account of the Bacor family and their Paris workshop.

Notes on the Contributors

Christa C. M. Thurman
Curator, Department of Textiles
The Art Institute of Chicago

Christa Thurman is a Fellow of the American Institute for Conservation and a member of the International Council of Museums, Centre International d'Etude des Textiles Anciens, and The Costume Society of America. She is author of *Masterpieces of Western Textiles*, 1969; coauthor with Mildred Davison of *Coverlets*, 1973; and author of *Raiment for the Lord's Service: A Thousand Years of Western Vestments*, 1975. She also wrote the textile chapters for *Selected Works of the 18th Century French Art in the Collections of The Art Institute of Chicago*, 1976, and *The Antiquarian Society: The First One Hundred Years*, 1977.

Harold P. Lundgren
Chairman, Division of Textiles and Clothing
University of California, Davis

Harold P. Lundgren received his B.S. (in chemistry) from North Dakota State University and his Ph.D. from the University of Minnesota. After post-doctoral work at the University of Uppsala, Sweden, in 1935–37, he became a research associate in chemistry at the University of Wisconsin. From 1941 to 1974 he was Research Leader and Chief of the Wool and Mohair Laboratory, U.S. Department of Agriculture, Albany, California. In 1970 he was chairman of the 4th International Wool Textile Research Conference in Berkeley, California. He has held his present position since 1974. Dr. Lundgren belongs to the American Association of Textile Chemists and Colorists and The Fiber Society, among other professional organizations, and he is an elected fellow of The Textile Institute in England.

Liliane Masschelein-Kleiner
Institut Royal du Patrimoine Artistique,
Brussels

Liliane Masschelein-Kleiner earned her Ph.D. from the Université Libre de Bruxelles and worked two years for the National Research Council of Belgium. She joined the Institut Royal du Patrimoine Artistique in 1963, where she is now *chef de travaux*. Her main interests and publications have been in the fields of old paint media and organic dyestuffs. She has contributed to two articles published in *Studies in Conservation:* "Etude et identification du bleu Maya" (with R. Kleber and J. Thissen, 1967) and "Contribution à l'analyse des liants, vernis et adhésifs anciens" (with J. Heylen and F. Tricot-Marckx, 1968). In addition, her article "Microanalysis of hydroxy-quinones in red lakes" appeared in *Mikrochimica Acta* 6 (1967). Dr. Masschelein-Kleiner is an Associate of the International Institute for Conservation of Historic and Artistic Works and a member of the International Council of Museums and the Société Chimique de Belgique.

Nobuko Kajitani
Conservator, Textile Conservation
The Metropolitan Museum of Art, New York

Nobuko Kajitani received her early training in fiber craft in Japan. In 1964, she began studying the conservation and fiber technology of museum fabrics at the Textile Museum in Washington, D.C. She has been a conservator in Textile Conservation at The Metropolitan Museum of Art in New York since 1966 and has published a number of articles, among them, "Care of Fabrics in the Museum" in *Preservation of Paper and Textiles of Historic and Artistic Value*, Advances in Chemistry Series No. 164, published by the American Chemical Society in 1977; and "Physical Characteristics of Silk Fabrics Generally Classified as 'Buyid' "in *Irene Emery Roundtable, 1974*, published by the Textile Museum in 1975.

Wendy Hefford
Senior Research Assistant, Department
of Textiles
Victoria and Albert Museum, London

Wendy Hefford read History at St. Hugh's College, Oxford. She joined the staff of the Victoria and Albert Museum in 1960, later becoming a Research Assistant in the Department of Textiles. There she deals with woven and printed textiles, carpets and tapestries, with particular interest in the latter.

222

Larry Salmon
Curator of Textiles
Museum of Fine Arts, Boston

Born in Kansas, Larry Salmon was educated
at the University of Kansas and at Harvard
University, where he received his A.M. in
1968. He has been on the staff of the Department of Textiles, Museum of Fine Arts,
Boston, since September 1968. He is Vice-
President for America of the Centre International d'Etude des Textiles Anciens, a director
of The Costume Society of America, and a
member of the International Council of
Museums' Committee on Costumes and Textiles. His most recent publication is the
catalogue for the exhibition *A Medieval Tapestry in Sharp Focus* (Boston: Museum of Fine
Arts, Boston, 1977).

Geneviève Souchal
Professor, Department of Art History
Université de Poitiers, France

Geneviève Souchal received a *Licence ès-
lettres* and diplomas from the Ecole Nationale
des Chartes, and the Ecole du Louvre; she
was also awarded a technical librarian's di-
ploma. She was a curator at the Musée de
Tulle (1953–54) and was then affiliated with
the Centre National de la Recherche Scientifique (in literary history) from 1955 to 1958.
From that time until 1973, she was curator at
the Musée National de Cluny in Paris. She
has held her present position since 1973.
Madame Souchal is the author of several publications, primarily concerning Limoges
enamel and tapestry (particularly *Masterpieces
of Tapestry from the Fourteenth to the Sixteenth
Century* for the exhibition at the Grand Palais,
Paris, and The Metropolitan Museum of Art,
New York, 1973–74). She is a member of the
Société Nationale des Antiquaires de France,
among others.

Guy Delmarcel
Curator of Tapestries and Textiles
Royal Museums of Art and History, Brussels

Born in Mechelen, Belgium, Guy Delmarcel
received his M.A. in romance philology and
in history of art at the Catholic University of

Leuven (Belgium). Since 1969 he has been
Assistant Lecturer in Art History at Leuven,
and since 1975 he has been Curator in charge
of tapestries and textiles at the Royal
Museums of Art and History in Brussels
where he organized two major exhibitions in
this field: "Brussels Tapestries of the Early
Renaissance" (1976) and "Brussels Tapestries in the Time of Rubens" (1977). Mr.
Delmarcel's research is oriented mainly
toward iconography in sixteenth-century
Flemish tapestries.

Madeleine Jarry
Inspecteur principal
Mobilier National et Manufactures Nationales
des Gobelins, de Beauvais, et de la Savon-
nerie, Paris.

Madeleine Jarry is a specialist in decorative
arts, an international lecturer in this field of
study, and the author of several books on
French tapestries, carpets, and furniture.

Bertrand Jestaz
Conservateur, Département des Objets d'Art
Musée du Louvre, Paris

Bertrand Jestaz was educated at the Ecole
Nationale des Chartes, the Ecole du Louvre
(1958–62), and the Ecole Française de Rome
(1962–64). In 1962 he began work as an assistant in the Département des Objets d'Art at
the Louvre, later becoming Conservateur. He
has published works on bronzes and majolica
of the Renaissance, tapestries, and French architecture of the seventeenth century.

Edith A. Standen
Consultant, European Sculpture and
Decorative Arts
The Metropolitan Museum of Art, New York

Edith A. Standen (B.A. Oxon., 1926) was
secretary to the Widener Collection before
she served in the Monuments, Fine Arts and
Archives section of the U.S. Military Government in Germany after World War II.
From 1949 to 1970 she was in charge of the
Textile Study Room at the Metropolitan
Museum. Her special interest is post-
medieval tapestry.

1,000 copies of the *Acts of the Tapestry Symposium: November 1976* have been printed for The Fine Arts Museums of San Francisco.

Typography is Palatino, set by Custom Typography Service, San Francisco. Offset Lithography by Cal-Central Press, Sacramento. Black-and-white reproductions are in 150-line screen. Cover paper is Hearthstone, Laid Finish, basis 65; text paper is Hopper white, Smooth Opaque Finish, basis 70. Bindery work by Cardoza-James, San Francisco. Book Design by John Guard, San Francisco. Production work by Polly Bryson, San Francisco.